Contributions in Stock-flow Modeling

Also by the editors:

The Elgar Companion to Hyman Minsky, edited by Dimitri B. Papadimitriou and L. Randall Wray

Hyman P. Minsky's *John Maynard Keynes,* edited by Dimitri B. Papadimitriou and L. Randall Wray

Hyman P. Minsky's *Stabilizing an Unstable Economy,* edited by Dimitri B. Papadimitriou and L. Randall Wray

Government Spending on the Elderly, edited by Dimitri B. Papadimitriou

Distributional Effects of Government Spending and Taxation, edited by Dimitri B. Papadimitriou

Hyman P. Minsky's *Induced Investment and Business Cycles,* edited by Dimitri B. Papadimitriou

Modernizing Financial Systems, edited by Dimitri B. Papadimitriou

Advances in Monetary Policy and Macroeconomics, edited by Philip Arestis and Gennaro Zezza (Palgrave Macmillan 2007)

The Stock-Flow Consistent Approach: Selected Writings of Wynne Godley, edited by Marc Lavoie and Gennaro Zezza (Palgrave Macmillan 2012)

Contributions in Stock-flow Modeling

Essays in Honor of Wynne Godley

Edited by

Dimitri B. Papadimitriou
Levy Economics Institute of Bard College, US

and

Gennaro Zezza
Levy Economics Institute of Bard College, US, and University of Cassino, Italy

palgrave
macmillan

First published 2012 by
PALGRAVE MACMILLAN

Palgrave Macmillan in the UK is an imprint of Macmillan Publishers Limited, registered in England, company number 785998, of Houndmills, Basingstoke, Hampshire RG21 6XS.

Palgrave Macmillan in the US is a division of St Martin's Press LLC, 175 Fifth Avenue, New York, NY 10010.

Palgrave Macmillan is the global academic imprint of the above companies and has companies and representatives throughout the world.

Palgrave® and Macmillan® are registered trademarks in the United States, the United Kingdom, Europe and other countries.

ISBN 978–0–230–29445–5

This book is printed on paper suitable for recycling and made from fully managed and sustained forest sources. Logging, pulping and manufacturing processes are expected to conform to the environmental regulations of the country of origin.

A catalogue record for this book is available from the British Library.

A catalog record for this book is available from the Library of Congress.

10 9 8 7 6 5 4 3 2 1
21 20 19 18 17 16 15 14 13 12

Printed and bound in Great Britain by
CPI Antony Rowe, Chippenham and Eastbourne

Contents

List of Tables

List of Figures

List of Abbreviations and Acronyms

AMECO	Annual macroeconomic database
BBC	British Broadcasting Corporation
CBO	Congressional Budget Office
CEPG	Cambridge economic policy group
CGP	Cambridge growth project
CSO	Central Statistical Office
CUR	Current balance
CUSUM	Cumulative sum
DAE	Department of applied economics
DGSE	Dynamic stochastic general equilibrium
EBITDA	Earnings before interest, taxes, depreciation and amortization
ECB	European Central Bank
ECM	Error correction model
ESA95	European system of accounts of 1995
EMU	European Monetary Union
EU	European Union
FCI	Financial condition index
FDI	Foreign direct investment
GATT	General Agreement on Tariffs and Trade
GDP	Gross Domestic Product
GNP	Gross National Product
HRA	Housing revenue account
iid	Independent and identically distributed
IMF	International Monetary Fund
IS/LM	Investment saving/liquidity preference money supply
IVA	Inventory valuation adjustment

NAFA	Net acquisition of financial assets
NAFAP	Net acquisition of financial assets by the private sector
NIIP	Net international investment position
NIPA	National Income and Product Accounts
ONS	Office of National Statistics
OPEC	Organization of Petroleum Exporting Countries
P/E	Price/rent ratio
PE	Private expenditure
PIM	Perpetual inventory model
PK	Post-Keynesian
PPE	Philosophy, politics and economics
PSD	Public sector deficit
SFC	Stock-flow consistent
SGP	European Stability Growth Pact
SPs	Stability Programmes
SSRC	Social Science Research Council
TMC	Theory of the Monetary Circuit
VAR	Vector autoregression
WTO	World Trade Organization

Levy Economics Institute of Bard College

Founded in 1986, the Levy Economics Institute of Bard College is an autonomous nonprofit public policy research organization. It is nonpartisan, open to the examination of diverse points of view and dedicated to public service.

The Levy Institute believes in the potential for economic study to improve the human condition. Its purpose is to generate viable, effective public policy responses to important economic problems. It is concerned with issues that profoundly affect the quality of life in the USA, in other highly industrialized nations and in countries with developing economies.

The Levy Institute's present research programs include such issues as financial instability, economic growth and employment, international trade, problems associated with the distribution of income and wealth, the measurement of economic well-being, and gender equality, globalization and poverty.

The opinions expressed in this volume are those of the authors and do not necessarily represent those of the Levy Institute, its Board of Governors or the Trustees of Bard College.

Acknowledgements

The contributions included in this volume were especially commissioned from economists whose ideas and research have been influenced by the work of Wynne Godley. Some of the papers were presented at a conference held in Wynne's honor at the Levy Economics Institute in May 2011. The conference served as a forum in discussing them and the papers presented and included here have been revised in light of the discussion. We would like to thank Eve Taylor, Wynne's daughter, for her support for this volume and conference. We are grateful to Deborah C. Treadway for copyediting the entire volume, managing the final details of collating the changes by the authors and overseeing all tasks of proofreading. Our greatest debt, however, is to our friend and mentor Wynne Godley.

Dimitri B. Papadimitriou
Gennaro Zezza

Notes on Contributors

Philip Arestis is Director of Research, Cambridge Centre for Economics and Public Policy, Department of Land Economy, University of Cambridge, UK; Professor of Economics, Department of Applied Economics V, Universidad del País Vasco, Spain; Distinguished Adjunct Professor of Economics, Department of Economics, University of Utah, US; Senior Scholar, Levy Economics Institute of Bard College, New York, US; Visiting Professor, Leeds University Business School, University of Leeds, UK; Professorial Research Associate, Department of Finance and Management Studies, School of Oriental and African Studies (SOAS), University of London, UK; and holder of the British Hispanic Foundation 'Queen Victoria Eugenia' British Hispanic Chair of Doctoral Studies. He is Chief Academic Adviser to the UK Government Economic Service (GES) on Professional Developments in Economics. He has published as sole author or editor, as well as co-author and co-editor, a number of books, contributed in the form of invited chapters to numerous books, produced research reports for research institutes, and has published widely in academic journals.

Jörg Bibow is Associate Professor of Economics at Skidmore College, New York, and Research Associate at the Levy Economics Institute of Bard College, New York. Previously he held lecturing positions at Cambridge (UK) and Hamburg (Germany) Universities, and at Franklin College (Switzerland). He received a BA Honors degree in economics from the University of the Witwatersrand, a diplom-volkswirt from the University of Hamburg, and MA and PhD degrees in economics from the University of Cambridge. Recent publications include: *Euroland and the World Economy: Global Player or Global Drag?* (Palgrave, 2007) and *Keynes on Monetary Policy, Finance and Uncertainty* (2009).

Michael Brecht is a graduate student of economics at the University of Jena, Germany. His study interests include financial markets, German and European economic policies and statistics.

Vincent Duwicquet holds a PhD in economics from Paris North University and is Associate Professor at CLERSE-CNRS. Lille 1 University.

James K. Galbraith is a Senior Scholar with the Levy Economics Institute of Bard College. He holds the Lloyd M. Bentsen Jr. Chair in Government/Business Relations at the Lyndon B. Johnson School of Public Affairs, The University of Texas at Austin. His most recent book is *The Predator State: How Conservatives Abandoned the Free Market and Why Liberals Should Too*, and his next one will be *Inequality and Instability*, forthcoming from Oxford University Press. He was a student at Cambridge in the early 1970s when Wynne Godley joined the Department of Applied Economics.

Saed Khalil is a Senior Researcher at the Palestine Monetary Authority and a Professor at Birzeit University. He has a PhD in Economics and Management from the University of Trento under Prof. Stephen Kinsella and his research interests are in Stock Flow Consistent Macroeconomics, Macroeconomics, and Monetary Economics.

Stephen Kinsella is a Lecturer in Economics at the University of Limerick. He is the author of *Ireland in 2050: How We will be Living* and *Understanding Ireland's Economic Crisis: Prospects for Recovery*. His research spans the area of computable economics, stock-flow consistent macroeconomics, and experimental economics.

Marc Lavoie is Professor in the Department of Economics at the University of Ottawa, where he started teaching in 1979. He has published over 175 book chapters and journal articles as well as a number of books, among which *Foundations of Post-Keynesian Economic Analysis* (1992), *Introduction to Post-Keynesian Economics* (2006), and *Monetary Economics: An Integrated Approach to Money, Income, Production and Wealth* (2007) with Wynne Godley. With Mario Seccareccia, he has been the co-editor of a book on the works of Milton Friedman (1993) and of *Central Banking in the Modern World: Alternative Perspectives* (2004). With Gennaro Zezza, he is preparing an edition of the *Selected Works of Wynne Godley*.

Edwin Le Heron is Professor in Economics at the Bordeaux Institute of Political Studies, France, and Researcher at the CED (Centre Émile Durkheim) there. He is also President of the ADEK (French Association for Development of the Keynesian Studies), which gathers French economists interested in Keynes and in post-Keynesian works. The research interests are monetary policy, post-Keynesian monetary theory, SFC modeling and the history of economic thought.

Bill Martin is a Senior Research Associate of the Centre for Business Research at the University of Cambridge, UK. Previously, he was a Specialist Adviser in the UK Cabinet Office Central Policy Review Staff (1981–83) and a Specialist Adviser to the House of Commons Treasury Committee (1986–97). Between 1983 and 2004, he held senior roles, including that of chief economist, at the investment banking and fund management arms of the Swiss bank UBS. He collaborated formally and informally with Wynne Godley over many years.

Tiago Mata is a Research Fellow at Center for the History of Political Economy, at Duke University, USA. In 2008–10, he was Assistant Professor at the Amsterdam School of Economics in the Netherlands. His research interests are on the sociology of economics and on the post-World War II history of the social sciences with a particular concern for the role played by social science knowledge in mass culture. He concluded his doctoral work at the London School of Economics in 2005 and his thesis is forthcoming as a book. He has published in the journals *History of Political Economy*, *Science in Context* and *Journal of the History of the Behavioral Sciences*.

Jacques Mazier is a Professor of Economics at the University Paris 13 (since 1983) and a Researcher at CEPN-CNRS. He is a former Research Fellow in the forecasting department of the French Ministry of Finance (1970–75), Professor at the University of Rennes (1976–81), Economic Adviser at the French Planning Commission (1981–85), and Head of IRES (1985–88). He has published on international macroeconomics, exchange rates, European integration, economic policies in Europe, and macroeconomic modelling.

Jo Michell is a PhD candidate in the Economics Department at SOAS, University of London. His research is on macroeconomics and finance. Michell's research interests include monetary theory, stock-flow consistent modeling and the financial development of contemporary China.

Dimitri B. Papadimitriou is President of the Levy Economics Institute of Bard College, and Executive Vice President and Jerome Levy Professor of Economics at Bard College. His research includes financial structure reform, fiscal and monetary policy, community development banking, employment policy, and the distribution of income, wealth, and well-being. He heads the Levy Institute's macroeconomic modeling team studying and simulating the US and world economies. He has served as vice-chairman of the congressional US Trade Deficit Review Commission. Papadimitriou is general editor of the Levy Institute's book series, a member of the editorial boards of *Challenge*, *The Bulletin of Political Economy* and the *Journal of Economic Analysis* and the author of many articles and books. He received his BA from Columbia University and a PhD in Economics from the New School for Social Research.

Malcolm Sawyer is Professor of Economics, University of Leeds, UK, and formerly Pro-Dean for Learning and Teaching for the Faculty of Business. He is managing editor of the *International Review of Applied Economics* and the editor of the series 'New Directions in Modern Economics' published by Edward Elgar. He is the author of 11 books, has edited 25 books and published over 100 papers in refereed journals and contributed chapters to over 100 books. His research interests are in macroeconomics, fiscal and monetary policy, the political economy of the European Monetary Union, nature of money, causes and concepts of unemployment and the economics of Michal Kalecki.

Anwar Shaikh is Professor of Economics at the Graduate Faculty of Political and Social Science of the New School University, Associate Editor of the *Cambridge Journal of Economics*, and was a Senior Scholar and member of the Macro Modeling Team at the Levy Economics Institute of Bard College from 2000 to 2005. He is the author of three books, the most recent being *Globalization and the Myths of Free Trade* (2007). Recent articles include 'The First Great Depression of the 21st Century', *Socialist Register* (2011) and 'Reflexivity, Path-Dependence and Disequilibrium Dynamics', *Journal of Post Keynesian Economics* (Fall 2010).

Silke Tober is a senior researcher at the Macroeconomic Policy Institute (IMK) at Hans-Boeckler-Foundation, Dusseldorf, Germany. Her research focus lies on monetary policy issues and the longer-term effects of macroeconomic policy.

Jan Toporowski is Professor of Economics and Finance and Chair of the Economics Department in the School of Oriental and African Studies, University of London. Jan Toporowski has worked in fund management and international banking, and for the international consultancy agency, the Economist Intelligence Unit. In 2005, he was Visiting Research Fellow at the Bank of Finland. Toporowski is the author of a large number of books and papers on monetary and financial economics, and he has written for the *Financial Times, Challenge, Monthly Review* and other newspapers and magazines.

Achim Truger is a Senior Researcher for public finance and taxation at the Macroeconomic Policy Institute (IMK) at Hans-Boeckler-Foundation, Dusseldorf, Germany. He has taught public economics and macroeconomics at the Universities of Cologne and Oldenburg, Germany. His current research interests include macroeconomic policy, fiscal policy and tax reform. He is currently very active as a fiscal policy and tax policy advisor in Germany.

Till van Treeck is a senior researcher at the Macroeconomic Policy Institute (IMK) at Hans-Boeckler-Foundation, Dusseldorf, Germany. He has taught macroeconomic policy at the University of Hamburg, Germany. His research interests include macroeconomic theory, European economic policies and applied econometrics.

L. Randall Wray is Professor of Economics and Research Director, the Center for Full Employment and Price Stability at the University of Missouri-Kansas City, and Senior Scholar at the Levy Economics Institute of Bard College. Wray has focused on monetary theory and policy, macroeconomics, financial instability, and employment policy. He has published widely in journals and is the author of *Understanding Modern Money: The Key to Full Employment and Price Stability* (1998) and *Money and Credit in Capitalist Economies* (1990). He is the editor of *Credit and State Theories of Money* (2004) and co-editor of *Contemporary Post Keynesian Analysis* (2005), *Money, Financial Instability and Stabilization Policy* (2006), and *Keynes for the Twenty-first Century: The Continuing Relevance of The General Theory* (Palgrave Macmillan, 2008). He has served as a Visiting Professor at the University of Rome, the University of Paris, and UNAM (Mexico City).

Gennaro Zezza is Associate Professor of Economics at the University of Cassino, and Research Scholar at the Levy Economics Institute of Bard College. He is a member of the Levy Institute's Macro-Modeling Team and co-author of its Strategic Analysis reports. Zezza worked with the late Distinguished Scholar Wynne Godley in the United Kingdom, Denmark and Italy, as well as at the Levy Institute. His other research interests include economic growth, innovation, and regional convergence. Zezza is also involved in projects on distance learning. His recent publications include 'US Growth, the Housing Market, and the Distribution of Income', *Journal of Post Keynesian Economics* (2008); and 'The US Housing Market: A Stock-flow Consistent Approach', *Ekonomia* (2007). He holds a degree in economics from the University of Naples.

1
Wynne Godley's Economics

Dimitri B. Papadimitriou

The death of Wynne Godley silences a forceful and very often critical voice in macroeconomics. Wynne's own strong view, that although his work was representative of the non-mainstream Keynesian approach to economics and especially economic policy was important nevertheless, has been confirmed time and time again as evidenced in the fortunes of the UK, US and Eurozone economies. His writings, reflecting the sharpness of his mind and intellectual integrity, have had a considerable impact on macroeconomics and have aroused the interest of scholars, economic journalists and policymakers in both mainstream and alternative thought. In a review of Wynne's last book with Marc Lavoie (2007), Lance Taylor had this to say: 'Wynne's important contributions are foxy – brilliant innovations... that feed into the architecture of his models' (2008, p. 1).

Godley's intellectual endeavors were wide-ranging and his contributions revealed his deep understanding of Keynesian economic theory and policy. The essays in this volume deal, too, with interpreting and modeling Keynesian theory and policy – a critical area of his research. As Wynne did, the contributors view economics as a persistent process, in which healthy debate and dissent play a crucial role.

Wynne Alexander Hugh Godley, born in London in 1926, was the younger brother of a hereditary Labour peer, and went to school at Rugby and New College at Oxford. His undergraduate education there was strongly influenced by two of his teachers, Isaiah Berlin and P.W.S. Andrews.

In the early 1950s he pursued a career as an oboist, having studied at the Conservatoire de Musique in Paris. He earned his living as a performer at the St James' Theatre in London and subsequently as principal oboist for the BBC Welsh Symphony Orchestra. Eventually he abandoned his professional career as an artist, but never his love and interest in music practicing the oboe every morning while at the Levy Institute for almost a decade (1994–2004) and having served on the Board of Directors of the Royal Opera House. His intense blue eyes, and facial expression, led his father-in-law, the distinguished sculptor Sir Jacob Epstein, to use him as a model for the sculpture he did for the rebuilt Coventry Cathedral, of 'St Michael triumphing over the Devil.' Godley, responding to a journalist from the *Observer* in 1992, as to which one of the two he was, he replied: 'You will be disappointed to hear that I'm on the godly side as St Michael, although only his face is mine. His body's an athlete who worked as a quantity surveyor, whose own face was for some reason thought more fitting for the devil.' 'But your features, at least, are cast in stone for all time?' the journalist asked. 'Well, bronze actually,' Wynne, retorted. 'But apart from that, I suppose so.'

When the stage fright became unbearable, Wynne turned to economics, landing an appointment as an economist at HM Treasury where he became a kind of a high flier working out the exact percentage of the Wilson government's 1967 sterling devaluation. Recalling this event, Wynne once told me, that the work was top secret, and he was forced into isolation in an empty room with a pad, a pencil and a slide rule, and was told he could not come out before he had the answer.

After 14 years at the Treasury, ultimately becoming its Chief Economic Forecaster, at the urging of Nicholas Kaldor, with whom he developed an increasingly close relationship and friendship, Wynne left the Treasury to become Director of the Department of Applied Economics and Fellow of King's College at Cambridge University. In the autobiographical note included in Arestis and Sawyer's *A Biographical Dictionary of Dissenting Economists* (2000), he tells the reader that his principal objective in leaving the Treasury for Cambridge was to carry out the same work in public that he did perforce in secrecy and in so doing to raise the level of the public discussion of economic policy.

In Cambridge, along with Francis Cripps, he formed the Cambridge Economic Policy Group which developed a coherent macroeconomic accounting model, what we now call 'stock-flow consistent' in which the accounting had no 'black holes.' Although both Godley and Cripps were identified as 'New Cambridge School' they 'preferred to talk of a new Cambridge model or a new Cambridge equation' (Maloney 2010, p. 3). They produced forecasts that questioned the viability of the Heath–Barber boom and the Thatcher–Howe policies of 1979–81 destined to generate the biggest post-war slump from which no recovery could occur without a 'U-turn.' But the Group's doom-laden scenarios in the early 1980s upset the Thatcher government that made sure the group's funding was cut off. Wynne remained disappointed and bitter for many years. In a *Sunday Times* interview in 1992, this is how he put it. 'What they did in 1982 was say there is only one way to forecast. I am not a high-grade idiot. I wasn't doing things that I knew to be wrong.' At the end, as is by now well known, his forecasts confirmed the boom was unsustainable and that the economy was heading for deep trouble.

Wynne's intellectual achievements were considerable not only in macroeconomic forecasting, but also in many other areas, including his work on pricing, profits, public expenditures, inflation, employment, the macroeconomic textbooks with Francis Cripps (1983) and Mark Lavoie, the more than fifty or so articles in peer-reviewed journals and many columns in the *Observer* and the *New Statesman & Society*.

During his sabbatical year in 1991, Wynne Godley came to the Levy Institute as a visiting distinguished scholar. After a year's stay, he returned to Cambridge and upon his retirement in 1993, returned to the Levy Institute. During the 1992–3 year in Cambridge, he enjoyed a period of very considerable success, mainly because both the strategic forecasts he had been making for years and also his short-term forecasts had come to pass and he was, at last, recognized by the British establishment as a maverick economist who had won the forecasting game hands down. While in Cambridge he was named one of the six wise men to advise the Chancellor of the Exchequer.

He and his wife, Kitty, eventually made their home in Rhinebeck in Upstate New York in what Kitty thought was an acceptable, but poor rendition of their true cottage at Cavendish in the UK. Writing in January 1991 to Hyman Minsky, who introduced him to me, Godley considered it strange that as a professor in Cambridge, England he felt the need to emigrate to be in an intellectually sympathetic environment.

While in Cambridge, during the year between his stays at the Levy Institute, he was pleased to report that he continued to work on the US model he had began constructing, and was ecstatic to announce in a letter he sent me 'I have succeeded in the main task I had set for myself, which has been to remove all the secret skeletons from the secret cupboards in my US model. In its revised form, there is no cheating at all – so I will not be ashamed to let other people look at it critically. I am very pleased because the process of strengthening its logical architecture has also improved the simulation properties of the model. It now simulates the period 1971–89 with a RMS error of only 1 per cent with endogenous inflation and without dummy variables.'

Re-reading the Godley papers, the older on the British economy and the later on the US, one cannot but observe his flair for economic forecasting. Not only did he forecast the scale and duration of Britain's early 1990s recession and the corresponding recessions in 2001–02 and 2007–09 in the US quite accurately and at an early stage, but he also wrote about the future in a circumstantial way documenting, before they happen, the same reasons that were given by everyone to explain them after they had occurred.

When the mainstream thought was vastly overoptimistic, Godley – the Cassandra of Cambridge as he had come to be known – recognized the coming of a chaotic and very difficult long-term future for both Britain and the US. In many of the Levy Institute's Strategic Analysis reports he authored (Godley 1999; Godley and Izurieta 2001; Godley 2003; Godley, et al. 2005; Godley et al. 2007a; Godley et al. 2007b; Godley et al. 2008), he warned that unless the US takes action to increase exports and reduce imports, her large and growing trade deficit will produce structural imbalances that would become unsustainable and lead to long recessions and high unemployment. He also warned of the bias of the fiscal policy stance toward surplus and the explosion of private sector indebtedness that would also become unsustainable predicting what has come to be known as the Minsky crisis of 2007–08.

He was often described as a doomsayer. But as Andrew Smithers once remarked not long ago, 'Cassandra was a sound analyst. Her forecasts were correct, she made no claims about their timing and her views were largely ignored. But what made her hopping mad was a headline in the *Troy Times* that read: "Queen Hecuba asks 'Why did no one warn us about the wooden horse?'"'

He foresaw the flaws of the Maastricht Treaty early on and the consequences in adopting a single currency with results that several countries of Southern Europe are currently enduring. Writing in the *Observer* in 1997, he noted that 'if a government stops having its own currency, it doesn't just give up 'control over monetary policy' as normally understood; its spending powers also become constrained in an entirely new way. If a government does not have its own central bank on which it can draw cheques freely, its expenditure can be financed only by borrowing in the open market in competition with businesses, and this may prove excessively expensive or even impossible, particularly under conditions of extreme emergency.'

Wynne's writings have made a distinctive contribution to the current discussion, effectively refuting the fashionable view that markets always know best and must never be tampered with. He thought that the most important part of modern economies is not millions of people working as free agents, but institutions such as governments, companies, banks and trade unions which operate in a number of unique ways and cannot be fitted into 'dangerous and pernicious' theories of free choice.

Since markets are neither free nor do they clear in the relevant time, governments must take responsibility for social goals including high levels of employment, a fair system to distribute income and 'ensuring that people who are ill or old or very poor are cared for.' It is not necessary, I think, to convince the readers of this book that at present, we are on the road of continuous growth recession with intolerable mass unemployment affecting millions of people in the US, Europe and elsewhere for the foreseeable future – in order to reach the conclusion that all ways in which governments can play an active role in economic management deserve urgent reconsideration.

This introductory chapter does not summarize adequately those that follow, but in a few sentences attempts to demonstrate how each chapter connects to Godley's ideas. The reader will need to go to each contribution to discover its individual message. In the opening chapter, Tiago Mata provides a portrait of Godley as an economist, a civil servant and adviser who continuously challenged the conventional account of knowledge of the structure of the UK economy first, and later of that in the US. He was a master forecaster with an economic judgment and insight acquired over the years 'by doing economics' that competed with formal theories. But Godley's forecasts were not the result of a model working independently of his 'mind' enabling him to 'get it right.' L. Randall Wray, in the next chapter, extends Mata's portrait of Godley by focusing mostly on Wynne's development of the Levy Economics Institute's three-sector model and his discovery of the unsustainable processes that provided him with a masterful insight of the US economy in the critical decades of the 1990s and 2000s. Godley warned repeatedly, in a series of papers, policy briefs and reports published by the Levy Economics Institute, that the euphoric nature of the global economy would be short-lived and that the US federal budget surplus of which the Clinton Administration was so proud would vanish. Alas, his warnings were not seriously considered as the prevailing neoclassical wisdom at the time had determined that the economic expansion was not caused by rising demand, but rather because growth had become 'structural' (Phelps 2000). As Wray points out, Godley predicted the 'Great Recession' accurately and proposed policy options to avert it. Wynne's powerful insight on the impending financial and economic crises that began in 2007 is eloquently echoed in the chapter that follows by James Galbraith. Galbraith compares his depth of analysis to the feebleness of mainstream economists in analyzing economic events.

Subsequent chapters deal with Godley's contributions to private sector expenditure behavior, his views on money and credit, structural aspects of his 'New Cambridge' stock-flow consistent modeling exercise of the UK and later the US economies, and theoretical extensions of it to countries in the Eurozone. Bill Martin's chapter is the logical starting point for this group of papers, since it is specifically devoted to a re-examination of the private sector's behavioral relationship between private financial wealth and disposable income – a research and policy area of immense significance and focus to Wynne's work. Martin's meticulously detailed econometric results based on a specially constructed historic database of the UK private sector expenditure aggregates show ample evidence of this relationship between *stocks* of financial wealth and *flows* of income and expenditure, albeit not always stable but dependent on shifting trends. What is important, however, is that his findings support Wynne's 1970s and 1980s 'New Cambridge' model of the mean reversion of the private sector's financial surplus and that there appears to be a strong connection between private expenditure and house prices. The private sector expenditure behavior is also the focus of the next chapter by Anwar Shaikh who compares Wynne's contribution on this topic to those of Richard and Nancy Ruggles for the US. National income accounts can be expressed in terms of three sectoral gaps between expenditures and income, relative to GDP. If the private sector balance tends to be small and stable, then it follows that foreign trade deficit would mirror the government deficit. This policy implication became the core of the 'New Cambridge' hypothesis. Godley and Cripps in their book aimed at providing a theoretical justification of the existence of a stable and desired norm between private sector net financial assets and private disposable income. The adjustment process they proposed, however, was unstable in the presence of endogenous growth. Shaikh attempts to generalize the Godley and Cripps hypothesis and shows that a modification of their adjustment process can lead to a stable convergence of the actual net financial assets ratio to the desired norm. His results imply that the private sector balance is proportional to the growth rate of GDP – a conclusion that is in concert with the Richard and Nancy Ruggles findings in the US. The received policy implication from these findings is that for a stable and positive value of the private sector balance, an increase in the government deficit will be largely mirrored in a corresponding increase in the current account balance.

Marc Lavoie takes up Godley's ideas on money and credit, and on pricing and profits as these are linked with business inventories. He traces the refinement and further development of Godley's architecture of thought through his various papers published from the publication of his textbook with Cripps to the writing of their book. As Lavoie points out, this was Wynne's long voyage in which he wanted 'to show how the whole system fits together and cast banks in a realistic role' (Godley 1996, p. 14). During this 25-year period, Wynne's treatment of money and credit was the same as that of the monetary circuit view, and he was able to refine his ideas on pricing, properly define profits and develop coherence in inventory valuations. The effort to integrate Augusto Graziani's monetary circuit theory into Godley's stock-flow consistent model comes through in Gennaro Zezza's chapter. In doing so, Zezza identifies the apparent inconsistency that exists in the money circuit theory in explaining how profits are determined within a single production period when firms are faced with interest payments on their initial loan – a condition known as the paradox of profits. Zezza shows how the paradox is resolved when in constructing a Godley consistent stock-flow model of the banking sector – the time period of the circuit is longer than the period of production beginning with the time of the initial loan and ending when the loan payment is made – banks' income from interest payments is treated as either a source of demand for goods and services or demand for financial assets emanating from another sector. Godley's approach and the monetary circuit theoretic become compatible once it is recognized that while the first uses end of the period stock of loans, the latter centers on the start of financing. Both the Lavoie and Zezza chapters are relevant to the discussion of the money and credit debate among post-Keynesian thinking – a theme that comes up again, from different perspectives, in later chapters. In the next chapter, Jan Toporowski and Jo Michell deal with related issues of firm behavior in the financing of investment and how these can be integrated in a Godley stock-flow consistent model. Here Toporowski and Michell try to document the difficulties of incorporating financing modes of investment, that is, bank loans, retained earnings, and effects of firm overcapitalization either as excess capital in the form of bank deposits or excess capital in the form of financial securities. These finance-guided cases reminiscent of the Minskyan classifications are illustrated in the transaction matrices, Toporowski and Michell provide, consistent with stock-flow methodology from which various policy implications are drawn.

The next three chapters, by Vincent Duwicquet and Jacques Mazier, Stephen Kinsella and Saed Khalil, all tackle various issues from Godley's stock-flow consistent perspective. Duwicquet and Mazier construct a model, along the lines of the Godley and Lavoie model, of monetary union involving two countries and compare it with the approach known as 'international risk sharing.' As is by now well understood from the financial crisis afflicting the Southern European economies in the monetary union, adjustments face asymmetric processes and are more difficult to deal with because of the fixed intra-zone exchange rates. If well-integrated capital markets exist with portfolio diversification and intra-zone credit, then, they can be brought about through international risk sharing. This type of adjustment mechanism has been advocated, as we have seen, by European Union policymakers to promote deeper financial integration even in the absence of a Eurozone budget. Duwicquet and Mazier raise theoretical and econometric methodology questions of this approach. To answer these questions, their stock-flow consistent model uses alternative structures, that is, with or without foreign financial assets, intra-zone credit and intra-zone capital income transfers with or without rationing. Each version of their model yields strong or weak stabilization results as compared with the 'risk-sharing' approach. Stephen Kinsella and Saed Khalil tackle a different issue involving, again, two countries. Their aim is to map out the macroeconomic effects of sustained debt deflation within a small open economy. They build a two-country stock-flow consistent model and show the effects of a debt deflation cycle on households, firms, banks, the government, and the central bank in each country. Their findings demonstrate that price declines across the economy can sustain a downturn, even as other areas of the economy experience a return to growth. The policy implications drawn from their results suggest that in a currency union, with one country experiencing deflation, only transfers from the larger country and increased government expenditure can bring the smaller economy out of the deflationary spiral contrary to the advice presently being dispensed in the countries of Southern Europe. Le Heron's chapter focuses on fiscal policy neutrality – a debate he apparently began with Wynne in 2006. The debate centers on the question of how to neutralize fiscal policy so as to measure the effects of monetary policy. Wynne's response was that neutrality of fiscal policy was tantamount to the steady or stationary state of growth. Le Heron tests a number of (six, including Wynne's) propositions of fiscal policy neutrality and obtains different (naturally) results of monetary policy effectiveness on growth rates, fiscal deficit and debt, firms' debt, consumption and finance rationing – all illustrated in well-drawn figures. His results are interesting and valuable for policy formulation and the reader will draw his or her own conclusions.

The last three chapters belong to the field of applied economics. As was mentioned above, Godley avoided the strict specialization, so common to mainstream economists. He was interested in the practical relevance of theoretical debates. In their chapter, Philip Arestis and Malcolm Sawyer concentrate on the Levy Economic Institute's model that Godley developed in the late 1990s (1999), to explore the impact of fiscal policy on the level of economic activity. They derive the scale of fiscal and monetary multipliers and effects of fiscal and monetary policy on the level of economic activity and other important variables. They compare their results with other estimates of the effects of fiscal policy and explore the reasons for the differences and similarities, and conclude that fiscal rather than monetary policy is shown to be an important and effective instrument of economic policy stabilization. Jörg Bibow, too, in his chapter, makes use of the Levy Institute's model as a starting point to analyze Godley's key insights into economic developments that alerted him to flaws in other, more optimistic assessments made before the global crisis of 2007. Bibow finds that Godley's diagnosis of the looming economic and financial difficulties ahead of their occurrence was prescient with regard to US domestic developments – a theme that came up in the chapters by Wray and Galbraith. But Bibow takes issue with Wynne's assessment of the US external balance being unsustainable. He notes that the US investment position and income flows are more or less in balance and he attributes this phenomenon to the safety of the US Treasury securities and the dollar functioning as the reserve currency. Even if this is so, it cannot continue indefinitely, Wynne would have replied. The last chapter in the volume, by Michael Brecht, Silke Tober, Till van Treeck and Achim Truger, test another application of Godley's stock-flow framework relating to Eurozone countries. They simulate the effects of Europe's various stability programs directed at reducing current account imbalances, public deficits and unemployment for the 2010–13 period, and find disappointing results. The stability programs appear to be based on optimistic assumptions about private sector demand and GDP growth, given the degree of fiscal consolidation imposed, and, moreover, there is the implication that current account imbalances in the euro area as a whole would improve its external balance with the rest of the world. The authors' conclusions based on their use of Godley's operational framework of the three balances suggest that the only way to achieve the assumed GDP growth would be for the governments of surplus countries to be prepared to run higher deficits over the next few years. This is in concert with the public outcry against the current focus on deficit reduction imposed harshly on the countries of Southern Europe.

The chapters in this book contribute to the rethinking of macroeconomics without microfoundations – as Wynne would have argued absolutely. Whatever may be thought of Wynne's legacy, it will not only be in his books, papers, and columns, but also in the personal memories that his friends and colleagues will remember. Whatever we might think of the old-style Keynesianism Wynne represented, he has left a more lasting impression than most of his kind, his immortality in the figure of St Michael's notwithstanding.

References

Godley, W. (1996) 'Money, Finance and National Income Determination,' Working Paper No. 167 (Annandale-on-Hudson, NY: Levy Economics Institute of Bard College).

Godley, W. (1997) 'Curried EMU: The Meal that Fails to Nourish,' *The Observer*, 31 August.

Godley, W. (2000) 'Seven Unsustainable Processes: Medium-Term Prospects and Policies for the United States and the World,' Strategic Analysis, October 2000 (Annandale-on-Hudson, NY: Levy Economics Institute of Bard College).

Godley, W. (2000) 'Wynne Godley,' in P. Arestis and M.C. Sawyer (eds) *A Biographical Dictionary of Dissenting Economists* (Cheltenham, UK: Edward Elgar Publishing), pp. 232–40.

Godley, W. (2003) 'The US Economy: A Changing Strategic Predicament,' Strategic Analysis, March 2003 (Annandale-on-Hudson, NY: Levy Economics Institute of Bard College).

Godley, W. and F. Cripps (1983) *Macroeconomics* (London: Fontana).

Godley, W. and A. Izurieta (2001) 'The Developing US Recession and Guidelines for Policy,' Strategic Analysis, October 2001 (Annandale-on-Hudson, NY: Levy Economics Institute of Bard College).

Godley, W. and M. Lavoie (2007) *Monetary Economics: An Integrated Approach to Credit, Money, Income, Production and Wealth* (Basingstoke, UK: Palgrave Macmillan).

Godley, W., D. B. Papadimitriou, C. H. Dos Santos and G. Zezza (2005) 'The United States and her Creditors: Can the Symbiosis Last?,' Strategic Analysis, September (Annandale-on-Hudson, NY: Levy Economics Institute of Bard College).

Godley, W., D. B. Papadimitriou and G. Zezza (2007a) 'The US Economy: What's Next?,' Strategic Analysis, April (Annandale-on-Hudson, NY: Levy Economics Institute of Bard College).

Godley, W., D. B. Papadimitriou, G. Hannsgen and G. Zezza (2007b) 'The US Economy: Is There a Way Out of the Woods?,' Strategic Analysis, November (Annandale-on-Hudson, NY: Levy Economics Institute of Bard College).

Godley, W., D. B. Papadimitriou and G. Zezza (2008) 'Prospects for the United States and the World: A Crisis That Conventional Remedies Cannot

Resolve,' Strategic Analysis, December 2008 (Annandale-on-Hudson, NY: Levy Economics Institute of Bard College).

Maloney, J. (2010) 'The Treasury and the New Cambridge School in the 1970s', Working Paper, Department of Economics, Exeter University Business School.

Phelps, E. (2000) 'Europe's Stony Ground for the Seeds of Growth,' *Financial Times*, August 9.

Taylor, L. (2008) 'A Foxy Hedgehog: Wynne Godley and Macroeconomic Modeling', *Cambridge Journal of Economics* 32(4): 639–63.

2

Godley Moves in Mysterious Ways: The Craft of Economic Judgment in Post-war Britain

*Tiago Mata**

2.1 Knowledge ways

Economists are not memorialized in monuments. Wynne Godley is the exception, his likeness is cast in bronze upon Coventry Cathedral as archangel Michael ('St Michael's Victory over the Devil', 1958) in a sculpture by his father-in-law Jacob Epstein. On his passing, Godley was remembered in obituaries in the major British broadsheets, that recalled his dotted career, his engagement with the arts, his grace as a host and his tragic family history.[1] At the venerable age of 75, Godley penned an essay to the *London Review of Books* on his battles, four decades earlier, with an abusive psychoanalyst (Godley 2001). If one were to write Godley's biography (and I know of no such plans) the defining features of his character would be taken from this autobiographical account: a search for his true voice, and as he took many public roles, a nagging fear that he might disappoint such responsibilities. The tensions that made up the intimate structures of his psychoanalytic self help also to describe his approach to economics: an anxious affirmation of voice and judgment.

One can read Godley's 2007 book with Marc Lavoie, *Monetary Economics*, as setting between covers the likeness of his economics. In this chapter I take the view that Godley's life work has more to teach us if we dispose of narratives of incremental progress and closure. The record shows Godley's continued efforts to enunciate a knowledge that was for him

*I interviewed Wynne Godley in 2006 while working on an earlier version of this chapter with very different purposes. The insights gained from that short but delightful conversation were critical for the present writing. I thank Marc Lavoie, David Laidler, Teresa Thomas Rangil, Harro Maas, Avi Cohen, John King, Roger Backhouse, and John Maloney for comments and suggestions to this chapter.

tacit. This record offers the historian a glimpse of economics as a craft. Like the artisans of all ages, and in sociological accounts the natural scientists of today,[2] economists are enjoined on a long apprenticeship in the developing of models that are able to speak to economic issues. It is a knowledge acquired 'by doing.' Yet Godley was different, because his craft was not in the design of models, but in offering judgment about the prospects of the economy, its challenges, its outcomes. His principal resource was not model building, but an interpretive understanding of the workings of the national accounts system shadowing the workings of the British economy – a skill he honed with public drama throughout his professional life.

My aim in this chapter is to outline a narrative of Wynne Godley's work that probes his ways to knowledge. The chapter challenges a conventional account of knowledge, as first produced in academic quarters and later applied beyond their threshold. In contrast, I argue that Godley developed his understanding of the economy in civil service, and popular media, as well as in academic settings. His core insights were gained prior to his university appointments, in public surroundings. Furthermore, Godley's greatest achievement was not to add to a body of literature but to develop his own, embodied, understanding of the economy in its uncertain dynamic, beyond the enunciation of facts, simulations or model results. The residual and crucial component was Godley's judgment. From my perspective, Godley was always the civil servant and the adviser, so the narrative begins with his tenure at the Treasury.

2.2 Forecaster: An education at the Economic Section

By his own account, Godley abandoned a promising career as a professional musician, principal oboist at the BBC Welsh Symphony Orchestra, because of his increasing stage fright. He had earned a PPE degree from Oxford, and although he recalled more vividly his interactions with Isaiah Berlin, it was his economics teacher, P.W.S. Andrews, who brokered for him an alternative career: first as economist at the Metal Box Co. in 1954, and two years later moving to the Economic Section, the principal institution for economic advice in the British government (Godley, 2000).

The Economic Section was Godley's graduate school and his tutor there was Sir Robert Hall.[3] When Hall took over the role of director from James Meade, the Economic Section was still housed in the Cabinet Office, and was on call to give advice to any branch of government. In 1953, its operations moved to the Treasury, and its influence had to be channeled through the Chancellor of the Exchequer's personality and prominence in the Cabinet. Hall adapted well to these changes. Whereas Meade was an academic first and an adviser second, Hall resisted the allure of doctrinal disputation and scholarly subtlety. He was of the 'one handed school of advisers,' famously saying that 'it is not much use giving advice to Ministers unless it is very loud and clear' (Cairncross and Watts, 1989, pp. 137, 135). In now dated terms, Samuel Brittan noted that 'at his best Hall had an almost feminine intuition for the way the economy was moving' (Brittan, 1971, p. 95). For Hall, the goal was always to grasp a comprehensive view of the whole, the general economic situation (Jones, 1994). The ability to grasp the landscape, and the flexibility to speak about all fields of government action were requisite skills for employment in the Treasury. The institutional set-up in which Godley entered privileged *unambiguous commentary on the general economic situation.* Godley was to make this bureaucratic mandate into his professional voice.

Hall held the longest and most distinguished of tenures at the Economic Section, serving for 14 years. He was a principal in shaping the institutions of government advice, arguing that the number of economists in government was insufficient and that both their quality and their commitment to public service were variable.[4] Retiring in 1961, it was Hall's replacement, Alec Cairncross, who saw the realization of the dreams of reform. On Godley's arrival in 1956, Hall's section was a small operation of about 15 professional economists. For a further decade it was a tight collaborative community, holding a monopoly over advice. In 1965 the new Labour administration created the Government Economic Service and overnight all ministries were staffed with economists. From under 20 economists in service the numbers leaped to 209, and kept on rising to 390 by 1979 (Coats, 1981). The partitioning of economic advice was the Labour government's design to break the monopoly by the Treasury and its economist advisers over the shaping of policy. It gave every ministry its own intellectual ammunition and installed the Department of Economic Affairs as the clearing house and planning bureau for policymaking. The Department was initially asked to outline supply-side policies to halt Britain's industrial decline. But, less than a year after beginning its operations, such plans were abandoned for more conventional policies, such as those met by the advice of the Treasury's Economic Section (Middleton, 2000).

Among the new arrivals were those known at the time as 'political economists': university faculty that took advising roles with the expressed goal of changing government policy. The welcomed addition of more skilled economists was accompanied by the unwelcomed prospect of competition for the attention and trust of ministers. Reading Cairncross' diary, one finds him in continuous and often strained debate with Robert Neild, adviser to the Chancellor, and Nicholas Kaldor, adviser at large on taxation (Cairncross, 1997). Thomas Balogh advised the prime minister. The presence of the academics did not change Godley's responsibilities:[5] to hold the most up-to-date outlook on the economic situation, anticipating official estimates and statistics, on wages, productivity, public expenditure and the balance of payments.[6]

However, Godley found himself more than ever a participant in a policy debate, an increasing element of which was a competition over conflicting claims to economic knowledge and theory.

It is a challenge for the historian to track how a deep understanding of data develops. There is no paper trail of how it arises over many years of looking at how data match, change, and what they mean. It is embodied knowledge. Sociologists of science have recorded this kind of knowledge through participant observation, whereby the sociologist tracks his own difficulties in joining a research community and assimilating their fast-paced and tacit acting.[7] The second-best approach is to locate the mutual puzzlement between historical actors who have the tacit skill and those that don't. The character of Godley's contribution to the Economic Section can be unpacked by looking at his relationship with Cairncross. Cairncross's mandate was to field the requests of ministers and to react to the grand designs of the multitude of economist advisers. Cairncross had to converse with policy players, about forecasts and statistics that were not his own.

Excerpts from Cairncross's published diaries testify to bonds of trust. Cairncross reports on a lunch with Godley, in July 1967, at which Godley complained about the public sector statistics 'prepared by junior clerks who don't appreciate any of the nicer points' (Cairncross, 1997, p. 223). The communication was done informally, over a meal, yet seems to have been an issue that should have preoccupied Cairncross, since statistics were the basis upon which his recommendations were grounded. But there is no further record of what the 'nicer points' might be, or what might be done to correct the juniors. Cairncross trusted that Godley could find his way to the necessary information. Indeed, the diaries are noteworthy for their brief references to issues of data.

Three months after their lunch, Godley once again complained about public sector statistics. Cairncross writes in his diary that:

> W.G. [Wynne Godley] very interesting on statistics of public expenditure. CSO [Central Statistical Office] use data for local authority

> investment quarterly which they disregard completely once they get capital spending figures once a year but these don't really relate to actual investment so we don't get either quarterly or annually any reliable guide of what is happening; and tend every year to be thrown off previous interpretation by annual data. (Cairncross, 1997, p. 239)

This comment provides a sense of how Godley worked, looking for patterns of connection and consistency in the data. In the case at hand, he discovered a glaring mismatch between quarterly and yearly series, arriving at the Economic Section as 'local authority investment' but really being inconsistent. Neither the quarterly nor the annual data gave the information required. A sense of 'what is happening' had to be gained with other sources. The annual data would arrive as a surprise, undermining the Section's standing interpretation. Routinely, for his short-term forecasts, Godley had to rely on incomplete or biased data, on data that swapped definitions depending on the time frame.[8] His forecasts were no conjurer's trick, but an accounting insight gained from toiling at the numbers for over one and a half decades, grasping for a big interpretative insight.

Godley's role at the Treasury was to provide short-term forecasting. In the late 1960s, he was recruited to a more unusual role, but one that drew on his understanding of the economic landscape. He produced the statistical classification upon which Kaldor's Selective Employment Tax was applied, selecting those industries that would be subsidized and those that would be subject to tax. More famously, Godley did the calculations for the package of policies accompanying the 1967 devaluation of the pound from $2.80 to $2.40 (Godley, 2000). In his final years at the Treasury Godley played a more active role in policy design, as the deputy director of the Economic Section. When Godley agreed, at some financial cost, to abandon his civil service job in order to move to Cambridge, he traveled with the expectation that he would remain engaged in policy debates and be free to express his policy views – a discretion that he had been denied as a civil servant.

2.3 New Cambridge: Publicity against the Keynesian consensus

Godley was an outsider to the town and to university life, but in joining Cambridge and King's College he saw plenty of familiar faces. Close by was Kaldor, who was the force behind Godley's appointment, and Robert Neild, who had rejoined the Cambridge faculty. Godley's closest collaborator, Francis Cripps, had been Kaldor's assistant. Besides the network of people, there are other aspects of continuity between the Treasury and the Cambridge periods. As Director of the Department of Applied Economics (DAE),[9] Godley set up the 'Cambridge Economic Policy Group' which issued a yearly forecast of the British economy. The initiative was in the spirit of the National Institute of Economic and Social Research, where Godley had worked on secondment from the Treasury. That institute was another of Robert Hall's contributions wanting 'an official set of forecasts' to counter Treasury ones and create an 'independent view on the state of the economy and its forecasts' (Jones 1994, p. 175). Godley believed that this independent view could be nurtured in an academic setting like Cambridge. He was soon proved mistaken.

From the mid-1950s to the mid-1970s, the troubles facing the British economy and the policy tools of government were well identified. The direct controls inherited from the war were quickly dismantled and the exchange rate, budget and monetary policy became the instruments of economic policy. When Godley joined the Treasury in 1955 a deteriorating balance of payments was a primary concern (Jones, 1994). When Godley traded the Treasury for the University of Cambridge, the subject was again in the spotlight. The so-called 'Barber boom', characterized by tax cuts and easy credit, led to record deficits in the balance of payments, which were compounded with the 1973 oil shock (Middleton, 2000). These were times of national urgency.

On January 22–3, 1974, Godley and Cripps authored a two-part article for the *London and Cambridge Economic Bulletin* which was also published in the *Times*.[10] They painted a picture of impending catastrophe, calling for the implementation of 'a new set of principles.' The fundamental mistake was the short-term focus that blinded everyone to the 'predominant source of imbalance' for the economy: the government's fiscal and monetary policies. According to Godley and Cripps, the fundamental error of the orthodoxy was the assumption that private sector surplus was income elastic. In fact, the private sector's 'net acquisition of financial assets, is small and fairly stable.' Consequently, the likely effect of the budget deficit was to aggravate trade imbalances (such as those that occurred in the wake of the 1973 OPEC price hike) and failing to stimulate the private sector. Godley and Cripps argued that Britain should aim to improve its export potential through policies to increase industrial productivity and rely on external demand for growth. Devaluation was ruled out as potentially worsening inflation – export subsidies and import restrictions were preferable.

In print, there was no immediate response to Godley and Cripps' proposals.[11] A month later, on February 26, Neild wrote a letter to the *Times* titled: 'Reversing Keynes on budgetary policy.' It addressed a controversy prompted by an editorial divining the shape of the Budget.[12] Neild began: 'I and a number of my colleagues at Cambridge believe that the orthodox [Keynesian] view, to which many of us used to subscribe, is wrong and that its application in policy-making has been a major cause of Britain's postwar economic troubles.' Strikingly, he summarized this policy position as contrary to the Keynesian wisdom: 'the Budget should be used to determine the foreign balance and the exchange rate to determine the level of activity.' Neild made no explicit mention either of the Policy Group research or of the earlier articles by Godley and Cripps.

Neild's polemical reversal of Keynesianism was a catalyst for a response by others in the Cambridge faculty. Richard Kahn and Michael Posner's 'Challenging the "Elegant and Striking" Paradoxes of the New School'[13] grouped together Kaldor, Neild, Godley, and Cripps distinguishing them from an Older Keynesian School at Cambridge.[14] Godley and Cripps' policy brief was being read as a statement in economic theory. Kahn and Posner distinguished the schools in terms of their composition of the multiplier. Using the scenario of a depreciation of the exchange rate, they argued that the 'new school' only considered the 'leakage' of increased imports following external demand-induced growth. The 'new school' ignored the parallel effects of increased savings, increased profits and improvements in the state's budget deficit. They argued that only by disregarding these effects was it plausible for the 'new school' to claim that the trade balance was insensitive to the exchange rate instrument. Within this setting the 'old' Keynesian view encompassed the 'new' as a restricted and implausible case.

Reflective of his new location, Godley's policy intervention, even in such a worldly publication as the *Times*, was overtaken by an academic debate about the progeny and classification of economic theory. The Kahn and Posner article concerned the Cambridge 'new-comers.' In late May, Godley wrote to Kahn that: 'I am really very sorry that we should be in the position of having a confused debate in public without trying harder to make contact between ourselves and nearer agreement.' Godley's request was soon heeded, and Nicholas Kaldor, Kahn, and Posner had a heated exchange of letters.[15]

Kaldor has been credited as the originator of many of the New Cambridge proposals, typically with references to Kaldor (1955, 1955–56). The account that has Kaldor as the prime mover has been confirmed by his biographers that take for granted the theorist/practitioner hierarchy (Targetti, 1992; Thirlwall, 2004). That account has Kaldor outsourcing public advocacy to the Policy Group because he was bound to silence by his advisory post (Turner, 1993). The relationship between the protagonists is far more complex. John Maloney, studying Treasury documents only recently opened to the public, reveals that Kaldor, Cripps, who had become adviser to Tony Benn, Minister of Industry, and Godley were not always, or often, in agreement. The punchline in Godley and Cripps' proposal was import controls, a proposal that Benn would argue for in the Cabinet. Kaldor was never supportive of this solution (Maloney, forthcoming). What the standard account also misses is the nature of Godley's relationship with Kaldor. While at the Treasury, Godley was not shy from criticizing Kaldor. Cairncross (1997), with some amusement, notes meetings in which by force of argument he beat Kaldor into silence, confiding that: 'This was the only time I have seen it done' (Cairncross, 1997, p. 210). Yet Cambridge was not the Treasury, a different set of values and rules applied, and Godley would have been happy had Kaldor taken charge in the private correspondence to bring the dons to some agreement.

Kaldor, however, only stoked the fire. In a long letter, he criticized the Kahn and Posner *Times* article as 'unnecessarily argumentative and rather tortuous.' He further imputed misunderstanding of the 'new school' position. Posner and Kahn responded in an equally ill-tempered tone. Each side sought to expose the theoretical limitation of the other by attributing the vice of unacknowledged assumptions such as full employment (by the 'old') or a disregard for important multiplier effect (by the 'new').[16] In two subsequent letters in late May, Kahn and Posner refrained from engaging in longer arguments. They concluded in a 28 May letter that:

> We did not – and do not now – seek to make a great fuss about passing comments made by you [Kaldor] or other of your friends, we were driven to write our articles only because Robert, Wynne and Francis seemed to be collecting together these passing comments into a theoretical structure that seems to us unacceptable.

The correspondence was being copied to Neild, Godley, Posner, Cripps, Luigi Pasinetti, Adrian Wood, Douglas Wass, and Kenneth Berrill. Of these spectators, it was Cripps that drew a line under the discussion, stating that 'disagreement between any of us is on the behaviour of the private sector. ... The argument is whether there is a tendency to stability, in the form of some corrective response to abnormal surpluses or deficits.' He added that the DAE was doing 'detailed empirical work' on the question and once these results were out further discussion would be 'useful.' He 'fear[ed] that little is to be gained by a "theological" debate with attendant dangers of misrepresentation and misunderstanding.' After his early outburst, Kaldor confessed to having other 'pre-occupations' preventing him from fully engaging the debate with Kahn and Posner. On June 6, Kahn conceded to Cripps that the 'theological' debate was unproductive.[17]

The discussions of 1974 testify to Godley's difficult initiation into Cambridge Keynesian quarters. In the articles in the *Times* and the bulletins of the Policy Group, Godley identified the perils and choices facing the British economy. In contrast to his time at the Treasury, however, his expertise was no longer trusted and his statements were read against the academic standards of 1970s Cambridge. They asked how Keynesian was he?[18] To have a voice in these new settings he would have to refashion his insights to the current economic situation into a theoretical structure. He had to build a model.

2.4 Modeling: Obtaining academic credentials

Godley and Cripps were eager to strike a settlement with Kahn and Posner and benefitted from Kaldor's lack of interest in continuing the argument. The debate in the Cambridge correspondence had already moved to academic fora and to the halls of government.[19] Following the *Times* controversy, Godley and Cripps adopted the 'New Cambridge' label with a twist. They did not call themselves the 'New Cambridge school' but instead they referred to a 'New Cambridge hypothesis' and later a 'New Cambridge equation.' The semantic difference defused any challenge to Cambridge's Keynesian heritage, and made their work evidence of Cambridge's vitality. It also hinted at the increasing difficulties they were facing in establishing their claims.

In the wake of the May 1974 correspondence, Godley and Cripps' statements began referring to empirical findings resulting from econometric research. They thus appeared to steer themselves away from doctrinal debate. With the appointment of Denis Healey as Chancellor, the Policy Group was called in for discussions with the Treasury. That month, the Tory-led Commons Expenditure Committee set up an inquiry on the effect of public expenditure on the balance of payments and making direct reference to 'the propositions set out by Godley and Cripps in *The Times* on 22 January 1974.'[20] In the hearings, Godley and

Cripps placed their emphasis on empirical evidence. They estimated the private sector's net acquisition of financial assets as a stable function of disposable income (with minor variables of personal hire purchase debt outstanding, change in personal bank advances, and change in book value of stocks), which they called the 'New Cambridge equation' (Cripps et al., 1974). The attention and credibility afforded by these hearings was short-lived.

The empirical claims of Godley–Cripps were soon undermined, in 1975, by the retiring editor of the *National Review* (the journal of the National Institute for Economic and Social Science Research). Marking his departure for the Bank of England, J.A. Bispham made a firm defense of the 'conventional school' of policymaking and forecasting. The targets of the article were the 'New Cambridge Economics' and 'The "Monetarist" Position' (advanced from Manchester's M. Parkin and D. Laidler).[21] The Bispham critique was particularly severe because it deployed the authority of the National Institute's data and estimations in attacking New Cambridge.[22] There were two kinds of empirical counter-evidence. First, the New Cambridge equation did not perform any better than the 'conventional' alternatives in use. Second, it did not hold after 1972. Bispham concluded that: 'The New Cambridge equation has broken down massively' (Bispham, 1975, pp. 42, 47). Bispham argued that New Cambridge theory was built on short-term circumstances and chance alone explained that, in previous years, the balance of payments had seemed unresponsive to devaluation (there had been an independent rise in import prices, also known as oil shock) (Bispham, 1975, p. 44). This criticism greatly concerned Godley. The National Institute had been the first independent forecasting and policy institution that had inspired his Cambridge Policy Group. Godley himself had been at the National Institute in the early 1960s.

From 1975 onward, policy debate and advice began to be seized by doctrine. Despite their media visibility and access to the halls of power, the New Cambridge claims were resisted by Treasury economists. In less than two years of joint seminars and efforts at mutual understanding and appreciation, the only point of consensus was the embargo on fine-tuning. The Treasury's reluctance can be explained as an attempt to protect its field of action from the visitations of foreign academic advisers. But equally important was the emergence of a competitive public debate between University-based policy groups, each wielding their own doctrinal brand and distinct model of the British economy: the National Institute, the Cambridge and Manchester groups, and the London Business School (Budd, 1975).[23] As the *Times* controversy had hinted, all policy claims were promptly deconstructed by academics for their theoretical plausibility. Denied an empirical relationship by the National Institute, and resisted at the Treasury, the DAE needed a model that would represent as a structure the relationships they were seeing in the data and consolidate their academic authority.[24]

Aware of their competitors' strengths, the Cambridge Policy Group wrote for *Economica* (Cripps and Godley, 1976). Against the critics – Kahn, Posner, and Bispham – Godley and Cripps lined up a list of 'qualified supporters,' from the empirical economics camp. Their article was the first translation of the Policy Group's views into a macroeconomic model. The main feature of this translation was the replacement of the consumption and investment functions by a single private expenditure function, the New Cambridge equation (estimated in 1974). The model balanced the Cambridge Policy Group's distinctiveness from – and communality with – other approaches. The authors embraced an unorthodox 'Keynesianism.' They also hedged their policy prescriptions by stating that: 'The effects of inflation and real growth in the above formulation are regarded by the CEPG as relatively uncertain, while the link between the steady-state budget deficit and balance of payments is more clear-cut.' '[T]he exchange rate, export subsidies, import tariffs and import quotas can all be considered potentially effective methods ... assessment of the efficacy of different trade policy instruments depends on assumptions about the determinants of inflation' (Cripps and Godley, 1976, pp. 339, 341).

My claim is that Godley and his associates were attempting to establish academic credentials for their policy interpretations. There was pressure for them to present a model that could be related to other competing representations of the British economy. But 'modeling' was not Godley's strength, as became apparent in 1977, with a conference on 'Public Policies in Open Economies' held in collaboration between the University of Rochester and Carnegie-Mellon University. Half of the conference volume was devoted to American economists examining the 'New Cambridge' model. Disconnected from the British policy context, Godley argued for the doctrinal character of his approach – that is, how it superseded the raging monetarism versus Keynesian controversies. Thus, three years on from the *Times'* altercation, New Cambridge was engaging in 'theological' debate.[25]

At the American meetings, Fetherston and Godley (1978) contributed a simulation model of the UK economy, illustrating their 'Keynesian-type macroeconomic model' of the 'medium-term framework.' They noted that most of their model's specifications were not essential to

'New Cambridge' and were shared by other models of the UK economy. What was distinctive about their approach was the modeling of total private disposable income and expenditure (Fetherston and Godley, 1978, p. 36). They used the model to study three policy scenarios: a step reduction in imports, or quotas, an increase in public expenditure, and a devaluation of the sterling. They argued that their model saved Keynesianism from much of the recent Monetarist criticism and that New Cambridge models were consistent with the analysis of stock equilibrium in asset markets. They concluded that 'introduction of asset market considerations gives us no reason to alter our view that the principal questions of economic strategy in an open economy concern the appropriate uses of fiscal policy and trade policy' (Fetherston and Godley, 1978, pp. 55, 56).[26]

The American commentators were unsupportive.[27] The principal complaint was that New Cambridge resembled too much the old-style Keynesianism that had lost currency in the United States – 'a simple "Keynesian cross" model' or a 'crude Keynesianism' (Blinder, 1978, pp. 76–7).[28] Blinder concluded that:

> I am struck by how many aspects have already been jettisoned here [in America], often after a great controversy: the completely passive supply side, the fixed interest rate, the interest-inelastic investment demand, the trivialization of monetary policy, and so on. Revising any of these hypotheses would seem to be taking a step backward.

Following Blinder, two comments defending Monetarism offered further reasons to reject the New Cambridge approach: a flawed conception of the long-run (Frenkel, 1978); a lack of empirical evidence; and failure to comply to the standard of modeling maximizing agents in a coherent general equilibrium framework (Russell and Wakeman, 1978, pp. 96–8).

In 1980, Godley was appointed to the faculty at Cambridge as Professor of Applied Economics. Even if he never thought much of the American criticisms, his writings in popular, policy and academic publications, after early influence and celebrity, were being rejected. Denied allies beyond Cambridge, he was facing academic defeat. As Godley reminisced decades later:

> I did find myself badly outflanked by the rise in influence of monetarism . . . It was not, as I now see it, that the monetarists

> won any argument in the sense that they made propositions which I was forced to concede, on reflection, were correct. They won it for a different reason which I now admit with some shame and frustration – namely because in my own thinking I was only just beginning to incorporate balance sheet concept systematically and therefore found myself unable, at the elementary level of accountancy, to give convincing answers to perfectly simple questions about where money 'was' in my model. (Godley, 2000, p. 236)

Candidly, Godley acknowledged that his policy advocacy suffered as a consequence of his flawed modeling efforts. And they failed because he had been unable to give a formal analysis of that which he knew best, the national accounts.

2.5 Cassandra: Publicity against monetarism

Throughout the early and mid-1970s, the Cambridge Policy Group was acclaimed in the editorial and business pages of the *Times*. Peter Jay called its contribution a 'brave message of hope' (February 17, 1975). The following year the discourse suddenly changed and Cambridge proposals were derided as 'radical' (March 29, 1976). On March 22, 1977, the editorial column of the *Times* attacked their proposals as fallacious, with the invitation that: 'Those who disagree as completely as we do with their prescriptions have a duty to explain where we think the fallacies lie in their argument.' The change of fortune for the Cambridge Policy Group was part of the ideological shift undergone by the business press during the 1970s towards varied forms of 'monetarism' (see Parsons, 1989).

Matters got worse on March 13 1981, when Frank H. Hahn and Robert R. Neild, on University of Cambridge notepaper, circulated a letter of protest against the 1981 contractionist Thatcher budget. The protest letter was published with 364 signatures, a near clean sweep of the British economics profession. It was an awkward coalition of voices, from conservatives to radicals. The professional economists were most likely reacting to Thatcher's dismissiveness of academic guidance and advice, rather than expressing opposition to specific budget plans. The largest number of signatures was from Cambridge, Godley among them.[29] Although tenured, Godley's DAE relied on operating grants, and notably on Social Science Research Council funding. In 1982, the funding was withdrawn by a specially appointed Consortium including the SSRC, the Treasury, the Bank of England and academic consultants from the UK and overseas. The mandate of the Consortium was to bring some order into the rapid multiplication of models and forecasting approaches. It created the Warwick Macroeconomic Modelling Bureau headed by Kenneth Wallis to conduct comparative analysis of the different models, and it outlined cuts to several programs.[30] That the consortium included representatives of the Treasury suggested to many in the press, and at Cambridge, that it was payback for their antagonism, but there were also plausible claims to New Cambridge's academic isolation, as I have argued. The effects of the cut were profound, since it made it impossible for the Cambridge Policy Group to function (Godley, 2000, p. 235).[31]

Godley's grim forecasts in the late 1970s and 1980s clashed with the optimism of the new economic opinion makers. In a series of letters to the *Times* he antagonized the new cadre of advisers. He repeatedly wrote to contradict the lagged correspondence, established by Milton Friedman and others, between the growth of the money supply and inflation. One such statement came on June 6, 1980, recalling an article in the newspaper four years earlier by William Rees-Mogg:

> That inflation is now accelerating after a long period of relatively low growth in the excess money supply strengthens the case I made in my original letter – monetarism is completely failing to achieve the main objective claimed for it. At the same time, every day brings more evidence that the Government's policy is inflicting immense and perhaps permanent damage on British industry.

On October 22, 1980, he asked in the *Times* 'How far will the Government let unemployment go?' The article was full of indignation, firing questions such as 'If not two million is it three million? If not three million is it five million? If not five million...' One can argue the case that Godley's 1970s fiscal proposals for the medium term were not so different from those of Thatcher's governments. One difference in content was that Godley believed the Thatcher policies would undermine British industry and the long-term prospects of the economy. Another aspect was that the government seemed to make policy choices on the grounds of doctrinal conviction alone, without presenting clear forecasts of policy scenarios. He asserted that 'unless a government is merely capricious, its policy is essentially based on a forecast, otherwise it can have no grounds for doing one set of things rather than another.' Godley was depressed that forecasters, those that imagined economic futures, had been removed from the policy debate.

References to 'New Cambridge' soon disappeared, and efforts to establish a doctrinal brand were abandoned. Godley continued his modeling efforts but settled for creating toy models to aid in thinking through the range of policy options. As he explained in his 1983 book, *Macroeconomics*:

> The analytic solutions are used to generate numerical simulations of the development of the whole economic systems by making specific assumptions about policies and behavioral relationships. We attach great importance to these simulations as they can always be reproduced using only a pocket calculator. . . . By carrying out their own simulations readers may also gain a sense of what is involved in macroeconomic forecasting for policy purposes. (Godley and Cripps, 1983, p. 18, emphasis in original)

This was an abandonment of modeling as representation and as a contribution to theoretical disputation, to endorse a much weaker, didactic use of modeling.[32] Godley might have wished his readers (and students) to 'play' with his model economy, but few did, and the book had limited impact.

2.6 Wise man: Simulating the worst case scenario

The narrative that I have outlined appears to be one of defeat. But I argue that it is no indictment on Godley and his economics. In moving from the Treasury to academia, and to secure his academic credibility, Godley was asked to codify into theory and models his understanding of the economy. The record shows him hesitating and equivocating about whether his contribution was an empirical claim, an equation on a model, a model, or a theory. What Godley saw was a changing picture that could not rest on any set of first principles and, in due course, he gave up on the codifying enterprise.

By 1982, the Cambridge Policy Group had lost its funding. Godley and Cripps' 1983 book had little impact. Four years later, Godley retired from his post as director of Cambridge's DAE, and spent a year away as a visiting professor in Denmark. His status in Britain's academic community was not great. But on his return, Monetarism and Thatcher economics began to unravel. The signal event for my argument was the pound's withdrawal from the European Exchange Rate Mechanism in 1992.

The British pound joined the Exchange Rate Mechanism in October 1990 at the instigation of the then Chancellor, John Major. A month later, Thatcher was forced to resign and Major replaced her as Prime Minister. Major had another victory two years later, winning the general election in April, but on September 16, 1992 he lost the economy. With a record of high interest rates to maintain parity with the German Deutschemark, Britain was facing recession. Learning that the situation was unsustainable, a wave of short selling forced the government to announce defeat. A decade earlier, Thatcher had successfully played against the economics profession. Major, facing economic humiliation, instead tried to bring the economists into the fold. The Treasury set up a Panel of Independent Forecasters, known as the 'six wise men.' Godley was one of them, between 1992 and 1995.

The return to the Treasury was a vindication of Godley's expertise as a forecaster. The record of the 1970s, reviewed here, shows a man seeking to make his voice heard outside the academy in polemical performances in newsprint and cautiously inside the academy.

Godley expressed a more unified attitude toward public life and science in an interview with sociologist Robert Evans in the mid-1990s. He was dismissive of the consensus in academic modeling. When queried by Evans about micro-foundations in economic models he replied: 'Well, ... when people speak of micro-foundations they tend to mean by that a very special thing, which is it's all deducible in terms of the optimizing behaviour of individual rational agents, and I don't accept that as an appropriate concept' (Godley in Evans, 1997, p. 414). More importantly, Godley was unequivocal that an accurate and complete model of the economy can never be attained. He remarked that

> There's a fantasy that you're going to introduce more and more complexity and more and more realistic features and apply better and better ... and eventually it will work, and it will give you the answer. You see it's all been a great failure, all of that, and forecasting isn't done better, it makes no progress as a result. (Godley in Evans, 1997, p. 436)

For him models were aids to the analyst, and 'the forecasts I publish are not the result of a model working independently of my mind' (Godley in Evans 1997, p. 410).

In the interview, Godley insisted that forecasting is an effort at capturing the economic landscape. Knowing the weaknesses of data he derides the aim of numerical precision. That 'tables of numbers are the enemies of good forecasting; [forecasts] should be judged by whether or not they give a good idea of what the whole situation is going to be like, what character it will have' and that 'a forecast ought to convey the whole character of the forthcoming period; it shouldn't be thought of as being an entirely quantitative thing' (Godley in Evans, 1997, p. 411, 416). The origins of this insistence on the general economic outlook was an insight Godley gained in his time at the Treasury. But the ability to use models for illustration and reflection was a skill he honed at Cambridge. Faced by the uncertainty of the economic future, Godley relied not on models or on theory, but on his expert judgment, and on his voice.

2.7 Craft and judgment

In this biographical chapter I have purposely omitted Godley's work on stock-flow consistency, his focus after 1994 at the Levy Economics Institute of Bard College. Some of this research originated in the mid-1970s in attempts to provide a non-monetarist account of inflation and had been a secondary subject in his 1983 book. Godley dedicated himself to this research as his real and lasting contribution: a representation of his accounting understanding of the British economy. Although he argued that these insights were more of a method than a theory (Lavoie, 2011), Godley shared the assumptions of his profession that his insights could and should find some inscription.

At the time of this writing, there is robust interest in the formulations of his and Lavoie's *Monetary Economics*, and it might be that Godley will earn, posthumously, the fame of the theorist. By placing the 'six wise men' as the final moment of the narrative, I am dramatizing Godley's affirmation of his voice in public affairs, in deciphering uncertainty in economic futures. The record shows Godley finding his voice without deferring to formal models, through an interpretive and flexible insight into aggregate balances and imbalances of the macroeconomy.

Not all economic judgment (and knowledge) can be codified into theories, maxims, or theorems. Some is embodied and tacit. Godley's work teaches us that some knowledge need not be codified. By Godley's own account, his contributions to macroeconomic theory, which occupied him in the mid-1970s, were unremarkable. What he knew evaded formalism. This insight is ironically lost, even to his close colleagues. Hashem Pesaran, a Cambridge econometrician, told the *Financial Times* how Godley would take a vast spreadsheet of numbers, study them for sometimes hours at a time and then pronounce: 'That figure is wrong.' He was 'invariably found to be right.' Pesaran explained that 'he had what amounted to a full macroeconomic model in his head, which, by some sort of subconscious process, he computed.'[33]

Most economists today find it hard to conceive of economic insight without some model as ultimate foundation of knowledge. Even more puzzling is that Godley's informal insight was into that most formal of realms, the national accounts, as he could see the patterns of their interconnectedness.

What Godley knew was not born of genius. He learned it 'by doing economics,' initially at the Treasury, working through the national accounts as the sole forecasting effort in the UK, and later at Cambridge, competing with many alternative (academic) accounts of economic futures. What we learn from Wynne Godley is that to inform public policy and debate it is not enough to build monuments to theory and its formal logic. We must also rely on the men and women that make it their job and lives reading the data and looking for the big picture.[34]

Notes

1. 'Wynne Godley, British economist, died on May 13th, aged 83,' *The Economist*, May 29, 2010. 'Economist known for accuracy of his pessimism,' *Irish Times*, May 29, 2010. William Keegan, 'Obituary: Wynne Godley: Economist with a flair for anticipating and responding to crises,' *The Guardian*, May 21, 2010. 'Professor Wynne Godley; Controversial Cambridge economist and one of the Treasury's "six wise men" in the 1990s who foresaw the 2008 global financial crash,' *The Times*, May 17, 2010. 'Professor Wynne Godley; Obituaries: Maverick Treasury economist who launched devastating attacks on the policies of Labour and the Tories alike,' *The Daily Telegraph*, May 22, 2010.
2. The awareness of the craft-like quality is often credited to Michael Polanyi, a chemist and philosopher, and his notion that much of scientific knowledge is tacit (Polanyi 2009). The consequences of this insight, for our understanding of scientific practices and its public authority, are developed in Collins and Evans (2002).
3. Hall has a claim to fame in the History of Economic Thought due to his and C.J. Hitch's 'Price Theory and Business Behaviour', see Lee (1981), with a connection to Oxford and Andrews. I thank Marc Lavoie for bringing it to my attention.
4. Hall was not alone in his campaign for more economic expertise in government, see Middleton (1998, p. 234).
5. Kaldor was the consummate academic. Neild, however, had a more mixed career, having been at the Economic Section in the period 1951–6, and as deputy director of the National Institute for some time thereafter. Neild and Godley were no strangers. In 1963 Neild worked on factors determining real personal income in order to improve forecasting methods. He states that 'we owe a great deal to Mr. W.A.H. Godley, of H.M. Treasury, who first suggested the pricing hypothesis which the study set out to test' and was then working at the Institute (Neild, 1963).

6. Cairncross's diary provides a record of Godley's contributions, see, for instance, Cairncross (1997, pp. 66, 84, 62).
7. The foremost study of this kind is found in Collins (1974), a participant observation study of a team of experimental physicists.
8. Godley would at times codify changes to data collection and calculation. In December 1969, *The Public Expenditure White Paper*, Godley attempted to overhaul the construction of public accounts, so that forward estimates of revenues and expenditures could be made consistent (Brittan, 1971).
9. From the Second World War, economists at the University of Cambridge had been divided between the Faculty of Economics and Politics and the Department of Applied Economics (DAE). The department was headed by a director. The first was Sir Richard Stone, who was in charge from its founding in 1945 to 1955. He was followed by W.B. Reddaway until 1970, and then Godley until 1987. The last director of the DAE was D.M.G. Newbery, until 2004, when the division between the faculty and the DAE was abolished, with the Faculty of Economics and Politics being renamed the Faculty of Economics.
10. The *Bulletin* originated during the Second World War when the London School of Economics was in residence at Cambridge. It was published in the mass distribution broadsheet the *Times* from November 26, 1965.
11. The claims of Godley and Cripps received immediate response in government.
12. 'The right shape for a budget' *The Times*, January 26, 1974, p. 15; Neild 'Letters to the Editor', January 31, p. 17; Professor Little's 'Letters to the Editor', February 6, p. 15.
13. Richard Kahn and Michael Posner, 'Challenging the "elegant and striking" paradoxes of the New School' and 'Theory dogged by its assumptions,' *The Times*, April 17–18, 1974.
14. Kahn and Posner certified that the label of 'Cambridge Economics' was legitimate, in as much as the Neild–Godley proposals rested in a Keynesian meta-structure: 'Although – for convenience – we call ourselves the Old School, we are highly appreciative of the efforts of the New School to force a reappraisal. Their elegant paradoxes, which have evolved strictly within the Keynesian structure of thought, are striking and seem to call into question accepted views.'
13. In Joan V. Robinson papers, Kings' College Cambridge, Wynne Godley to Richard Kahn, May 23, 1974. JVR/vii/228/3/3.
14. Nicholas Kaldor to Richard F. Kahn, May 20, 1974, JVR/vii/228/3/15–16; Richard Kahn and Michael Posner to Nicholas Kaldor, May 24, 1974, JVR/vii/228/3/17–20.
15. In Joan V. Robinson papers, Kings' College Cambridge, Wynne Godley to Richard Kahn, May 23, 1974, JVR/vii/228/3/3.
16. Nicholas Kaldor to Richard F. Kahn, May 20, 1974, JVR/vii/228/3/15–16; Richard Kahn and Michael Posner to Nicholas Kaldor, May 24, 1974, JVR/vii/228/3/17–20.
17. In Joan V. Robinson papers, Kings' College Cambridge, Michael Posner and Richard Kahn to Nicholas Kaldor, May 28, 1974, JVR/vii/228/3/24; Francis Cripps to Richard Kahn, May 1974, JVR/vii/228/3/25; Nicholas Kaldor to Richard Kahn and to Michael Posner, May 29 and 30, 1974, JVR/vii/228/3/26; Richard Kahn to Francis Cripps, June 6, 1974, JVR/vii/228/3/27.

18. Godley was often less knowledgeable of Keynes than one might expect, as evidenced in an exchange in the *London Review of Books* where he misremembered the policies contained in 'How to Pay for the War': 'I transposed a course of action which Keynes discussed into one which (I for a moment wrongly imagined) he had advocated' (Godley, 1992).
19. This is not to say that there was no continued debate about New Cambridge in the press. There were several letters to the editor critiquing the Neild–Godley–Cripps proposals (c.f. August 22, 1974 in the *Financial Times* and January 28, 1974 in *The Times*).
20. The committee concluded rather meekly that the Treasury should educate itself on New Cambridge ideas through a series of joint seminars; see Maloney (forthcoming) for more.
21. The Manchester group coalesced around a SSRC research program on 'Inflation, its Causes, Consequences and Cures.' The diverse group included Keynesians. The conviction that it was Monetarist in outlook came from a contemporaneous review by Laidler and Parkin (1975) on 'inflation' in the *Economic Journal*. Here again, the doctrinal academic frame took precedent over all other typologies.
22. Bispham (1975, p. 45) was aware of Cambridge's recent revising of earlier claims, as he stated: 'By the time evidence was presented to the Expenditure Committee in mid-1974 the simple relationship suggested at the start of the controversy had become considerably more complex, implicitly weakening the argument substantially' (Bispham, 1975, p. 45).
23. To this list, Evans (1997, p. 400) adds the Cambridge Growth Project (CGP) and Southampton University as engaged in macroeconomic modeling. The Social Science Research Council had been giving financial support to these groups since 1965.
24. New Cambridge was not without advocates. The Australian Treasury economist C.I. Higgins (1976, p. 201) believed that: 'the distinction between the New and Old School, ... is an empirical question and depends both on the particular economy and the length of time period being considered.' Higgins believed with New Cambridge, that private expenditure stability, although microeconomically problematic, was plausible in the aggregate. He further suggested channels that tied fiscal policy to balance of payments management as proposed by the 'New School'. With sympathy for the 'New School' was another paper by David Vines in 1976. Vines refers to the Kahn and Posner model introducing to it a New Cambridge equation of private expenditure replacing the traditional consumption and investment functions (Vines, 1976, p. 208). Vines concluded: 'a "New School assignment" of the exchange rate to the level of income and the budget deficit to the balance of trade is appropriate as long as domestic leakages are less than foreign leakages' (Vines, 1976, p. 227, although this is a weak result, see his footnote 26 on p. 226).
25. Posner wrote the introductory article for the conference volume, sharing his experience as civil servant and government adviser. He briefly presented New Cambridge, in what he labeled a 'bastardized' version, and for the American reader concluded favorably: 'These seem to me undisputed gains from an innovation in theory' (Posner, 1978, pp. 19–20). There was no reiteration of the 1974 criticisms.

26. In 1976, Vines had denied the New Cambridge school the attribute of Keynesian. He wrote that

    > the instability of expectations is the very basis of the Keynesian 'investment determines savings' doctrine; savings adjusts to whatever investment entrepreneurs' animal spirits give rise to, via changes in the level of economic activity. The New School appear to deny this. (Vines 1976, p. 227)

    Years later, Dixon maintained in equal strong terms that:

    > There can be no doubt that both in its analytical core and in its policy assignment, doctrines associated with the New Cambridge School represent a dramatic break with the ideas of Keynes. New Cambridge theory seems to be more pertinent to long-run equilibrium than the world in which we have our being. (Dixon, 1982–83, p. 291)

    For yet another comparison of 'New Cambridge' and 'Chicago monetarist' models of the economy, one of which Godley and Cripps approved of – see McCallum and Vines (1981).

27. The only lukewarm support came from Robert E. Hall that considered that some of 'New Cambridge' formulations may be acceptable on empirical grounds for the British case (Hall, 1978).
28. Blinder argued that it was unclear how the New Cambridge expenditure function could be divided into constituents' consumption and investment; that it was unreasonable to assume that monetary policy can successfully peg the interest rate; or that demand for money was insensitive to GNP. On the issue of prices he charged that they were solely determined by supply factors – 'In the land where the Phillips curve was first discovered, it apparently exists no more'; and that Britain was portrayed as setting the price of its imports. Finally, he noted the absence of any aggregate supply side; and no consideration of efficiency losses arising from import quotas. (Blinder 1978, pp. 69, 73, 74, 76 and 78).
29. There is a poisonous debate about the assessment of this letter, particularly as British libertarians have used the episode to try to undermine the credibility of academic economics. A far more balanced assessment is provided in Wickham-Jones (1992).
30. I thank David Laidler for bringing this to my attention.
31. Evans (1997, p. 400) notes that Southampton University and the Cambridge Growth Project also lost their funding. Grants to the National Institute and London Business School were reduced, and new grants awarded to, and subsequently withdrawn from, Liverpool University and City University Business School.
32. Even sympathetic reviewers found it difficult to forgive Godley and Cripps' disregard for the current literature, and were critical of their insularity (Vines, 1984).
33. Sue Cameron and John Llewellyn 'Maverick who endured with ideas undimmed' *Financial Times*, May 14 2010.

34. Great Britain has a better record than most countries in acknowledging this insight. As scholars in science studies have noted, the British polity is acceptant of elite insight into scientific controversies. Those that serve that state, and exhibit a record of independence (and eloquence!) are trusted by public and politicians alike (see Fourcade, 2009; Jasanoff, 2005).

References

Bispham, J.A. (1975) 'The New Cambridge and "Monetarist" Criticisms of "Conventional" Economic Policy-Making,' *National Institute Economic Review* 74: 39–55.

Blinder, A.S. (1978) 'What's "New" and what's "Keynesian" in the "New Cambridge" Keynesianism?,' *Carnegie-Rochester Conference Series on Public Policy* 9: 67–85.

Brittan, S. (1971) *Steering the Economy: The British Experiment* (New York, NY: Library Press).

Budd, A.P. (1975) 'The Debate on Fine-tuning: The Basic Issues,' *National Institute Economic Review* (74): 56–9.

Cairncross, A. (1997) *The Wilson Years: A Treasury Diary, 1964–1969* (London, UK: The Historians' Press).

Cairncross, A. (1996) *Managing the British Economy in the 1960s: A Treasury Perspective* (London, UK: Macmillan).

Cairncross, A. and N.G. Watts (1989) *The Economic Section, 1939–1961: A Study in Economic Advising* (London, UK: Routledge).

Coats, A.W. (1981) 'Britain: The Rise of the Specialists,' in *Economists in Government: An International Comparative Study* (Durham, NC: Duke University Press), pp. 27–66.

Collins, H.M. (1974) 'The TEA Set: Tacit Knowledge and Scientific Networks,' *Science Studies* 4(2): 165–85.

Collins, H.M. and R. Evans (2002) 'The Third Wave of Science Studies: Studies of Expertise and Experience,' *Social Studies of Science* 32: 235–96.

Cripps, T., M. Fetherston and W. Godley (1974) 'Public Expenditure and the Management of the Economy,' in *Public Expenditure, Inflation and the Balance of Payments*, Ninth Report from the Expenditure Committee, Session July 1974, HC328, London, Her Majesty's Stationery Office.

Cripps, F. and W. Godley (1976) 'A Formal Analysis of the Cambridge Economic Policy Group Model,' *Economica* 43(172): 335–48.

Dixon, R. (1982–83) 'On the New Cambridge School,' *Journal of Post Keynesian Economics* 5(2): 289–94.

Evans, R. (1997) 'Soothsaying or Science?: Falsification, Uncertainty and Social Change in Macroeconomic Modelling,' *Social Studies of Science* 27(3): 395–438.

Fetherston, M.J. and W. Godley (1978) '"New Cambridge" Macroeconomics and Global Monetarism: Some Issues in the Conduct of UK Economic Policy,' *Carnegie-Rochester Conference Series on Public Policy* 9: 33–65.

Fourcade, M. (2009) *Economists and Societies: Discipline and Profession in the United States, Britain, and France, 1890s to 1990s* (Princeton, NJ: Princeton University Press).

Frenkel, J.A. (1978) '"New Cambridge" Macroeconomics and Global Monetarism,' *Carnegie-Rochester Conference Series on Public Policy* 9: 91–4.
Godley, W. and F. Cripps (1983) *Macroeconomics* (London, UK: Fontana).
Godley, W. (1992) 'Maastricht and All That,' *London Review of Books* 14(19): 3–4.
Godley, W. (2000) 'Wynne Godley,' in P. Arestis and M.C. Sawyer (eds) *A Biographical Dictionary of Dissenting Economists* (Cheltenham, UK: Edward Elgar Publishing), pp. 232–40.
Godley, W. (2001) 'Saving Masud Khan,' *London Review of Books* 23(4): 3–7.
Hall, R.E. (1978) 'A Comment on the Fetherston and Godley and Posner Papers,' *Carnegie-Rochester Conference Series on Public Policy* 9: 87–9.
Higgins, C.I. (1976) 'Some Observations on the Cambridge New School of Economic Policy,' *Australian Economic Papers* 15(27): 201–6.
Jasanoff, S. (2005) *Designs on Nature: Science and Democracy in Europe and the United States* (Princeton, NJ: Princeton University Press).
Jones, K. (1994) *An Economist Among Mandarins: A Biography of Robert Hall (1901–1988)* (Cambridge, UK: Cambridge University Press).
Kaldor, N. (1955) *An Expenditure Tax* (London, UK: Allen and Unwin).
Kaldor, N. (1955–56) 'Alternative Theories of Distribution,' *Review of Economic Studies* 23(2): 83–100.
Laidler, D. and M. Parkin (1975) 'Inflation: A Survey,' *The Economic Journal* 85(340): 741–809.
Lavoie, M. (2011) Private communication.
Lee, F.S. (1981) 'The Oxford Challenge to Marshallian Supply and Demand: The History of the Oxford Economists' Research Group,' *Oxford Economic Papers* 33(3): 339–51.
Maloney, J. (forthcoming) 'The Treasury and the New Cambridge School in the 1970s,' *Cambridge Journal of Economics*. (Available at: http://ideas.repec.org/p/exe/wpaper/1008.html) (Accessed April 4, 2011.)
McCallum, J. and D. Vines (1981) 'Cambridge and Chicago on the Balance of Payments,' *Economic Journal* 91(362): 439–53.
Middleton, R. (1998) *Charlatans or Saviours? Economists and the British Economy from Marshall to Meade* (London, UK: Edward Elgar Publishing).
Middleton, R. (2000) *The British Economy Since 1945: Engaging with the Debate* (London, UK: Palgrave Macmillan).
Neild, R.R. (1963) 'Pricing and Employment in the Trade Cycle: A Study of British Manufacturing Industry, 1950–61,' National Institute of Economic and Social Research Occasional Paper 21 (New York: Cambridge University Press).
Parsons, W.E. (1989) *The Power of the Financial Press: Journalism and Economic Opinion in Britain and America* (Aldershot, UK: Edward Elgar).
Polanyi, M. (2009) *The Tacit Dimension* (Chicago, IL: University of Chicago Press).
Posner, M. (1978) 'Problems of the British Economy,' *Carnegie-Rochester Conference Series on Public Policy* 9: 5–32.
Russell, T. and L.M. Wakeman (1978) '"New Cambridge" – Economics Without Markets: A Comment,' *Carnegie-Rochester Conference Series on Public Policy* 9: 95–101.
Targetti, F. (1992) *Nicholas Kaldor: The Economics and Politics of Capitalism as a Dynamic System* (New York: Oxford University Press).

Thirlwall, A. (2004) 'Nicholas Kaldor,' in D. Rutherford (ed.) *Biographical Dictionary of British Economists* (Brighton, UK: Thoemmes Press).

Turner, M.S. (1993) *Nicholas Kaldor and the Real World* (Armonk, NY: M.E. Sharpe).

Vines, D. (1976) 'Economic Policy for an Open Economy: Resolution of the New School's Elegant Paradoxes,' *Australian Economic Papers* 15(27): 207–29.

Vines, D. (1984) 'Macroeconomics (Book Review),' *The Economic Journal* 94(374): 397–9.

Wickham-Jones, M. (1992) 'Monetarism and Its Critics: The University Economists' Protest of 1981,' *The Political Quarterly* 63(2): 171–85.

3
Godley Got It Right

L. Randall Wray

The Queen of England famously asked her economists why 'no one saw it coming' – referring, of course, to the global financial collapse that began in early 2007. In fact, many economists, market participants, and even policymakers did recognize problems. Since the beginning of the crisis, I have been arguing that Hyman Minsky had been studying the transformation of the economy toward fragility since the late 1950s, so in some sense he had seen 'it coming' a half century ago. I have also argued that we should not try to locate the origins of the crisis in the subprime-lending-fueled housing bubble since 2000; rather, it should be viewed as resulting from the long-term trends over the entire post-war period. In that sense, I claimed that we should see this not as a 'Minsky moment' or even a 'Minsky crisis' but rather as a Minsky 'half century.' I will not repeat any of those arguments here (see Wray, 2009).

Instead, I will focus on the specific unsustainable processes of the decade that preceded the collapse. Minsky died in 1996, just at the beginning of that decade of a truly historic and rapid transformation of the financial structure of the US economy. Hence, while the following analysis fits in well with the post-war transformation that Minsky identified as the rise of 'money manager capitalism,' it was Wynne Godley who closely studied those specific processes that brought about a collapse of the global economy. Unfortunately, Wynne is no longer here to say 'I told you so' and it is the goal of this piece to make the case that he certainly deserves the accolades (see Bezemer, 2011). In my view, no one else came close to providing such a trenchant analysis. All of us at Levy benefitted tremendously from his insights and we miss his wisdom.

3.1 My introduction to Godley

We did not hit it off well in the beginning. Wynne was careful, methodical, and proper – almost an exact opposite to Minsky, the other distinguished scholar at the Levy Institute, who was gregarious, confident, and, by comparison, highly productive. I did not at first appreciate Wynne's methodology – modeling with heroic simplifications to produce numerical simulations. While Hy knew (or at least maintained the appearance that he knew) financial institutions and instruments, Wynne admitted that he understood next to nothing about the financial system. (Even after the global financial collapse was well underway, Wynne would call on me for the most basic details about mortgage securitization.) His models overlooked too much that I thought important. And for a follower of Minsky's 'financial Keynesian' approach (that was more closely related to Institutionalism than to anything else), Godley's methodology looked too orthodox.

So when Godley began a series of papers laying out his model, my focus was on what was left out rather than on what he had accomplished. We had something of a showdown in my office that ended with his explosion, demanding more respect from me, and slamming of my door. It was in retrospect the start of a wonderful relationship. I began to read him more carefully, and he tried to improve the financial aspects of his model. We began to write together – a journal article, a policy note for Levy, and some op-eds for the *Financial Times*. He was, without question, a brilliant analyst and was by far the best writer I have ever known. He would take a piece I considered to be finished, and then worry over it for an interminable period. There was never an extra word, and every sentence was always phrased just right.

Wynne was meticulous where I was rash; he was methodical where I was intuitive. In the early 2000s as household debt and debt service were growing rapidly, he once came to my office to ask whether there might be a theoretical limit to the portion of income a household or firm could devote to debt service. I responded immediately and intuitively: no, it could go to 99.99 per cent and above so long as one could find a willing lender. Wynne returned to his office and worked it through his complete stock-flow consistent model and came back several hours later: 'you are right.' It was a disappointing result because we could not say for sure when the unsustainable debt-spree might end. Another time he came by to discuss an investment opportunity: we should short the mortgage market (shades of John Paulson!). I reminded him of Keynes' admonition that markets can stay irrational a lot longer than we could stay solvent. Another disappointment – but a reminder that debt and price ratios, and sectoral balances, cannot tell us when an unsustainable trend will end.

Wynne was influenced by three disturbing experiences. First there was his upbringing and treatment by a psychoanalyst – recounted in Wynne's own remarkable autobiographic essay (Godley, 2001). Second, he felt as if he had been cast off by the neoliberals who took over policymaking in the UK, after having spent much of his life as a valued public servant. Cambridge University followed suit in – what seemed to him – a reprehensible manner. Those experiences made him highly sensitive to criticism, and led to a search for approval. I recall a particular panel on which he had presented a strategic analysis of US sectoral balances, showing that at projected growth rates the private sector's borrowing would have to grow faster than GDP. Goldilocks's growth was unsustainable. A prominent self-described Keynesian textbook writer was the discussant. He dismissed Wynne's presentation with the comment that things would probably turn out better than suggested. He offered no analysis, not even an attempt at justification for this view. I expected Wynne to tear him apart as it would have been easy enough to do. Instead, Wynne refused to respond. He was furious but too much of an English gentleman to show it. (Years later I had the pleasure to hear Charles Goodhart provide a well-deserved public rebuke to Wynne's tormentor. Following that individual's presentation on a plenary panel, Goodhart announced for all to hear that he had never witnessed such an embarrassing performance. Touché!) In addition to his sensitivity, Wynne engaged in an eternal search for assistants and co-authors for his books. (Many of these partnerships did not work out, but Wynne did (finally) find a superb partner in Marc Lavoie.) The problem was that Wynne was all-consuming. His own effort was at least 120 per cent and what he really needed was a similar commitment from all those around him – in other words, disciples, not colleagues. I am sure all of this had a lot to do with the life-long insecurities he perceptively analyzed in his autobiography.

Finally, his economic outlook was highly influenced by exchange rate crises in the UK. It was the last of these experiences that led to the only sustained disagreement that we had. Wynne always insisted that the US current account deficit was unsustainable. In his writing over the years, it became clear that this was meant as a contingent statement – if the US private sector will run, on average, a surplus and if the government deficit is constrained, then a large and persistent current account deficit cannot be sustained. In his belief, what would give would be economic growth – the US would be doomed to slow growth to reduce its trade imbalance. However, as the domestic private sector's balance moved to large and growing deficits, Wynne and I came together to argue that was the more important of the unsustainable processes. Still, he was convinced – where I was not – that the US would ultimately have to reduce its trade deficit.

In this chapter, much of the focus will be on the growth of private sector deficits and debt. Wynne's 'three sectoral balances' approach was adopted by all of us at Levy when the federal budget went into surplus in the mid- to late 1990s. In the next section I will quickly recount how that changed my own views as I came to embrace Wynne's approach. I will then address Wynne's methodological approach and then will turn to the specific analyses and projections of crisis.

In what follows, I am pulling material from working papers, Policy Notes, and Strategic Analyses published at the Levy Institute. I am including pieces I authored, some authored by Wynne, and a couple of co-authored pieces (one with Wynne, one with Dimitri Papadimitriou). Except where indicated, I am retaining the original wording throughout, with editing and a few added comments to help with the flow. My goal is to demonstrate that 'Wynne got it right' and by using the original exposition I can make it clear that this is not an *ex post* interpretation. To be sure, I am quoting selectively – potentially leaving out analysis that does not hold up to the test of time – but I am presenting the main thrust of the argument as it developed from 1995. I will conclude with a final assessment of Wynne's analysis that allowed us to 'see it coming'.

3.2 Godley's three balances approach

In this section, I explain how I came to adopt Godley's three balances approach as a more useful alternative to the Keynes/Kalecki/Levy approach I was taught. What follows is an excerpt from a piece I wrote for Levy in 2000. It introduces the three balances approach that Wynne imparted to us. It is in some sense an alternative to the usual Keynesian 'leakages and injections' approach as well as to the Kalecki (et al.) 'profits equation'. While it took me a while to embrace it, I found it to be a useful way to ensure stock-flow consistency – something I had struggled with from the early 1980s and through to my exposure to both 'endogenous money' and the 'circuit approach'.

> In the early 1980s, when I was one of Minsky's students, he introduced us to the Kalecki equation, which he, and we, later found to

be similar to Jerome Levy's profits equation. In the Kalecki version, aggregate profits = private sector investment + government deficit + export surplus (− export deficit) + consumption out of profits (capitalists' consumption) − saving out of wages (workers' saving). In his exposition, Minsky quickly jumped to what is called the classical case, in which capitalists do not consume and workers do not save, so that aggregate profits would be equal to investment plus the government deficit minus the trade deficit. The early 1980s was interesting because the United States was struggling to break free from the Reagan recession, with almost no private investment and a growing trade deficit. Thus, according to the equation, the only source of profits was the burgeoning federal budget deficit. ... (Wray 2000, p. 1)

In 1984, as the economy was recovering and consumers were becoming sufficiently confident to increase debt, Minsky and I discussed a non-classical version of the Kalecki equation. Minsky had emphasized the role that government transfers play in fueling consumption, but what if consumers simply borrowed to keep consumption up? In other words, the Kalecki equation subtracts worker saving from aggregate profits, but what if worker saving were negative, that is, what if workers spent more than their income? In that case, even with a trade deficit and sluggish investment, aggregate profits could be positive without a government deficit. We even considered a more extreme version of the Kalecki equation. What would happen if the government budget moved toward surplus? In the US case, with a trade deficit, profits would have to be generated by capitalist spending (both on investment and consumption) as well as by worker deficit spending. Minsky recognized that theoretically this could happen, but he doubted that it was sufficiently likely to warrant further investigation. ... (Wray 2000, pp. 1–2)

Fortunately for our analysis, two things happened over the next 15 years. First, Wynne Godley came up with a much more fruitful way of looking at the whole matter. Godley simply consolidates all levels of government into a public sector, similarly consolidates households and firms into a domestic private sector, and, for completion, adds a foreign sector. It is clear that if the public sector is spending more than its income (that is, is running a deficit), at least one other sector must be spending less than its income. The United States has been running a trade deficit over the past two decades, and one that has generally been rising. A public sector in deficit tends to generate a private sector surplus – some of which is drained off through a trade deficit. In theory, all of the government sector's stimulus could be drained off that way, but, in practice, the trade deficit has not generally been large enough to do so. With Godley's approach, we do not need to allocate saving between profits and wages; the relevant breakdown is between households and firms, and those data are readily available. (Wray 2000, p. 2)

The second thing that happened is that the real world cooperated by generating unprecedented private sector deficits. What seemed unlikely to Minsky in 1984 became a reality, albeit in a slightly altered form. If one compares the 1980s expansion with that of the 1990s, one can see that large government deficits helped initiate both. In both cases, once the expansion was under way, the private balance dropped from large, recession-period surpluses toward deficits. In the 1980s the private balance fell from a surplus of about 4.5 per cent of GDP to a deficit of about 1.5 per cent of GDP – a swing of 6 percentage points. In the 1990s the private balance fell from a surplus of 4 per cent of GDP to a deficit of 5.5 per cent... a swing of almost 10 percentage points. (Wray 2000, p. 2)

A swing of such magnitude is entirely unprecedented in the postwar period. It was brought about by the combination of a large trade deficit (although the 1980s expansion saw a similar deterioration in the balance of payments) and an unprecedented shift of the government budget toward large surpluses. How can the economy boom in the presence of large and growing government surpluses, and how can we explain the willingness of the private sector to spend in excess of its income to the tune of 5.5 percent of GDP, and rising? [In other words, what] processes brought the economy to this point, and what [are] the prospects for continued Goldilocks growth? (Wray 2000, pp. 2–3)

First, ... consumers became able and willing to borrow to a degree not seen since the 1920s. Credit cards became readily and widely available; lenders expanded credit to subprime borrowers; publicity about redlining provided the stick and the Community Reinvestment Act provided the carrot to expand the supply of loans to lower income homeowners; deregulation of financial institutions enhanced competition. All these things made it easier for consumers to borrow. Consumers were also more willing to borrow. As memories of the Great Depression faded, people became less reluctant to commit future income flows to debt service. The last general debt deflation is beyond the experience of almost the whole population and the last recession was almost half a generation ago. With only one recession

> in nearly a generation, it is not hard for people to convince themselves that downside risks are small. Add to that the stock market's irrational exuberance and the wealth effect, and you can pretty easily explain consumer willingness to borrow. (Wray 2000, p. 3)

> I would add one more point, which is that until recently the average American family had not regained its real 1973 income. Even during the Clinton expansion, real wage growth has been low. Americans are not used to living through a quarter of a century without rising living standards. The first reaction to the slow growth was to increase the number of earners per family, but that has resulted in only a small increase in real income. Thus, it is not surprising that consumers ran out and borrowed as soon as they became reasonably confident that the expansion would last. (Wray 2000, p. 3)

> The private sector balance is expected to continue to deteriorate. Looking to the public sector, the consolidated government balance is over 2 per cent of GDP. The federal budget surplus was 1.4 per cent of GDP in 1999, but, according to CBO projections, that will increase to 2.8 per cent by 2010. By then, government spending will equal only 16.9 per cent of GDP and tax revenue will still equal nearly 20 per cent. The federal debt held by the public will decline from 40 per cent of GDP to a little over 6 per cent by 2010. It is important to note that this growth of the surplus is projected to occur as economic growth slows down – from about a 4 per cent growth rate today to an average of 2.7 per cent. In other words, fiscal policy is supposed to tighten substantially over the next 10 years, so that it will be heavily biased toward running government surpluses even when the economy grows far below its long-run average, which is closer to 3.5 per cent. So the public sector has gone from a budget that was biased toward huge deficits at moderate rates of growth during the peak of the 1980s expansion to one that is biased toward huge surpluses at even lower growth rates. (Wray 2000, pp. 3–4)

We now return to the implications of this tight fiscal stance. We consistently argued it could not be sustained – growth would falter and the deficit would return.

3.3 Godley's approach to methodology

In what follows I deal explicitly with Wynne's development of his three balances approach. In addition, it will be shown that at the same time he was presenting a critique of the inconsistencies present in mainstream macroeconomics. In retrospect, I would count his contribution in this area as among the most important critiques of orthodoxy that I have encountered. What is particularly important is that his criticism did not rely on particular financial institutions or practices – it really was fundamental, and devastating. By carefully accounting for flows and stocks, he showed that the orthodox treatment of money was flawed. A couple of generations of work by orthodox economists on 'money demand' was in a single stroke destroyed. At the same time, he rigorously showed that the Post Keynesian 'endogenous money' was on the right track – but had failed to convincingly demonstrate its fundamental conclusion that money supply is not independent of money demand.

3.3.1 Methodological approach, part 1: The treatment of money

> Modern textbooks on macroeconomics treat money in a remarkably uniform – and remarkably silly – way. In the primary exposition the stock of 'money' is treated as exogenous in the two senses a) that it is determined outside the model and b) that it has no accounting relationship with any other variable. The reader is then invited to assume, *pro tem*, that the central bank controls 'the money supply' so that it is constant through time. When the operations of banks are described, typically some thirty chapters later, the quantity of money is some multiple of commercial banks' reserves as a consequence of these institutions having become 'loaned up'. (Godley 1996, p. 1)

> Silly? The money stock, as revealed in real life financial statistics, is as volatile as Tinkerbell – for good reasons, as I shall argue below. How can it be sensible to undertake a thought experiment in which the flickering quantity called 'money' is literally constant through periods at least long enough for capital equipment to be planned, built and commissioned – and for lots of other things to happen as well? And the other, 'money multiplier', story has the strange defect that, while giving some account of how credit money might be created, it completely ignores the impact on spending of the counterpart changes in bank loans which are assumed to be taking place... (Godley 1996, p. 1)

> There is a reason for all this. It is that mainstream macroeconomics postulates in its basic model that macroeconomic outcomes are all determined by relative prices established in Walrasian markets. Individual agents are held to engage in a market process of which the outcome is to find prices for product, labor and money which clear all three markets plus, by Walras's law, the market for 'bonds'.

But as is now well known, there is no use for money in the Walrasian world even though, paradoxically, 'money' is a logical necessity if the model is to be solved.... (Godley 1996, p. 2)

A radically different macroeconomic tradition does exist although this is largely, for the time being, ignored. The names which come first to (my) mind are Wicksell, D.H. Robertson, Keynes (when not writing the General Theory), Kaldor, Graziani and Hicks, particularly Hicks (1989) as well as a large number of authors in the post-Keynesian tradition (for example, Chick, Davidson, Sheila Dow, Wray, Minsky and Moore). Threads linking these authors, and distinguishing them sharply from today's mainstream, is first their perception that investment, production and distribution are processes which take up historical time – a period which must elapse before sales can take place, hence generating a systemic need for finance. (Godley 1996, p. 2)

A second thread is the perception that all decisions have to be taken in a state of uncertainty, without agents knowing what their sales or incomes are going to be. In what follows I am going to present a greatly simplified, but within its limitations realistic, model of how a modern monetary economy may work. Looked at one way, it contains nothing new. Keynes, Kaldor and Hicks all had very well worked out notions as to how economies – extremely complicated interdependent systems changing through historical time – function. (Godley 1996, pp. 2–3)

The trouble is that none of these authors chose to formalize their systems, so it is extremely difficult to teach them reliably or rigorously, and there remains a penumbra of ambiguity around too much of what they wrote; for instance, there is still much room for argument about 'what Keynes really meant'. (Godley 1996, p. 3)

I shall instead adopt the methodology pioneered by James Tobin wherein a whole model is set out formally and then subjected to numerical simulation; it is perhaps the only way in which the properties of a very complicated dynamic system can be ascertained with precision. The model is large by the standards of theoretical models, having about eighty equations. But even so, a great many simplifying assumptions have been made to prevent the scale of this (preliminary) operation from getting completely out of hand. I am all too aware that for some people *the model* will have simplified away some of the features of a monetary economy which they regard as crucially important. (Godley 1996, p. 3)

The two most important things which a model of this kind does are first, simply to show with precision how all the

> concepts – a comprehensive system of stocks and flows at constant and current prices – fit together. Then, with numerical solutions easy to obtain, we can gain insights into how the system as a whole functions, by first obtaining a base solution and then changing one exogenous variable at a time to see what difference is made. It might seem as though any particular model 'run' depends so much on the particular numbers used that the results are completely arbitrary and have no general application at all. However, it is my experience that repeated simulation, combined with iterative modification of the model itself, does progressively lead to improved understanding, for instance of what the stability of the system turns on, what combinations of parameters are plausible and how the whole thing responds when subjected to shocks. (Godley 1996, pp. 22–3)

This piece really drove home for me the usefulness of Wynne's method – a simplified stock-flow consistent model would demonstrate coherently the point we had been trying to make about endogenous money.

3.3.2 Methodological approach, part 2: Refinement of the model

In this piece, Godley digs deeper. He advances a stock-flow analysis in which money is endogenous. In my view this is especially important because Tobin's portfolio balance approach had already made some move in the direction of endogenous money with impacts on portfolios. Here Wynne carefully lays out the conditions for stock-flow consistency. This could then form the basis for his analysis of sectoral balances – a huge step beyond Tobin's economics. I must say that in conversations with Wynne, I always insisted that what he was doing was heads and shoulders above anything Tobin had accomplished. I believe Godley's analysis will withstand the test of time.

> Some endogenous money writers, for instance Graziani (1989), have outlined an extension of the theory of credit and money to cover national income determination and distribution. However none of them has yet set out a comprehensive, fully articulated, theoretical model which could provide the blueprint for an empirical representation of a whole economic system. There exists no macroeconomic textbook based on Kaldorian or EM ideas. This paper takes a step in the right direction by incorporating EM ideas into a complete, if very much simplified, model of a whole economy. Writings on monetary theory commonly rely solely on a narrative method which puts a strain on the reader's imagination and makes disagreements difficult

> to resolve. The narratives in this paper will all describe simulations which are grounded in a rigorous model which will make it possible to pin down exactly why the results come out as they do. (Godley 1998, pp. 2–3)

> [T]he model has four sectors, firms, households, the government and banks. Each row and column of the flow matrix sums to zero on the principle that every flow comes from somewhere and goes somewhere. The financial balance of any sector – the gap between its income and expenditure – is always equal to the total of its transactions in financial assets. Changes in the value of financial asset stocks... include nominal capital gains and losses on bonds as well as flow transactions. The change in the value of inventories includes both the value of their physical change and also stock appreciation. The stock of household wealth is given alternatively by the sum of all the financial assets or by the sum of government debt and inventories... (Godley 1998, pp. 5–6)

> We now have so many accounting identities and behavioral assumptions that all the banks' remaining transactions must be passive responses to the transactions of other sectors. Given the other assumptions of the model, banks passively exchange any form of money (cash, demand and time deposits) for any other form. It is also implied that banks passively provide loans to firms on the security of inventories, which results in an addition to the money holdings of wage earners as wages become due and are paid. Banks automatically extinguish loans when cash or checks are deposited by firms as sales are realized except to the extent that new loans, in an ongoing situation, will be needed to keep up the flow of production. (Godley 1998, p. 9)

> The 'supply' of money is a redundant concept – there is no such thing. Even the term 'demand' for money strains language; for it badly describes a situation where people aim to keep their holdings of money within some normal range but where the sums they end up with are determined in large part by impulse purchases, windfalls and other unexpected events. It is unfortunate that the stock of money, measured expost, should have become generally known as 'the money supply' – a term which invites the supposition that a supply exists independently from what people wish to hold. (Godley 1998, pp. 9–10)

In short, Godley had rigorously shown that 'money demand' is accommodated by 'money supply' – there is no justification for treating the 'functions' as independent. This was an unexpected but important result that came out of stock-flow modeling.

3.4 Godley's analysis of the Goldilocks economy

In the following series of excerpts, we see Godley developing his analysis of what came to be called the Goldilocks economy – supposedly a sustainable economic structure that fell fortuitously between the extremes of too hot and too cold. These pieces begin in 1995 and run through to the collapse of Goldilocks. In my view, Wynne got it exactly right: Goldilocks was doomed to fail. What he (and we) did not realize was that she would rise from the ashes, fueled by an even greater speculative and unsustainable boom. In many important respects the period from 1996 through to 2001 served as a precursor to the later boom and more spectacular crash in 2007.

3.4.1 Goldilocks part 1: The three balances

Godley had to spend years sifting through official data to construct the three balances behind the macro identity. He emphasized that one can infer causation because underlying a sector's balance are a number of behavioral equations. His stock-flow consistent modeling ensured coherency – in other words, it made sure that behavior conformed to macro constraints.

> [T]he difference between the PSD (public sector deficit) and the current account deficit is related, by accounting identity, to the aggregate spending behavior of the private sector relative to its income. Total national income is identically equal to total private expenditure plus government expenditure plus any surplus of exports and income received from abroad less imports. Subtracting transfers (mainly taxes and interest payments) from both sides of the equation, we have that private disposable income (GNP less taxes and transfers) less total private expenditure (consumption plus investment) is always exactly equal to the PSD (government expenditure less transfers) less the balance of payments deficit. The gap between total disposable income and expenditure also measures the net acquisition of financial assets by the private sector (NAFA). As the NAFA is identically equal to the PSD less the balance of payments deficit, the two deficits would be identical twins if, and only if, the NAFA were always zero; they would look quite like twins if NAFA were nearly constant as a proportion of GDP. (Godley 1995, pp. 11–12)

This is more than an identity, as one can say something about causation: Private expenditure, as one might expect, falls relative to income during the peak to trough periods and rises again during the trough to peak periods, partly because of the pattern of the investment cycle.

3.4.2 Goldilocks part 2: Outlook for Goldilocks as of the end of 1999

In this piece, Godley laid out seven points about the US economy at the end of the millennium. The end of Goldilocks was near, and policy choices were limited. What would be required was a very large fiscal relaxation – too large to be politically feasible. Hence, aggregate demand would be reduced. Godley was particularly worried about the external imbalance – a topic I will return to in the conclusion.

1. The United States has a balance of payments deficit worth nearly 4 per cent of GDP and negative net foreign assets (or foreign debt) worth nearly 20 per cent of GDP. If US growth is sustained in the medium term, it is quite likely that the balance of trade in goods and services will not improve. The United States is the only major country, or country 'bloc,' to have a substantial trade deficit and this is proving of great advantage to the rest of the world.

2. If the balance of trade does not improve, there is a danger that over a period of time the United States will find itself in a 'debt trap,' with an accelerating deterioration both in its net foreign asset position and in its overall current balance of payments (as net income paid abroad starts to explode). Such a trap would call imperatively for corrective action if it is not at some stage to unravel chaotically.

3. The emergence of a debt trap is put forward as a possibility that must be taken seriously rather than as a forecast of what is most likely to happen. Policymakers are advised to ensure that adequate instruments are available should things start getting out of hand.

4. Whether the outflow of property income starts to accelerate depends critically on the rate of return earned on internationally owned assets and liabilities. The well-known condition for exploding payments on debt is that the rate of interest exceeds the growth rate. At present the United States' negative position is worth about $1,500 billion while the net foreign income outflow is only about $10 billion, so it might be supposed that there is nothing to worry about. But this is deceptive. The low rate of return overall,

measured ex post, is the consequence of the extremely low return so far earned on foreign direct investments in the United States. However, the bulk of any change in the net asset position, in the future as in the past, is likely to take the form of financial investment, which has been earning a much higher rate of return and one that already slightly exceeds the growth rate. Also, the return on foreign direct investment in the United States may improve.

5. There have recently been extremely heavy direct investments by foreign firms in the United States, but a high proportion of these have been financed by exchange of shares and, to that extent, make no contribution at all to the financing of the deficit. The analysis of capital account flows and rates of return would be greatly facilitated if acquisitions financed by share exchange were identified separately in the accounts.
6. Policy responses in principle come down to:
   a. Reducing domestic demand
   b. Raising foreign demand
   c. Reducing imports and increasing exports relative to GDP, preferably by changing relative prices
7. The danger is that resort (perhaps by default) will be had to remedy (a), in other words, that chronic and growing imbalances between the United States and the rest of the world come to impart a deflationary bias to the entire system, with harmful implications for activity and unemployment. Remedy (b) reads hollow when neither appropriate institutions nor agreed upon principles exist, but should not be dismissed out of hand. As for remedy (c), currency depreciation is the classic remedy. But, in view of the way global capital markets work, depreciation has ceased to be a policy instrument in any ordinary sense, and 'floating' cannot be counted on to do the trick. Policymakers should be aware of the possibility of using nonselective (nondiscriminatory) control of imports in extremis in accordance with the principles set out in Article 12 of the WTO. Such a policy is to be sharply distinguished from 'protectionism' as commonly understood. (Godley 2000b, p. 1)

3.4.3 Goldilocks part 3: Medium-term prospects for the US economy, viewed from the end of 1999

This excerpt summarizes Godley's conclusion on US growth prospects. Given the likely government and external balances, the economy would grow only if the private sector engaged in continued deficit spending. This, in turn, would require an 'extremely large' increase in growth of private sector debt. As we now know in retrospect, growth of debt did resume after the recession – through to 2007 when the economy collapsed.

> The central contention is that, given unchanged fiscal policy and accepting the consensus forecast for growth in the rest of the world, continued expansion of the US economy requires that private expenditure continues to rise relative to income. Yet while anything can happen over the next year or so, it seems impossible that this source of growth can be forthcoming on a strategic time horizon. The growth in net lending to the private sector and the growth in the growth rate of the real money supply cannot continue for an extended period. Moreover, if, *per impossibile*, the growth in net lending and the growth in money supply growth were to continue for another eight years, the implied indebtedness of the private sector would then be so extremely large that a sensational day of reckoning could then be at hand. In sum, if a truly strategic view is taken, covering the next 10 to 15 years, one is forced to the conclusion that the present stance of policy is fundamentally out of kilter and will eventually have to be changed radically. (Godley 2000, p. 5)

3.4.4 Goldilocks part 4: Goldilocks meets the three bears

What follows is not Godley, but rather it is my analysis based on his approach. It was one of the first pieces projecting the end of Goldilocks, written at the end of summer 1998. As can be seen it drew heavily on Godley.

> Since the early 1990s the United States has enjoyed reasonably robust economic growth and low unemployment with low and stable inflation. The economy has been neither too hot to induce inflation nor too cold to allow unemployment to rise... And, as late as July 1998 – well after the growls of the three bears had been clearly heard – Chairman Greenspan was still warning of the dangers of inflation... The US stock market stumble in the summer of 1998 was said to be just a momentary correction... (Wray 1998, p. 1)

> As the market fell, financial advisers appeared on all the talk shows trying to calm small-time investors and assure them that no matter how far the market might fall, it is always best to stay in because stocks beat bonds over the long run. At the same time, the advisers got out. (Wray 1998, p. 3)

> Eventually, everyone will recognize that it is better to earn 4 per cent on government bonds over the short run than to lose 50 per cent on stocks – no matter what the long run might bring. Besides, the Fed has only a few more hundred basis points of room to move. As David A. Levy recently said, 'Never since World War II has it been more appropriate for investors to emphasize preservation of capital over other objectives.'... (Wray 1998, p. 3)

> As Wynne Godley has been arguing for some time, the Clinton-era expansion is unusual because of the extent to which expansion has been financed by private borrowing and the size of the private sector deficit – which is now larger as a percentage of GDP than at any time during the last 35 years. Godley argues that given the fiscal surplus and the trade deficit, the US economy can continue to expand only as long as the private sector deficit increases; as soon as private expenditure stops rising relative to income, the boom will end. Since consumer debt is already at record levels, consumer saving has fallen to depression levels, and market 'corrections' are wiping out financial wealth, it is highly unlikely that firms can look to consumer demand to be a source of the spending that would be required to turn around the financial situation of firms. (Wray 1998, p. 4)
>
> Many commentators have presumed that the movement toward a fiscal surplus fueled the boom, but as Papadimitriou and I have argued, this is a presumption that reverses cause and effect. Economic booms generally do reduce fiscal deficits (through the automatic stabilizers), but the reduction then acts as a fiscal drag on the economy. It is not surprising that the official announcement of the surplus achieved in the last fiscal year comes precisely as commentators finally are recognizing signs that the economy is slowing. (Wray 1998, p. 4)

3.4.5 Goldilocks part 5: Clinton's budget surpluses as far as the eye can see

This piece, also by me, again leans heavily on Wynne's analysis in order to critique Clinton's policy and projections, carrying on from the analysis above. I argue that the budget surpluses will be short-lived, and will play an important role in the demise of Goldilocks. Hence, rather than celebrating the achievement of a budget surplus, Clinton should have moved to relax policy. The argument included analysis of the plan to devote surpluses to rescuing Social Security – what became one of Candidate Gore's main policy proposals. I argue that this completely misunderstands the nature of a budget surplus. Anyone who understood Godley's sectoral balance approach would have rejected the Clinton–Gore plan as nonsense, yet, many economists signed on to it. No wonder few prominent economists 'saw it coming' – they did not see Goldilocks's demise coming, either! Importantly, several of those economists who endorsed the plan were rewarded with positions in the Obama Administration. While this excerpt is long, it provides an explanation of the details behind the government balance – in other words, it explains what impact the resulting budget has on the private sector's income and wealth. I should note that Wynne came to explicitly adopt my 'government-centered' view of money, concisely stated as 'taxes drive money'. He proposed to write a textbook in which money entered the first chapter as the means of paying tax liabilities.

> According to President Clinton's State of the Union address, we are on a course to run federal government budget surpluses for the next 15 to 25 years. ... The publicly held debt would be cut by more than two-thirds, dropping the debt-to-GDP ratio from 44 percent today to just over 7 per cent by 2014 – heralded as 'its lowest level since 1917' – and completely eliminating publicly held debt by 2018. (Wray 1999, p. 1)
>
> The plan was well received. A number of prominent economists, including six Nobel winners at last count, have been circulating an open letter dubbing the president's plan 'good economics' and stating that 'Although no one can predict how large the budget surpluses will turn out to be, we can be sure that saving them by reducing outstanding government debt is an excellent way to ease the burden on future workers of supporting an aging population.' In 'Saving the Surplus Will Protect Retirees' (*Wall Street Journal*, February 18, 1999), Lawrence Summers, deputy secretary of the Treasury, and Janet Yellen, chair of the President's Council of Economic Advisers, assured us that the president's proposal to 'lock away' most of the projected budget surpluses in the Social Security Trust Fund is based on 'sound accounting' and that it will extend Social Security's solvency through 2055. David Broder's *Washington Post* article (February 7) proclaimed the plan to be 'the greatest gift to our children' because it will 'help grow the economy' by 'raising national savings.' ... (Wray 1999, p. 1)
>
> Unfortunately, the accounting is not sound, and a policy that would preserve surpluses in an attempt to retire Treasury debt held by the public is anything but a gift to our children. The federal government has been in debt every year but one since 1776. Far from viewing

government debt as a horror to be avoided, at least some of the founding fathers recognized the benefits. Thomas Paine proclaimed that 'No nation ought to be without a debt' for 'a national debt is a national bond.' Alexander Hamilton asserted that 'A national debt, if it is not excessive, will be to us a national blessing.' Andrew Jackson, however, labeled the public debt a 'national curse' and, like President Clinton, set out to retire it. By January 1835, for the first and only time in US history, the public debt was retired, and a budget surplus was maintained for the next two years in order to accumulate what Treasury Secretary Levi Woodbury called 'a fund to meet future deficits.' (Wray 1999, p. 1)

In 1837 the economy collapsed into a deep depression that drove the budget into deficit, and the federal government has been in debt ever since. Since 1776 there have been six periods of substantial budget surpluses and significant reduction of the debt. From 1817 to 1821 the national debt fell by 29 per cent; from 1823 to 1836 it was eliminated (Jackson's efforts); from 1852 to 1857 it fell by 59 per cent, from 1867 to 1873 by 27 per cent, from 1880 to 1893 by more than 50 per cent, and from 1920 to 1930 by about a third. The United States has also experienced six periods of depression. The depressions began in 1819, 1837, 1857, 1873, 1893, and 1929. (Wray 1999, p. 1)

Every significant reduction of the outstanding debt has been followed by a depression, and every depression has been preceded by significant debt reduction. Further, every budget surplus has been followed, sooner or later, by renewed deficits. However, correlation – even where perfect – never proves causation. Is there any reason to suspect that government surpluses are harmful? At the macroeconomic level, government expenditures generate private sector income; taxes reduce disposable income. When government spending exceeds tax revenue (a budget deficit), there is a net addition to private sector disposable income. This addition may well have secondary and tertiary and even further effects (for example, households may spend on goods produced domestically or abroad, thereby raising consumption or imports as measured in national GDP accounts). When the Treasury sells bonds, some of that extra disposable income is devoted to saving, accumulated as private sector wealth held in the form of government debt. Even if the Treasury did not sell the bonds, however, the private sector would be wealthier by an amount equal to the government's deficit, but this would be held in the form of non-interest-earning cash (and bank reserves) for the simple reason that the total value of checks issued by the Treasury to finance expenditures would exceed the total value of checks written by the private sector to pay taxes. ... (Wray 1999, pp. 1–2)

Movements of the budget position are largely automatic. Rapid economic growth, such as that experienced in the United States since 1992 or in Japan previous to 1990, tends to cause tax revenues to rise faster than government spending, resulting in surpluses. Recessions and depressions tend to cause tax revenues to fall as spending rises, resulting in deficits. Many economists focus on the secondary or tertiary effects of government deficits and surpluses. While they might agree that deficits increase disposable income and private sector wealth, they argue that deficits also increase interest rates and thus depress investment or that households reduce consumption on the expectation that tax rates will be increased in the future. They argue that while surpluses might reduce disposable income and private sector wealth, they also lower interest rates and thus spur private capital formation. (Wray 1999, p. 2)

While I believe these arguments are based on faulty reasoning, it is possible that under some conditions the secondary effects might outweigh the primary effects so that, at least for a while, deficits might depress the private sector and surpluses might stimulate it. However, history suggests that over the longer run, deficits stimulate the economy and surpluses are harmful. ... (Wray 1999, p. 2)

Those who believe that a surplus can be 'saved' for the future or 'used' to finance tax cuts or spending increases do not understand the nature of a surplus. There is no 'surplus' there for the purpose of 'saving' or 'use.' A surplus is measured as a flow, with tax receipts over the year greater than government spending. The stock or balance sheet implication is that outstanding government debt (whether that be in the form of cash, bank reserves, or interest-earning debt) is reduced. (Wray 1999, p. 4)

If the government were to retire all the outstanding debt and then continue to run surpluses, these could be accumulated only in the form of claims on the private sector (that is, private sector indebtedness). During any period the government can always choose to spend more (or less), in which case the surplus over the period may be lower (or higher); similarly, it can increase (or decrease) taxes, in which case the surplus may rise (or fall)... It is difficult to take seriously any analysis that begins with the projection that our government will run surpluses for the next 15 or 25 years. Part of our

> skepticism comes from the inherent difficulty in making projections. Summers and Yellen note, 'Today, the US debt held by the public is $1.2 trillion less than was projected in early 1993.' A projection made just six years ago missed the mark by more than a trillion dollars. A few trillion here and a few trillion there can really add up to big errors over a couple of decades. (Wray 1999, p. 4)
>
> Even more important, our economy cannot continue to grow robustly as the government sucks disposable income and wealth from the private sector by running surpluses. When the economy slows, the surpluses will disappear automatically – and because the private sector will eventually demand that the government stop draining income from the economy. Tax cuts will be rushed through Congress and the president will put forward spending initiatives. (Wray 1999, p. 4)

3.4.6 Goldilocks part 6: Can Goldilocks be sustained?

In this excerpt, co-authored with Wynne, we argued that Goldilocks growth was unsustainable. It is closely based on Wynne's approach and it was one of the first publications to 'get it right'. To be sure, as explained above, the Goldilocks crash did not lead to restoration of sustainable processes. As we now know, the following recession was temporary – quickly ended by the 'jobless recovery'. Yet, the unsustainable processes that generated growth after the Bush recession would lead to the current financial crisis. For that reason, I would not conclude from the following excerpt that we got it wrong; indeed, I would argue that the crisis that began in 2007 resulted from a continuation of the unsustainable processes already apparent in the late 1990s.

Note that the budget surpluses soon ended, the economy went into recession, and a budget deficit was restored. Not only that, the new President Bush did rush through the tax reductions I predicted above. During his campaign tax cuts had been sold as good old supply-side economics. However, he quickly converted to Keynesianism and argued for tax cuts for their stimulative value. Given his anti-government ideology, he did not explicitly endorse Keynesian-style spending programs, but his 'predator state' (as Jamie Galbraith later called it) did funnel plenty of spending to favored sectors of the economy, such as the military. In any event, Clinton's projected surpluses and retirement of the outstanding debt never came to pass, although the Democrats came to misinterpret the whole budget surplus episode. Clinton's economists, including Yellin, Summers, and Rubin linked the relatively robust growth of the Clinton years to the budget surplus, reversing causation to claim that surpluses somehow generate good growth. This would later come back to haunt them as President Obama's hands were tied by these same economists – who had become his advisors. Hence stimulus packages after 2008 were always too small to do much good, in large part due to deficit fears.

> Recent economic statistics confirm that our Goldilocks economy continues to grow at a relatively swift pace, in spite of financial turmoil in Asia, Latin America, and Russia and economic recession in a third of the world. The longevity of the expansion is record-setting; it is already the longest peacetime expansion in US history and is about to break the record set by the 1960s Vietnam-era expansion. The expansion's longevity and its strength have tightened labor markets, allowing unemployment rates to remain below 4.5 per cent for the past year and raising real wages at a good clip for the first time in a generation. (Godley and Wray 1999, p. 1)
>
> Perhaps the most potent symbol of the strength of the expansion has been the remarkable turnabout of the federal government's budget, from a chronically large deficit to a substantial surplus. One has to go all the way back to the demilitarization of the economy after World War II to find a comparable shift in the fiscal stance. By most accounts, the surplus will continue indefinitely. The Congressional Budget Office (CBO) is projecting a rise in the federal budget surplus through the next 10 years from 1.2 per cent of GDP for 1999 to 2.8 per cent for 2009. (Godley and Wray 1999, p. 1)
>
> Such projections are, of course, contingent on continued economic growth and unchanged budget policies. What we wish to do here is to take the CBO's projections (which are not substantially different from those used by the administration) at face value and determine what they mean for the private sector. ... Government budget surpluses imply that the private sector must have an offsetting deficit. The financial situation of the domestic private sector is made worse because of the United States' international payments imbalance. ... (Godley and Wray 1999, p. 1)
>
> One might then ask, if the fiscal and trade stances are so restrictive, how can Goldilocks appear so robust? The answer is suggested by our accounting identity: the private sector is running a record deficit. Since the end of 1991 private expenditure has persistently risen more than income; indeed, the private sector deficit of the past three years is entirely unlike any that has occurred before. Today, the private sector deficit is 4.5 per cent of GDP, with the consolidated government

> surplus equal to 2 per cent of GDP and the balance of payments deficit equal to 2.5 per cent of GDP. (The sum of the government and trade balances, of course, equals the private sector deficit.) Before 1992 a private sector deficit was rare, never persisted for more than 18 months, and never exceeded much more than 1 per cent of GDP. (Godley and Wray 1999, p. 3)

> We are thus in uncharted territory, with a private sector deficit that is (relative to GDP) nearly five times greater than ever before and has already persisted twice as long as any deficit in the past. If we take the CBO forecasts of a GDP growth rate of 2.0 to 2.4 per cent per year indefinitely and an increasing government budget surplus over the next decade and then make reasonable assumptions about the continued deterioration of the US trade account, this implies that the private sector deficit must continue to worsen. In order to validate the CBO's projections, the private sector deficit would have to rise, by our reckoning, to about 8 per cent of GDP. Continued economic expansion in the presence of unprecedented fiscal restriction is possible only if the private sector increases spending faster than its income grows. The balance sheet implication is that private sector borrowing must also grow to the point that the ratio of private debt to disposable income increases to 2.5 from the current ratio of 1.6, which is already a record. We dismiss this projection based on CBO forecasts as implausible in view of the absurd increase in the private deficit and indebtedness that the forecasts require. (Godley and Wray 1999, p. 3)

3.5 Can 'it' happen again?

What follows is an analysis that Dimitri Papadimitriou and I prepared by taking Wynne's analysis and applying it to the prospects for another debt deflation; in addition, we were concerned with policy that could deal with what we expected to be a deep crisis. Yes, it did turn out that we were in some sense overly pessimistic – we did not foresee the spectacular serial bubbles in housing, commodities, and equities that would fuel growth. But the other side of that coin was the tremendous build-up of debt that would finally crash the economy. Hence, we really did not face the deflationary forces we discuss in this excerpt until the global meltdown after 2007.

> Could 'it' (debt deflation) happen again? Yes, Minsky thought, it might. Let us quickly review developments that might have made that worst-case scenario more possible. First, the federal government

has been 'downsized' – partly because of devolution of more responsibilities to state governments, partly because of reduced military spending, and partly because of the attempts to balance the budget. By the end of the 1990s, federal government spending had declined to just over 17 per cent of GDP, a fall of some 3 percentage points below what was common in the postwar period. And, importantly, tax revenues had not fallen much: they were still running about 20 per cent of GDP, in spite of the much-vaunted tax cutting efforts of President Reagan a decade earlier. This meant that a demand gap of nearly 3 percentage points had opened up. To be sure, slower economic growth since then has eliminated the budget surplus and generated a large deficit. (Papadimitriou and Wray 2003, p. 16)

However, the government budget has been structured to run surpluses at adequate rates of growth, so as to act as a drain on demand (called 'fiscal drag' in the early 1960s), and this tight fiscal stance exerts a chronic drain on disposable incomes and profits, making debt that was emitted in each expansion harder to service. These deflationary conditions have been aggravated by another development over the past two decades: the chronic and growing trade deficit. This deficit now runs some 5 per cent of GDP. When we add together the full-employment budget surplus and the trade deficit, we have a 'leakage' of aggregate demand that reaches to 6 or 7 per cent of GDP when the economy grows robustly. This leakage must be made up by a private sector 'injection,' that is, through spending in excess of income by households and firms taken as a whole. (Papadimitriou and Wray 2003, p. 16)

It is thus no coincidence that the Clinton boom was characterized by a private (business and personal) sector deficit that reached above 6 per cent of GDP. Meanwhile, exposure to fierce foreign competition has made it more difficult for businesses to maintain prices of final output, and, hence, to service their debt. ... (Papadimitriou and Wray 2003, p. 16)

While the pace of personal borrowing has subsided a bit in recent months, it is no secret that consumers have carried the economy since 2000, largely by borrowing against home equity. As late as the first half of 2003, household debt was still growing at 10 per cent per year: household debt now stands at 83.5 per cent of national income, up from 76 per cent in 2000. The Federal Reserve has recently reported that as of August 2003, the overall level of consumer credit outstanding (revolving and nonrevolving credit, excluding mortgages) stood at an all-time high of $1.96 trillion. (Papadimitriou and Wray 2003, p. 17)

In discussing deflation, the aftermath of the bursting of Wall Street's bubble is also noteworthy. Many households lost financial wealth as equity values plummeted, creating some financial distress and leading to some moderation of consumption. What is only now being realized, however, is the long-term damage that has been done to the private pension system. About 44 million private sector workers and retirees are covered by 'defined benefit' plans, which pay a preset amount at retirement and typically hold portfolios biased toward equities holdings. The three-year bear market has already forced some of these defined benefit plans into default, and estimates place the remaining plans some $400 billion short. Unless Congress approves relief, companies will have to contribute $125 billion next year; because there is a long lag built into the system – even if the autumn equity price rally continues – firms will have to continue to make such contributions for several years to come... (Papadimitriou and Wray 2003, p. 17)

The final point we would make here concerns the financial position of state budgets. ... Unlike the federal government, state and local governments can be (and occasionally are) forced to default on their debts. Even if they do not, budget cutting, layoffs, and tax increases will begin to take a greater toll on the economy this year for the simple reason that states already made the least painful adjustments during the past three years. The financial straits of states have already been proclaimed as the worst since the Great Depression. But if our prognosis is correct, things are likely to get very much worse before they get better. (Papadimitriou and Wray 2003, pp. 18–19)

We believe that the probability of significant deflation of output prices, even as imperfectly measured by conventional indices, is not great. Nor do we believe that falling output prices alone would be sufficient to wreak havoc on the economy. (Papadimitriou and Wray 2003, p. 19)

Rather, the real danger comes from the possibility of a deflation of asset prices. Stock prices are still down significantly from their 2000 prerecession peak... (Papadimitriou and Wray 2003, pp. 19–20)

Real estate prices also appear to be excessive compared to long-term trends. Given the rising leverage ratios that are increasingly accepted by financial markets, the margins of safety have been reduced considerably over the past two decades. Therefore, fairly small negative movements

> of the value of real estate (and other) assets can reduce their value below the debt issued in their purchase. (Indeed, the effects of a real estate market crash would be more widespread across American households than were the effects of the stock market tumble after 2000.) In a worst-case scenario, this would lead to 'fire sales' of assets, pushing their prices down farther and setting off a classic Minsky–Fisher debt-deflation spiral. (Papadimitriou and Wray 2003, p. 20)

3.6 Conclusion

It can be seen from this analysis that Wynne's coherent stock flow provided the basis for a prescient analysis of US unsustainable processes. Many of us followed in his footsteps, using the three balances approach to analyze Goldilocks growth and her demise. Further, after the 2000s recovery we continued to warn that growth was based on continued unsustainable processes. Serial bubbles encouraged private sector borrowing that kept the economy on that fragile path toward accumulation of debt that was far too large to service. A crash was inevitable, although the exact timing was impossible to project. That was an important lesson we all learned, which reminded us (again) of Keynes's caution that things can stay irrational a lot longer than we might think. I believe that those analyses from the late 1990s described in all important respects the similar processes underway in the 2000s that finally collapsed into the Great Recession. Further, the warnings of the dangers of a Minskyan debt deflation process still apply. While some already see recovery, what I see in Spring of 2011 reminds me of the respite we got after Goldilocks – but with an even more fragile financial structure. And while the private sector has retrenched – and the government budget has relaxed – high debt ratios (and bad debts) remain. With high unemployment and falling real estate prices, I do not believe a real recovery is underway. Further, we are witnessing (yet again) a boom of commodities and equities prices. Finally, with all the deficit hysteria in Washington (and the real fiscal crises at state and local government areas), we cannot look to proactive fiscal stimulus. While budget deficits may continue to widen (in spite of balanced budget attempts) this will only slow the deterioration of the economy, as the deficits result from falling revenue rather than from discretionary stimulus.

Over all the years we worked together, the only substantial difference that persisted between Wynne's views and my own concerned the external balance. It must be remembered that Wynne lived through exchange rate crises in the UK that led to quite painful adjustments.

However, these occurred on the Bretton Woods system or on managed but unsustainable exchange rate systems. The UK suffered for decades with unrealistically high exchange rates in conjunction with uncompetitive sectors; austerity was the only way to maintain exchange rates at desired levels because growth would worsen the trade balance and threaten the pound. In some sense, the UK was always trying to relive its glory days as source of the international reserve currency – but it was a relatively small economy with an outsized financial sector. By contrast, the US is a much larger economy (with a growing financial sector that certainly did become outsized in the 2000s) with a floating exchange rate. It is much better suited to its role as provider of the international reserve currency. I will not attempt here to defend my belief that the US position was, and is, sustainable – its current account deficits provide the reserves the rest of the world desires. The transition from the UK position to the US position was a bridge too far for Wynne. We had to agree to disagree.

Hence, while I would always agree with his three sector analysis, and while it is identically true that the US current account deficit must be made up by a domestic 'injection,' I always believed that the federal government deficit could be the balancing item. Hence, domestic private surpluses plus external deficits would equal government budget deficits. I do admit that we now face a horrific political constraint on budget deficits. Yet so far as the economics goes, there is no reason why persistent federal budget deficits cannot allow both our domestic private sector and our foreign partners to 'net save' in the form of US government debt (cash, reserves, and treasuries). But a detailed examination of that would take us too far afield.

Minsky always spoke of the 'giants' on whose shoulders we stand. Wynne Godley was truly one of those giants. Just as Minsky's analysis of the financial structure of the economy has never enjoyed more interest, Godley's stock-flow consistent modeling is growing in popularity. I expect that it will revolutionize macroeconomics, serving as a much more useful tool than the 'microfoundations of macroeconomics' that was so popular a couple of decades ago.

References

Bezemer, D. (2011) 'The Credit Crisis and Recession as a Paradigm Test,' *Journal of Economic Issues* 45(1): 1–18.

Galbraith, J. (2008) *The Predator State: How Conservatives Abandoned the Free Market and Why Liberals Should Too* (New York: The Free Press).

Godley, W. (1995) 'US Foreign Trade, the Budget Deficit and Strategic Policy Problems: A Background Brief,' Working Paper No. 138 (Annandale-on-Hudson, NY: Levy Economics Institute of Bard College).

Godley, W. (1996) 'Money, Finance and National Income Determination,' Working Paper No. 167 (Annandale-on-Hudson, NY: Levy Economics Institute of Bard College).

Godley, W. (1998) 'Money and Credit in a Keynesian Model of Income Determination,' Working Paper No. 242 (Annandale-on-Hudson, NY: Levy Economics Institute of Bard College).

Godley, W. (2000) 'Interim Report: Notes on the US Trade and Balance of Payments Deficits,' Strategic Analysis, January 2000 (Annandale-on-Hudson, NY: Levy Economics Institute of Bard College).

Godley, W. (2000) 'Seven Unsustainable Processes: Medium-Term Prospects and Policies for the United States and the World,' Strategic Analysis, October 2000 (Annandale-on-Hudson, NY: Levy Economics Institute of Bard College).

Godley, W. (2001) 'Saving Masud Khan,' *London Review of Books* 23(4): 3–7.

Godley, W. and L.R. Wray (1999) 'Can Goldilocks Survive,' Policy Note 1999/4 (Annandale-on-Hudson, NY: Levy Economics Institute of Bard College).

Graziani, A. (1989) *Production, Circulation et Monnaie* (Paris: Presses Universitaires de France).

Hicks J.R. (1989) *A Market Theory of Money* (Oxford: Clarendon Press).

Minsky, H.P. (1986 [2008]) 'Stabilizing an Unstable Economy' (New Haven, CT: Yale University Press, republished in D.B. Papadimitriou and L.R. Wray (eds), *Hyman P. Minsky's Stabilizing an Unstable Economy* (New York: McGraw-Hill).

Papadimitriou, D.B. and L.R. Wray (2003) 'Understanding Deflation: Treating the Disease, Not the Symptoms,' Public Policy Brief No. 74 (Annandale-on-Hudson, NY: Levy Economics Institute of Bard College).

Wray, L.R. (1998) 'Goldilocks and the Three Bears,' Policy Note 1998/7 (Annandale-on-Hudson, NY: Levy Economics Institute of Bard College).

Wray, L.R. (1999) 'Surplus Mania: A Reality Check,' Policy Note 1999/3 (Annandale-on-Hudson, NY: Levy Economics Institute of Bard College).

Wray, L.R. (2000) 'Can the Expansion be Sustained: A Minskian View,' Policy Note 2000/5 (Annandale-on-Hudson, NY: Levy Economics Institute of Bard College).

Wray, L.R. (2009) 'The Rise and Fall of Money Manager Capitalism: A Minskian Approach,' *Cambridge Journal of Economics* 33(4): 807–28.

4
Who Are These Economists, Anyway?

James K. Galbraith

> Of course, there were exceptions to these trends: a few economists challenged the assumption of rational behavior, questioned the belief that financial markets can be trusted and pointed to the long history of financial crises that had devastating economic consequences. But they were swimming against the tide, unable to make much headway against a pervasive and, in retrospect, foolish complacency. (Paul Krugman, *New York Times Magazine*, September 6, 2009)

Amen.

While normal ecclesiastic practice places this word at the end of the prayer, on this occasion it seems right to put it up front. In two sentences, Professor Paul Krugman, Nobel Laureate in Economics for 2008 and in some ways the leading economist of our time, has summed up the failure of an entire era in economic thought, practice and policy discussion.

And yet, there is something odd about the role of this short paragraph in an essay of over 6,500 words. It's a throwaway. It leads nowhere. Apart from one other half-sentence, and three passing mentions of one person, it's the *only* discussion – in the entire essay – of those economists who got it right. They are not named. Their work is not cited. Their story remains untold. Despite having been right on the greatest economic question of a generation – they are *unpersons* in the tale.

This chapter provides a survey of the unpersons. Among these, the late great Cambridge economist of Irish origin, Wynne Godley, holds a central place, having deployed his stock-flow consistent accounting framework far in advance to demonstrate why a crisis would come. However, though central Godley was not unique: there were at least five distinct frameworks within which the dangers could be clearly identified, and of these at least three were developed within the guidelines of well-developed – though little-known – economic theory.

Krugman's essay is about two groups, both entrenched at what (they believe to be) the top of academic economics. Krugman calls them 'saltwater' and 'freshwater' economists; they tend to call themselves 'new classicals' and the 'new Keynesians' – although one is not classical and the other is not Keynesian. One might speak of a 'Chicago School' and an 'MIT School.' In truth there are no precise labels, because the differences are both secondary and obscure.

The two groups share a common perspective, a preference for thinking along similar lines. Krugman describes this well, as a 'desire for an all-encompassing, intellectually elegant approach that also gave economists a chance to show off their mathematical prowess.' Exactly so. It was in part about elegance – and in part about showing off. It was not about... the economy. It was not a discussion of problems, risks, dangers, and policies. In consequence, the failure was shared by both groups. This is the extraordinary thing. Economics was not riven by a feud between Pangloss and Cassandra. It was all a chummy conversation between Tweedledum and Tweedledee. And if you didn't think either Tweedle was worth much – well then, you weren't really an economist, were you?

Professor Krugman contends that Tweedledum and Tweedledee 'mistook beauty for truth.' The beauty in question was the 'vision of capitalism as a perfect or nearly perfect system.' To be sure, the accusation that a scientist – let alone an entire science – was seduced by beauty over truth is fairly damaging. But it's worth asking, what exactly was beautiful about this idea?

Krugman doesn't quite say. He does note that the mathematics used to describe the alleged perfection was 'impressive-looking' – 'gussied up' as he says, 'with fancy equations.' It's a telling choice of words. 'Impressive-looking'? 'Gussied up'? These are not terms normally used to describe the Venus de Milo.

To be sure, mathematics is beautiful, or can be. I'm especially fond of the complex geometries generated by simple non-linear systems. The clumsy algebra of the modern economics journal article is not like this. It's more like a tedious high school problem set. The purpose, one suspects, is to intimidate and not to clarify. And with reason: an idea that would come across as simple-minded in English can be made 'impressive-looking' with a sufficient string of Greek symbols. Particularly if the idea – that 'capitalism is a perfect or nearly-perfect system' – would not withstand the laugh test once stated plainly.

As it happens, the same John Maynard Keynes of whom Krugman speaks highly in his essay, had his own view of the triumph of the economists' vision – specifically that of the first great apostle of drawing policy conclusions by deductive reasoning from first principles, that of David Ricardo over Thomas Robert Malthus. He wrote:

> It must have been due to a complex of suitabilities in the doctrine to the environment into which it was projected. That it reached conclusions quite different from what the ordinary uninstructed person would expect added, I suppose, to its intellectual prestige. That its teaching, translated into practice, was austere and often unpalatable, lent it virtue. That it was adapted to carry a vast and logical superstructure, gave it beauty. That it could explain much social injustice and apparent cruelty as an inevitable incident in the scheme of progress, and the attemp to change such things as likely on the whole to do more harm than good, commended it to authority. That it afforded a measure of justification to the free activities of the individual capitalist, attracted to it the support of the dominant social force behind authority. (Keynes, 1936)

Note that Keynes does not neglect the element of beauty. But he embeds this point in a much richer tapestry of opportunism, venality, and apologetics. To this day, seduction-by-deduction is known, in some corners of economics at least, as 'the Ricardian Vice.'

Keynes also wrote:

> But although the doctrine itself has remained unquestioned by orthodox economists up to a late date, its signal failure for purposes of scientific prediction as greatly impaired, in the course of time, the prestige of its practitioners. For professional economists... were apparently unmoved by the lack of correspondence between the results of their theory and the facts of observation; – a discrepancy which the ordinary man has not failed to observe...

Nothing much changes, and it is interesting to ask, why not?

The reason is not that there has been no recent work into the nature and causes of financial collapse. Such work exists. But the lines of discourse that take up these questions have been marginalized, shunted to the sidelines within academic economics. Articles that discuss these problems are relegated to secondary journals, even to newsletters and blog posts. The scholars who betray their skepticism by taking an interest in them are discouraged from academic life – or if they remain, they are sent out into the vast diaspora of lesser state universities and liberal arts colleges. There, they can be safely ignored.

Let us venture out into the nether wastes of economics, and attempt a brief survey of the main currents that didn't get it wrong. My method is far from comprehensive. It consists of surveying my own habitual reading, augmented by suggestions from a large list of economists – almost none of them in so-called 'top departments.' Many of the examples given below were volunteered, at my request, by their authors or by admirers of those authors. And numerous examples are not cited, for want of space.[1]

As noted earlier, I will offer five categories; the categories are my own invention. Of the first two, one is deep without being (in my view) sufficiently operational, and the other is operational, without being deep. The remaining three strike a better balance between theoretical appreciation and practical application. All are, however, a considerable improvement over the supposed mainstream on this question.

4.1 Habitual cassandras: the radical theory

For a generation or more – as a relic of the radical movements of the 1960s, at a time when Keynesianism was King – the token dissident tolerated in many economics departments has been a strand of Americanized Marxism, much of it developed in the 1970s at the University of Massachusetts – Amherst, after the radicals were expelled from Harvard. For this tradition, class struggle and power relations generally remain at the heart of economic analysis, and crisis is inevitable – sometime.

The South African economist Patrick Bond in 2004 summarized the major Marxian crisis-is-inevitable arguments as being of two major types: one based on cut-throat competition (Brenner, 2003), and another based on the over-accumulation of capital (Wood, 2005; Harvey, 2005) with various qualifying views (Arrighi, 2003). In a paper that gives the financial history in detail, Brenner (2009) recapitulates that the crisis 'manifests huge, unresolved problems in the real economy that have been literally papered over by debt for decades, as well as a financial crunch of a depth unseen in the postwar epoch.'

The focus on an underlying 'real economy' means that the radical tradition does not truly provide a theory of *financial* crisis. In this respect, the radicals resemble the mainstream: for them, finance is largely a veil over deeper forces. And thus the specific character of the impending crisis, and the way it might arrive, is not terribly important. (In 2004 the crisis Bond anticipated would be set off by a collapse of the dollar, due to unsustainable

US current account deficits and the exhaustion of the American imperial mission in Iraq. This was one crisis that might have happened, but so far has not.) The radicals also lack interest in policy: at the heart of things, they do not believe that the existing system can be made to work.

4.2 The practice of bubble detection

A second perspective seeks to identify financial bubbles – the peculiar indicia of an imminent crash. Dean Baker of the Center for Economic Policy Research in Washington is the pre-eminent practitioner of this craft, with a clear claim to having seen the housing bubble when academic economists largely could not. As far back as 2002, Baker wrote:

> If housing prices fall back in line with the overall rate price level, as they have always done in the past, it will eliminate more than $2 trillion in paper wealth and considerably worsen the recession. The collapse of the housing bubble will also jeopardize the survival of Fannie Mae and Freddie Mac and numerous other financial institutions. (Baker, 2002)

This was spot on,[2] by a simple method. It is to identify economic indicators – usually a ratio of two underlying variables – that are departing sharply from their historical norms, so as to suggest a temporary and unsustainable condition. An example would be the price/earnings ratio in the stock market, say for technology stocks in the late 1990s. More recent analogs include the price/rental ratio in the housing market, the ratio of housing price changes to inflation, the vacancy rate, and so forth. (The extent of deviation, coupled to the scale of the housing stock, gives a measure of the scale of the bubble itself – something Baker eventually calculated at about $8 trillion for housing.) The word 'bubble' is basically a label, applied to the out-of-normal-range rise of an asset price. There is not much more to it than that.

Underlying this method is the idea that market *institutions and relationships* are generally stable, in the sense that normal values exist. That being so, the most likely thing, when a ratio of this kind departs radically from its normal ranges, is that it will return to them eventually – and in a rush. The departure is a bubble and the rush is a crash. Those who bought high will be forced to sell low, and therefore ruined – something against which Baker warned repeatedly for six years.

The method of bubble detection has an important virtue: it works, much of the time. But the method does not depend in a systematic way on theory. The possibility exists, in any particular case, that it will fail. Institutional relationships – the 'normal' price/rent ratio (P/E) – *might* change. It is not quite enough to assert, in effect, that the claims of history are eternal. Maybe there is a 'new paradigm' at work, after all?

4.3 Godleyness is next to Keynesliness

The work of John Maynard Keynes is linked closely to the accounting framework that we call the National Income and Product Accounts (NIPA). Total product *is* the flow of expenditures in the economy; the change in that flow *is* what we call economic growth. The flow of expenditures is broken into major components: consumption, investment, government and net exports, each of them subject to somewhat separable theories about what exactly determines their behavior.[3]

Accounting relationships state definite facts about the world in relational terms. In particular, the national income identity (which simply states that total expenditure is the sum of its components)[4] implies, without need for further proof, that there is a reciprocal, offsetting relationship between public deficits and private savings. To be precise, the financial balance of the private sector (the excess of domestic saving over domestic investment) must always just equal the sum of the government budget deficit and the net export surplus. Thus increasing the public budget deficit increases net private savings (for an unchanged trade balance), and conversely: increasing net private savings increases the budget deficit.

The late Cambridge (UK) economist Wynne Godley and a team at the Levy Economics Institute built a series of strategic analyses of the US economy on this insight, warning repeatedly of unsustainable trends in the current account and (most of all) in the deterioration of the private financial balance (Godley, 2008). They showed that the budget surpluses of the late 1990s (and relatively small deficits in the late 2000s) corresponded to debt accumulation (investment > savings) in the private sector. They argued that the eventual cost of servicing those liabilities would force private households into financial retrenchment, which would in turn drive down activity, collapse the corresponding asset prices, and cut tax revenues. The result would drive the public budget deficits through the roof. And thus – so far as the economics are concerned – more or less precisely events came to pass.

Godley's method is similar to Baker's: an unsustainable condition probably exists when an indicative difference (or ratio) deviates far from prior values. The difference is that Godley's approach is embedded explicitly in a framework of accounts, so that there is a structured approach to figuring out what is and what is not tolerable. This is a definite advance.

For example: public sector surpluses were (not long ago) driven by private sector debt accumulation. This raises the question, how can such accumulation be sustained and what happens when it stops? Conversely in a downturn: very large public sector deficits are made inevitable by the private sector's return to net saving. But how long will public policymakers, who are not accustomed to thinking about these relationships, tolerate those deficits? The question is important, since if for political reasons they do not, the economy may collapse. Thus a failure to understand the elementary accounting that Godley so strongly emphasized stands as one of the greatest dangers to recovery from the Great Crisis.

On the international side, the willingness of foreigners to hold US government bonds as reserve assets creates a counterpart in the US public deficit: US budget deficits are inevitable so long as the world wishes to add to its reserves of Treasury bonds. But this raises another focused question: what drives the reserve asset decisions of foreign central banks? Will anything ever decide them to sell their Treasury bonds for euro assets, or anything else? In this way the Godley framework very usefully focuses our attention on the critical questions: the things we know about and the things we need to know about. Unfortunately again, policymakers rarely exhibit either trained or intuitive understanding of these issues.

4.4 Minsky and non-linear financial dynamics

The work of Hyman Minsky approaches the problem of financial instability from a different angle. Minsky's core insight was that *stability breeds instability.* Periods of calm, of progress, of sustained growth render financial market participants malcontent with the normal rate of return. In search of higher returns, they seek out greater risk, making bets with greater leverage. Financial positions previously sustainable from historical cash flows – hedge positions – are replaced by those which, it is known in advance, will require refinancing at some future point. These are the speculative bets. And then there is an imperceptible transition, as speculative positions morph into positions that can only be refinanced by new borrowing on an ever-increasing scale. This is the Ponzi scheme, the end-stage, which must collapse once it is recognized to exist.

Minsky's analysis showed that capitalist financial instability is not only unavoidable, but intrinsic: instability arises from within, without requiring external disturbances or 'shocks'. There is no such thing as an equilibrium growth path, indefinitely sustained. Short of changing the system, the public responsibility is to regulate financial behavior, limiting speculation and stretching out for as long as possible the expansionary phase of the cycle.

A strong line of descent runs from Minsky to recent work in non-linear dynamics, for example the work of Peter Albin (1998), Rosser, Gallegati and Palestrini (2011) and Ping Chen (2010). A key property of non-linear systems is the appearance within them of phase transitions: from single equilibria, to two-, four- and eight-period repeating cycles, and finally to deterministic chaos. These *phase transitions* – analogous to the solid-liquid-gas phases of water and other chemicals – are qualitatively distinct, internally stable, and characterized by definite boundaries. The crossing of a boundary, we are now given to understand, is never a 'new paradigm.' It is merely the change of a single integrated system from one state to another. Thus the regulatory problem can be seen as that of maintaining the system within a stable (and relatively desirable) phase – either hedge or speculative – and well away from the phase boundary associated with Ponzi finance and inevitable collapse.

It's a simple idea. But it played no role in the mainstream's thinking about the appropriate posture of policy toward financial crisis. Ping Chen (2010, epilogue) first quotes and refutes Robert Lucas, the leading Chicago School economist, on this point:

> The main lesson we should take away from the EMH for policymaking purposes is the futility of trying to deal with crises and recessions by finding central bankers and regulators who can identify and puncture bubbles. If these people exist, we will not be able to afford them'. This is the Lucas impossibility theorem in crisis management. However, this impossibility theorem has... obvious flaws. First, there are reliable methods to identify and punch asset bubbles in our theory of the viable market ... For example, sudden changes of trading volumes in Wall Street signal speculative activities by big investors and herd behavior of noise traders. The regulating agency could easily take counter- cyclic measures, such as increasing the capital reserve requirement, restricting leverage ceiling, increasing the transaction tax rate.

In the mainstream, insouciance and fatalism combined to justify inaction. This pattern explains the pathological willingness of some economists – such as Lawrence Summers – to countenance the dismantling of regulatory barriers (such as Glass–Steagall) that helped keep the system shy of the Ponzi phase. It shows up as grotesque Alan Greenspan's public encouragement for the mass adoption of speculative mortgages. Clearly, incorporating Minsky-thought into regulatory practice would be an enormous advance. But it would still leave an open question: how exactly do we decide which regulations to adopt?

4.5 Galbraith, institutional form and the new criminology

The point of departure for work in this area is John Kenneth Galbraith's *magnum opus, The New Industrial State* (2007). A huge popular success when it appeared in 1967, this book was the target of a sustained and largely successful assault by mainstream economists, and it disappeared from view during the neoliberal revival. It represented a vast threat to their modes of thought, for it sought to replace (in part) an economics of markets with an economics of organizations – of corporations, governments, unions and other parties, with the focus on internal structures of governance, countervailing power and the efficacy of group effort toward shared objectives.

In *The Predator State* (2008), I argue that after 1970 the large American corporation was pushed into crisis by 'stop–go' macroeconomic policies, international competition, technological change and, especially, the weakening of internal controls over the abuse of the corporate form by executive officers within the firm. In financial firms, it is precisely the weakening or corruption of controls, both internal and those imposed by external regulation, that leads toward disaster.

For this kind of work, close observation can be superior to statistics. Gary Dymski's 2005 examination of subprime credit markets provides an example, and demonstrates that it was very far from impossible to foresee the crisis. It was entirely sufficient, just to look:

> ... The likelihood in market after market is that potential borrowers will break into two prototypical groups: one group whose assets and position are secure ... and a second group, whose wealth levels are so low that contracts are written with the hope of extracting sufficient returns in the short run to compensate for what will inevitably be (for most) longer-term insolvency problems... The financial crisis that is familiar from Minsky's work involves the collapse of expectations and of conditions for refinancing in the formal market ... A second type of crisis, however, involves a collapse of the conditions required for financial reproduction in the

> informal market. .... This does not mean that these participants will cease to function or to borrow: they have no choice but to borrow and to get ever deeper into hopelessly high levels of debt. When asset exhaustion makes it impossible to renew activities, so that more time cannot be bought, then life and financial crisis can become indistinguishable.

Dymski's work also noted at an early stage the class- and race-based strategies of the major banks and mortgage originators as they laid their traps for the meager assets of the poor. It raises, inevitably, the question of responsibility. And this brings us to an important line of new research, focused on economic behavior and the law, and specifically on the conditions that generate epidemics of financial fraud.

In this area a key reference is William K. Black's (2005) systematic study of the savings and loan crisis and his development of the concept of 'control fraud' – fraud committed on organizations by those who control them.[5] An effort to bring this to the attention of mainstream economists also exists, in the work of Akerlof and Romer (1993), itself greatly informed by Black's practical experience as an investigator and whistle-blower in the savings and loan affair.

In the present crisis, the vapor trails of fraud and corruption are everywhere: from the terms of the original mortgages, to the appraisals of the houses on which they were based, to the ratings of the securities issued against those mortgages, to the gross negligence of the regulators, to the notion that the risks could be laid off by credit default swaps, a substitute for insurance that lacked the critical ingredient of a traditional insurance policy, namely loss reserves. None of this was foreseen by mainstream economists, who generally find crime a topic beneath their dignity. In unraveling all this now, it is worth remembering that the resolution of the savings and loan scandal saw over a thousand industry insiders convicted and imprisoned. Plainly, the intersectionof economics and criminology remains a vital field for research going forward.

4.6 Conclusions

Paul Krugman did great service by training his guns on the failures of the club of which he has been, for many years, a most distinguished member. So, I am inclined to forgive the headline writer of *The New York Times Sunday Magazine* for borrowing, almost word for word, the title of an article of mine – published nine years previously (Galbraith

2000). I nevertheless will not resist the temptation to quote my own words from back then:

> Leading active members of today's economics profession... have formed themselves into a kind of Politburo for correct economic thinking. As a general rule – as one might generally expect from a gentleman's club – this has placed them on the wrong side of every important policy issue, and not just recently but for decades. They predict disaster where none occurs. They deny the possibility of events that then happen. ... They oppose the most basic, decent and sensible reforms, while offering placebos instead. They are always surprised when something untoward (like a recession) actually occurs. And when finally they sense that some position cannot be sustained, they do not reexamine their ideas. They do not consider the possibility of a flaw in logic or theory. Rather, they simply change the subject. No one loses face, in this club, for having been wrong. No one is dis-invited from presenting papers at later annual meetings. And still less is anyone from the outside invited in.

This remains the essential problem. As I have documented – and only in part – there is a rich and promising body of economics – theory and evidence – entirely suited to the study of the real economy and its enormous problems. This work is significant in ways in which the entire corpus of mainstream economics – and including recent fashions like the new 'behavioral economics' – simply is not. And it brings great clarity to thinking about the implications of the Great Crisis through which are still passing today. But where is it, inside the economics profession?

Essentially, nowhere.

It is therefore pointless to continue with conversations centered on the conventional economics. The urgent need is instead to expand the academic space and the public visibility of ongoing work that is of actual value when faced with the many deep problems of economic life in our time. It is to make possible careers in those areas, and for people with those perspectives, that have been proven worthy by events. The followers of John Kenneth Galbraith, of Hyman Minsky and of Wynne Godley can claim this distinction; the task now is to increase their numbers and to reward their work with the public recognition and academic security it deserves.

This is – obviously – not a matter to be entrusted to economics departments. It is an imperative, instead, for university administrators, for funding agencies, for foundations, and for students and perhaps their parents. The point is not to argue endlessly with Tweedledum and Tweedledee. It is to move past them toward the garden that must be out there, *that in fact is out there,* somewhere.

Notes

1. I pass over the world of business economists, including Nouriel Roubini, whose methods I cannot clearly discern, and Nassim Taleb, whose nihilism in this case seems to me excessive, in suggesting that things cannot be predicted when in fact they were. I also do not deal here with grand theorists, such as Paul Davidson (2003) or Joseph Stiglitz. Both offer general reasons to expect crisis, but less on the specific causes of the present one.
2. As was Jane D'Arista, in work based on the flow of funds (2002): '...The bursting of the mortgage bubble could unleash broader financial disruptions with deeper macroeconomic implications than the shakeout following the S&L crisis of the 1980s.'
3. As Mirowski (1991) pointed out, one may consider that in Keynes's economics, total expenditure is the standard-of-value for which the equivalent in earlier theories was gold or labor or psychological welfare.
4. C + I + G + X − M = Y. In the standard notation, Y is income, C is consumption, I is investment, G is government spending, X is exports, M is imports, T is total tax revenue, and S is saving. The second relationship is (S − I) = (G − T) + (X− M), where S is defined as Y − C − T. To know any two of the terms within brackets is, by definition, to know the third.
5. There are important parallels between the study of organizational looting in advanced western and decrepit eastern economies, developed by Janine Wedel (2001).

References

Akerlof, G. and P.M. Romer (1993) 'Looting: The Economic Underworld of Bankruptcy for Profit,' *Brookings Papers on Economic Activity* 24: 1–74.

Albin, P.S. (1998) *Barriers and Bounds to Rationality* (Princeton, NJ: Princeton University Press).

Arrighi, G. (2003) 'The Social and Political Economy of Global Turbulence,' *New Left Review* (March–April).

Baker, D. (2002) 'The Run-Up in Home Prices: Is It Real or Is It Another Bubble?'August 5, http://www.cepr.net/documents/publications/housing_2002_08.htm.

Black, W.K. (2005) *The Best Way to Rob a Bank is to Own One* (Austin, TX: University of Texas Press).

Bond, P. (2004) 'Crunch Time for US Capitalism?,' *Z-Net Commentary* (December 4).

Brenner, R. (2003) *The Boom and the Bubble* (New York, NY: Verso).

Brenner, R. (2009) 'The Origins of the Present Crisis,' http://www.sscnet.ucla.edu/issr/cstch/.

Chen, P. (2010) *Micro Interaction, Meso Foundation, and Macro Titality: Essays on Complex Evolutionary Economics* (London, UK: Routledge).

D'Arista, J. (2002) 'The Overheated Mortgage Machine,' *Flow of Funds Review & Analysis* (December).

Davidson, P. (2003) *Financial Markets, Money and the Real World* (London, UK: Edward Elgar).

Dymski, G. (2005) 'Financial Globalization, Social Exclusion and Financial Crisis,' *International Review of Applied Economics*, 19(4): 439–57.

Galbraith, James (2000) 'How the Economists Got it Wrong,' *The American Prospect* (February).

Galbraith, J.K. (2008) *The Predator State* (New York: Free Press).

Galbraith, J.K. (2007) *The New Industrial State* (Princeton, NJ: Princeton University Press).

Godley, W. (2008) 'Prospects for the United States and the World: A Crisis That Conventional Remedies Cannot Resolve,' Strategic Analysis (Annandale-on-Hudson, NY: Levy Economics Institute of Bard College).

Harvey, D. (2005) *The New Imperialism* (Oxford, UK: Oxford University Press).

Keynes, J.M. (1936) *The General Theory of Employment, Interest, and Money* (London: Macmillan).

Minsky, H.P. (1986 [2008]) *Stabilizing an Unstable Economy* (New Haven, CT: Yale University Press) republished in D.B. Papadimitriou and L.R. Wray (eds) *Hyman P. Minsky's Stabilizing an Unstable Economy* (New York, NY: McGraw-Hill).

Mirowski, P. (1991) *More Heat Than Light* (New York, NY: Cambridge University Press).

Rosser, B., M. Gallegati and A. Palestrini (2011) 'The Period of Financial Distress in Speculative Markets: Interacting Heterogeneous Agents and Financial Constraints,' *Macroeconomic Dynamics* 15(1): 60–79.

Wedel, J. (2001) *Collision and Collusion: The Strange Case of Western Aid to Eastern Europe* (London, UK: Palgrave Macmillan).

Wood, E.M. (2005) *Empire of Capital* (New York: Verso).

5
A New Look at New Cambridge: Will the UK Private Expenditure Function Stand Up?

*Bill Martin**

5.1 Introduction

Long before it became a mainstay of real business cycle theory, the idea of an aggregate private sector expenditure function had come to prominence in Britain during the 1970s, promoted by the so-called 'New Cambridge' School of Keynesian economists led by Wynne Godley. The New Cambridge private expenditure function was an innovative empirical relationship with dramatic policy implications. Rapid adjustment of private spending to private income, it was claimed, meant that UK fiscal policy had the power swiftly to affect the level of output and the balance of payments.

After a brief, fiery existence marked by econometric controversy, the New Cambridge function fell prey to changes in theoretical fashion and, latterly, to the disappearance of the UK historic sector national accounts dataset.[1] Over the last two decades or so, very little empirical work has been published in a similar vein; extensive searches reveal just five examples for three overseas economies (Bangladesh, France and the US) and none for the UK.[2] This general disinterest is a pity, for at least three reasons.

First, the New Cambridge relationship rests on an axiom of behavior that usefully challenges the mainstream emphasis on micro-founded macroeconomic models populated by optimizing households and firms with rational expectations. Underlying the New Cambridge relationship is the notion of a rule-of-thumb target norm between the flow of private disposable income and the stock of private financial wealth,

* For very helpful comment on earlier drafts and general discussion, I am indebted to Robert Rowthorn, Hashem Pesaran, Graham Gudgin and Wynne Godley, whose original work inspired this re-examination. None of them is responsible for the final result.

an approach seemingly in sympathy with Akerlof's (2007) critique of mainstream theory. Akerlof contends that the existence of social norms, omitted from the mainstream calculus, helps to explain the otherwise puzzling influence that household *current* disposable income and corporate *current* cash flow exercise over expenditure decisions.

The second point of interest is the unusually high level of aggregation at which the New Cambridge function is struck, conflating the expenditure decisions of households and companies. This feature runs counter to the separation of consumption and investment relationships found both in mainstream macroeconomic models, in which agents typically optimize, and in more recent post-New Cambridge theoretical models populated by rule-of-thumb agents (Godley and Lavoie, 2007).[3]

One justification for a high level of aggregation rests on the heroic assumption that perspicacious households, as shareholders, 'pierce the corporate veil', adjusting their decisions to offset the saving done on their behalf by corporations. Perhaps surprisingly, this proposition enjoys some empirical support;[4] the most striking finding, not confined to the UK, is that 'corporate retentions have a well-determined impact on measured consumers' expenditure' (Sumner, 2008). The pierced corporate veil rationale for across-sector aggregation has a limited following, however.

An alternative rationale rests on the gains from aggregation that can result in practice from grubbier considerations: the misspecification of micro-relationships and data measurement errors. That aggregation may have practical advantages is a possibility long recognized by econometricians[5] and has particular relevance in the UK context. Well-known problems of measuring saving and the separate incomes of households and corporations[6] are aggravated by the likelihood of related sectoral measurement errors that cancel out, or become less potent, at the aggregate level. Sumner (2004a, 2008) notably finds evidence in support of his theory that official statisticians inadvertently fail to exclude some intermediate purchases by corporations of consumer goods and services from the official UK measure of household final consumption. He maintains this measurement error explains the empirical connection between measured consumers' expenditure and corporate retentions.

Contemporary concerns provide a third reason to re-examine New Cambridge. The related phenomena of sectoral financial imbalances, rising levels of indebtedness, and asset price booms and busts have been features of the British economy, and of some overseas, for the last two decades. Notwithstanding extensive research, the connection between these developments and private spending decisions remains empirically uncertain and the topic of considerable controversy, not least in monetary policy circles.[7] The New Cambridge approach has the potential to throw some light from a neglected angle.

The present chapter's contribution is wholly empirical. It develops, first, a new historical database describing UK sectors' income, expenditure and balance sheets. Using econometric techniques that have since become standard, I test the implications of the original New Cambridge view for the time-series properties of sectoral financial balances and associated stocks of wealth. This exploration prompts a reappraisal of the specification of an aggregate expenditure function. A tentative, estimated function is then presented and evaluated.

5.2 Historical dataset

This study would not be possible without a long-run dataset of sectoral income and expenditure flows and related wealth stocks. Alas, the UK national accounts historic record is subject to large gaps and discontinuities, mainly before 1987, the year chosen by the UK Office for National Statistics (ONS) from which to begin comprehensive sectoral estimates consistent with the European System of Accounts of 1995 (ESA95).[8] Balance sheet information is also patchy.[9] Much of the data used in this study have therefore been reconstructed.

Data sources and methods are described in an appendix and in detail in Martin (2007b, 2009). It suffices to stress that the resulting estimates for income and expenditure flows and associated balance sheets are more reliable at higher levels of sector aggregation: the private, government and Rest of the World sectors. By contrast, historic data for households and companies are much less reliable. Moreover, measurement errors in the former will feed across to the latter, though with opposite sign, as a result of unavoidably crude estimation methods used to reconstruct historic data before 1987.

The definitions used in this study are largely conventional. The private sector comprises households – including non-profit institutions serving households – and private corporations, both non-financial and financial. The public corporations sector is added to form a 'market' sector, for which the counterpart state sector is the general government sector, comprising local and central government. Although the terms 'market' and 'private' are used interchangeably where the argument is unaffected, the 'market' sector definition is preferred empirically as it circumvents most, though not all,[10] of the data distortions that arise from Britain's history of nationalization and privatization. The Rest of the World sector records, with few exceptions, transactions that take place between UK residents and non-residents.

Private disposable income (Y^d) can be broadly construed as the sum of household disposable income and corporations' retained profits. Disposable income comprises factor incomes, like wages and profits, and transfer payments and receipts, such as property income, direct taxes, social benefits and current and capital transfers.[11] Private sector total expenditure (E) comprises final consumption, capital expenditure (fixed capital investment and the change in inventories) and 'land' transfers.[12]

The corresponding financial surplus (or financial balance, F), also known somewhat confusingly in official parlance as 'net lending', is identically equal to disposable income less total expenditure:

$$F \equiv Y^d - E \tag{1}$$

With the state (or government) and Rest of the World sectors designated respectively by subscripts s, and w (but, for descriptive ease, leaving the private or market sector symbol unadorned), conventional national income accounting gives the across-sector adding-up identity:

$$F + F_s + F_w + \Gamma \equiv 0 \tag{2}$$

where Γ denotes the national accounts residual error, the excess of the expenditure measure over the income measure of the gross domestic product (GDP). Adjusted measures of the market sector financial surplus and disposable income are defined to include the residual error. In this case, the three counterpart financial surpluses sum to zero.

5.3 Long-run tendencies under New Cambridge

Tests of New Cambridge can usefully begin with an examination of its long-run predictions. The basic hypothesis holds that, over the long run, private expenditure decisions are taken in order to keep steady the ratio of private financial wealth to private disposable income. This axiom has the important implication that the ratio to income of the private financial surplus tends to a constant. From identity (2) it can be inferred that the sum of the same ratios of the financial surpluses of government and the Rest of the World should tend to the same constant, irrespective of the behavior of the individual balances. The basic theory is similarly silent on the behavior of the financial balances of households and companies.

These predictions are not unique to New Cambridge. Other sets of behavior could be envisaged which would lead to the same steady state. For example, a government in a closed economy could set fiscal policy to deliver a fixed long-run ratio to GDP of government debt, a ratio that the private sector accepted passively. Observational equivalence means that tests of long-run tendencies have the power to reject the basic New Cambridge view but cannot establish its dominance over other theories.

Exposition of the New Cambridge steady state is straightforward. In its simplest form, the postulated target for the stock of end-period financial wealth (V) may be written:

$$V^* = \varpi Y^d \tag{3}$$

The superscript asterisk denotes the target level. ϖ is the target ratio of financial wealth to disposable income. The equation describes a long-run aim from which it is acknowledged there might be temporary deviations.[13]

For ease of presentation, variables are defined in constant price terms, equal to the corresponding nominal values, denoted where necessary by a diacritical tilde, divided by the private expenditure price deflator (P); for example, $Y^d \equiv \dfrac{\tilde{Y}^d}{P}$.

It is helpful to begin with an assumption of price stability in markets for goods and assets in order to equate the financial surplus with the one-period change in financial wealth in constant prices:

$$F = \frac{\tilde{V} - \tilde{V}_{-1}}{P} = \frac{\tilde{V}}{P} - \frac{\tilde{V}_{-1}}{P_{-1}} = \Delta V \tag{4}$$

The numerical subscript indicates the time period and Δ denotes the one-period change. By assumption: $P = P_{-1}$.

Under these conditions and in a steady growth state it is assumed that:[14]

$$Lim(F) = \Delta V^* \tag{5}$$

The combination of equations (3) and (5) and identity (1) yields a long-run relationship between total expenditure and disposable income:[15]

$$Lim(E) = \left(1 - \frac{g}{1+g}\varpi\right)Y^d \tag{6}$$

where g is the steady-state constant rate of income growth. The corresponding ratio to disposable income of the financial surplus is given by:

$$Lim\left(\frac{F}{Y^d}\right)=\frac{g}{1+g}\varpi \tag{7}$$

Equation (7) shows that the long-run ratio to income of the private financial surplus is a constant approximately equal to the product of the target wealth ratio and the steady state rate of growth.

The same points can be stated in the language of cointegration. Under the New Cambridge null, the three variables – the stock of private financial wealth, private disposable income and private expenditure – follow long-run trends that are separated only by constant proportionate differences. The variables should therefore cointegrate.[16] The ratios to disposable income of the private sector financial surplus and financial wealth should be stationary variables, reverting to their respective means.

It is worth emphasizing that stationarity of the financial surplus ratio does not guarantee stationarity of the financial wealth ratio. For the financial wealth ratio to be stationary, it would be necessary for the financial surplus ratio to revert to the mean described by equation (7).

More generally, a stationary financial surplus ratio may accompany a financial wealth ratio that is rising or falling depending on the pace of income growth and the outstanding level of the wealth ratio. For it is identically true that:

$$\Delta\left(\frac{V}{Y^d}\right)\equiv\frac{F}{Y^d}-\left(\frac{g}{1+g}\right)\frac{V_{-1}}{Y^d_{-1}} \tag{8}$$

In the long run, the wealth ratio stabilizes – $Lim\left\{\Delta\left(\frac{V}{Y^d}\right)\right\}=0$ – only if:

$$Lim\left(\frac{F}{Y^d}\right)=\left(\frac{g}{1+g}\right)\frac{V^{\star}}{Y^d} \tag{9}$$

These propositions have been derived assuming constant prices. The introduction of goods price inflation complicates the story but leaves unchanged the essential message. With the price level changing, equation (4) does not hold: the financial surplus in constant prices is not equal to the change in financial wealth in constant prices. Instead:

$$F = V - \left(\frac{P_{-1}}{P}\right)V_{-1} = \Delta V + \frac{\pi}{1+\pi}V_{-1} \tag{10}$$

where π denotes the rate of inflation defined by: $\pi \equiv \dfrac{\Delta P}{P_{-1}}$.

The basic New Cambridge propositions go through, however, if disposable income and the financial surplus are adjusted by deducting an 'inflation tax' approximately equal to the product of goods and services price inflation and the stock of financial wealth.[17] Specifically:

$$Y^a \equiv Y^d - \left(\frac{\pi}{1+\pi}\right)V_{-1} \tag{11}$$

$$F^a \equiv F - \left(\frac{\pi}{1+\pi}\right)V_{-1} \tag{12}$$

where the superscript a denotes an inflation-tax adjusted measure. Steady states equivalent to those given in equations (6) and (7) follow once the financial wealth target is re-expressed in terms of Y^a.

Additional allowances could be made for capital gains and losses on financial wealth, although these adjustments would involve a further departure from standard national income accounting concepts of income. Growing capital gains or losses would insert a wedge between the conventional or inflation tax-adjusted measures of the financial surplus, on the one hand, and the change in financial wealth on the other. As a result, long-term trends in either measure of income and in expenditure could diverge, even under the New Cambridge null.

5.4 Testing long-run tendencies

Standard unit root tests can be employed to test these long-run propositions, but with the caveat that the tests too often indicate non-stationarity. This well-known problem of low 'power' is somewhat mitigated by the maximal length of my reconstructed annual dataset which runs from 1948 to 2009. Shiller and Perron (1985) argue forcibly that the power of unit root tests depends more on the span of the data than on the frequency of the observations. Haug (2002), however, stresses the importance of using the highest frequency of data over a long time span. In the light of these arguments, the unit root tests performed here are repeated, where possible, using quarterly data, although these are less reliable than the annual figures and begin in 1955.

Unit root tests are also sensitive to the impact of events that create outlying observations in the series under examination. In some cases, the effect can be to cause substantial 'size' distortions, predisposing conventional unit root tests towards rejection of a null hypothesis of non-stationarity; in other cases, the impact is unclear.[18] Standard recommended approaches to overcome this problem comprise the detection and exclusion of outliers or the use of robust estimation techniques. In the series of interest here, outliers occur after 2007, coincident with the recessionary impact of the global banking crisis. In 2009, the private sector financial surplus was extraordinarily large. As it is not knowable whether this shock will prove transitory or permanent, I truncate the sample period for all unit root tests in 2007, and then examine the effect of extending the sample to 2009.

Conventional tests are also used to examine the possibility of breaks in series mean and variance. Flow relationships, represented by financial balances, are examined before turning to the financial wealth target, the key stock-flow relationship.

5.4.1 Financial balances

Visual inspection of the behavior of Britain's financial balances over the last 60 years provides some support for the original New Cambridge view. Figure 5.1 shows the market sector financial surplus with and without the addition of the national accounts residual error, each series being expressed in relation to market sector disposable income (MDI).[19] The figure suggests mean reversion, albeit of series whose oscillations increase in size after the mid-1970s. Within these larger oscillations, fluctuations in year-to-year changes diminish from the mid-1980s onwards, an artefact possibly resulting from the adoption by the ONS of new techniques to balance the national accounts (Officer, 2008).

Similar characteristics are seen in the case of the government's financial balance shown in Figure 5.2, but there is a hint of a mild upward trend in the Rest of the World financial surplus. Shifting trends are more easily discerned in the behavior of the household sector financial surplus in Figure 5.3, an uptrend in the 1950s and 1960s giving way to an apparent downtrend beginning in the early 1990s and ending in 2007. These putative trends find their mirror image in the behavior of the company sector financial surplus.

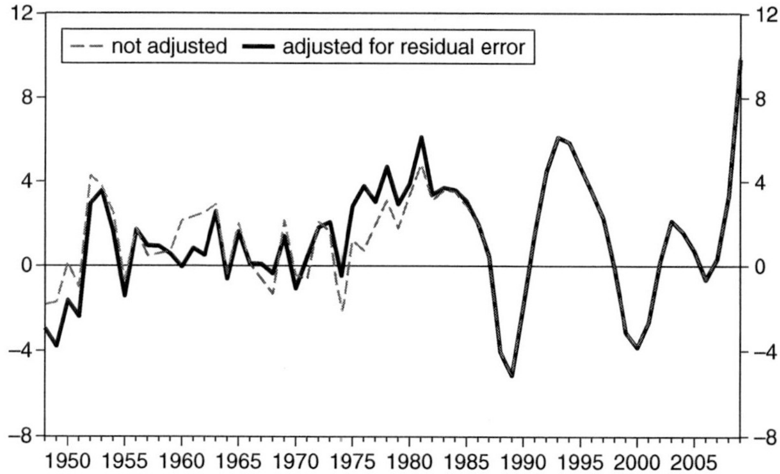

Figure 5.1 Market sector financial surplus, per cent of MDI

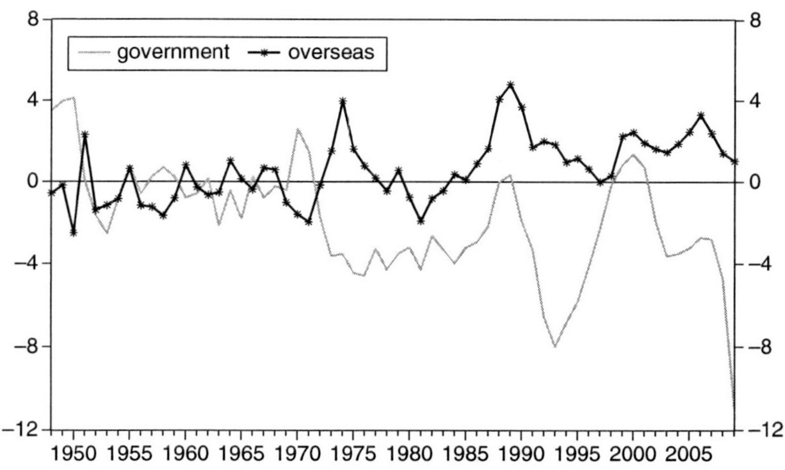

Figure 5.2 Government and overseas financial surplus, per cent of MDI

Although formal unit root tests do not always speak as one, a not uncommon finding, those in Table 5.1 using annual data broadly match the visual evidence. They do not reject the hypothesis that the market sector financial balance mean reverts. The same is true for the government and Rest of the World sectors and possibly for two of the three

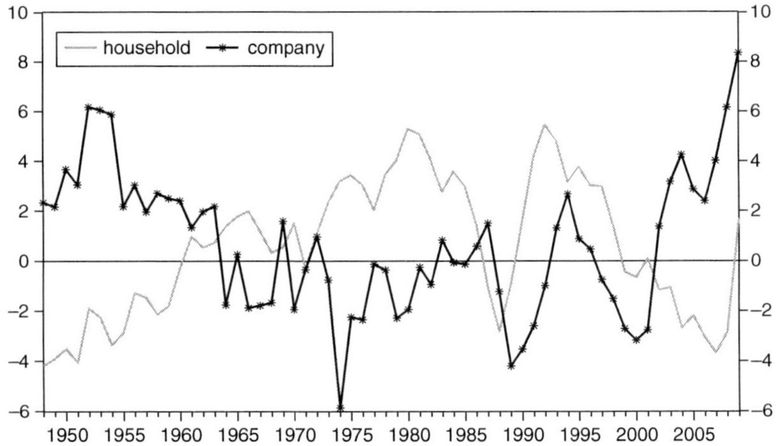

Figure 5.3 Household and company financial surplus, per cent of MDI

Table 5.1 Univariate stationarity tests – annual data to 2007

Financial surplus, % of market disposable income	**Unit root test**		
	ADF	PP	KPSS
Market sector	−3.52	−3.67	0.07
Market sector adjusted	−3.32	−3.48	0.09
General government	−4.30	−3.64	0.36
Rest of the World	−3.09	−3.68	0.66*
Market sector components:			
Household sector	−2.31*	−1.99*	0.25
Company sector, of which:	−2.90*	−2.81*	0.31
Private non-financial	−3.00	−2.95	0.37
Financial	−2.44*	−2.56*	0.45
Public corporations	−3.87	−3.87	0.60*

Source: Author's calculations. Unit root tests estimated with a constant and no trend: ADF – Augmented Dickey-Fuller; PP – Phillips Perron; KPSS – Kwiatkowski, Phillips, Schmidt and Shin. Lag length and residual spectrum at zero frequency determined using the default settings in the software program Eviews 7.1 by Quantitative Micro Software, LLC. Estimated over a period (1951 to 2007) that ensures an equal number of observations per test (57 observations). Critical values for ADF and PP (null of non-stationarity): −2.91; for KPSS (null of stationarity): 0.46, both at the 5 per cent level of significance. * indicates non-rejection of the ADF or PP null or rejection of the KPSS null.

sub-sectors that comprise the company sector (although data quality concerns seriously qualify any conclusion at that level of disaggregation). Two out of three tests indicate non-stationarity in the case of the household and the total company sectors.

Table 5.2 Univariate stationarity tests – quarterly data to 2007

Financial surplus, % of market disposable income	**Unit root test**		
	ADF	**PP**	**KPSS**
Market sector	–3.89	–6.31	0.07
Market sector adjusted	–3.68	–5.44	0.12
General government	–2.69*	–5.28	0.42
Rest of the World	–3.26	–4.11	0.84*
Market sector components:			
Household sector	–2.23*	–3.03	0.28
Company sector	–4.15	–6.69	0.22

Source: Author's calculations. See Table 5.1 for details. Estimated over a period (1955Q4 to 2007Q4) that ensures an equal number of observations per test (209 observations). Critical values for ADF and PP: –2.88; for KPSS: 0.46, both at the 5 per cent level of significance. * indicates non-rejection of the ADF or PP null or rejection of the KPSS null.

Results shown in Table 5.2 using quarterly data paint a slightly different picture. The null of non-stationarity is not rejected on one test in the case of the government sector. On the other hand, the financial surplus ratios of both the household and total corporate sectors appear to mean revert, although the conclusion for households is borderline. Whether the contrast between the annual and quarterly results is informative or the product of measurement error is a question left for future study.[20]

Of immediate importance is the unequivocal nature of the findings for the market sector: irrespective of the frequency of the data, its financial surplus appears to be stationary. This conclusion is robust to an extension of the sample period to include the exceptional events of 2008 and 2009.[21]

Less formal than unit root tests, but perhaps as revealing, are the descriptive statistics and related tests in Tables 5.3 and 5.4, which show sometimes marked changes in the average level and volatility of sectors' financial surpluses across three periods of roughly equal length: 1948–69, 1970–89 and 1990–2007. The dates broadly demarcate the period of the UK's 'Golden Age' in the 1950s and 1960s, the period of rising and falling inflation in the 1970s and 1980s, and the steady growth, low inflation years of stability that emerged after the early-1990s until the global banking crisis of 2008 and 2009.

Average financial surplus ratios shifted significantly between the Golden Age and each of the last two periods in all sectors, *except* the market sector (measured before addition of the national accounts

Table 5.3 Financial surplus period means and standard deviations

% of market dis. inc. **no. of observations**	**1948–1969** **22**	**1970–1989** **20**	**1990–2007** **18**	**1948–2007** **60**
Market sector				
annual average	1.2	1.5	1.4	1.3
standard deviation	2.2	3.4	3.7	3.0
Market sector adj.				
annual average	0.3	2.3	1.4	1.3
standard deviation	2.4	3.6	3.7	3.3
General government				
annual average	0.1	–3.1	–3.6	-2.1
standard deviation	2.2	2.6	3.2	3.1
Rest of the World				
annual average	–0.4	0.8	2.2	0.8
standard deviation	1.3	2.4	1.2	2.0
Market sub-sectors:				
Household sector				
annual average	–1.4	2.8	1.1	0.8
standard deviation	2.6	2.7	3.5	3.4
Company sector				
annual average	2.5	–1.4	0.3	0.6
standard deviation	3.0	2.3	3.3	3.2

Source: ONS, author's calculations. The table shows averages and sample standard deviations of annual observations. The adjusted market sector financial surplus includes the national accounts residual error. The financial surpluses of the adjusted market sector, general government and the Rest of the World sum to zero, subject to rounding error.

residual error).[22] Period averages for the market sector financial surplus ratio remain insignificantly different from the 60-year average: 1.3 per cent of market sector disposable income (equivalent to 1.1 per cent of GDP). The historic average for the market sector surplus rises when the sample is extended to include the extreme observations after 2007 but the hypothesis of across-period constancy is still not rejected.

Equally striking is the contrasting pattern of volatility. Whereas there is no evidence of a shift in the case of households and companies, the variance of the market sector financial surplus ratio increases after 1970, and remains high even during the post-1990 period of general stability.[23] The volatility history of counterpart sectors is less remarkable: an increase, though not of statistical significance, in the case of the government sector and a rise and fall in the case of the Rest of the World.

The contrast in the volatility behavior of the market sector and its sector components reflects a shift in the correlation between the

Table 5.4 Financial surpluses – mean and variance equality tests**

Period mean and variance equality test probability	Periods compared		
	1948–1969 v 1970–1989	1970–1989 v 1990–2007	1948–1969 v 1990–2007
Market sector			
mean	0.74	0.93	0.84
variance	0.08	0.74	0.05*
Market sector adj.			
mean	0.04*	0.41	0.31
variance	0.07	0.96	0.08
General Government			
mean	0.00*	0.64	0.00*
variance	0.49	0.41	0.13
Rest of World			
mean	0.05*	0.03*	0.00*
variance	0.01*	0.00*	0.66
Market sub-sectors:			
Household sector			
mean	0.00*	0.09	0.02*
variance	0.85	0.29	0.21
Company sector			
mean	0.00*	0.08	0.03*
variance	0.24	0.14	0.70

Source: See Table 5.3. **Welch–Satterthwaite mean-equality t-test (allows for unequal variances) and variance-equality F-test. * rejects null hypothesis of equality across periods at 5 per cent level of significance.

financial balances of households and companies. Normally offsetting, these financial balances moved together between the mid-1980s and late-1990s, amplifying the volatility of the aggregate market sector balance. The offsetting behavior of household and company financial balances reappears thereafter until 2007, although not to the extent seen in earlier years.

The conclusion is that the ratio to disposable income of the market sector financial surplus exhibits a behavior over the last six decades that is not demonstrably shared by other sector balances: broad constancy of mean combined with increased volatility. These properties, taken with the formal evidence of stationarity, are not inconsistent with New Cambridge thinking, and help justify its focus on the private sector aggregate.

The increase in volatility of the private financial surplus requires further explanation, however. One plausible answer is inflation, which is known to have affected the changing volatility of GDP. Mention may therefore be made, but briefly since little light is shed, of results obtained after adjusting the financial surplus ratio for the 'inflation tax'. As before, the hypothesis of stationarity is not rejected but the post-1990 level of the market sector inflation-tax adjusted financial surplus ratio appears to be significantly above previous period averages and there is no upbreak in variance. The behavior of the financial wealth stock is more informative.

5.4.2 Financial wealth to income ratio

On tentative estimates, the financial wealth of the market sector at the end of 1948 was nearly double annual disposable income. Ignoring capital gains and losses, the market sector would have had to run a financial surplus worth about 12 per cent of income to achieve the same wealth ratio in 2007, before the global banking crisis. But the financial surplus ratio averaged only 1.3 per cent.

The financial wealth ratio duly fell, precipitously until the mid-1970s, less sharply thereafter but with large oscillations, as Figure 5.4 shows. By the end of 2007, market sector financial wealth was about a fifth of disposable income. The wealth ratio rose to about a third by end-2009. This behavior appears to be wholly inconsistent with the New Cambridge concept of a constant long-run wealth target, even one subject to occasional deviations.

A not unreasonable response would be to question the verity of the facts, which could be seriously afflicted by measurement error in a number of ways. The historic data are taken from different sources and spliced together. Before 1957, financial wealth stocks are derived less than ideally from accumulated financial surpluses, albeit with an allowance back to 1952 for capital gains and losses on government debt. Furthermore, crude but necessary adjustments have been made to put the official (book value) record of the UK's net assets from foreign direct investment (FDI) onto the same basis of market valuation used for other financial assets and liabilities.

The main counter to these concerns is the magnitude of the change in the financial wealth ratio recorded in Figure 5.4: it seems highly improbable that measurement errors alone could obscure these major trends. Moreover they are replicated in Figures 5.5 and 5.6 using different measures. Figure 5.5 shows that a market sector wealth ratio calculated from accumulated financial surpluses (and therefore without allowance for poorly measured capital gains or losses) follows the same general pattern traced by the wealth ratio derived using balance sheet figures. Figure 5.6 shows the UK balance sheet measure with FDI valued

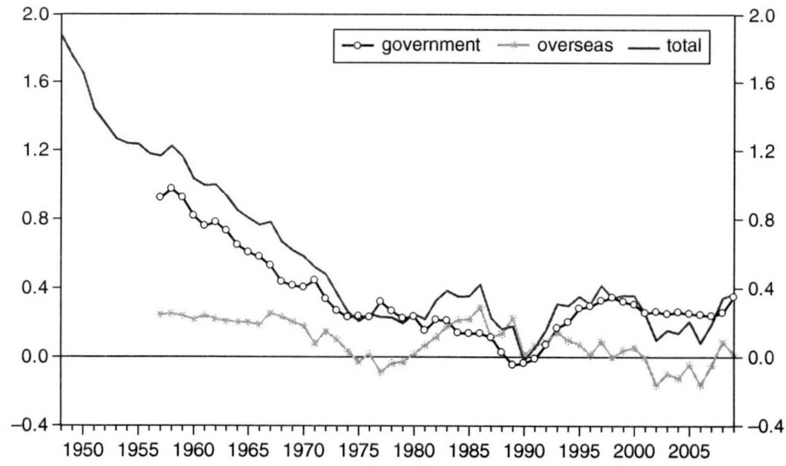

Figure 5.4 Market sector financial wealth, ratio to disposable income

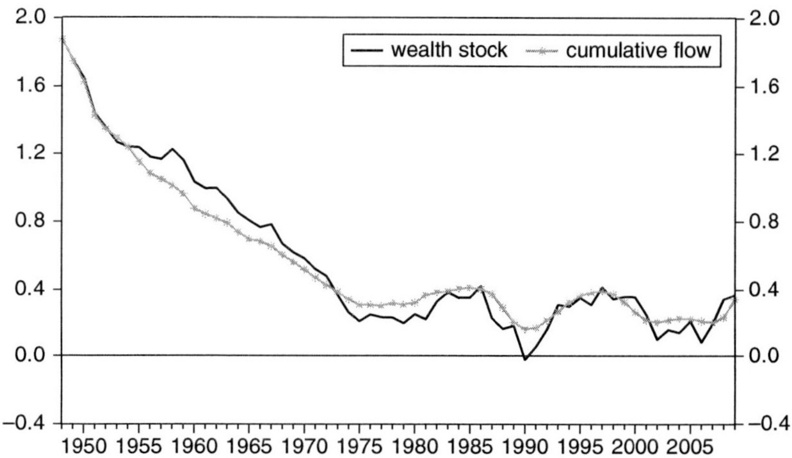

Figure 5.5 Financial wealth versus accumulated flows, ratio to MDI

at book value. The chart also shows that the UK experience is not unique. The private wealth ratio fell sharply in the US until the early-1970s, and again after the mid-1990s, a pattern also seen in US data corrected for FDI misvaluation.[24]

Further reassurance about the verity of the UK evidence comes from the timing and composition of the break in the post-war downtrend in

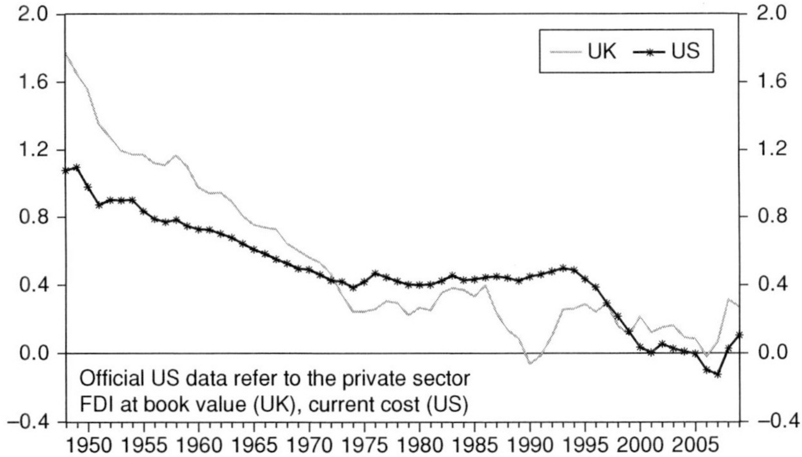

Figure 5.6 Financial wealth UK versus US, ratio to disposable income

the wealth ratio. Statistical tests corroborate the visual evidence that the trend break occurs in the early-to-mid-1970s,[25] largely the result, as Figure 5.4 and Table 5.5 show, of the behavior of market sector holdings of government net debt. This timing fits with the analysis of financial historians Homer and Sylla (1996, p. 451) who note, 'In 1946 began the long retreat of the English bond market, which lasted, with occasional cyclical interruptions, until 1974.'

To complete the evidence, Tables 5.6 reports formal tests for the stationarity of the financial wealth ratio.[26] The full sample test using annual data up to 2007 allows for a structural break in the mid-1970s, a procedure due to Perron (1989; Perron and Vogelsang 1993). Perron's test is known to suffer from a 'size' defect, too frequently rejecting the null hypothesis of non-stationarity when, as in this case, the dating of the structural break has little independent justification (Christiano, 1992). Even so, the null of a unit root in the financial wealth ratio is not rejected. The same holds when the sample period is extended to include the banking crisis years of 2008 and 2009.[27]

In the second set of tests, the full sample period is split before and after the mid-1970s break. There is evidence, using quarterly data of dubious reliability, that the financial wealth ratio is stationary around a declining trend until the mid-1970s. This conclusion is not borne out by the tests on annual data, however. Suitably adjusted for the subsequent (and unexplained) disappearance of this trend, the majority of

Table 5.5 Market sector financial wealth, ratio to disposable income

End-year wealth, ratio to annual MDI	1948	1957	1974	2007	2009
Total, of which counterpart net liabilities of:	1.87	1.17	0.26	0.19	0.37
Government	n.a.	0.92	0.23	0.24	0.35
Rest of World, of which:	n.a.	0.24	0.03	–0.05	0.02
foreign direct investment	n.a.	0.20	0.09	0.37	0.39
other	n.a.	0.04	–0.06	–0.42	–0.37

Source: Author's calculations, including FDI misvaluation adjustment (see Appendix). n.a. – not available. Totals subject to rounding error.

Table 5.6 Financial wealth ratio stationarity tests

Market sector financial wealth, End-year ratio to annual MDI	Unit root test		
	ADF	PP	KPSS
Annual data			
Full sample: 1949–2007**	–3.54*	n.a.	n.a.
Split sample:			
1951–1974	–2.97*	–3.16*	0.18*
1975–2007	–2.46*	–2.58*	0.08
Quarterly data			
1956Q2–1974Q4	–0.79*	–5.50	0.13
1975Q1–2007Q4	–2.18*	–2.67*	0.10

Source: Author's calculations. See Table 5.1 for details. **Perron's ADF-equivalent test run on the residuals from a regression with a (significant) time trend split after 1974. Lag length to produce white noise disturbances based on the modified Akaike information criterion recommended by Ng and Perron (2001). Split sample periods chosen to ensure an equal number of observations for each test: constant and linear trend in first period; constant in second period. Critical values: for Perron: –3.92; for ADF and PP: –3.61 (1951 – 1974), –2.95 (1975 – 2007), –3.47 (1956Q2 – 1974Q4), –2.88 (1975Q1 – 2007Q4); KPSS: 0.15 (1951 – 1974, 1956Q2 – 1974Q4), 0.46 (1975 – 2007, 1975Q1 – 2007Q4), all at the 5 per cent level of significance. * indicates non-rejection of the Perron, ADF or PP null or rejection of the KPSS null. n.a. – not applicable.

the tests for the period beginning in the mid-1970s do not reject the hypothesis that the financial wealth ratio does not mean revert. The same tests applied to two alternative measures of financial wealth – one using balance sheet data uncorrected for FDI misvaluation, the other calculated from accumulated financial surplus flows – give similar verdicts over sample periods ending in both 2007 and 2009.[28]

5.5 The New Cambridge wealth target reconsidered

The unexplained shifting trends and non-stationarity of Britain's private wealth to income ratio pose a major challenge to the New Cambridge view, one that surprisingly has not been addressed in previous published research. The evidence rejects the basic specification of the private wealth target, even with its provisos.[29] Without this axiom, the history of the wealth ratio invites a prosaic interpretation in terms of changing fiscal policy, notably the emergence of large budget deficits in the 1970s and 1980s. A rethink is required.

At least two issues warrant investigation. The first concerns the notion of the financial wealth target itself. Although a wealth-income norm is consistent with several theories of consumers' behavior, it is not clear that the same motivations can be ascribed to the private sector as a whole.[30]

An important reason for doubt concerns the nature of private financial wealth. The private sector aggregate is formed by *consolidating* the accounts of households and companies, including the banking system, with all intra-private sector transactions netted off. Consolidation means that 'inside' financial instruments, such as money deposits and equity securities, which are an asset of one sub-sector but the liability of another, cancel out at the aggregate level. Private sector financial wealth comprises *only* those net financial assets that are counterparts of the net liabilities of the government and the Rest of the World.

It is not self-evident that private sector agents would wish to stabilize, in relation to their disposable income, the sum of their holdings of government net debt and of overseas securities: deposits, loans and stocks of FDI. Empirical demand functions for investment securities like government bonds are typically specified as portfolio decisions unrelated to the level of income, unless the latter proxies for wealth (Spencer, 1981). There are many forces that drive FDI: tariff hopping, trade friction avoidance, cost-minimizing vertical integration and so on (Blonigen, 2005). None suggests a link with domestic income alone.

The second issue deserving further consideration is the role played by competing rates of return on non-financial capital. Matthews and Minford (1980) usefully develop a theoretical model in which private sector agents divide total wealth between non-financial and financial capital depending on the discounted value of future income or utility streams from each asset type. In the authors' world, firms are construed as 'financial holding companies with a multinational and multiasset perspective' while households obey 'similar principles of asset disposition.'

Alas, empirical implementation of this idea has foundered on the severe problems of measuring properly total wealth and expected rival rates of return. In perhaps the most successful of the econometric studies of the New Cambridge function, Bennett (1986, 1987) is forced to assume that the return on non-financial capital is an unobserved constant.

Nevertheless, there appears to be merit in treating private non-financial and financial wealth as substitutes. Table 5.7 and Figure 5.7 show the ratio to the disposable income of the market sector of its total wealth split between asset types. Non-financial capital comprises residential

Table 5.7 Market sector wealth, ratio to disposable income

End-year wealth, ratio to annual MDI	**1948**	**1957**	**1974**	**2007**	**2009**
Total, of which:	5.04	3.96	5.22	5.50	5.10
Financial	1.87	1.17	0.26	0.19	0.37
Non-financial, of which:	3.16	2.80	4.96	5.31	4.73
housing	1.21	1.01	1.97	3.80	3.37
other	1.95	1.79	2.99	1.51	1.36

Source: See Table 5.5 notes. Totals subject to rounding error.

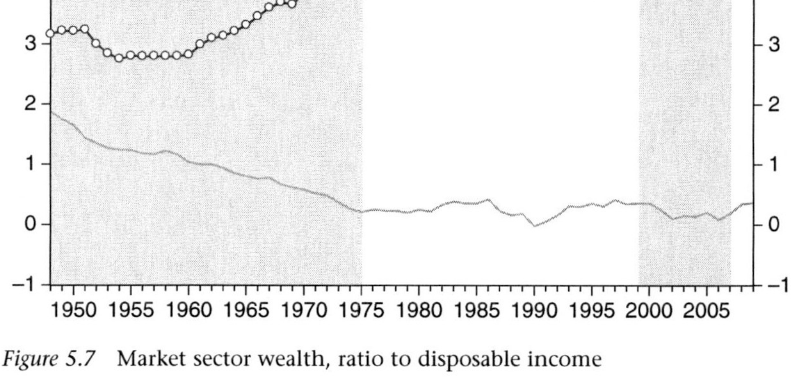

Figure 5.7 Market sector wealth, ratio to disposable income

dwellings ('housing'), and other non-housing capital such as business equipment, structures and inventories. The data appendix describes the problems of estimating the value of these assets at market prices.

The figure shows two broad tendencies. First, the ratios to disposable income of total and non-financial wealth, like the financial wealth ratio, are non-stationary, whether or not allowance is made for a linear time trend (Table 5.8).[31] Second, and more important, there appears to be an inverse relationship between the financial and non-financial wealth ratios that suggests substitution. Several phases can be roughly distinguished.

In the first phase that lasts until the mid-1970s, the downtrend seen in the financial wealth ratio coincides with an uptrend in the non-financial wealth ratio, the latter beginning in the mid-1950s as the impact of wartime disruption and early peacetime controls abated.[32] These inverse trends are associated with the Golden Age investment boom, itself propelled by several forces – a large backlog of investment opportunities, technical progress including catch-up with the US, and a low cost of capital. These were circumstances also conducive to a run-down of companies' excess liquid financial assets (Matthews, 1968; Matthews, Feinstein and Odling-Smee, 1982).

In the second phase from the mid-1970s to the late-1990s, there is little discernible trend in either the financial or non-financial wealth ratios. The latter is much more variable, however, largely as a result of oscillations in housing wealth, which continued to rise in relation

Table 5.8 Total and non-financial wealth ratios stationarity tests

Market sector wealth, End-year ratio to annual MDI	**Unit root test**		
	ADF	PP	KPSS
Detrended:			
Total wealth	–3.14*	–2.62*	0.11
Non-financial wealth	–2.68*	–2.07*	0.16*
Demeaned:			
Total wealth	–2.06*	–1.56*	0.60*
Non-financial wealth	–1.76*	–1.45*	0.71*

Source: See Table 5.1 for details. Tests run with a constant and linear trend ('detrended') and with a constant alone ('demeaned'). Sample period 1955 to 2007 excludes data likely to be materially affected by post-war controls and measurement error. Critical values: for ADF and PP –3.50 (detrended), –2.92 (demeaned); for KPSS: 0.15 (detrended), 0.46 (demeaned), all at the 5 per cent level of significance. * indicates non-rejection of the ADF or PP null or rejection of the KPSS null.

to disposable income while the ratio for other non-financial capital trended lower. These oscillations are associated with the increased variability of the market sector financial surplus ratio seen in Figure 5.1, a timing that fits with the gradual liberalization of Britain's mortgage market. The financial wealth ratio displays weaker, mirror image, oscillations.

In a third phase beginning in the late-1990s, an upward movement sustained until 2007 in the non-financial wealth ratio, wholly attributable to housing wealth, is associated with a downward drift in the financial wealth ratio. The position reverses after 2007: the financial wealth ratio rises and the non-financial wealth ratio falls.

Were markets in capital goods perfect, with prices set consistently with discounted future income and utility streams, the non-financial wealth ratio would help capture the changing incentives to invest in non-financial as opposed to financial assets. Conceptually, this wealth ratio can be compared to the ratio of a stock price to a firm's earnings: the PE reflects investors' expectations of the uncertain rate of return on the firm's assets set against the yield on safer alternatives.[33] In practice, significant measurement error impairs the ability of the non-financial wealth ratio to act as a suitable proxy. But formal tests for cointegration are nevertheless suggestive.

The salient results of an investigation using the Johansen procedure with different measures of financial wealth, disposable income and non-financial wealth are summarized in Table 5.9. The dependent variable is the end-year stock of market sector financial wealth in constant prices (V) calculated either from balance sheet data or from the accumulated flow of financial surpluses, the latter benchmarked to the balance sheet data in 1947. The other two variables in the potentially cointegrating relationship are market sector disposable income in constant prices and the ratio to income of non-financial wealth.

Income is defined consistently with the measure of financial wealth. In the case of the balance sheet measure, constant price disposable income, denoted Y^{aa}, is adjusted for the inflation tax and includes capital gains, calculated from the change in the difference between the measures of financial wealth based on balance sheet data and cumulative flows. For specifications (2) and (3) using the cumulative flows measure of financial wealth, constant price disposable income, Y^{a}, is calculated after adjustment for the inflation tax alone. The ratios to income of non-financial wealth are defined symmetrically: $k'' \equiv \frac{K}{Y^{aa}}$ and $k \equiv \frac{K}{Y^{a}}$, where K is non-financial wealth in constant prices.

Table 5.9 Cointegration summary results – Johansen method

Dependent variable *V*	Cointegrating vector		Error Correction
Equation specifications	Y^{aa}, Y^{a}	100(k'', k)	$\bar{R}^2$
1 Balance sheet data			
coeff	−0.03	−1013.1	0.12
t-statistic	−0.7	−8.2	
2 Cumulative flows data			
coeff.	0.07	−687.7	0.65
t-statistic	3.0	−9.8	
3 Y^a, k weakly exogenous			
coeff.	0.11	−710.6	0.70
t-statistic	5.0	−11.5	

Source: Author's calculations using a second order VAR selected on the basis of the Schwarz Bayesian and Akaike information criteria, with a constant but no trend in the cointegrating vector and no constant in the VAR. The number of non-collinear cointegrating vectors is set at 1 based on the maximum eigenvalue and trace statistics. Sample period: 1955 to 2007. Pre-tests indicate that all variables are $I(1)$ (see Appendix).

These definitions ensure that the specifications reported in Table 5.9 are stock-flow consistent: the change in financial wealth is identically equal to the difference between disposable income, suitably defined, and expenditure. The table does not report the results of experiments using components of the non-financial wealth ratio or stock market proxies, which added nothing of interest. To avoid inclusion of observations materially affected by post-war controls and measurement error, and latterly by the global banking crisis, the estimation period runs annually from 1955 to 2007.

Results from the Johansen procedure come with familiar caveats. Precise results are sensitive to the order of the vector autoregression (VAR) and choice of deterministic components, although the broad message of Table 5.9 is robust to different selections. More important, finite-sample bias in a systems approach could result were the implicit equations for income or non-financial wealth misspecified.[34] Accordingly, the Johansen procedure is used in this study to guide the choice of cointegrating vector that could be included with less risk of spuriousness in a single equation error correction model (ECM) of private expenditure.

The key features of the results in Table 5.9 are straightforward.

First, disposable income forms part of the cointegrating vector when financial wealth and income exclude capital gains, but is insignificant and incorrectly signed when capital gains are included. The coefficients on income in specifications (2) and (3), which use the cumulative flows measure of financial wealth, are statistically significant but small, a finding not inconsistent with the doubts raised over the notion of a private sector financial wealth target.

Second, the null hypothesis that financial wealth cointegrates with the ratio to income of the non-financial wealth stock is not rejected. The ratio is highly significant and correctly (negatively) signed in all specifications.

Third, the relationship between the variables is far tighter when financial wealth is calculated from cumulative flows rather than from balance sheet data. Table 5.9 reports the adjusted coefficient of determination ($\bar{R}^2$) for the Johansen systems estimate of the error correction model for the change in financial wealth. The fit is poor in the case of the balance sheet measure but acceptable in the case of the cumulative flows measure ($\bar{R}^2$ of 65 per cent). The result is important since the Johansen systems estimate ECM can be construed as a restricted version of a private expenditure function.[35]

The poor performance of the balance sheet measure is puzzling. Measurement error is one possibility. Another explanation is that holders of government and overseas securities target their nominal holdings and largely ignore the effect of market revaluations. This possibility finds empirical support in the study of the UK gilt-edged market by Davidson, Madonia and Westaway (1994). The implication is that the cumulative flows measure of financial wealth is more likely than the balance sheet measure to represent a targeted variable to which private sector agents adjust.

The last finding of significance is given by specification (3) in Table 5.9. The hypothesis that the changes in disposable income and the non-financial wealth ratio do not respond to departures from the long-run desired level of financial wealth (measured by cumulative flows) cannot be rejected.[36] Equation fit is also improved by this restriction ($\bar{R}^2$ of 70 per cent). Income and the non-financial wealth ratio can therefore be treated as weakly exogenous, justifying the estimation of a private expenditure function within a single-equation framework.

5.6 An augmented New Cambridge expenditure function

The methodology of Hendry (1995) is used to nest a long-run relationship between market sector financial wealth (measured by cumulative flows) and the ratio to income of non-financial wealth within an error correction model for market sector total expenditure of the general form:

$$\Delta E = A(L)\Delta X + \tau_0\{E_{-1} - \tau_1 Y^a_{-1} - \tau_2(V_{-1} + \tau_3 k_{-1} + \tau_4)\} \qquad (13)$$

where X is a vector of regressors, $A(L)$ is a vector polynomial in the lag operator L such that $L^i(\Delta X) \equiv \Delta X_{-i}$. $A(L)\Delta X$ comprises up to two lags of differenced variables that are integrated of order zero (denoted $I(0)$) whereas all the levels variables are $I(1)$ (see Appendix). Granted cointegration of the latter and weak exogeneity, the variables in the ECM are stationary and inference can be based on standard distributions.

The differenced variables in ΔX comprise changes in total expenditure and in inflation-tax adjusted disposable income[37] and components of the change in the non-financial wealth ratio. In addition, allowance is made for the impact of monetary and inflation shocks by including terms in the change in the level of the short-term (three-month) nominal interest rate, i, and in the inflation rate of the market sector expenditure deflator.

The change in the non-financial wealth ratio that forms part of ΔX is decomposed into three parts using an identity that takes advantage of the available data on non-financial asset prices, here confined to house prices. The nominal stock of housing wealth is divided by a house price index to form a series for the volume of the dwelling stock, $\bar{H}$, and its ratio to disposable income $h \equiv \frac{\bar{H}}{Y^a}$. The level of house prices in relation to the market sector expenditure deflator is denoted q^h; h and nh superscripts denote housing and non-housing non-financial wealth respectively, and a diacritical dot denotes rates of change (so that, for example, $\dot{q}^h \equiv \frac{\Delta q^h}{q^h_{-1}}$). An Appendix shows that:

$$\Delta k \equiv [\dot{q}^h + \dot{h}(1 + \dot{q}^h)]k^h_{-1} + \Delta k^{nh} \qquad (14)$$

The component $\dot{q}^h k^h_{-1}$ can be regarded as a measure of the ratio to income of real capital gains on the housing stock.

Using annual data from 1955 to 2007, estimation of the expenditure function by ordinary least squares begins with a general specification that is subsequently pared down to a more parsimonious form. An Appendix summaries the tests applied, and passed, to delete insignificant variables (including lags of ΔE, ΔY^a and several terms in Δk), to restrict coefficients and to examine the assumed exogeneity of the contemporaneous terms ΔY^a and $\dot{q}^h k^h_{-1}$.

It is of note that these tests decisively reject a restriction that imposes equal coefficients (of opposite sign) on the lagged levels of expenditure and income. With unequal coefficients, the level of income plays some, albeit small, role in the determination of the long-run desired level of financial wealth. The result should be taken with a degree of circumspection, however, in view of data quality concerns. The equality restriction is accepted over the 1955 to 2002 sample period. In addition to normal revisions, question marks are raised over more recent figures by changes to the method by which the ONS balanced the national accounts from 2004 (Akers and Clifton-Fearnside, 2008).

The preferred results are shown in Table 5.10. As expected, the change in expenditure is related positively to the change in income, housing capital gains, past levels of financial wealth and the non-financial wealth ratio and related negatively to interest rate and inflation shocks and to past differences between the level of expenditure and income. The fit is acceptable ($\bar{R}^2$ of 86 per cent) and residuals appear to be normally distributed, free of serial correlation, first and higher order (not reported), and of heteroscedasticity. There is no evidence of functional misspecification.

With the last 15 years of the estimation sample period set aside, the equation passes standard Chow tests for the adequacy of out-of-sample predictions and parameter stability. The same conclusion is drawn from the CUSUM test (not reported) based on the cumulative sum of one-step-ahead residuals resulting from recursive estimation. The CUSUM of squares test (not reported) based on the cumulative sum of the same residuals squared indicates some variance instability in the late 1970s. But the departure from the null hypothesis is negligible and the CUSUM of squares generally stays well within the 5 per cent confidence limits.

A test for cointegration can be based on residuals calculated by deducting from the level of expenditure the algebraic long-run static-state solution, E^S, derived by setting to zero the difference variables in equation (13):

$$E^s = \tau_1 Y^a + \tau_2(V + \tau_3 k + \tau_4) \tag{15}$$

The estimated solution is:[38]

$$E^s = 0.87Y^a + 1.41[V + 689.2(100k) - 417{,}283] \tag{16}$$

In static stock-flow equilibrium, the financial surplus is also zero ($E^s = Y^a$). In this case, the estimated level of financial wealth, V^s, is:

$$V^S = 0.09Y^a - 689.2(100k) + 417{,}283 \tag{17}$$

Table 5.10 Estimation results using inflation-tax adjusted disposable income

	Regressors									Regression statistics						
	ΔY^a	$\dot{q}^h k^h_{-1}$	Δi_{-1}	Δi_{-2}	$\Delta^2 \pi_{-1}$	E_{-1}	Y^a_{-1}	V_{-1}	$100k_{-1}$	$\bar{R}^2$	Z1	Z2	Z3	Z4	Z5	Z6
a	0.32	234.0	−1772.7	−1561.1	−733.4	−0.19	0.17	0.27	187.6	0.86	0.98	0.83	0.53	1.02	0.88	0.96
t	3.8	4.1	−2.7	−2.8	−2.6	−3.7	3.3	8.8	6.5	*p*	0.33	0.37	0.77	0.44	0.59	0.50

Note: See text for definition of variables. The coefficient on real capital gains on housing assets is divided by 100. Ordinary least squares regression for the dependent variable ΔE using annual data from 1955 to 2007 including an intercept (not reported). *a* – coefficient value, *t* – t-statistic, p – p-value. Regression statistics: $\bar{R}^2$ – coefficient of determination adjusted for degrees of freedom; Z1 – F-version of Breusch–Godfrey Lagrange Multiplier (LM) test for first-order serial correlation; Z2 – F-version of Ramsey's RESET test for functional form; Z3 – LM version of Jarque-Bera's normality test; Z4 – F-version of White's heteroscedasticity test; Z5 – F-version of Chow's predictive failure test (Chow's second test) for the adequacy of the predictions; Z6 – F-version of Chow's (first) test for the stability of the regression coefficients. Stability tests use the last 15 years of the full sample period ending 2007. The equation specification is a transformation of equation (13), which can be estimated directly using nonlinear least squares with equivalent results.

Table 5.11 Estimation results using conventional measure of disposable income

	Regressors									Regression statistics						
	ΔY^d	$\dot{q}^h k'^h_{-1}$	Δi_{-1}	Δi_{-2}	$\Delta^2 \pi_{-1}$	E_{-1}	Y^d_{-1}	V_{-1}	$100k'_{-1}$	$\bar{R}^2$	Z1	Z2	Z3	Z4	Z5	Z6
a	0.37	228.1	−1764.9	−1196.1	−795.3	−0.20	0.17	0.27	186.4	0.87	1.00	0.37	0.55	0.91	0.99	1.15
t	4.2	4.0	−2.8	−2.3	−2.8	−4.1	3.7	9.1	6.4	*p*	0.32	0.55	0.76	0.52	0.49	0.36

Note: See notes to preceding table. $k'^h \equiv K^h/Y^d$ and $k' \equiv K/Y^d$.

a result not dissimilar to the Johansen-based estimates in Table 5.9. Tests on the residuals formed by deducting these solutions from the levels of expenditure and financial wealth respectively reject the unit root null, consistent with a stationary error correction mechanism (see Appendix).

To the best of my knowledge, there are no recent published results for a UK private sector expenditure function with which these estimates can be compared. However, it is feasible to examine two alternative hypotheses, the first concerning the correct measurement of income, the second concerning linearity.

Table 5.11 shows estimation results using the conventional measure of income, not adjusted for the inflation tax. Equation fit and performance are very similar to those in Table 5.10. Non-nested hypothesis tests reported in an appendix suggest a modest preference for the conventional measure of income but do not reject use of the inflation-tax adjusted measure, which is analytically purer. The same appendix records non-nested tests of the linear model in Table 5.10 set against a model linear in logarithms. Although not suggested by the stock-flow accounting, a logarithmic specification might prove a better approximation were the true underlying model non-linear.[39] However, the log-linear model is decisively rejected in favor of the linear specification.

5.7 New Cambridge comparisons

Although an extended disquisition would be inappropriate, there is merit in drawing comparisons between the original New Cambridge view and my augmented specification. The implications of the estimates in Table 5.10 are considered once allowance is made for the feedback between the accumulation of financial wealth and spending.

The first comparison of note concerns *steady state properties*. Under New Cambridge, the ratio to income of the financial surplus tends to a constant, as shown by equation (7). It is perhaps surprising that the alternative approach has a similar implication. Even though the long-run impact on desired financial wealth of a change in the level of income is very small (equation (17)), the steady state of the augmented specification is characterised by non-negligible ratios to income of financial wealth and the financial surplus. The main reason is that desired financial wealth is sensitive in the long run to income growth.

The point can be explained intuitively. According to the estimates in Table 5.10, a £100 increase in income raises expenditure initially by £32, thereby adding £68 to financial wealth. The latter is then drawn down as expenditure continues to respond. For there to be a material long-run impact on financial wealth, changes in income would need to persist, implying a relationship between the wealth ratio and the rate of income growth.

The precise relationship derived in an appendix is a function of the steady rate of growth, g, the size of the initial impact on expenditure of an increase in income a_0, the impacts of income and financial wealth on the level of the long-run desired level of expenditure, as measured by τ_1 and τ_2 in equation (13), and the speed of adjustment of expenditure to departures for this long-run level, as measured by τ_0. Assuming a constant non-financial wealth ratio, the steady state financial wealth ratio under the augmented specification is described by:

$$Lim\left(\frac{V}{Y^a}\right)=\frac{(1+g)\{g(1-a_0)-\tau_0(1-\tau_1)\}}{g(g-\tau_0(1+\tau_2))-\tau_0\tau_2} \tag{18}$$

It follows that:

$$Lim\left(\frac{F^a}{Y^a}\right)=\frac{g\{g(1-a_0)-\tau_0(1-\tau_1)\}}{g(g-\tau_0(1+\tau_2))-\tau_0\tau_2} \tag{19}$$

These results are framed in terms of inflation-tax adjusted disposable income, but equivalent steady state results can be derived in terms of the conventional measure of income granted a constant rate of inflation. To illustrate, Table 5.12 compares hypothetical steady state financial surplus ratios under the New Cambridge paradigm and under the augmented specification. Growth of disposable income is set at 3 per cent a year, close to the 20-year average, while the financial wealth to annual income ratio relevant to New Cambridge is set at one fifth, close to the low end-2007 value. On this figuring, the steady state financial surplus ratio under the augmented specification is likely to be small but positive and only somewhat below that predicted by New Cambridge.

The second comparison of note concerns the *speed of adjustment* of expenditure to changes in income. New Cambridge controversially claimed that private expenditure responded very rapidly indeed.[40] According to the School's novel 'mean lag theorem', which Taylor (2008), following Dorfman (1959), refers to as the 'bathtub theorem', the mean lag response of private expenditure to a change in private disposable income is equal to the (low) target financial wealth ratio. An Appendix provides a formal proof, which can be understood in terms of the analogy of a bathtub of water – financial wealth – to which income adds and from

Table 5.12 Hypothetical steady state solutions

Private financial surplus,	**Inflation rate %**		
% of MDI	**0**	**2**	**4**
New Cambridge view	0.58	0.96	1.32
Augmented specification	0.47	0.78	1.07

Note: Calculations assume 3 per cent p.a. real income growth and a financial wealth to annual income norm under New Cambridge of 0.2.

which expenditure subtracts. The smaller the bathtub, the less time an inflow of income would be detained before flowing out as expenditure.

As New Cambridge acknowledged, the mean lag theorem loses its power if the adjustment of expenditure to income is oscillatory. In this case, the mean lag comprises an average of positive and negative effects, and ceases to have meaning (Solow, 1983; Godley and Lavoie, 2007). Since private expenditure includes consumption of durable goods and fixed investment, oscillatory and drawn out dynamics would not be surprising.

The augmented specification does not surprise. Under it, the response of expenditure to a change in income is subject to persistent overshooting and undershooting, as Figure 5.8 shows. As with New Cambridge, the long-run impact is one-for-one. An almost one-for-one response also occurs rapidly – within three years of the income shock – but expenditure continues to rise for another two years, before subsiding. Further damped oscillations ensue with no less than 11½ years separating successive peaks in the response of expenditure, a protracted adjustment to which the corresponding mean lag of less than five *weeks* gives no clue. An Appendix provides formal details.

The final comparison of note concerns the *causes of the historic increase in the variability of the private sector financial surplus* noted in section 5.4. The original New Cambridge function offers an explanation in terms of inflation, but variations in the inflation tax cannot explain the continued volatility of the financial surplus during the post-1990 period of general macroeconomic stability. The augmented specification offers an additional explanation based on the role played by asset prices, notably those of residential dwellings. According to the Table 5.10 estimates, a change in house prices relative to prices in general has a marked impact: a 10 per cent relative price fall curtailing private expenditure by 1½ per cent over a two year period. This finding may be compared with the Bank of England's previous contention that house prices have little effect on consumers' spending (Benito et al., 2006).

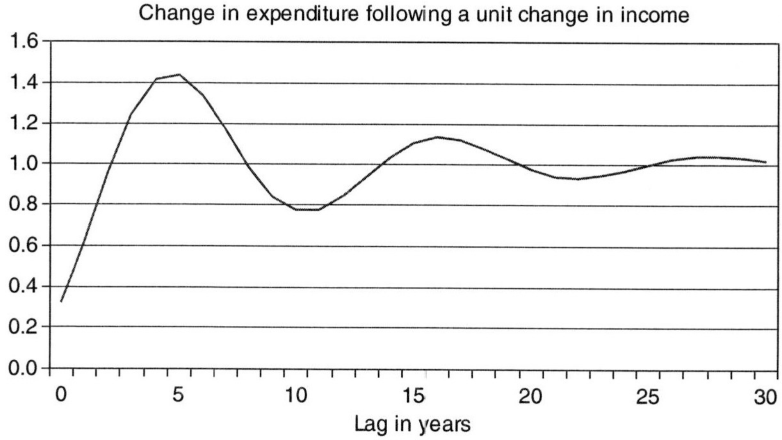

Figure 5.8 Estimated response of expenditure to income
Source: Author's calculations of the impact of an income stock, ceteris paribus.

Table 5.13 Proximate impact of house price variations

Market sector financial surplus,	**1955–1979**	**1980–2007**	
% of disposable income*	**actual**	**actual**	**simulated****
annual average	1.4	1.6	1.9
standard deviation	1.9	4.0	2.0

Note: *adjusted for national accounts residual error. **actual less simulated impact of variations in relative house prices around their post-1955 trend.

Table 5.13 reports a simple calculation that removes the simulated impact of off-trend variations in relative house prices from the post-1979 record of the market sector financial surplus. The average financial surplus in relation to income is little affected but the impact on variability is marked. With off-trend house price movements removed, the variability of the financial surplus ratio is substantially reduced to a level little different from that seen before 1979.

5.8 The banking crisis

Although providing a useful interpretation of post-war developments until 2007, the augmented New Cambridge specification fails to explain the collapse in private spending in the UK that occurred during the banking crisis of 2008 and 2009. The regression forecasts flat spending over this two-year period as against a measured fall of 10 per cent.[41]

In 2008, the forecast error for the change in spending is over four times the regression standard error; the equivalent figure in 2009 is nearly 18 times. The use of alternative measures of private wealth, including stock market valuations, does not resolve this problem. The regression reported in Martin (2010), reached after extensive investigation, 'succeeds' in eliminating the outsized forecast error in 2008, but the over-prediction in 2009 is more than 20 times the regression standard error.[42]

This failure should not be surprising. An equation estimated under one regime, in which the banking system works, may prove uninformative under a new regime, when the banking system fails.[43] The private spending function's ability to capture the impact of the banking collapse is confined to the role played by wealth effects, arising from, for example, changes in property or stock market prices. But in 2008 and 2009, the wealth shocks were neither large enough nor long enough sustained – asset prices recovered after spring 2009 – to provide an adequate explanation of the dramatic fall in private spending.

As Bean (2009) forcibly argues, the problem is a general one that applies to all explanations reliant on wealth effects. On Bean's calculation, the wealth losses associated with the global banking crisis, and the related impact on consumption, account for only a very small fraction – he suggests less than 10 per cent – of the output loss in the advanced economies. He concludes, 'we cannot come near to explaining the 'Great Contraction' in terms of wealth effects'.

Resolution of these model failures is in its infancy but there are two promising lines of enquiry. The first stresses the role played by the provision of credit: a leftward shift in banks' credit supply curve may have forced private sector agents to curtail expenditure. Such forced saving is consistent with original New Cambridge thinking and Wynne Godley's advocacy of the inclusion of measures of credit flows in the private spending function. His and others' estimates suggest such an approach works empirically in the case of the US, but extensive tests fail to replicate that success in a UK context.[44] Moreover, as Rowan (1976) noted, the inclusion of credit flows is inconsistent with the level of aggregation postulated by New Cambridge: the credit flows are largely 'inside' and should net off against counterpart private financial asset flows.

A second line of enquiry stresses the impact of deep uncertainty on precautionary saving. As Caballero (2010) argues, under conditions of Knightian uncertainty, private sector agents may place 'extreme emphasis on tail outcomes and worst-case scenarios.' The banking crisis was arguably an event that invited extreme pessimism, and high levels of precautionary saving. The empirical problem is that 'pessimism,' as measured by financial market risk premiums and survey evidence of consumer and business confidence, did not persist at extreme levels, and therefore does not provide as yet a powerful explanation of the 2009 spending collapse.[45]

5.9 Conclusions

The New Cambridge model of UK private sector spending was ahead of its time in formalizing empirically the relationship between *stocks* of financial wealth and *flows* of income and expenditure. Stock-flow consistency was combined with a novel high-level aggregation that overcame serious defects of national accounting, a lesson still lost on applied economists who treat household disposable income as a suitable measure of consumers' budget constraint.

Using a specially reconstructed historic database, I find evidence that helps to justify the New Cambridge focus on the private sector aggregate, notably the mean reversion of the private sector financial surplus. However, the evidence rejects the underlying axiom that posits a simple long-run norm linking financial wealth and private current disposable income. The ratio to income of financial wealth is instead subject to shifting trends and persistent oscillations.

An alternative hypothesis, not without merit, is that the private sector chooses between non-financial and financial assets on the basis of competing expected rates of return.[46] These, alas, are not observable but experimentation with a proxy leads to a tentative augmented private spending function with interesting attributes. Like New Cambridge, it suggests the possibility of stable steady-state ratios to income of financial wealth and of the financial surplus, but only if competing expected rates of return are constant. The adjustment of expenditure to changes in income is quick but also oscillatory, a feature that robs the New Cambridge mean lag theorem of usefulness. The results also reveal a powerful connection between house prices and expenditure, a relationship absent from the original New Cambridge function and distrusted by the Bank of England. But like other empirical relationships, the augmented function cannot properly explain the collapse in spending associated with the post-2007 banking crisis.

Future research needs to focus on the theory of portfolio choice adumbrated in this study to discover in what way investments in financial and non-financial assets can be regarded as substitutes; and the net advantage, which may vary over time, in the postulated high level of aggregation. The roles that credit conditions and Knightian uncertainty play are also likely to prove the key to understanding the post-2007 recession in private spending – a challenge that goes far wider than New Cambridge.

Appendix A

Data sources and methods

Flow data in current prices

The construction of government, Rest of the World and private sector income and expenditure flow data is largely explained in Martin (2007b, 2009). A correction is applied to remove errors in the official national accounts related to a reclassification of the Housing Revenue Account (HRA), which distort local government and public corporations data from 1974.

The derivation of historic data for households and companies is problematic. Pre-1987 figures for the financial surplus of households are derived using an ONS series for disposable income and saving of dubious quality and now partly suspended (Martin, 2007a, 2007b), and own estimates of the household capital account that draw on available data for housing investment and pre-ESA95 figures consistent with the 1997 national accounts Blue Book. Pre-1987 data for private corporations as a whole and for private financial corporations separately are derived by residual using estimates for the private sector, for households and for private non-financial corporations. Historic estimates for the latter use ONS-suspended, ESA95-consistent data back to 1965 and, before then, scaled pre-ESA95 data for industrial and commercial companies.

Table 5.A.1 compares the stationarity properties of the reconstructed data for the financial surplus of the household and private company sectors (as a share of GDP) with the last available pre-ESA95 estimates taken from the 1997 Blue Book. There is, perhaps, some reassurance to be had from the fact that these properties are not dissimilar, despite the large revisions and changes in statistical definitions

Table 5.A.1 Stationarity tests – latest data versus 1997 Blue Book data

Financial surplus,	**Unit root test**		
% of GDP	**ADF**	**PP**	**KPSS**
Household or personal sector			
Latest data	–2.57*	–2.06*	0.58*
1997 Blue Book data	–2.70*	–2.34*	0.42
Private non-financial corporations**			
Latest data	–2.84*	–2.73*	0.54*
1997 Blue Book data	–2.97	–2.86*	0.46*
Financial corporations			
Latest data	–2.18*	–2.28*	0.53
1997 Blue Book data	–3.26	–3.20	0.18

Note: See Table 5.1, main text, for details of tests. Estimated over a period (1951 to 1996) that ensures an equal sample for each test (46 annual observations). Critical values for ADF and PP: –2.93; for KPSS: 0.46, both at the 5 per cent level of significance. *indicates non-rejection of the ADF or PP null or rejection of the KPSS null. **Industrial and commercial companies in 1997 Blue Book.

and concepts, which are especially marked for the household sector (Dolling, 1998). Over the 1951 to 1996 interval, there is evidence of non-stationarity in the comparable series for households and private non-financial companies. Only the results for financial companies diverge.

Expenditure data in constant prices

Constant-price equivalents of market sector expenditure, comprising consumption and capital spending, are derived where necessary using ONS chain-linking methodology (Robjohns, 2006) with corrections for errors in the published official data. General government fixed investment data are chain-subtracted from the economy total to give equivalent estimates for the market sector. The general government investment price deflator is estimated from pre-ESA95 sources and national totals prior to 1987.

Balance sheet in current prices: financial assets and liabilities

Official figures are available for the stocks of financial assets and liabilities of each sector from 1987, but not on a consolidated basis. Before 1987, private and market sector net financial asset stocks are inferred from public sector and Rest of the World counterparts. With some corrections, the official data can be taken back to 1966 and spliced to estimates in Roe (1971) available from 1957.

Before 1957, cumulative financial surpluses are used to backcast figures for government and Rest of the World net financial asset stocks with an allowance, in the case of central government, for revaluations of the debt stock. The revaluation adjustments, available back to 1952, are based on a comparison of the nominal and market values of British government securities.

A major qualification concerns the valuation of foreign direct investment (FDI). Official figures that value FDI stocks at book value are likely substantially to underestimate market values, the yardstick used for other financial assets and liabilities. To convert the FDI figures to market values, a valuation adjustment is applied from 1957 using infrequent benchmark market-to-book valuation estimates (Reddaway, 1968; Pratten, 1996). The inferred market values are backcast and extended using stock market indices with a correction for reinvested FDI earnings.

Balance sheet in current prices: non-financial assets

Non-financial assets comprise residential buildings, other structures (such as commercial buildings), equipment (such as plant and machinery), inventories and various intangible assets. Official valuation methods vary. Market valuations are given for residential dwellings and some structures and, in part, for transport equipment. But where second-hand markets are thin or absent, as in the case of much plant and machinery, the ONS reports the replacement cost of assets calculated using its Perpetual Inventory Model (PIM).

Historic data for each major asset category are derived by splicing the latest Blue Book estimates to pre-ESA95 1997 Blue Book figures back to 1957. Prior to 1957, estimates for the household sector residential dwelling stock are linked to those for the personal sector given in Solomou and Weale (1997). Holdings of public corporations are inferred by residual from a national total based on figures for the total dwelling stock given in Blake and Orszag (1999). These historic estimates are adjusted to reflect movements in house price data published by the Department of Communities and Local Government.

Before 1957, figures for the non-housing tangible asset stocks of households are pro-rated backwards using Solomou and Weale's estimates. ONS PIM data, generally available from 1947, are used to backcast national accounts structures and equipment data. The main qualification concerns the backcast of structures data, where the PIM estimates exclude the value of land that is implicit in the national accounts figures. For inventories, a national figure is estimated from the cumulative value of changes in the book value of inventories recorded in the 1997 Blue Book and attributed to sectors based on 1957 shares.

Quarterly data

The estimation of the quarterly dataset uses exact quarterly equivalents to the annual series where available. In other cases, recourse is made to interpolation based on closely related quarterly series and straight-line methods. A number of series are seasonally adjusted using the software package 'Demetra' but with its output calendar-year constrained.

US data

Official data are taken from the National Income and Product Accounts and Flow of Funds Accounts.

All data include official revisions published up to November 2010.

Appendix B

Detailed econometric results

Table 5.B.1 Integration tests of market sector regression variables

ADF statistic	**Variable expressed in**	
Variables in constant prices (unless noted *)	**Levels**	**First differences**
Financial wealth		
balance sheet data	–2.44	–8.57
cumulative flows data	–2.77	–4.53
Non-financial wealth to income ratio		
conventional income measure	–1.75	–4.99
inflation-tax adjusted income measure	–1.88	–5.04
Disposable income		
conventional measure	4.12	–5.21
inflation-tax adjusted measure	3.84	–5.73
Total expenditure	2.73	–3.81
Weighted relative house price inflation*	–3.97	–7.46
Weighted growth in housing to output ratio*	–4.59	–9.66
Residual change in k*	–6.69	–6.52
Nominal short-term interest rate*	–1.98	–6.81
Inflation rate*	–1.87	–6.45

Note: See notes to Table 5.1 in main text. Sample period 1955–2007. Critical value of ADF statistic at 5 per cent level: –2.92.

Table 5.B.2 Hypothesis tests on ΔE error correction model

Test	F-statistic*	Probability
Restrictions:		
1) Drop insignificant variables	0.71	0.73
2) Restrict coefficients on E_{-1} & Y^a_{-1}	10.20	0.00
3) Restrict coefficients on $\Delta\pi_{-1}$ & $\Delta\pi_{-2}$	0.15	0.70
4) All accepted restrictions	0.67	0.78
5) Wu-Hausman test for exogeneity	0.21	0.81
6) ADF test on $E - E^s$	–5.18	0.0
7) ADF test on $V - V^s$	–5.32	0.0

Notes on tests:- (1): F-test for the redundancy in the unrestricted ECM of lagged values of ΔE, ΔY^a, $\dot{q}^h k_{-1}$, $\dot{h}k_{-1}$, ΔK^{nh}_{-1} and contemporaneous values of Δi and $\Delta\pi$; (2) and (3): F-version of Wald tests for equality, with opposite sign, of coefficients on E_{-1} and Y^a_{-1} (2), $\Delta\pi_{-1}$ and $\Delta\pi_{-2}$ (3); (4): combined effect of restrictions (1) and (3); (5): exogeneity test based on redundancy of residuals from auxiliary regressions for ΔY^a and $\dot{q}^h k_{-1}$ (all test statistics based on likelihood ratios give similar results); (6) and (7): ADF on residuals derived using the algebraic long-run solutions; critical values: –4.32 and –3.92 at the 5 per cent level. * unless stated.

Table 5.B.3 Non-nested tests for alternative income definitions

Statistic (probability) Test type	Model using Y^a versus model using Y^d	Model using Y^d versus model using Y^a
Adjusted Cox	–1.36 (0.17)	0.36 (0.72)
Wald	–1.32 (0.19)	0.37 (0.71)
Encompassing	1.18 (0.34)	0.72 (0.58)

Note: See Godfrey and Pesaran (1983) for an evaluation of these tests. Model specifications are shown in Tables 5.10 and 5.11 of the main text.

Table 5.B.4 Non-nested tests for linear versus log-linear models

Statistic (probability) Test type	Linear model versus log-linear model	Log-linear model versus linear model
Simulated Cox	–1.60 (0.11)	–7.32 (0.00)
MacKinnon et al.	1.46 (0.14)	3.23 (0.00)
Bera-McAleer	1.00 (0.32)	2.09 (0.04)
Davidson-MacKinnon	1.85 (0.07)	4.22 (0.00)

Note: The log-linear model substitutes logarithmic equivalents for all variables in the specification in Table 5.10 except for $\dot{q}^h k^h_{-1}$ and terms in Δi and $\Delta\pi$. The tests are explained in Pesaran and Pesaran (2009).

Appendix C

Detailed proofs

Decomposition of Δk

The change in the non-financial wealth ratio comprises changes in its housing and non-housing components, the former being the product of the relative house price and the ratio to constant-price income of the (own-price deflated) housing stock.

The change in the housing wealth ratio is given by:

$$\Delta k^h \equiv q^h h - q^h_{-1} h_{-1} \equiv \Delta q^h h_{-1} + \Delta h q^h \tag{C1}$$

The two expressions on the right-hand side can be re-arranged as follows:

$$\Delta q^h h_{-1} \equiv \dot{q}^h q^h_{-1} h_{-1} \equiv \dot{q}^h k^h_{-1} \tag{C2}$$

$$\Delta h q^h \equiv \dot{h}\left(h_{-1} q^h_{-1}\right) \frac{q^h}{q^h_{-1}} \equiv \dot{h}\left(1 + \dot{q}^h\right) k^h_{-1} \tag{C3}$$

Identity (14) in the text combines identities (C1) to (C3) and adds Δk^{nh}.

Dynamic path of V

The estimated equation in Table 5.10 can be written in the form:

$$\begin{aligned} \Delta E = {} & a_0 \Delta Y^a + a_1 \dot{q}^h k^h_{-1} - a_2 \Delta i_{-1} - a_3 \Delta i_{-2} - a_4 \Delta^2 \pi \\ & - a_5 E_{-1} + a_6 Y^a_{-1} + a_7 V_{-1} + a_8 k_{-1} - a_9 \end{aligned} \tag{C4}$$

where each coefficient a takes a positive value.

Equation (C4) re-written using the lag operator becomes:

$$E = \frac{\{a_0 + (a_6 - a_0) L\} Y^a + \Delta B + a_7 V_{-1} + a_8 k_{-1} - a_9}{1 - (1 - a_5) L} \tag{C5}$$

where $\Delta B \equiv a_1 \dot{q}^h k^h_{-1} - a_2 \Delta i_{-1} - a_3 \Delta i_{-2} - a_4 \Delta^2 \pi$.

The identity for the change in financial wealth is:

$$\Delta V \equiv (1 - L) V \equiv Y^a - E \tag{C6}$$

Substitution for E in identity (C6) using equation (C5) yields after rearrangement:

$$V = \frac{(1 - a_0) \Delta Y^a + (a_5 - a_6) Y^a_{-1} - \Delta B - a_8 k_{-1} + a_9}{1 - (2 - a_5 - a_7) L + (1 - a_5) L^2} \tag{C7}$$

The inverse characteristic equation in the lag operator has these estimated values: $2 - a_5 - a_7 = 1.53$ and $1 - a_5 = 0.81$. The discriminant is negative: $(2 - a_5 - a_7)^2 - 4(1 - a_5) = -0.87$. The roots are therefore complex, implying oscillatory dynamics, but with an absolute value less than unity since $\sqrt{1-a_5} < 1$. The system is thus convergent.

The periodicity of the cyclical response, the time that elapses between successive peaks, is determined by the value of $\frac{2pi}{\theta}$ where the angular frequency, θ, measured in radians. is given by:

$$\theta = \cos^{-1}\left\{\frac{2-a_5-a_7}{2\sqrt{1-a_5}}\right\} = 0.55$$

This estimate implies cycle periodicity of 11.5 years.

Dynamic path of *E*

The first difference of equation (C7) gives an expression for ΔV, which substituted into the identity $E \equiv Y^a - \Delta V$, yields the following equation for the level of expenditure:

$$E = \frac{\{a_0-(2a_0-a_6-a_7)L+(a_0-a_6)L^2\}Y^a+\Delta^2 B+a_8\Delta k_{-1}}{1-(2-a_5-a_7)L+(1-a_5)L^2} \tag{C8}$$

Steady-state solutions

Division of equation (C7) by Y^a gives the following expression for the financial wealth ratio when income grows at a constant rate g:

$$\frac{V}{Y^a} = \left(\frac{1-a_0}{1+g}\right)\frac{\Delta Y^a}{Y^a_{-1}} + \frac{a_5-a_6}{1+g} + \left(\frac{2-a_5-a_7}{1+g}\right)\frac{V_{-1}}{Y^a_{-1}} - \left(\frac{1-a_5}{(1+g)^2}\right)\frac{V_{-2}}{Y^a_{-2}} - \Phi \tag{C9}$$

where $\Phi \equiv \frac{\Delta B + a_8 k_{-1} - a_9}{Y^a}$.

Granted a constant non-financial wealth ratio and assuming $Lim(\Phi) = 0$, the financial wealth to income ratio converges in the steady state to a constant given by:

$$Lim\left(\frac{V}{Y^a}\right) = \frac{(1+g)\{g(1-a_0)+a_5-a_6\}}{a_7+g(a_5+a_7+g)} \tag{C10}$$

The steady state financial surplus ratio also tends to a constant. The combination of the identity:

$$\frac{F^a}{Y^a} \equiv \left(\frac{g}{1+g}\right)\frac{V}{Y^a} \tag{C11}$$

and equation (C10) gives the following expression:

$$Lim\left(\frac{F^a}{Y^a}\right)=\frac{g\{g(1-a_0)+a_5-a_6\}}{a_7+g(a_5+a_7+g)} \tag{C12}$$

Formulae reported in the text use the substitutions:

$$a_5 = -\tau_0, \quad a_6 = -\tau_0\tau_1, \quad a_7 = -\tau_0\tau_2.$$

These expressions in terms of inflation-tax adjusted disposable income may be re-expressed in terms of conventionally measured income assuming a constant rate of inflation.

Re-arrangement of identity (11) in the main text gives:

$$Lim\left(\frac{Y^d}{Y^a}\right)=1+\frac{\pi}{(1+\pi)(1+g)}Lim\left(\frac{V}{Y^a}\right) \tag{C13}$$

The reciprocal of which can be used in combination with equation (C10) to derive the conventional financial wealth ratio:

$$Lim\left(\frac{V}{Y^d}\right)\equiv Lim\left(\frac{V}{Y^a}\right)Lim\left(\frac{Y^a}{Y^d}\right) \tag{C14}$$

Similarly for the financial surplus ratio, re-arrangement of identity (12) in the main text gives:

$$Lim\left(\frac{F}{Y^d}\right)=\left\{Lim\left(\frac{F^a}{Y^a}\right)+\frac{\pi}{(1+\pi)(1+g)}Lim\left(\frac{V}{Y^a}\right)\right\}Lim\left(\frac{Y^a}{Y^d}\right) \tag{C15}$$

The mean lag theorem

Assume the adjustment of financial wealth to its target level determined by the New Cambridge norm (equation (3)) is described by:

$$V = \lambda(L)V^* \tag{C16}$$

The lag polynomial is subject only to the restriction $\lambda(1)=\sum_{i=0}^{i=\infty}\lambda_i=1$ where $\lambda(1)$ denotes the value of the lag polynomial with $L=1$.

The first difference of equation (C16) combined with the New Cambridge norm and the identity for expenditure yields:

$$E = (1-(1-L)\lambda(L)\varpi))Y^d \tag{C17}$$

The mean lag response, Ω, is defined as (Dhrymes, 1971):

$$\Omega_{E,Y^d} \equiv \sum_{i=0}^{i=\infty} i\beta_i = \frac{\beta'(1)}{\beta(1)} \tag{C18}$$

where $\beta(L) = 1 - (1 - L)\lambda(L)\varpi$ and $\beta'(1)$ is the first derivative of $\beta(L)$ with respect to L $(= \lambda(L)\varpi - (1 - L)\lambda'(L)\varpi)$ evaluated at $L = 1$. It follows that:

$$\Omega_{E,Y^d} = \frac{\beta'(1)}{\beta(1)} = \frac{\lambda(1)\varpi}{1} = \varpi \tag{C19}$$

The same procedure applied to equation (C8) produces a mean lag equal to $\frac{a_5 - a_6}{a_7}$.

Notes

1. For claims and counter-claims during this controversy in approximate chronological order see, for example: Cripps, Fetherston and Godley (1974, 1976); Bispham (1975); Rowan (1976); Fetherston and Godley (1978); Blinder (1978); Chrystal (1981, 1983); Anyadike-Danes (1983); Godley (1983); Godley and Cripps (1983). Alternative econometric estimates are given in Bennett (1986) and Matthews and Minford (1980).
2. Bennett (1987); Hossain (1991); Godley (1999); Godley, Papadimitriou and Zezza (2008); Zezza (2009). The list excludes empirical investigations not freely in the public domain.
3. Godley and Lavoie (2007, p. 25) argue against the theoretical amalgamation of households and firms into a single private sector: '... households and production firms take entirely different decisions.'
4. Feldstein (1973) finds that US households pierce the corporate veil almost completely. For the UK, Feldstein and Fane (1973) find only a partial piercing. Poterba's (1991) somewhat inclusive results for Britain, Canada and the US suggest the presence of a veil; those by Auerbach and Hassett (1983) for the US and by Koskela and Virén (1986) for the US and UK do not (though results for other countries vary). Pitelis (1987) finds the veil almost intact in the UK, a result rejected by Sumner (2004a). Sumner (2004a, 2008) finds strong evidence that retained profits have a significant impact on measured UK consumption.
5. See, for example, Grunfeld and Griliches (1960); Aigner and Goldfeld (1974); Pesaran, Pierse and Kumar (1989); Lee, Pesaran and Pierse (1990).
6. Acute problems of separating household from company income arise in the case of defined-benefit pension schemes, which are deemed to be the property of households but are materially controlled by the sponsoring company. Other difficulties result from the distinction between income and capital: whereas share repurchases and capital gains are excluded from the system of accounts, equivalent dividend payments and related capital taxes are not. Chamberlin and Dey-Chowdhury (2008) discuss the difficulties encountered in the context of the UK national accounts.

7. The compendious cross-country study by Altissimo et al. (2005), citing around 150 relevant references, finds little evidence that asset prices affect investment but concludes in favour of a link between wealth and consumers' spending in a number of economies, including the UK. The link with housing wealth is questioned in Bank of England research (Benito et al., 2006).
8. See Martin (2007a, 2007b and 2009) for details.
9. Recent historic estimates usefully published by the ONS (Sbano, 2008) do not observe the basic constraint that, adjusted for the government's holdings of monetary gold and Special Drawing Rights, stocks of financial asset less liabilities should sum to zero across sectors.
10. Transfers of activity between public corporations and general government distort market sector data.
11. The official definition of disposable income is struck before taking account of capital transfers.
12. Land transfers are formally known as the net acquisition of non-produced, non-financial assets (land and subsoil assets like oil and gas).
13. Godley (1983) acknowledges that the target norm might be sensitive to the rate of interest and subject to shocks.
14. In the earliest versions of New Cambridge, this equality was assumed to hold over one period with $F \equiv \Delta V = V^*$ (Blinder, 1978). Later expositions deployed partial adjustment of the form: $\Delta V = \lambda(V^* - V_{-1})$. It was perhaps not sufficiently stressed that the implied steady growth state is not one of equality between actual and target financial wealth but rather a constant proportionate relationship such that: $Lim(F) = \frac{\lambda(1+g)}{\lambda+g}\Delta V^*$. The corresponding long-run financial surplus ratio – $Lim\left(\frac{F}{Y^d}\right) = \frac{\lambda g}{\lambda+g}\varpi$ – is stationary but implies persistent targeting errors. Flemming (1976) argues that the adjustment process could 'change gear', targeting growth rates rather than levels. With suitable parameter values, an adjustment process such as: $\Delta v = \lambda_1(g - v_{-1}) + \lambda_2\left(\frac{V_{-1}^*}{V_{-1}} - 1\right)$ where v is the growth rate of V, would ensure $Lim(F) = \Delta V^*$ in the steady growth state.
15. Use is made of the definitions: $Y^d \equiv (1+g)Y_{-1}^d$ and $\Delta Y^d \equiv \frac{g}{1+g}Y^d$.
16. Standard definitions are used. A time series with no deterministic component which has a stationary, invertible, auto-regressive moving average representation after differencing d times is said to be integrated of order d, denoted $x \sim I(d)$. Variables are cointegrated if a linear combination of them exists which is $I(0)$ with zero mean (Engle and Granger, 1987). The New Cambridge hypothesis is an example of multicointegration (Granger and Lee, 1989) for which specialised estimation techniques exist (Engsted, Gonzalo and Haldrup, 1997).
17. See, for example, Godley and Lavoie (2007, p. 293). Although the rationale is different, the adjustment is similar to that used in a seminal article by Taylor and Threadgold (1979).
18. See, for example, Lucas (1995); Yin and Maddala (1997).
19. Nothing of substance would alter were GDP chosen as the denominator.

20. Rowthorn and Glyn (2006) argue that measurement error in the dependent variable causes negative autocorrelation of the disturbance terms, and 'may therefore exaggerate the appearance of stationarity.'
21. For example, the Phillips-Perron test statistic for the market sector financial surplus ratio is −3.28 using annual data and −5.19 using quarterly data to end-2009. Retesting using the logarithmic ratio of constant price private spending to private disposable income produces similar results.
22. The average market sector financial surplus inclusive of the national accounts residual error shows less stability across periods, but some part of this error should be apportioned to other sectors.
23. The precise date at which behavior changes has not been exactly identified. At the 5 per cent level of significance (critical value of the F-statistic of 4.7), the heteroskedasticity-robust Quandt likelihood ratio (QLR) test indicates an evolving breakdown in the coefficients of a time-varying autoregressive representation of the market sector financial surplus ratio beginning in 1976 (F-statistic 7.7) – or in 1972 in the case of the ratio adjusted for the national accounts residual error (F-statistic 4.9) – and reaching a maximum in 1986.
24. Bureau of Economic Analysis FDI data at market value are available from 1982.
25. According to a QLR test, an autoregressive trend stationary representation of the financial wealth to income ratio breaks during the first half of the 1970s, with a QLR statistic (maximum F-statistic) of 5.8 in 1976.
26. It is of note that the null hypothesis of a unit root in the wealth ratio series over the full sample period is rejected at the 5 per cent level of significance according to the augmented Dickey-Fuller statistic. This inference is false, however. Disturbances in the difference of the wealth ratio series contain a moving average process with a large negative root, a feature known to create severe size distortions and over-rejection of the unit root null in standard tests (Schwert, 1989; DeJong, Nankervis, Savin and Whiteman, 1992).
27. The same holds for the logarithmic wealth ratio.
28. Tests on annual data using the cumulative flows measure reject the hypothesis of non-stationarity around a linear trend in the period to 1974.
29. Fetherston and Godley (1978) assume the wealth target responds positively to the real rate of interest, a proposition that finds empirical support in Bennett (1986). A relationship of this sort survives in my data over Bennett's sample period (1967 to 1980), but not before or since.
30. Solow (1983) and Vines (1984) question the form of the wealth target on other grounds.
31. This conclusion is robust to an extension of the sample period to 2009 and to a re-specification in terms of the logarithmic ratio of wealth to income.
32. The downtrend in the non-financial wealth ratio until the mid-1950s can be significantly attributed to the unwinding of an aberrantly high level of capital goods prices in relation to consumer prices in the late-1940s, the result of wartime dislocation of the construction industry and post-war rent and food price controls. Statistical error is also probable. See Matthews, Feinstein and Odling-Smee (1982), Appendix H.
33. Under highly simplified conditions of constancy of the retention rate, the expected rate of growth, the expected rate of return (γ) and the required rate of return on investment (δ), comprising the return on safer assets plus a risk

premium, the PE can be expressed as $\frac{1}{\delta}\left(1-\frac{g}{\gamma}\right)/\left(1-\frac{g}{\delta}\right)$ (Kopcke, 1997). The PE ratio rises if the expected rate of return rises or the required rate of return falls.

34. See, for example, Bredin and Cuthbertson (2002); Sumner (2004b).
35. The systems ECM can be written: $\Delta V = c_0\Delta V_{-1} + c_1\Delta Y^a_{-1} - c_2\Delta k_{-1} + c_3\,(V^*_{-1} - V_{-1})$ where the coefficients c_i are positive. In the case of financial wealth calculated from cumulative flows, $\Delta V \equiv Y^a - E$. The ECM may be re-written

$$E = c_0\,E_{-1} + (1-c_0)Y^a + c_0\Delta Y^a - c_1\Delta Y^a_{-1} + c_2\Delta k_{-1} - c_3\,(V^*_{-1} - V_{-1}).$$

36. The asymptotically Chi-square distributed likelihood ratio test statistic for this restriction conditional on the presence of a single cointegrating vector is 2.2 (probability 0.33).
37. Also inclusive of the national accounts residual error.
38. Non-linear least squares estimation gives t-statistics on the parameters τ_1, τ_2 and τ_3 of 20.1, 3.5 and 11.1 respectively.
39. I am indebted to Hashem Pesaran for this point.
40. The School's original claim regarding lag length was based on the controversial finding that financial wealth adjusted fully to its desired level within one year (Blinder, 1978). The mean lag theorem holds irrespective of the lags in the financial wealth adjustment process.
41. The forecasts referred to are one-step ahead or static forecasts.
42. The regression is estimated over a shorter sample period (1979 to 2008) with separate terms in housing, non-housing-non-financial, and stock market wealth. Martin (2010) discusses the regression's strengths and weaknesses.
43. The closest post-war comparator in a UK context is the 'secondary' banking crisis in the mid-1970s, but this did not cause system-wide failure.
44. For US evidence, see, for example, Godley (1999) and Zezza (2009). Credit flow terms, either for total credit or bank credit, are either insignificant or significant but incorrectly signed when added to the Table 5.10 specification, even without allowance for potentially flattering simultaneity bias.
45. Note that the specification reported in Martin (2010) includes a measure of consumer confidence but still fails to account for the 2009 spending fall. The problem is symmetric with the one noted by Adam and Vines (2009) in their commentary on the dynamic stochastic general equilibrium model simulations performed by McKibben and Stoeckel (2009): the temporary rise in risk premiums does not provide an adequate explanation of the scale of the crisis.
46. This theory offers an interpretation, not mentioned by the authors, of the term in relative stock market prices that appears in the US private expenditure functions estimated by Godley, Papadimitriou and Zezza (2008) and Zezza (2009) who, like Godley (1999), also finds a role for house prices.

References

Adam, C. and D. Vines (2009) 'Remaking Macroeconomic Policy After the Global Financial Crisis: a Balance Sheet Approach,' *Oxford Review of Economic Policy* 25(4): 507–52.

Aigner, D. and S. Goldfeld (1974) 'Estimation and Prediction from Aggregate Data when Aggregates are Measured More Accurately than Their Components,' *Econometrica* 42(1): 113–34.

Akerlof, G. (2007) 'The Missing Motivation in Macroeconomics,' *American Economic Review* 97(1): 5–36.

Akers, R. and A. Clifton-Fearnside (2008) 'Blue Book 2008 – Balanced Estimates of Gross Domestic Product using a Supply and Use Approach,' ONS website http://www.statistics.gov.uk/about/methodology_by_theme/inputoutput/articles_and_analyses.asp.

Altissimo, F., E. Georgiou, T. Sastre, M. Valderrama, G. Sterne, M. Stocker, M. Weth, K. Whelan and A. Willman (2005) 'Wealth and Asset Price Effects on Economic Activity,' Occasional Paper No. 29 (Frankfurt, Germany: European Central Bank).

Anyadike-Danes, M. (1983) 'A "Comment" on Chrystal,' *Journal of Monetary Economics* 11: 133–5.

Auerbach, A. and K. Hassett (1991) 'Corporate Savings and Shareholder Consumption,' in B. Bernheim and J. Shoven (eds) *National Saving and Economic Performance* (Chicago, IL: University of Chicago Press).

Bean, C. (2009) 'The Great Moderation, the Great Panic and the Great Contraction,' Schumpeter Lecture, Annual Congress of the European Economic Association, Barcelona, Bank of England, August.

Benito, A., J. Thompson, M. Waldron and R. Wood (2006) 'House Prices and Consumer Spending,' *Bank of England Quarterly Bulletin*, Summer, 142–54.

Bennett, A. (1986) 'Expenditure, Wealth and the Rate of Interest,' *Economic Modelling* (January): 72–80.

Bennett, A. (1987) 'Wealth, Expenditure and the Demand for Money: The Case of France,' Working Paper No. 26 (Washington, DC: International Monetary Fund).

Bispham, J. (1975) 'The "New Cambridge" and "Monetarist" Criticisms of "Conventional" Economic Policy Making,' *National Institute Economic Review* (November): 39–55.

Blake, D., and J. Orszag (1999) 'Annual Estimates of Personal Wealth Holdings in the United Kingdom since 1948,' *Applied Financial Economics* 9: 397–421.

Blinder, A. (1978) 'What's "New" and What's "Keynesian" in the "New Cambridge" Keynesianiam?,' *Carnegie-Rochester Conference Series on Public Policy* 9(1): 67–85.

Blonigen, B. (2005) 'A Review of the Empirical Literature on FDI Determinants,' *Atlantic Economic Journal* 33(4): 383–403.

Bredin, D. and K. Cuthbertson (2002) 'Liquidity Effects and Precautionary Saving in the Czech Republic,' *Applied Financial Economics* 12: 405–13.

Caballero, R. (2010) 'Macroeconomics after the Crisis: Time to Deal with the Pretense-of-Knowledge Syndrome,' Working Paper No. 16429 (Cambridge, MA: National Bureau of Economic Research).

Chamberlin, G. and S. Dey-Chowdhury (2008) 'Household Saving Ratio,' *Economic & Labour Market Review* 2(3): 55–61.

Christiano, L. (1992) 'Searching for a Break in GNP,' *Journal of Business and Economic Statistics* 10: 237–50.

Chrystal, A. (1981) 'The "New Cambridge" Aggregate Expenditure Function,' *Journal of Monetary Economics* 7: 395–402.

Chrystal, A. (1983) 'The New Cambridge Aggregate Expenditure Function: Reply,' *Journal of Monetary Economics* 11: 137–8.

Cripps, T., M. Fetherston and W. Godley (1974) 'Public Expenditure and the Management of the Economy,' in *Public Expenditure, Inflation and the Balance of Payments*, Ninth Report from the Expenditure Committee, Session July 1974, HC328, London, Her Majesty's Stationery Office.

Cripps, T., M. Fetherston and W. Godley (1976) 'What is Left of New Cambridge?,' *Economic Policy Review*, March, no. 2, Cambridge Department of Applied Economics.

Davidson, J., G. Madonia and P. Westaway (1994) 'Modelling the UK Gilt-Edged Market,' *Journal of Applied Econometrics* 9(3): 231–3.

DeJong, D., J. Nankervis, N. Savin and C. Whiteman (1992) 'The Power Problems of Unit Root Tests in Time Series with Autoregressive Errors,' *Journal of Econometrics* 53: 323–43.

Dhrymes, P. (1971) *Distributed Lags: Problems of Estimation and Formulation* (San Francisco, CA: Holden-Day).

Dolling, M. (1998) *Introducing the European System of Accounts 1995 in the UK* (London, UK: The Stationery Office).

Dorfman, R. (1959) 'Waiting and the Period of Production,' *Quarterly Journal of Economics* 73(3): 351–72.

Engle, R. and C. Granger (1987) 'Co-integration and Error Correction: Representation, Estimation, and Testing,' *Econometrica* 55(2): 251–76.

Engsted, T., J. Gonzalo and N. Haldrup (1997) 'Testing for Multicointegration,' *Economics Letters* 56: 259–66.

Feldstein, M. (1973) 'Tax Incentives, Corporate Saving, and Capital Accumulation in the United States,' *Journal of Public Economics* 2: 159–71.

Feldstein, M. and G. Fane (1973) 'Taxes, Corporate Dividend Policy and Personal Savings: the British Postwar Experience,' *Review of Economics and Statistics* 55(4): 399–411.

Fetherston, M. and W. Godley (1978) '"New Cambridge" Macroeconomics and Global Monetarism: Some Issues in the Conduct of UK Economic Policy,' *Carnegie-Rochester Conference Series on Public Policy* 9(1): 33–65.

Flemming, J. (1976) *Inflation* (Oxford, UK: Oxford University Press).

Godfrey, L. and M. Pesaran (1983) 'Tests of Non-Nested Regression Models,' *Journal of Econometrics* 21: 133–54.

Godley, W. (1983) 'Keynes and the Management of Real National Income and Expenditure,' in D. Worswick and J. Trevithick (eds) *Keynes and the Modern World* (Cambridge, UK: Cambridge University Press), pp. 135–57.

Godley, W. (1999) 'Seven Unsustainable Processes: Medium-Term Prospects and Policies for the United States and the World,' Special Report (Annandale-on-Hudson, NY: Levy Economics Institute of Bard College).

Godley, W. and F. Cripps (1983) *Macroeconomics* (Oxford, UK: Oxford University Press).

Godley, W. and M. Lavoie (2007) *Monetary Economics: An Integrated Approach to Credit, Money, Income, Production and Wealth* (London: Palgrave Macmillan).

Godley, W., D. Papadimitriou and G. Zezza (2008) 'Prospects for the US and the World: A Crisis That Conventional Remedies Cannot Resolve,' Strategic Analysis (Annandale-on-Hudson, NY: Levy Economics Institute of Bard College).

Granger, C. and T. Lee (1989) 'Investigation of Production, Sales and Inventory Relationships Using Multicointegration and Non-Symmetric Error Correction Models,' *Journal of Applied Econometrics* 4 (supplement): 145–59.

Grunfeld, Y. and Z. Griliches (1960) 'Is Aggregation Necessarily Bad,' *The Review of Economics and Statistics* 42(1): 1–13.

Haug, A. (2002) 'Temporal Aggregation and the Power of Cointegration Tests: a Monte Carlo Study,' *Oxford Bulletin of Economics and Statistics* 64(4): 399–412.

Hendry, D. (1995) *Dynamic Econometrics* (Oxford, UK: Oxford University Press).

Homer, S. and R. Sylla (1996) *A History of Interest Rates* (New Brunswick, NJ: Rutgers University Press).

Hossain, A. (1991) 'An Aggregate Private Expenditure Function for the Bangladesh Economy,' *World Development* 19(8): 1107–16.

Kopcke. R. (1997) 'Are Stocks Overvalued?,' *New England Economic Review*, Federal Reserve Bank of Boston, September/October, pp. 21–40.

Koskela, E. and M. Virén (1986) 'Testing the Direct Substitutability Hypothesis of Saving,' *Applied Economics*18: 143–55.

Lee, K., M. Pesaran and R. Pierse (1990) 'Testing for Aggregation Bias in Linear Models,' *The Economic Journal*, Conference Papers 100: 137–50.

Lucas, A. (1995) 'An Outlier Robust Unit Root Test with an Application to the Extended Nelson–Plosser Data,' *Journal of Econometrics* 66: 153–73.

Martin, B. (2007a) 'UK Historic Sector National Accounts: Memorandum to the Statistics Commission,' June, Statistics Commission, http://www.statscom.org.uk/S_19.aspx.

Martin, B. (2007b) 'Resurrecting the UK Historic Sector National Accounts,' Working Paper No. 356 (Cambridge, UK: Centre for Business Research, University of Cambridge).

Martin, B. (2009) 'Resurrecting the UK Historic Sector National Accounts,' *Review of Income and Wealth* 55(3): 737–51.

Martin, B. (2010) 'Rebalancing the British Economy: A Strategic Assessment' (Cambridge, UK: Centre for Business Research, University of Cambridge).

Matthews, K. and P. Minford (1980) 'Private Sector Expenditure and Financial Asset Accumulation in the UK,' *Journal of Money, Credit and Banking* 12(4): 644–53.

Matthews, R. (1968) 'Why Has Britain Had Full Employment Since the War?,' *The Economic Journal* 78: 555–69.

Matthews, R., C. Feinstein and J. Odling-Smee (1982) *British Economic Growth, 1956–1973* (Oxford, UK: Clarendon Press).

McKibben, W. and A. Stoeckel (2009) 'Modelling the Global Financial Crisis,' *Oxford Review of Economic Policy* 25(4): 581–607.

Ng, S. and P. Perron (2001) 'Lag Length Selection and the Construction of Unit Root Tests with Good Size and Power,' *Econometrica* 69(6): 1519–54.

Officer, L. (2008) 'What was the UK GDP Then? A Data Study,' MeasuringWorth, http://www.measuringworth.org/ukgdp/.

Perron, P. (1989) 'The Great Crash, the Oil Price Shock and the Unit Root Hypothesis,' *Econometrica* 57(6): 1361–401.

Perron, P. and T. Vogelsang (1993) 'The Great Crash, the Oil Price Shock and the Unit Root Hypothesis: Erratum,' *Econometrica* 61(1): 248–9.

Pesaran, H. and B. Pesaran (2009) *Time Series Econometrics using Microfit 5.0* (Oxford, UK: Oxford University Press).

Pesaran, M., R. Pierse and M. Kumar (1989) 'Econometric Analysis of Aggregation in the Context of Linear Prediction Models,' *Econometrica* 57(4): 861–88.

Pitelis, C. (1987) 'Corporate Retained Earnings and Personal Sector Saving: a Test of the Life-Cycle Hypothesis of Saving,' *Applied Economics* 19: 907–13.

Poterba, J. (1991) 'Dividends, Capital Gains, and the Corporate Veil: Evidence from Britain, Canada, and the United States,' in B. Bernheim and J. Shoven (eds) *National Saving and Economic Performance* (Chicago, IL: University of Chicago Press).

Pratten, C. (1996) *The Valuation of Outward and Inward Direct Investment: A Report for the CSO* (Cambridge, UK: University of Cambridge, Department of Applied Economics).

Reddaway, W. (1968) *Effects of UK Direct Investment Overseas: Final Report* (Cambridge, UK: University of Cambridge, Department of Applied Economics).

Robjohns, J. (2006) 'Methodology Notes: Annual Chain-Linking,' *Economic Trends* 630: 25–8.

Roe, A. (1971) *The Financial Interdependence of the Economy 1957–1966* (London, UK: Chapman and Hall).

Rowan, D. (1976) 'Godley's Law, Godley's Rule and the "New Cambridge Macroeconomics",' *Banca Nazionale del Lavoro Quarterly Review* 117: 151–74.

Rowthorn, R. and A. Glyn (2006) 'Convergence and Stability in US Employment Rates,' *Contributions to Macroeconomics* 6(1), www.bepress.com/bejm/contributions/vol6/iss1/art4.

Sbano, T. (2008) 'New Historical Data for Assets and Liabilities in the UK,' *Economic & Labour Market Review* 2(4): 40–6.

Schwert, G. (1989) 'Tests for Unit Roots: A Monte Carlo Investigation,' *Journal of Business & Economic Statistics* 7(2): 147–59.

Shiller, R. and P. Perron (1985) 'Testing the Random Walk Hypothesis: Power versus Frequency of Observation,' *Economics Letters* 18(4): 381–6.

Solomou, S. and M. Weale (1997) 'Personal Sector Wealth in the United Kingdom,' *Review of Income and Wealth* 43(3): 297–318.

Solow, R. (1983) 'Comment' on W. Godley 'Keynes and the Management of Real National Income and Expenditure,' in D. Worswick and J. Trevithick (eds) *Keynes and the Modern World* (Cambridge, UK: Cambridge University Press), pp. 162–8.

Spencer, P. (1981) 'A Model of the Demand for British Government Stocks by Non-Bank Residents 1967–1977,' *The Economic Journal* 91: 938–60.

Sumner, M. (2004a) 'Corporate Retentions and Consumers' Expenditure,' *The Manchester School* 72(1): 119–30.

Sumner, M. (2004b) 'A Cautionary Note on Cointegration Testing,' *Applied Economics Letters* 11: 275–8.

Sumner, M. (2008) 'Corporate Consumption: A Postscript,' *The Manchester School* 76(2): 196–203.

Taylor, C. and A. Threadgold (1979) '"Real" National Saving and its Sectoral Composition,' Discussion Paper No. 6 (London, UK: Bank of England).

Taylor, L. (2008) 'A Foxy Hedgehog: Wynne Godley and Macroeconomic Modelling,' *Cambridge Journal of Economics* 32(4): 639–63.

Vines, D. (1984) 'Review' of *Macroeconomics* by Wynne Godley and Francis Cripps, *The Economic Journal* 94: 397–9.

Yin, Y. and G. Maddala (1997) 'The Effects of Different Types of Outliers on Unit Root Tests,' in T. Fomby and C. Hill (eds) *Advances in Econometrics*, Volume 13 (Greenwich, CT: JAI Press).

Zezza, G. (2009) 'Fiscal Policy and the Economics of Financial Balances,' Working Paper No. 569 (Annandale-on-Hudson, NY: Levy Economics Institute of Bard College).

6

Three Balances and Twin Deficits: Godley versus Ruggles and Ruggles

Anwar Shaikh

6.1 Introduction

Wynne Godley was my colleague at the Levy Economics Institute of Bard College, a mentor on macroeconomics, and a co-author on one paper. Most of all, he was a dear friend. We shared many interests over the years, from peering endlessly at data to eating well and taking long walks on the beautiful grounds of Bard College. My first interaction with him was when I happened to be walking past his office and he summoned me in to look at the simulation runs of his model – which of course I found completely fascinating. Very many subsequent hours were spent doing that. Wynne had a wonderful intuitive feel for empirical patterns. He could 'see'. Like Joan Robinson, he had a limited background in math and was therefore 'obliged to learn how to think,' which he did very well indeed. And he was not afraid to conclude that he had been wrong: I can remember conversations, in person or on the phone, which began with the phrase 'Look here, I have been talking absolute nonsense.' The subsequent discussion was often punctuated by long silences which I learned to accept with equanimity. On the other hand, where Wynne felt the error was mine, he was far more polite. This chapter is a small tribute to his memory, in partial thanks for the many things I learned from him.

Wynne's adoption of the GDP national accounting identity in terms of three sectoral balances always played a crucial role in his macroeconomic analysis. In keeping with the post-war empirical evidence at the time, the earliest version of the three balance approach assumed that the private sector (household plus business) balance was essentially zero. Then the two remaining sectoral balances would offset each other. This led to the famous 'twin deficit' hypothesis of the New Cambridge approach delineated in Fetherston and Godley (1978). In their fascinating macroeconomic text, Godley and Cripps (1983) attempted to provide a theoretical justification for the empirical finding that the private sector balance tends to be small. They posited that the private sector as a whole had some desired ratio of the stock of financial assets to the flow of income. Changes in the aggregate savings rate were then the means of maintaining the actual ratio at its desired level. This in turn implied that in a static economy the equilibrium private sector balance would be zero.

On the other side of the Atlantic, over a similar interval of time Richard and Nancy Ruggles (Ruggles and Ruggles, 1992) had arrived at very similar results on the private sector balance, albeit by a different route and with a different focus. The Ruggles' empirical investigation of US post-war savings led them to conclude that average household savings was zero because households' income not spent on consumer nondurables was largely spent on consumer durables (that is, for what they called household 'capital formation'), so that in the end all household income was used for consumption. At the same time, business savings was essentially aimed at financing business capital formation (investment). Their dual-capital-formation hypothesis implied that the private savings equaled private investment, so that the private sector balance was essentially zero. What is particularly interesting in this history is that both sides emphasized that the *flow* of savings has a *stock* purpose. This turns out to imply that the aggregate savings rate is endogenous in the short run – not exogenous as is so often assumed in both orthodox and heterodox macroeconomic analysis (Shaikh 2009, pp. 476–82).

6.2 The three balances

It is useful to approach the famous three balances relation sideways, so to speak, in order to understand its true import. Aggregate demand for domestically available goods (D) is the sum of consumption (C), investment in desired stocks of fixed capital and inventories (I), government (G) and export (X) demands, while domestically available supply (Q) is the sum of domestic supply (Y) and imports (M). Let T = total private sector (households and business) taxes. Then over any time period, aggregate excess demand (E) is the difference between aggregate supply and demand. This can in turn be written in terms of three sectoral contributions to excess demand: the private sector deficit, which is the excess of its expenditures over its disposable (that is, post-tax) income

$[(C + I) - (Y - T)]$; the government deficit $[G - T]$; and the foreign trade surplus $[X - M]$.

$$\begin{aligned} E \equiv D - Q &= (C + I + G + X) - (Y + M) \\ &= [(C + I) - (Y - T)] + [G - T] + [X - M] \end{aligned} \tag{1.1}$$

There is nothing in this *ex ante* relation which requires that the three balances add up to zero. If aggregate demand happened to exceed aggregate supply at given prices, then the excess demand would lead to undesired changes in inventories: $E = -\Delta INV_u$. National accounts incorporate the undesired inventory change into 'investment,' redefined as the sum of desired fixed investment and desired inventory change *and* unplanned inventory change. This accounting device converts the *ex ante* non-zero balance in equation (1.1) into an *ex post* zero-balance identity.

$$\begin{aligned} &[(C + (I - E)) - (Y - T)] + [G - T] + [X - M] \\ &\quad = [(C + (I + \Delta INV_u)) - (Y - T)] + [G - T] + [X - M] = 0 \end{aligned} \tag{1.2}$$

The trouble is that *an* ex post *accounting identity is not a constraint*: any sum of three sectoral balances can be accommodated in equation (1.2). Theoretical economists therefore implicitly or explicitly add a further condition: that aggregate demand and supply gravitate around each other over some period of time called 'the short run'. The imposition of this equilibrium condition is what converts the three balanced identity in equation (1.1) into a constraint operative over some putative 'short run'. For convenience in subsequent use, the constraint is written to state that the sum of the private sector balance (the excess of income over expenditure) and trade deficit is equal to the government deficit.

$$E = -\Delta INV_u \approx 0 \tag{1.3}$$

$$\begin{aligned} &PB + [M - X] \approx [G - T] \quad \text{where } PB \equiv [(Y - T) - (C + I)] \\ &\quad = \text{the private sector balance} \end{aligned} \tag{1.4}$$

How long is the supposed short run? Neoclassical authors typically assume that equilibrium is instantaneous and continuous. Keynes generally focuses on comparative statics, so time disappears from view. But elsewhere he does recognize that production, and hence the working out of the multiplier, takes time. In his exposition he tends to switch back and forth between a given observational time period which is short enough to investigate the workings of the multiplier and a period long enough for the multiplier to work itself out and hence for short-run equilibrium to obtain (Asimakopulos 1991, pp. 52, 67–8). Modern macroeconomic analysis skips over these issues by simply assuming that supply and demand equilibrate fast enough to allow us to treat observed data (usually quarterly data in macroeconomics) as representing equilibrium outcomes (Godley and Lavoie 2007, p. 65; Pugno 1998, p. 155). Godley and Cripps implicitly do the same thing by treating the identity as a 'budget constraint' within the annual or quarterly time period defined by available data (Godley and Cripps 1983, pp. 33, 60–1). On the other hand, from Walras' Law the mutual adjustment between aggregate demand and aggregate supply is linked to the adjustment between money supply and money demand. One estimate of the latter yields a 50 per cent closure in two quarters, so that it takes about 12 quarters to achieve a 99 per cent adjustment (McCulloch 1982, p. 27). Finally, given that excess demand is expressed through unplanned change in inventories, it is useful to note that what we now call the 'business cycle' refers to the three–five-year (12–20-quarter) inventory cycle (van Duijn 1983, pp. 7–8). Continuous balance versus three–five-year balance obviously have very different implications for practical macroeconomics.

In preparation for what follows, it is useful to note that the private sector balance can be expressed in terms of the balance between aggregate private savings and investment. The excess of disposable private income over consumption expenditures is private savings $(Y - T) - C = S_p$, which can in turn be written as the sum of household savings (S_h) and business savings, that is, retained earnings (*RE*).

$$PB = S_p - I = S_h + (RE - I) \quad (1.5)$$

6.3 The twin deficit hypothesis of the New Cambridge approach

In the 1970s, Godley and his colleagues at the Department of Applied Economics (DAE) of Cambridge University transformed the three balance constraint into the Twin Deficit Hypothesis. They had discovered that at an empirical level the private sector balance in the UK, measured relative to income, was 'generally small and stable' (Dos Santos and Macedo e Silva 2010, p. 25). This led them to conclude that over the short run the other two balance ratios in equation (1.5) would tend to mirror each other. An increase in the government deficit would therefore lead to an increase the foreign trade deficit.

$$PB \approx 0 \text{ so } \frac{[M - X]}{Y} \approx \frac{[G - T]}{Y} \text{ [Twin Deficit Hypothesis]} \qquad (1.6)$$

In 1978 Fetherston and Godley (Fetherston and Godley 1978, p. 34) hypothesized that 'virtually all the disposable income in the private sector' was quickly 'spent on goods and services' (Dos Santos and Macedo e Silva 2010, p. 22). A few years later Godley and Cripps (1983) attempted to provide a theoretical foundation for this hypothesis. They posited that individual households and businesses had desired 'norms' concerning the ratio of net financial assets to income which translated into a stable aggregate norm (Godley and Cripps 1983, pp. 41–4, 60). The original Godley–Cripps argument was posed in terms of a series of highly abstract models in which various concrete factors were successively introduced and analyzed. It also was confined to a static economy (a constant level of income), because as they themselves point out their adjustment process was unstable in the context of exogenous growth (Godley and Cripps 1983, pp. 17–20, 49–51, 95–7). In what follows I will generalize both their argument and their adjustment process.

The first step is to recognize that the excess of any sector's spending over its income represents its *net* acquisition of financial assets (*NAFA*). Consider the private sector balance $PB = S_p - I = S_h + (RE - I)$. The Keynesian definition of household savings is the excess of household income over expenditures on nondurable and durable consumer goods, which is the change in household net financial assets (defined to include money and to count debt as a negative item). Similarly, the difference between business retained earnings and investment is the change in business net financial assets (which will be negative if the business sector is a net borrower). Hence the change in actual private sector net financial assets from the beginning to the end of the period is equal to the private sector balance over the period.

$$\Delta NAFA_{p_t} \equiv (S_p - I)_t = PB = \text{the private sector balance} \qquad (1.7)$$

Next comes the central Godley–Cripps behavioral hypothesis that the end-of-period desired stock of the private sector's net financial assets ($NAFA^*_{p_t}$) is proportional to the period's flow of the private sector's disposable income $(Y - T)_t$ – that is, that the desired stock-flow ratio is constant. Let t = the tax rate so that total tax revenue $T = tY$.

Then the Godley–Cripps hypothesis (Godley and Cripps 1983, pp. 22, 40, 43–4, 61) implies that the desired stock of net financial assets is

$$NAFA^*_{p_t} = \alpha(1 - t)Y_t \tag{1.8}$$

The desired net stock is only relevant if there is some process which makes the actual net stock conform to the desired one. Godley and Cripps proposed an adjustment mechanism of the form $\Delta NAFA_{P_t} = \phi(NAFA^*_{P_{t-1}} - NAFA_{P_{t-1}})$ where ϕ is some positive adjustment coefficient less than one. Note that since $\Delta NAFA_{P_t} \equiv (S_p - I)_t$, where investment is determined by profitability and income is given to the individual household or firm, this implicitly supposes that it is the *private savings rate* which does the adjusting. In any case, as Godley and Cripps themselves point out, their adjustment mechanism is only consistent with a constant level of income because the path becomes unstable when growth is endogenous.[1] A similar adjustment problem appears in Harrod and Domar (Domar, 1946; Harrod, 1957; Sen 1970, pp. 10–14). In all cases, there is a simple and sensible dynamic adjustment process which is perfectly stable (Shaikh 2009, pp. 464–7). The crucial step is to recognize that a dynamic path is a *moving* target. In order to hit such a target, it is necessary to track its path with adjustments based on past errors. In the present case, the target is the desired net stock $NAFA^*_{P_t}$ which will generally be growing when income is growing. Hence the changes in actual net stock must make adjustment relative to the dynamic path of the desired stock. This is a perfectly general principle derived from Hicks' stock-flow adjustment principle which encompasses a stationary path as a special case (Hicks 1985, pp. 97–107). Let ε_t represent some zero-mean error process which may incorporate all sorts of serial correlation (that is, which need not be iid). Then the Hicksian adjustment process shown below is completely stable around the moving equilibrium point $NAFA^*_{P_t} = NAFA_{P_t}$.[2] As we can see, it involves a simple extension of the Godley–Cripps adjustment mechanism.

$$\Delta NAFA_{P_t} = \Delta NAFA^*_{P_t} + \phi(NAFA^*_{P_{t-1}} - NAFA_{P_{t-1}}) + \varepsilon_t \tag{1.9}$$

The stability of the adjustment process in the face of equation (1.8) implies that $NAFA_{P_t} = NAFA^*_{P_t} = \alpha(1 - t)Y_t$, so

$$\frac{\Delta NAFA_{P_t}}{Y_t} = \frac{\alpha(1-t)(\Delta Y_t/Y_{t-1})}{(Y_t/Y_{t-1})} = \frac{\alpha(1-t)g_{Y_t}}{1+g_{Y_t}} \approx \alpha(1-t)g_{Y_t} \tag{1.10}$$

where $g_{Y_t} \equiv (\Delta Y_t / Y_{t-1})$ = the growth rate of aggregate output << 1. In light of equation (1.7) the foregoing result implies that the private sector balance will be essentially proportional to the growth rate of GDP. Godley and Cripps, like most macroeconomists of their time except for Harrod, Domar and Hicks, assume that the level of output is constant in the 'short run' (Godley and Cripps 1983, pp. 49–51). Then equations (1.4), (1.7) and (1.10) with $g_{Y_t} = 0$ imply a zero private sector balance and hence twin deficits. More generally, for given positive growth rate g_{Y_t}, we get 'sibling deficits':

$$\frac{[M-X]}{Y} \approx \frac{[G-T]}{Y} + \alpha(1-t)g_{Y_t} \tag{1.11}$$

6.4 The sectoral savings–investment hypothesis of Ruggles and Ruggles

Ruggles and Ruggles define household savings as the excess of income over the *nondurable* consumption goods. Their empirical analysis of the US economy then leads them to conclude that household savings so defined is roughly equal to household expenditures on *durable* consumer goods, that is, on 'household capital formation.' On the business side, Ruggles and Ruggles also find that total corporate and noncorporate business savings, that is, total retained earnings, is roughly equal to total business capital formation (investment).

The observations of Ruggles and Ruggles were rooted in their intimate knowledge of the intricacies of US national income and product accounts (NIPA). They point out that the NIPA 'personal sector' includes not only households but also non-profit enterprises, and the NIPA definition of personal savings is quite different from household savings. When they correct for these and other problems,[3] they find that over the period 1947–89 cumulative household gross 'savings' is almost exactly equal to 'household gross capital formation' (purchases of consumer durables and owner-occupied housing). As a corollary, transfers of funds between households and other sectors are relatively small (Ruggles and Ruggles 1992, pp. 119–26, 156). A similar finding obtains for business savings, which is roughly equal to business investment over the long run: 'the gross savings for many enterprise sectors has been equal to or greater than their gross capital formation', while for nonfinancial corporate business the ratio of retained earnings to gross capital formation is about 90 per cent (Ruggles and Ruggles 1992, pp. 119, 157). Ruggles and Ruggles point out that their findings undermine 'the usual functional approach' which assumes that households are net savers and businesses are net borrowers (Ruggles and

Ruggles 1992, p. 161). This leads them to the general principle that each sector saves just what it needs to fund its purchases of durable goods:

> with respect to sector saving and capital formation the general rule is that each tub tends to stand on its own bottom. The household sector is not, and historically has not been, a net supplier of funds to other sectors; furthermore, the manufacturing sector does not absorb more funds than it generates. (Ruggles and Ruggles 1992, p. 160)

Several remarkable implications follow from the Ruggles' findings. First of all, household savings, defined in Keynesian fashion as the excess of household income over total consumer purchases, is essentially zero while business saving is equal to business investment. It is striking that these are the standard characterizations of savings within the classical tradition and even some parts of the Keynesian one (Marx 1967, pp. 506–7; Marx 1977, ch. 4; Robinson 1965, p. 178; Shaikh, 1988, footnote 2, p. 85). Secondly, the two results imply that aggregate private savings equals private investment, so that the private sector balance is zero. Although the Ruggles' do not make this connection, this in turn implies that trade deficits and government deficits will be twins as in the New Cambridge hypothesis. Finally, on the assumption that 'capital formation' is determined by long-run factors, this implies that it is the private savings *rate* which adjusts in response to private sector investment needs.

$$PB = S_h + (RE - I) \approx 0 \text{ because } S_h \approx 0 \textit{ and } RE \approx I \qquad (1.12)$$

Ruggles and Ruggles end by focusing on a set of 'simple and rather obvious policy implications'. They conclude that 'measures designed to stimulate household savings in order to spur business investment will actually have the opposite effect because the resulting reduction in consumer spending will hurt profits and hence investment. Thus policy should focus on 'direct incentives which increase profits and induce enterprises to reinvest their own retained earnings'. In the latter regard, they note that 'from past evidence it is apparent that a high level of aggregate demand is needed for enterprises to undertake high levels of capital formation' (Ruggles and Ruggles 1992, pp. 161–2).

6.5 Summary and implications

This chapter has focused on the empirically derived notion that the private sector balance, relative to GDP, is driven by some general principles involving the motivations for household and business savings. Figure 6.1 depicts the path of this balance in the US in the period 1947–2010. We can see that it fluctuated around a constant level of about 4.7 per cent for almost half a century. A similar pattern held in the UK, except that the average balance was somewhat smaller.

In the UK, the existence of a small and stable private sector balance led Wynne Godley and his co-authors to the realization that the trade deficit would mirror the government deficit. This became known as the Twin Deficit Hypothesis of the New Cambridge view. In their 1983 book Godley and Cripps tried to provide a theoretical foundation for their empirical finding by hypothesizing that the private sector balance was driven by a stable norm between private net financial assets and disposable income. But their hypothesized adjustment process turned out to be unstable in a growth context. One of the contributions of the present paper is to show that there is a simple and sensible modification of their adjustment process which makes it wholly stable. This leads to the general conclusion that the private sector balance will be roughly proportional to the GDP growth rate.

In the US, Ruggles and Ruggles followed the same thread of evidence to a different set of conclusions. Upon carefully decomposing the

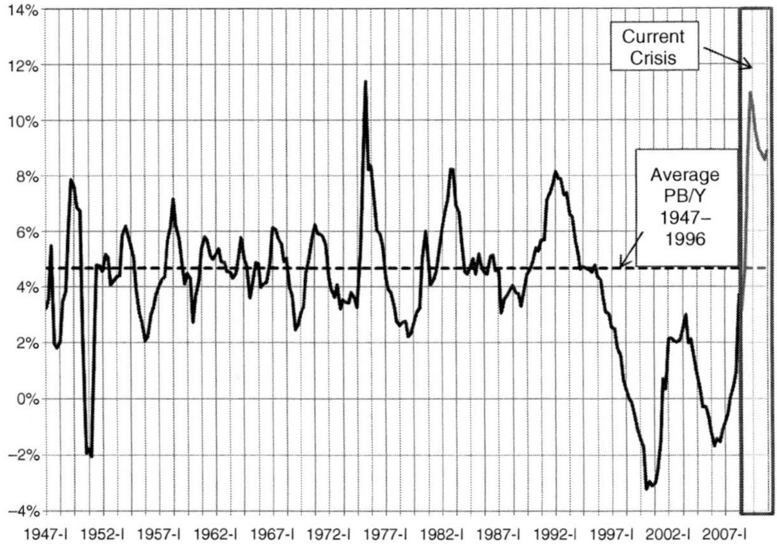

Figure 6.1 US private sector balance relative to GDP

empirical evidence on household and business savings, they found that over the post-war period the excess of household disposable income over nondurable consumer expenditures (which was their definition of savings) was roughly equal to household expenditures for durable consumer goods. Similarly, business saving (retained earnings) was close to business expenditures on new plant and equipment. This led them to hypothesize that each sector was driven by the common behavioral principle that the purpose of savings was to fund 'capital formation.' Note that from a Keynesian point of view, savings is defined as the excess of disposable income over *all* consumption expenditures. Then the Ruggles' findings imply that (under the Keynesian definition) the household savings rate is zero and the business savings rate is equal to the investment share in profit. It is striking that these are exactly the assumptions typically made by classical economists.

Both schools give rise to the implication that the savings rate adapts to investment needs. The endogeneity of the savings rate has contradictory implications for effective demand theories. On one hand, it reduces the scope of the multiplier argument. In the standard Keynesian case, any gap between investment and savings is filled by changes in the volume of output, because the savings *rate* is assumed to be unchanged. To the extent that the savings rate itself adjusts to the fill the gap, the multiplier is reduced.[4] In the Ruggles' and classical case in which households do not save and firms save what they need for investment, the multiplier is a *transient* whose duration depends on how long it takes for business savings to adapt to investment needs. On the other hand, an endogenous savings rate allow us to reinstate the notion that growth can be ruled by the expected profitability of investment as in Marx, Keynes, and Kalecki while retaining the sensible notion that actual capacity utilization will fluctuate around its normal level in the long, as in Harrod (Shaikh, 2009).

Figure 6.1 also illustrates why the notion of a stable private sector balance fell out of favor. After the mid-1990s this ratio plunged into negative territory as the private sector embarked upon a borrowing spree – with a corresponding large rise in household debt (Papadimitriou, Shaikh, Dos Santos and Zezza 2002, pp. 1, 3). The economic crisis which unfolded over the ensuing decade forced the balance sharply back into positive territory as debt reduction became paramount. While we cannot say yet where this will end up, it is certainly possible that the relative private sector balance will settle once again at some sustainable level. If so, we will be back to the era of sibling deficits: then liberal economic prescription for continued expansion in budget deficits to raise employment will result in larger trade deficits, while the conservative prescription for reduced deficits will lead to lower trade deficits but higher unemployment. These are the dilemmas of our time.

Notes

1. The Godley–Cripps adjustment mechanism $\Delta NAFA = \phi\ (NAFA^* - NAFA)$ where $0 < \phi < 1$ is in equilibrium when $\Delta NAFA = 0$, which implies that $NAFA^* = NAFA$ = constant. But since the desired net stock is proportional to aggregate income (equation (1.8), this implies that income must be constant. When inventories are made endogenous, growth also becomes endogenous. But then this particular adjustment mechanism leads to an unstable path (Godley and Cripps 1983, pp. 95–6).
2. Stability of the general adjustment process in equation (1.9) is easily proved. Define $x_t \equiv NAFA^*_{P_t} - NAFA_{P_t}$. Then the dynamic adjustment is $\Delta x_t = -\phi x_{t-1} + \varepsilon_t$, and this is stable for all $0 < \phi < 1$.
3. Ruggles and Ruggles make four major corrections: they separate households from non-profit enterprises; they remove the fictitious housing sector which arises because NIPA treats home-owners who live in their own homes as 'businesses' renting out their homes to themselves; they adjust for the fact that employer contributions to pension funds and even the earnings of these pension funds are treated as being paid out to individuals, while at the same time the actual pension payments are not counted in individual income; and they separate consumption expenditures into nondurables and durables, treating the expenditures on the latter as savings used to fund 'household capital formation' (Ruggles and Ruggles 1992, pp. 119–26).
4. Thus, if investment is greater than savings ($I > S = s \cdot Y$), with investment (I) and the savings rate (s) given, it is the level of output which must rise to bring savings into line with investment. Obviously, if the savings rate itself adjusts to the investment-savings gap, then this reduces the multiplier effect.

References

Asimakopulos, A. (1991) *Keynes' General Theory and Accumulation* (Cambridge: Cambridge University Press).

Domar, E. (1946) 'Capital Expansion, Rate of Growth, and Employment,' *Econometrica* 14(2): 137–47.

Dos Santos, C.H. and A.C. Macedo e Silva (2010) 'Revisiting "New Cambridge": The Three Financial Balances in a General Stock-flow Consistent Applied Modeling Strategy,' Working Paper No. 594 (Annandale-on-Hudson, NY: Levy Economics Institute of Bard College).

Fetherston, M.J. and W. Godley (1978) '"New Cambridge" Macroeconomics and Global Monetarism: Some Issues in the Conduct of UK Economic Policy,' *Carnegie-Rochester Conference Series on Public Policy* 9(1): 33–65.

Godley, W. and F. Cripps (1983) *Macroeconomics* (London: Fontana).

Godley, W. and M. Lavoie (2007) *Monetary Economics: An Integrated Approach to Credit, Money, Income, Production and Wealth* (Basingstoke: Palgrave Macmillan).

Harrod, R.F. (1957) *International Economics* (Chicago: University of Chicago Press).

Hicks, J.R. (1985) *Methods of Economic Dynamics* (Oxford: Clarendon Press).

Marx, K. (1967) *Capital, Vol. II* (New York: International Publishers).

Marx, K. (1977) *Capital, Vol. I* (New York: Vintage).

McCulloch, J.H. (1982) *Money & Inflation: A Monetarist Approach* (New York: Academic Press).

Papadimitriou, D., A. Shaikh, C.H. Dos Santos and G. Zezza (2002) 'Is Personal Debt Sustainable?,' Strategic Analysis, November 2002 (Annandale-on-Hudson, NY: Levy Economics Institute of Bard College).

Pugno, M. (1998) 'Harrod's Economic Dynamics As a Persistent and Regime-Changing Adjustment Process,' in G. Rampa, L. Stella and A.P. Thirlwall (eds), *Economic Dynamics, Trade and Growth: Essays on Harrodian Themes* (London: Macmillan Press), pp. 153–77.

Robinson, J. (1965) 'A Reconsideration of the Theory of Value,' in J. Robinson (ed.), *Collected Economic Papers* (Oxford: Basil Blackwell), pp. 173–81.

Ruggles, N. and R. Ruggles (1992) 'Household and Enterprise Saving and Capital Formation in the United States: A Market Transaction View,' *Review of Income and Wealth* 38(2): 119–62.

Sen, A. (1970) *Growth Economics* (London: Penguin Books).

Shaikh, A. (1988) 'Accumulation, Finance, and Effective Demand in Marx, Keynes and Kalecki,' in W.E. Semmler (ed.), *Economic Dynamics and Financial Instability* (New York: M.E. Sharpe).

Shaikh, A. (2009) 'Economic Policy in a Growth Context: A Classical Synthesis of Keynes and Harrod,' *Metroeconomica* 60(3): 455–94.

van Duijn, J.J. (1983) *The Long Wave in Economic Life* (London: Allen & Unwin).

7

From Macroeconomics to Monetary Economics: Some Persistent Themes in the Theory Work of Wynne Godley

Marc Lavoie

7.1 Introduction

I first met Wynne Godley in December 1999. Colin Rogers, from the University of Adelaide, was visiting Tom Rymes at the neighboring Carleton University, and the two of them, plus my colleague Mario Seccareccia and myself, decided to set up our own regular workshop in the fall of 1999, reading and discussing recently published works in monetary economics. One of these was Wynne Godley's paper, 'Money and Credit in a Keynesian Model of Income Determination,' which had been published during the previous summer in the *Cambridge Journal of Economics*. Despite all of us being full professors, none of us could figure one of the equations of the paper, so I sent an email to the author, asking for some explanation. It turned out there was a small mistake in the equation. But Wynne was quite excited to see that four researchers, unrelated to him or to the Levy Institute, were paying attention to his paper, so we agreed to have Wynne give a formal lecture at the University of Ottawa. Thus an error in an equation led to my first meeting with Wynne! Then, a few months later, another error, this time in a paper of mine, induced me to ask Wynne for help on a difficult accounting question. This eventually led to our collaboration on one book, one book chapter and four journal articles, as well as to an extremely large number of phone conversations and emails.

I have two regrets with regards to Wynne, both of which are related to missed meetings. In the fall of 1985, during my first sabbatical, I was in Cambridge for about four weeks. Tom Rymes was there as well as a visitor, and I had a good time with other visitors, notably Peter Skott and Warren Young. I also met or met again famous post-Keynesians – Geoff

Harcourt, Nicholas Kaldor, A.B. Cramp, John Eatwell. But when I suggested that I should get to talk with Wynne Godley, I was told not to waste my time meeting this 'ignorant fool.' Being still young and unsure of myself I did not pursue the matter any further, thus postponing my first meeting with Wynne Godley by nearly 15 years. My second regret is another missed encounter. In the spring of 2010, I started planning a visit to Northern Ireland, where Wynne lived with his daughter Eve and his son-in-law. I sought the advice of Gennaro Zezza, who had paid Wynne a visit a few months before, about how to get to the house. I had to go to France in May and to Luxembourg in June, so hesitating a bit between the two dates, I decided to get organized to go and see Wynne in June, after my Luxembourg presentation. On May 13, I flew back from Paris to Canada – on the very day that Wynne passed away. I had not seen him since May 2005, when we worked together for a week at King's College and when we both went to a post-Keynesian study group seminar, at the SOAS in London.

The reason I wanted to meet Wynne Godley in Cambridge back in 1985 is that I had read the 1983 book, *Macroeconomics*, which he had co-written with Francis Cripps. I had been fascinated by this highly original and ambitious work as well as the formal introduction of endogenous money through the need to accumulate inventories, but at the same time I was somewhat taken aback by its idiosyncratic presentation style and all the chapters on inflation accounting. As far as I can remember, I first made a reference to this book in a survey that I made on circuit theory (Lavoie, 1987), claiming that there were tight similarities between French and Italian circuit theory and the Godley and Cripps (1983) book – an assessment that turned out to be right since Wynne Godley himself became an *aficionado* and a good friend of Augusto Graziani, the leader of the Italian monetary circuit school. I also made two references to the book in my *Foundations of Post-Keynesian Economic Analysis* (1992), but I completely omitted to mention it in my survey of Cambridge views on endogenous money, prepared for the 1987 Kaldor conference in New York City and at the Levy Institute (Lavoie, 1991).[1]

The present chapter is in a sense a rectification of this omission. I wish to go through some of the main themes that appear in the *Macroeconomics* book of Godley and Cripps, as I see them following my experience in writing with Wynne our joint volume *Monetary Economics* (2007). We shall see that many of these themes discussed in 1983 reappear nearly 25 years later in either the same form or in a slightly different shape. I shall restrain myself to some of the main theoretical issues that appear in these two works, omitting purposefully the more practical literature that Wynne was involved in, most notably the so-called New Cambridge hypothesis in the 1970s and the forecast of unsustainable processes in 1999 and thereafter. In what follows I shall examine three themes: Godley's big picture, his views on money and credit, and his views on pricing and profits as well as their link with inventories. These will constitute the three sections of the chapter.

Despite its huge importance, both in relation to practical issues and in relation to the justification of some of the theoretical positions taken by the proponents of neo-chartalism or modern monetary theory, I will not deal with the famous fundamental identity, which Wynne has helped so much in making known, that links the accumulation of net financial assets by the private domestic sector with the government deficit and the current account balance. Neither will I deal with a theme that Wynne has defended throughout, even when it was not fashionable at all, a theme that has become of paramount importance during the current global financial crisis, that is, the dominance of fiscal policy and the relative weakness of monetary policy in depression times. Finally, another major theme will be left out, that of open-economy macroeconomics, which as Wynne said, needs to be tackled using models of closed systems (Godley, 1999b).

7.2 Broad themes

The *Monetary Economics* book, published in 2007, was the arrival point of a long voyage. For a long time, Godley (1996, p. 14) had been groping 'to show how the whole system fits together and cast banks in a realistic role'. Already in 1993, Godley (1993, p. 79) puts forward a summary 'of a substantial monograph in the course of preparation in collaboration with Ken Coutts'. We are also told that there exists 'a simulation model in which banks' operations are fully articulated with income, expenditure and transfer flows together with asset demand functions' (ibid., p. 72), and that the model 'has already been tested by simulation experiments' (ibid., p. 80). Thus, by then, one can say that Wynne had a fully-integrated model of the economy on his computer. But only the main equations of the model are being shown in the 1993 paper, with a steady state solution, along with justifications of the behavioral equations imposed on the various sectors – households, corporations, banks, and the government.

A full model, looking very much like the description found in the 1993 paper, with all its equations, and with a verbal description of a couple of experiments, will only be presented three years later, in Godley (1996), with the appearance, for the first time, of a full transaction flow matrix based on flow of funds at current prices. The 1996 paper does not show a balance sheet matrix, however. This is surprising because a complete stock matrix had appeared ten years earlier, in the Coutts, Godley and Gudgin (1985) paper. Perhaps in part because Godley had moved out of Cambridge in 1994, working at the Levy Institute in the United States, his partner in the writing of a full monograph had changed by then, as we are also told that the 1996 paper is part of a research program, undertaken in collaboration with George McCarthy, and that the paper 'owes a special debt to Ken Coutts and Anwar Shaikh' (Godley, 1996, p. 1). Indeed, it is Anwar Shaikh who brought my attention to this 1996 paper during one of his visits to Ottawa. After having read the paper, I remember telling my colleague Mario Seccareccia that this was how we ought to handle monetary economics from now on, despite being somewhat perplexed by the large number of equations.

It is only one year later, in an intermediate paper (Godley, 1997), that one finds the simultaneous presence of both the balance sheet matrix and the transactions flow matrix. This is an important step, as it solidifies and provides support for the stock-flow consistent approach, that is, a macroeconomics based on comprehensive accounting and without black holes (Godley, 1996, p. 7), which was already in the books when Godley and Cripps (1983, p. 44) wrote that macroeconomists ought to exploit the fact that 'every money flow comes from somewhere and goes somewhere'. The 1997 working paper is less well known, but as I understand it, it gave rise to its much modified published version, the *Cambridge Journal of Economics* 1999 paper.[2] In my opinion, the latter paper brought Wynne Godley back to the attention of his post-Keynesian colleagues, after having been partly forgotten after the dismissal of the New Cambridge research team, when its public funding got cut off in the early 1980s. In both the 1997 and the 1999 paper, Godley says that he owes 'a special debt to George McCarthy' because of his help and guidance 'in all manner of ways', 'through a long trek'. Acknowledgements are also made in both papers to Anwar Shaikh, Robert Solow and Lance Taylor. These papers were then followed by a 'Draft treatise/textbook', which was sent to a number of people in February 2000, and in which McCarthy is again thanked 'for extensive help with making these models at an early stage'. This draft already contained, in fairly familiar form, the first four models of chapters 3 to 6 of *Monetary Economics*. Ultimately, 14 years after its first announcement, the monograph was completed![3]

My view of Wynne's theoretical work is that his work is a quest for the Holy Grail of Keynesianism. When I was a graduate student in France, Keynesians kept mentioning the need to integrate the real and the monetary sides of economics. Integration was all the talk, but little seemed to be achieved. Stinted by the rise of monetarism in the 1970s, Godley wanted to discover how money got into the economy. I understand the Godley and Cripps book to be an exercise in finding some way to amalgamate the real and the financial sides. This is clearly stated in the introduction to their book, where Godley and Cripps (1983, p. 17) claim that 'our present synthesis may be broadly characterized by saying that we make a "monetarist" financial system (based on the behaviour of stocks of money, financial assets and debts) drive a "Keynesian" flow system based on the response of expenditure to income', and it is reiterated in the epilogue, when they claim 'to have provided a framework for an orderly analysis of whole economic systems evolving through time' (ibid., p. 305). Retrospectively, it seems that it would have been better to avoid the word 'monetarist', as the use of the word and that of long-run or steady-state positions, plus the critiques addressed against the Keynesian orthodoxy of the time, which was said to be 'incomplete and inadequate' because 'it did not properly incorporate money and other financial variables', led several contemporary Keynesians to wonder whether Godley and his associates were not some kind of Cambridge Monetarists. The confusion was so great that Francis Cripps, following the presentation by Godley at the Keynes Centenary conference, felt obliged to state that 'what they were doing was Keynesian monetary economics; it was not neoclassical let alone general equilibrium monetary economics' (Worswick and Trevithick, 1983, p. 176).

In their attempt to integrate the real and the monetary sides, Godley and Cripps and their colleagues 'found quite early on that there was indeed something deficient in most macroeconomic models of the time', including their own, 'in that they tended to ignore constraints which adjustments of money and other financial assets impose on the economic system as a whole' (Godley and Cripps, 1983, p. 16). Interestingly, Godley was aware of the work being carried out at about the same time by Tobin and his Yale colleagues, as well as that of others such as Buiter, Turnovsky, and Blinder and Solow, who emphasized, as did Godley and Cripps (1983, p. 18), that 'money stocks and flows must satisfy accounting identities in individual budgets and in an economy as a whole'. Still, Godley thought that their analysis was overly complicated. I also suspect that Godley and Cripps (1983, p. 15) were annoyed by several of the behavioral hypotheses found in the work of these more orthodox Keynesians, as they 'could only give vague and complicated answers to simple questions like how money is created and what functions it fulfils'. The Cambridge authors thus wanted to start from scratch, with their own way of integrating the real and the financial sides, thus avoiding these 'tormented replies'.

In line with the New Cambridge approach, Godley and Cripps (1983, p. 43) contend that stock-flow norms 'are crucial to determining how actual economic systems work' and that they 'exhibit a fair degree of stability'. They focus their attention on two stock-flow norms: the desired inventory to sales ratio and the desired financial assets to disposable income ratio. The stability of the latter has often been questioned in the past. However, it seems that it has not been realized that this wealth to income ratio target is constant as long as one assumes a constant propensity to consume out of disposable income and a constant propensity to consume out of wealth, as most Keynesians would when constructing a model. The link between this stable stock-flow ratio and the stable propensities to consume is first made, as far as I know, in Godley (1996), and then reappears in subsequent work.

7.3 Money and banking

The big difference in the theoretical work on money conducted by Wynne Godley in the early 1980s and the mid-1990s is the explicit introduction of asset choices in his later work. In the Godley and Cripps (1983) book, portfolio choice is discussed, but it is not modeled. We are told that there must exist a hierarchy of interest rates: 'bank lending rates must be higher than bond yields (otherwise banks would not want to lend to the private sector) and rates on interest-bearing bank deposits must be lower than bond yields (otherwise neither the public nor banks would want to hold bonds)' (Godley and Cripps, 1983, p. 160). This hierarchy in interest rates will remain embedded in the explicit models to be built later (as in Godley, 1993, p. 73).

What was most striking to me when I first read his 1996 paper was that Godley was putting together a monetary flow analysis, linking monetary income and expenditure with a flow demand for credit, and a portfolio analysis, that explained the various demand functions for financial assets, including the demand for a stock of money. Brought up in the tradition of the monetary circuit theory, where monetary flows and the flow demand for credit are most important and where stocks of financial assets were a side issue, I always had some difficulty in seeing how this approach could be reconciled with the more traditional

Keynesian portfolio approach based on stocks of financial assets. But Godley's 1996 paper integrated the two views, showing how flows and stocks would gradually change in line with each other through time. Godley's models could simultaneously determine the stock of money held by households and the flows of credit, investment and income. The same integration had already been achieved in the Godley and Cripps (1983) book, but the integration was only partial, the difference being that most of the book assumed that all financial assets held by households were detained in the form of bank deposits. With the introduction of the public sector, Godley and Cripps (1983) assumed that the non-bank private sector chose between government securities and bank deposits, but this choice was only described in words and not explicitly modeled.

In the French and Italian monetary circuit theory, as described earlier by Parguez (1980) and Graziani (1990), the production process starts with banks granting advances to production firms to pay for wages and intermediary products. This is initial finance. Firms are then able to pay back this initial finance as long as households do not accumulate new money balances in banks. Godley and Cripps (1983) have a similar view. For them, production takes time, and firms must borrow from banks to finance their new production. In both monetary circuit theory and the Godley and Cripps representation of the simplified circuit, the outstanding debt of firms towards banks will be equivalent to the money balances held by households. There are two innovations from Godley and Cripps (1983), compared to the monetary circuitists. The first one is that Godley shows that the outstanding debt of firms will be equal to the end-period inventories valued at cost. The second innovation is that he has an explanation of the size of the money balances. As recalled earlier, they were some stable proportion of disposable income. In his 1990s work, the proportion of money balances as a share of financial wealth was given an additional Tobinesque explanation.

As Godley points out on a number of occasions, he himself owed his formalization of portfolio choice and of the fully consistent transactions-flow matrices to James Tobin. Godley was most particularly influenced and stimulated by his reading of the paper by Backus et al. (1980), as he writes in Godley (1996, p. 5) and as he told me verbally several times. The discovery of the Backus et al. paper, with its large flow-of-funds matrix, was a revelation to Godley and allowed him to move forward. But as pointed out in Godley and Lavoie (2007, p. 493), despite their important similarities, there is a crucial difference in the works of Tobin and Godley devoted to the integration of the real and monetary sides. In Tobin, the focus is on one-period models, or on the adjustments from the initial towards the desired portfolio composition, for a given income level. As Randall Wray (1992, p. 84) points out, in Tobin's approach 'flow variables are exogenously determined, so that the models focus solely on portfolio decisions'. By contrast, in Godley and Cripps and in further works, Godley is preoccupied in describing a fully explicit traverse that has all the main stock and flow variables as endogenous variables. As he himself says, 'the present paper claims to have made ... a rigorous synthesis of the theory of credit and money creation with that of income determination in the (Cambridge) Keynesian tradition' (Godley, 1997, p. 48). Tobin never quite succeeds in doing so, thus not truly introducing (historical) time in his analysis, in contrast to the objective of the Godley and Cripps book, as already mentioned earlier. Indeed, when he heard that Tobin had produced a new book (Tobin and Golub, 1998), Godley was quite anxious for a while as he feared that Tobin would have improved upon his approach, but these fears were alleviated when he read the book and realized that there was no traverse analysis there either.

Another major difference between Tobin and Godley are their views about the role of banks. Again this is discussed in detail in Godley and Lavoie (2007, pp. 497–9). Banks in most of Tobin's writings are veils that provide households with a greater variety of asset choices: 'the raison d'être of Tobin's banks, so far as I can see, is to enlarge the asset choice of households and facilitate the agility with which it can be made' (Godley, 1997, p. 49). By contrast, in Godley's view, banks play a distinct and essential role, since 'bank loans are required to enable industry to function at all' (ibid., p. 49). Godley's banks are Kaldorian, responding to the financial needs of their creditworthy clients. As pointed out earlier, this is linked to his view of the production process, which, as we said, is similar to that of the French and Italian monetary circuitists. Within this framework, bank loans act as a necessary buffer for the fluctuations in inventories. The link between inventories and bank loans is preserved all the way from Godley and Cripps (1983) to Godley and Lavoie (2007).

There is another feature of banking behavior that survived the 25-year transition. Godley and Cripps (1983, p. 160) describe the mechanism through which deposit and lending rates will remain around bill rates. If the Treasury bill rate goes up, this will induce households to acquire bills from the banks and get rid of their money deposits. But if this is the case, the deposit to loans ratio will fall, and banks will feel that they are less liquid, holding relatively fewer of their assets in the form of safe bills. Banks will thus be induced to raise their deposit rate, so as to preserve their liquidity ratio norm, and consequently they will also raise their lending rates to maintain their profit margins. The mechanism is first formalized in Godley (1996, p. 21), and it can be found in a similar form in later works, including Godley and Lavoie (2007). It is interesting to note that Alfred Eichner (1986) had identified a very similar mechanism through his empirical work, arguing that interest rates tended to be higher when the deposit to loan ratio was high relative to its trend level, thus also arguing along the lines of some sort of bank liquidity mechanism. It is not clear that such a mechanism still exists in the real world, as banks tend to use securitization or liability management, marking up the overnight rate target of the central bank to set the prime lending rate. Unless banks desire to achieve a target deposit to loan ratio, a sudden increase in the amount of required loans will have no impact whatsoever on interest rates or interest rate differentials, a point that was made to me by John Smithin when we were together riding a cab in Berlin in 2001.

Godley was always puzzled by the standard neoclassical assumption, found in both the IS/LM model and among monetarists, of an exogenous or fixed stock of money, the worse example of which is Friedman's money helicopter drop. As Godley (1997, p. 4) says, 'governments can no more control stocks of either bank money or cash than a gardener can control the direction of a hosepipe by grabbing at the water jet'. In Godley and Cripps (1983), the essentials of a monetary economy are described in any case without a government or a central bank, so that we have a pure credit economy, where private agents can only hold their wealth in the form of bank deposits. Thus, 'in such a world there is only one way in which the stock of money can be changed – namely by banks increasing or decreasing the total value of their loans' (Godley and Cripps, 1983, pp. 76–7). Godley shows clearly that loans make deposits, but he also shows that changes in the desire to hold deposits have a feedback effect on outstanding loans. Thus, in that simple world, there can be no discrepancy between the stock of money and outstanding credit, just as there can be no discrepancy between saving and investment in the national accounts.

Also, 'there cannot be any problem about equating what is usually called the "supply" of money with the "demand" for it. Money is created when banks make loans' (ibid., p. 82). Thus, as the circuitists would put it, 'the act of money creation is also an act of expenditure and (therefore) of income creation' (ibid., p. 83). This is reiterated later in the book, even with a government sector, as Godley and Cripps (1983,

p. 126) claim that there cannot be 'any discrepancy between the amount of money created and the amount of money which people in some sense want to hold'. Bank loans will need to increase either because firms desire to hold more inventories relative to sales and because firms expect more sales, or because households desire to increase their wealth to disposable ratio, thus desiring larger bank deposits. But this desire to save more and hence to acquire more bank deposits will generate a reduction in the sales of production firms, and hence an increase in their inventories and the amount of loans required to finance unsold stocks. Thus an exogenous increase in the demand for money will generate a concomitant increase in the supply of loans and hence in the supply of money. All these ideas are found again in chapters 7 and 9 of Godley and Lavoie (2007), where the interdependence between loans and deposits and their necessary equality is explored in a similar simplified model. In the more sophisticated model of Godley (1999a), where banks hold several assets and liabilities, the necessary equality between bank deposits and bank loans vanishes, although their interdependence does not.

In the short term there may be a discrepancy between the stock-flow ratio targeted by firms and the wealth (bank deposits) to disposable ratio targeted by households, but the variations in output will eventually make these two ratios compatible with each other. Furthermore, at any period of time, there may be a discrepancy between the planned demand for money and the amount actually being held. But, in contrast to what several orthodox and heterodox economists have affirmed, this discrepancy is not due to some hypothetical excess supply of money that would arise as a consequence of an excessive supply of credit that would make bank deposits grow beyond the desires of households. As already pointed out by Godley (1996, p. 18), the discrepancy is caused instead by the fact that 'mistaken expectations about disposable income turn up as differences in holdings of [money deposits] compared with what was targeted'. Money deposits act as a buffer to absorb the consequences of these mistakes. (The point is further explored in Lavoie and Godley, 2001–02, pp. 294–6.) When, for instance, disposable income is underestimated, the end-of-period wealth will also be underestimated, so that the actual holdings of money will exceed the planned demand for money, hence signifying that the supply of money exceeds the planned demand for money. But this discrepancy is entirely due to mistaken expectations by deposit holders; it cannot be said to be the cause of some excess demand on the goods market. This thus vindicates Kaldor's (1982) position that there can never be an excess supply of money.

7.4 Profits and cash flows

When Godley left the Treasury and joined the Department of Applied Economics at the University of Cambridge, and when he wrote his book with Francis Cripps, the United Kingdom was facing high rates of inflation. The impact of inflation on real variables was thus of great concern to him. The Godley and Cripps (1983) book devotes several chapters to inflation processes, inflation accounting and to the conditions required to achieve inflation neutrality, in particular the kind of fiscal stance that will keep real demand constant despite wage and price inflation. While all these issues are present in the Godley and Lavoie (2007) book, they don't resonate so strongly.

Still, present in the latter book – in fact an entire chapter is solely devoted to these issues, just as it was in the earlier book – is the concern with price setting and the distinction between profits and cash flows. This distinction is all the more important when wage inflation runs high and when firms have to carry large inventories as a proportion of sales, because the value of inventories – unsold production – will be large and its increase will reduce the cash flow of firms. The distinction, as we shall see, also has a link with bank credit granted to firms and hence to the importance of truly describing a monetary economy. The interest of Godley in prices and pricing is well known from the book that he co-authored on industrial pricing (Coutts, Godley and Nordhaus, 1978). But this interest goes back further, with his first published paper in the early 1960s, and of course also to his encounters with two figures of the Oxford Economists' Research Group on pricing, P.W.S. Andrews, who was his teacher at Oxford University and Robert Hall (from Hall and Hitch), who was his senior colleague at the Treasury. Some of the discussions that slowed down the progress of our book were related to finding the best way to present pricing decisions and the various possible definitions of profits.

Godley's understanding of pricing is very close to that of Andrews and is thus one variant of the more generic full-cost pricing procedure – that is, the claim that firms set prices by adding a costing margin to some measure of unit costs. In the Godley and Cripps book, in my opinion, there are two features which obscure the presentation of pricing and income distribution. First, Godley, being used to working with statistical data provided by real statistical agencies, makes use of indices such as base-period market prices or base-period costs. The use of these indices, and the additional variables that they require, makes it even harder to comprehend ideas which are relatively difficult by themselves. It is only soon after we met that it dawned on Wynne that since we were building theoretical models, without tackling actual statistical data, we could assume that we knew volume measures, that is, we knew how many widgets were being produced! The second obscuring feature was the lack of clarity about whether Godley and Cripps (1983, ch. 9) were dealing with *ex post* unit costs when discussing pricing, thus making use of identities, or whether they meant to determine prices from some behavioral equation. I dare say that this distinction is clear in the Godley and Lavoie (2007) book.

Godley's original proposition is that firms set prices on the basis of historical unit costs, that is on unit costs that take into account the fact that part of the sold goods this period will have been produced at some unit cost in the current period while the rest will have been produced in the previous period at some other unit cost, plus (unitary) interest payments arising from the cost of financing the holdings of these inventories for the period.[4] Assuming that the inventories to sales ratio is smaller than unity, this means that the proportion of goods sold but produced in the previous period is equal to the inventories to sales ratio. But this proportion cannot be known in advance, since firms do not know how many widgets they will manage to sell. The proportion used in the calculation of historical unit costs, when prices need to be set by firms before they are actually being sold, must thus be either based on an expected level of sales or be equated by convention to the normal or target inventories to sales ratio. The latter solution is closest to normal-cost pricing in the Andrews tradition, since cost is based on some normal rate of capacity utilization and on a normal level of inventories. But whatever solution is adopted, pricing based on historical costs shows that Godley was very much concerned with disequilibrium phenomena, while steady states were less interesting to him despite their apparent clear-cut appeal.

A key feature of historical unit costs is that if unit costs this period go up by 10 per cent after a period of steady costs, prices will increase by less than 10 per cent in the current period. But, all else equal, by how much should they rise? Godley's answer (also found in Coutts, Godley and Nordhaus, 1978) is that this depends on the normal proportion of goods sold this period that have been produced this period. This will be the complement of the normal inventories to sales ratio. So if this normal ratio is 30 per cent, then 70 per cent of the current 10 per cent unit cost increase will be passed onto prices, so that prices would rise by only 7 per cent. Godley thus argued that the time lag between costs and prices could not be just about anything. He was against the econometric determination of time lags in pricing studies. He thought that the normal or average inventories to sales ratios that could be obtained from raw data provided the necessary information.

A contentious issue, at least in the mind of Godley, was the adoption of a proper definition of profits. At least four definitions could be used. Net business profits, or what we came to call entrepreneurial profits, are simply equal to sales less actual historical costs (including required interest payments on inventories). Gross business profits, or total business profits, not unlike the famous Earnings Before Interest, Taxes, Depreciation and Amortization (EBITDA), are equal to sales less actual historical costs, excluding interest payments. National Income and Product Accounts (NIPA) profits are total business profits less stock appreciation or Inventory Valuation Adjustment (IVA), which represents the increase in the value of the opening stock of inventories. Finally, the cash flow of firms is equal to entrepreneurial profits less the change in the value of inventories, or, considering it from another angle, it is equal to sales less current costs and interest costs. Thus, the accountant may tell the business owners that they are making big-time profits when in fact the firms needs to keep borrowing just to keep afloat or to be able to distribute dividends. This will happen when changes in the value of inventories are looming, either because the number of units in inventories is quickly rising, or because the production cost of each unit of inventory is exploding, presumably due to cost and price inflation. As ironically put by Godley and Cripps (1983, p. 71): 'how can the trader live? His accountant is telling him he is making a profit; but far from having money to buy bread for himself, he is out of pocket on a substantial scale.' This problem was an important one for Godley, one that starting businesses face and one that arose during the days of double-digit inflation.

Wynne Godley expressed great reluctance in accepting the definition of NIPA profits. Although he was fully aware that national accountants needed such a definition to equate the value of production to factor incomes, it took a long uphill battle to persuade him to include the NIPA definition in our book. Godley was convinced that the business definition of profits was closest to reality. He also argued that the business profits to sales ratio or, in other words, the share of profits so defined, was invariant or, it turned out, *nearly* invariant to large fluctuations in inventories and unit costs. This he found to be an interesting property, which he could link to his theory of conflicting-claims inflation. He grudgingly accepted to include the NIPA definition only when I showed him that the NIPA profits to sales ratio was *completely* invariant to fluctuations in inventories and their costs (Godley and Lavoie, 2007, p. 278) – a rather surprising result.

Godley also always insisted that coherence required that inventories be valued at production cost. National accountants value everything at market prices, except government services and inventories, which are indeed valued at production cost. If the flow-of-funds matrix is to be fully consistent, the value of inventories needs to be equal to the wage costs encountered in producing the goods and initially kept as money balances by the workers, and this means that the advances provided by banks to finance the production of the good will also be equal to the value of inventories, so that the flow of bank credit will equate the flow of bank deposits. Unfortunately, when reading other contributions, I have noted time and time again that the few sophisticated models that deal with inventories do not respect this accounting constraint.

7.5 Conclusion

As all those that worked with him, I learned a great deal from my ten-year collaboration with Wynne Godley. I used to tell him that I had learned more during the six years that led to the publication of our book than during the previous 20 years of my academic career. It was sometimes a frustrating experience, as no doubt my predecessors such as Ken Coutts and George McCarthy can attest, because Wynne could be incredibly stubborn on some issues, while changing his mind for a fleeting moment on some others, especially on matters of presentation.

One of the difficulties that we faced when writing our book was to choose our targeted audience. Eventually, after several long phone calls, we decided to seek out a post-Keynesian audience, despite the advice of a few of Wynne's friends. There was a stage where Wynne was aiming at a larger group of economists, as he was when writing his middle-term assessments of economic conjuncture. The same desire transpires in Godley and Cripps (1983, p. 305) when they say that their 'logical framework is neither "monetarist" nor "Keynesian"; it is non-denominational both in theoretical and in political terms'. Certainly the same can be said about the stock-flow consistent framework that informs Godley and Lavoie (2007). The framework, with its flow and stock matrices, can be put to use by orthodox economists. But we came to realize that post-Keynesians perhaps best needed the discipline of stock-flow consistency, and that in any case, since the rest of our message and our assumptions were essentially Keynesian, it was more realistic to presume that only fellow post-Keynesian or heterodox colleagues were likely to listen to us.

Wynne, notwithstanding some of his heterodox critics, was a true Keynesian. Godley and Cripps (1983, p. 305) conclude their book by saying that its main result is 'to re-establish the quintessentially Keynesian principle of effective demand as the determinant of real output and employment'. The principle of effective demand, applied both to the short period and to the long period, is in my view one of the essential two characteristics of post-Keynesian economics, the other one being a concern with the operation of economic systems through historical time, with the present dependent on the past. An analysis conducted in historical time was precisely a most fundamental concern of Wynne Godley who always wanted to track the interdependent evolution of variables through recursive relationships and sequences (Godley, 1993, p. 61), a concern that he also attributed to the older John Hicks (1989).

Wynne Godley often expressed his great admiration for several of his former colleagues, notably his former co-authors, but he had a particular appreciation for the work and ingenuity of Nicholas Kaldor. He often regretted in print (Godley, 1993, p. 63; 1996, p. 3) and in conversations, however, that Kaldor did not bother to attempt to put all of his ideas within a comprehensive scheme.[5] Wynne was no doubt a post-Keynesian of the Kaldorian variety, as exemplified by his work on money and credit, the main themes of which I have tried to develop here in the second section. I had myself high regards for the work of Kaldor, and was grateful to the fact that, unsolicited, he had offered his help following his reading of the preliminary version of a paper of mine (Lavoie, 1984) at a time when I did not have tenure. Wynne and I were thus fated to get along, because we were both influenced by the monetary circuit view and concerned with pricing issues, and because my own previous work was 'a mix of Kaldorian and Kaleckian economics'(Lavoie, 1992, p. 4).

Notes

1. I have recently realized that when Godley (1999a, p. 396) linked up his own work to the post-Keynesian views on endogenous money in general, he did cite an article of mine among others (Lavoie, 1984). For some reason, in the working paper version (Godley, 1998), the reference is instead to Lavoie (1985).
2. The 1996, 1997 and 1999a papers all have the same structure. The 1996 paper has the most complicated balance sheet: in addition, to cash, demand deposits and time deposits, it has equities and bonds. The 1999a paper removes equities, while the 1997 paper had removed both equities and bonds thus getting rid of the difficulties associated with capital gains.

3. I still remember the looks of puzzlement and friendly sarcasm when in 2001 I told staff members of the Levy Institute that Wynne and I were joining forces to get this book done.
4. In the simplified version that appears in the main text of Godley and Cripps (1983), but not in the formal appendix, it is assumed that there is a one-period lag for all of the sales, so that everything sold this period has been produced in the previous period. Some authors make this assumption, but it leads to all sorts of problems, instability and over-determination, since present sales can be no different from past production. The flexibility provided by inventories, of which John Hicks (1989) became so much aware, also disappears.
5. Very few post-Keynesian authors have attempted to do so, among which most notably are Alfred Eichner and Edward Nell.

References

Backus, D., W.C. Brainard, G. Smith and J. Tobin (1980) 'A Model of US Financial and Nonfinancial Economic Behavior,' *Journal of Money, Credit and Banking* 12(2) May: 259–93.

Coutts, K.J., W. Godley and G.D. Gudgin (1985) 'Inflation Accounting of Whole Economic Systems,' *Studies in Banking and Finance* [Supplement to *Journal of Banking and Finance*] (Amsterdam: North Holland), pp. 93–111.

Coutts, K.J., W. Godley and W. Nordhaus (1978) *Industrial Pricing in the UK* (Cambridge: Cambridge University Press).

Eichner, A.S. (1986) 'The Demand Curve for Money Further Considered,' in A.S. Eichner (ed.), *Toward a New Economics: Essays in Post-Keynesian and Institutionalist Theory* (London: Macmillan), pp. 98–112.

Godley, W. (1993) 'Time, Increasing Returns and Institutions in Macroeconomics,' in S. Biasco, A. Roncaglia and M. Salvati (eds) *Market and Institutions in Economic Development: Essays in Honour of Paolo Sylos Labini* (New York: St Martin's Press), pp. 59–82.

Godley, W. (1996) 'Money, Finance and National Income Determination: An Integrated Approach,' Working Paper No. 167 (Annandale-on-Hudson, NY: Levy Economics Institute of Bard College).

Godley, W. (1997) 'Macroeconomics Without Equilibrium or Disequilibrium,' Working Paper No. 205 (Annandale-on-Hudson, NY: Levy Economics Institute of Bard College).

Godley, W. (1998) 'Money and Credit in a Keynesian Model of Income Determination,' Working Paper No. 242 (Annandale-on-Hudson, NY: Levy Economics Institute of Bard College).

Godley, W. (1999a) 'Money and Credit in a Keynesian Model of Income Determination,' *Cambridge Journal of Economics* 23(4): 393–411.

Godley, W. (1999b) 'Open Economy Macroeconomics Using Models of Closed Systems,' Working Paper No. 285 (Annandale-on-Hudson, NY: Levy Economics Institute of Bard College).

Godley, W. and F. Cripps (1983) *Macroeconomics* (London: Fontana).

Godley, W. and M. Lavoie (2007) *Monetary Economics: An Integrated Approach to Credit, Money, Income, Production and Wealth* (Basingstoke, UK: Palgrave Macmillan).

Graziani, A. (1990) 'The Theory of the Monetary Circuit,' *Économies et Sociétés* 24(6) June: 7–36.

Hicks, J.R. (1989) *A Market Theory of Money* (Oxford: Clarendon Press).

Kaldor, N. (1982) *The Scourge of Monetarism* (Oxford: Oxford University Press).

Lavoie, M. (1984) 'The Endogenous Flow of Credit and the Post Keynesian Theory of Money,' *Journal of Economics Issues* 18(3): 771–97.

Lavoie, M. (1985) 'Credit and Money: The Dynamic Circuit, Overdraft Economics and Post-Keynesian Economics,' in M. Jarsulic (ed.) *Money and Macro Policy* (Boston: Kluwer-Nijhoff), pp. 63–84.

Lavoie, M. (1987) 'Monnaie et Production: Une Synthèse de la Théorie du Circuit,' *Économies et Sociétés* 21(9): 65–101.

Lavoie, M. (1991) 'Change, Continuity, and Originality in Kaldor's Monetary Theory,' in E.J. Nell and W. Semmler (eds) *Nicholas Kaldor and Mainstream Economics: Confrontation of Convergence?* (London: Macmillan), pp. 259–78.

Lavoie, M. (1992) *Foundations of Post-Keynesian Economic Analysis* (Aldershot: Edward Elgar).

Lavoie, M. and W. Godley (2001–02) 'Kaleckian Models of Growth in a Coherent Stock-flow Monetary Framework: A Kaldorian View,' *Journal of Post Keynesian Economics* 24(2): 277–311.

Parguez, A. (1980) 'Profit, Épargne, Investissement: Éléments pour une Théorie Monétaire du Profit,' *Économie appliquée* 33(2): 425–55.

Tobin, J. and S.S. Golub (1998) *Money, Credit and Capital* (New York: Irwin McGraw-Hill).

Worswick D. and J. Trevithick (1983) *Money and the Modern World* (Cambridge: Cambridge University Press).

Wray, L.R. (1992) 'Alternative Theories of the Rate of Interest,' *Cambridge Journal of Economics* 16: 69–89.

8
Godley and Graziani: Stock-flow Consistent Monetary Circuits

*Gennaro Zezza**

8.1 Introduction and motivation

As a student of Augusto Graziani, I learned about the Monetary Theory of Production in his lectures back in 1984. At the time, many researchers in the Department of Economics in Naples were involved in developing this line of research, under the strong influence of Graziani. I clearly remember some of the puzzles in a monetary circuit that Graziani showed us with very simple models. The simplest puzzle refers to a very simple economy, where firms need to borrow before production takes place, to pay for wages and other production costs. Banks are eager to provide loans, say in the form of overdraft deposit accounts: Graziani clearly showed us how loans create deposits, and not the other way round as mainstream scholars were teaching us, since the loan comes into existence only when firms actually use their overdraft facility to pay wages, which we can assume are immediately deposited in a bank. Any loan generates a deposit somewhere – possibly in the same bank – for the same amount, unless wage earners choose to keep their income in cash form. When a loan is made, money is created, and when the loan is paid back, as firms sell their goods to wage earners, money gets destroyed. The puzzle arises if firms have to pay interest on the loan: in the best case scenario, where firms have recovered from sales all the money they have paid out in wages, and the

* The author gratefully acknowledges financial support from MIUR. I am indebted to several people for discussion of these issues over the years. Most notably Anwar Shaikh, Augusto Graziani, Marc Lavoie, Marcello Messori and Alberto Zazzaro. I also wish to thank participants at a seminar at Université Paris Nord for comments, and Jamel Saadoui in particular. Any remaining errors are my responsibility.

initial amount of newly created money gets entirely destroyed, where do firms get the cash to pay for interest? And how can they possibly get a monetary profit?

Graziani's lectures were fascinating, but the existence of unresolved puzzles in the theory led me to pursue other avenues of research. Graziani encouraged me to visit Cambridge, and I went to introduce myself to the head of the Department of Applied Economics, Wynne Godley, who had accepted my application for visiting scholar. On our very first meeting, in 1986, Wynne proposed that we wrote a model using Italian economic data, and that marked the beginning of a long period of collaboration first in the UK, then later Denmark and the Levy Economics Institute in the US.

I did not follow the evolution of Graziani's Theory of Monetary Profit[1] in great detail until much later, in 2003, when I was asked to discuss a contribution by Louis-Philip Rochon at a conference in honor of Augusto Graziani in Benevento, Italy, on 'The Monetary Theory of Production'.[2] Reading Rochon's contribution, I realized that (at least some) *circuitists* knew little about Godley's stock-flow consistent methodology, which could provide a robust accounting framework for their models, while showing that some of the 'puzzles', as the one described above, are only apparent.

Zezza (2004) was an attempt to contribute to the *circuitists'* debate, but I failed to make my point clear enough, and the debate on the *circuitists'* 'puzzles' continued. In this chapter, I revise my early paper, trying again to show how Godley's approach can provide additional rigor to Graziani's analysis, and pay homage to my two mentors.

More in detail, following Lavoie (2004), and Godley and Lavoie (2007) we investigate the implications for the Theory of the Monetary Circuit (TMC) models of laying down the corresponding set of stock-flow accounting, which must imply that every monetary flow comes from somewhere and goes somewhere, so that there are no 'black holes'.[3] As the accounting is analyzed, it appears that several, if not all, contributors to the TMC fail to take properly into account how banks' profits can be spent in the goods or the financial markets. In several models, interest payments on loans made from firms to banks are not accounted for as part of national income, and simply disappear, instead of being treated as a possible source of demand for goods and/or financial assets. By ignoring the accounting and behavioral implications of interest payments, TMC models are usually characterized by a 'paradox of profits.' In a pure credit economy and considering a single production period, if firms receive an initial loan M to cover for their current expenditure, by selling goods and financial assets they can, at most, recover the amount of money M being injected into the economy at the beginning of the period. Firms can, therefore, pay back the principal to banks at the end of the period, but will not possibly have enough liquidity to pay for interests, unless (a) they pay interest in kind, or (b) at the end of the production period they remain indebted with banks, by an amount equal to interest payments. In our view, this result depends on interest payments disappearing from income or stock-flow accounting, and we will show how simple TMC models can be made consistent on this respect. In our approach, the TMC will also be reconciled with the Godley and Cripps (1983) approach, which laid the foundation for Godley's developments in stock-flow consistent modeling in the post-Keynesian tradition.

In section 8.2 we present the simplest possible model of the Monetary Circuit, in order to recall the major hypothesis and results for this approach, and we show in section 8.3 how to modify the approach in the literature to deal with interest payments. In section 8.4 we discuss implications of our approach, and compare our simple TMC model with consistent stock-flow models à la Godley. In section 8.5 we extend the model to an economy with two productive sectors, laying down the 'paradox of profits' in greater detail. Section 8.6 summarizes and concludes.

8.2 The simplest traditional monetary circuit

Let us consider the simplest possible model of the TMC, namely that of a single production period in a pure credit economy with no government.[4] Only a single good is produced, which is used for both consumption and investment.

At the heart of the TMC is the notion, shared by Godley,[5] that production requires time, and that costs of production have to be paid before receipts from sales can be obtained. Monetary wages must therefore be paid in advance, and this requires firms to have enough liquidity before production occurs. Firms as a whole need to obtain an initial loan (L_0), equal to the wage bill (W):

$$L_0 = W \tag{1}$$

Money, in the form of bank deposits, is created[6] as soon as firms pay wage earners.

When production is complete, wage earners may either buy consumption goods (C), or save, increasing their stock of financial assets (V). The budget constraint of households is thus

$$W = C + \Delta V \tag{2}$$

Let us assume that firms finance investment by issuing equities (E).

$$\Delta E^s = I \tag{3}$$

Financial assets are, therefore, given by bank deposits (D) and equities. It must be the case that

$$\Delta V = \Delta D^d + \Delta E^d = W - C \tag{4}$$

At the end of the production period, firms have to pay back the initial loan, plus interest. Firms' receipts are given by sales of consumption goods plus sales of investment goods (I). Firms' profits (Π) are thus given by

$$\Pi = C + I - W - r{\cdot}L \tag{5}$$

where $r{\cdot}L$ is interests paid on loans. Using (3) and (4) into (5) we obtain

$$\Pi = W - \Delta D^d + (\Delta E^s - \Delta E^d) - W - r{\cdot}L \tag{6}$$

and, therefore, when the supply of new equities from firms equals the demand from households, and assuming that the supply of bank deposits is perfectly elastic

$$\Pi = -\Delta D - r{\cdot}L \tag{7}$$

The best possible situation for firms is when the demand for new deposits from households is zero, and, therefore, firms get back the initial loan entirely either by selling consumption goods, or by selling equities. If this is the case, at the end of the production period firms will have enough liquidity to pay back the initial loan, but no liquidity to pay for interests, and there is no room for the realization of profits. This is a simple version of the 'profit paradox' of the TMC, which is very close to Marx's 'Scheme of Simple Reproduction'.[7] In Marx's terminology, the profit motive in capitalist production is to increase the capitalist amount of money holdings: M-C-M′ implies that an initial stock of liquidity *M* is used to start production (create commodities *C*) in order to obtain a larger stock of final liquidity *M′*. While it is straightforward to understand this process for the individual firm, how can firms *as a whole* recover more money from the production process than the money which has been injected in the system at the beginning of the process?

Proposals for solving the profit paradox have been reviewed in Parguez (2004), but none seemed entirely satisfactory, since more contributions on the same topic continue to appear.[8] Messori and Zazzaro (2004) show that either firms' debt with banks increases without limits, or that a given percentage of firms go bankrupt, and, therefore, do not reimburse their initial loan, while others earn profits. In Rochon (2005) the solution depends on assuming that part of the initial loan is long-term in nature, and does not require to be repaid in full at the end of the production period.

Bruun and Heyn-Johnsen (2009) again state that 'The paradox of monetary profits has been a recurrent theme in macroeconomics since the problem was first formulated by Marx. Capitalists as a whole can at most get from workers, what they already paid out in wages. Marx did not solve this problem, and neither did Keynes' (Bruun and Heyn-Johnsen 2009, abstract) and they conclude saying that 'Economics has not been able to capture what, at least Marx and Keynes, regarded as the most fundamental fact of capitalist economies – that firms produce in order to gain a monetary profit.' (Bruun and Heyn-Johnsen 2009, p. 22).

Keen (2010, p. 2) notes that 'The consensus to date has been that it is mathematically impossible for capitalists in the aggregate to make profits' and challenging this consensus suggests that 'In brief, "M becomes M+" via the price mechanism, which converts the sale of the physical surplus generated in production into money' (Keen 2010, p. 2) with a solution very close to what we will adopt in this chapter. Forges-Davanzati and Patalano disagree, stating that 'Assuming that workers have a unitary propensity to consume (and do not decide to keep a portion of their savings in the form of liquid balances), it is shown that firms as a whole recoup an amount of money exactly equal to their costs of production for whatever price level, which at the aggregate level equals the money wage bill' (Forges-Davanzati and Patalano 2011, p. 8). In our view, these authors – who state that 'it is logically impossible to imagine that the closure of the monetary circuit is made possible via banks' expenditure, since banks can spend only in the event firms as a whole have previously gained profits',[9] which is what we suggest in this chapter and in Zezza (2004) – derive their conclusion on the inconsistent hypothesis that firms' receipts are equal to money wages.[10]

Godley (2004) did not address this problem in his contribution to Graziani's conference, in our view because in his stock-flow consistent model monetary profits were always possible, as we will try to show in the next section.

8.3 The simplest consistent monetary circuit

In our view, the basic circuit described in the previous section is incomplete and inconsistent, mainly because interest payments, which constitute the income of bankers, disappear, in that they are not spent on goods or financial assets. This is both an accounting inconsistency and a logical inconsistency, since banks exist because they generate profits for their owners, while such profits disappear in the simple example described above.

A simple solution to close the circuit can be obtained by treating interest payments consistently. If we want to keep the model within a single production period, the only rationale for banks asking for interest payments is either to pay for their 'costs of production,' namely wages, or to distribute profits to bank owners, or to cumulate wealth, and since we can rule out that banks cumulate wealth in the form of their own deposits, we can safely assume that any level of undistributed profits obtained by the banking sector is used entirely to purchase equities.

We thus need a 'financial period' which is longer than the 'production period.' The former starts when a loan is made and money is created and ends when the loan is paid back and the money is destroyed. The production period starts immediately after the loan is received and wages are paid. When production is complete firms can sell the output, and as they recover liquidity from sales, they can pay the interest to banks, which in turn can use this liquidity to purchase goods or equities from firms. If effective demand is equal to output, at the end of the whole (financial) period, firms have received back the entire amount of money they own to the banks, including interest, and the value of their profits will equal the value of investment.

8.3.1 An economy with only consumption goods

Let us detail this logical sequence by examining how money circulates among firms, workers and the banks in an economy producing only a consumption good, where bankers' income is used to purchase such a good, and profit is the consumption of the capitalist class. A bank loan is made to firms in the form of bank notes printed by the bank, and widely accepted as means of payment. Assume that the price of goods is equal to \$1, wages are equal to \$100, the interest rate is 10 per cent and the value of production is \$150. This implies, of course, that the (real) value of production is greater than the (real) value of costs (wages plus interest), so that (real) monetary profits correspond to a physical surplus value.

If firms' profits are used to purchase consumption goods there will be a simultaneous payment and receipt for the firms sector as a whole, and cancel out in *ex post* balance sheets. So let us assume that two firms exist, that workers buy goods from each of them, while the owner of firm A uses profits to purchase goods from firm B and vice versa.

In Table 8.1 we report the deposit balance of each group at the different stages of the financial cycle. We want the circuit to close by the end of the financial cycle, and the only way this can happen is for income to be entirely spent before the circuit ends. This implies that monetary profits realized by both firms must be spent, as well as interest payments received by banks.

An assumption underlying Table 8.1, along with the idea that all income is spent, is that firms have perfect foresight on effective demand, so that the whole of production is sold at the current price level.

Assume instead that workers save 10 per cent of their income. In this case, workers money holdings at the end of the financial cycle will be equal to \$20, and both firms will be unable to pay back the entire loan, ending the cycle with a debt of \$10 each, and an unexpected increase in inventories of 10 goods each. In our view, this was the main concern of Godley's models. Godley focused on balance sheet accounts at the end of the period, rather than on the need for initial finance, and usually assumed that the change in bank loans outstanding would be equal to the change in inventories valued at costs. The two approaches to finance, Graziani's and Godley's, are therefore entirely compatible.[11]

Another issue worth noting from the example in Table 8.1 is related to the velocity of circulation. Some authors have suggested that monetary profits can be realized in the TMC only if the velocity of circulation is greater than one. This is indeed the case, since the same bank notes will be used once by wage earners, and a second time by capitalists or bankers. Transactions of bank notes among workers or firms, on the other hand, will not change the aggregate money holding of each sector. The logical closure of the circuit therefore requires that all income is spent, and this has implications on the velocity of circulation, but

Table 8.1 Money holdings at different stages of the financial cycle

Period	**Firm A**	**Firm B**	**Workers**	**Bankers**	**Firms debt outstanding**
Beginning: a loan is made to both firms	+\$100	+\$100	0	0	−\$200
Wages are paid	0	0	+\$200	0	−\$200
Production is complete and workers spend 80% of their income	+\$80	+\$80	+\$40	0	−\$200
Firms pay interest	+\$70	+\$70	+\$40	+\$20	−\$200
Owner of firm A purchases goods from firm B	+\$30	+\$110	+\$40	+\$20	−\$200
Bankers spend their income on consumption goods	+\$40	+\$120	+\$40	0	−\$200
Owner of firm B purchases goods from firm A	+\$80	+\$80	+\$40	0	−\$200
Workers spend the remaining 20% of their income	+\$100	+\$100	0	0	−\$200
The loan is paid back	0	0	0	0	0

assumptions about velocity alone are insufficient to close the circuit by extinguishing the initial loan.

8.3.2 Stock-flow accounting in a simple consistent model

The *ex post* flow accounting for a simple consistent model is reported in Table 8.2. Table 8.2 is organized, following Stone (1966), so that monetary payments from a sector are recorded in a column, while rows record receipts. Including a row and a column for transaction on capital account, accounting consistency requires that the total for each row to be equal, *ex post*, to the total for the corresponding column, yielding a system of accounting identities, one of which is linearly dependent from the others.

Table 8.2 Social accounting matrix – Model 1: The simplest monetary circuit

	Firms	Households	Banks	Capitala account	Total
1. Firms		C		I	S
2. Households	W		$Wb\ (+r{\cdot}D)$		Yh
3. Banks	$r{\cdot}L$				Yb
4. Capital account	Π	ΔV	Πb		SAV
Total	S	Yh	Yb	I	

Comparing the second row and column in Table 8.2, households budget constraint is now given by

$$W + Wb = C + \Delta V \tag{8}$$

While banks' profits are given, in the third row and column, by[12]

$$\Pi b = r{\cdot}L - Wb \tag{9}$$

Table 8.3 reports the *ex post* flow of funds related to flow accounting in Table 8.1.

Demand for equities arises from household savings and banks' profits

$$\Delta E^d = (\Delta V - \Delta D) + \Pi b \tag{10}$$

If we look at the budget constraint of banks, in the third column of Table 8.3, we will see that our assumption behind (10) implies that the end-of-period increase in the stock of loans will exactly match the end-of-period increase in the stock of banks deposits. We will turn to this issue later.

The value of firms' profits is given by

$$\Pi = C + I - W - r{\cdot}L \tag{11}$$

And using the identities (8) and (9)

$$\Pi = I - \Delta V - \Pi b \tag{12}$$

Using (10) which defines the demand for equities

$$\Pi = I - \Delta E^d - \Delta D \tag{13}$$

Table 8.3 Flow of funds for Model 1

	Firms	Households	Banks	Total
Deposits		$+\Delta D$	$-\Delta D$	0
Loans	$-\Delta L$		$+\Delta L$	0
Equities	$-\Delta E$	$+\Delta Eh$	$+\Delta Eb$	0
Capital	$+I$			$+I$
Total	$+\Pi$	$+\Delta V$	$+\Pi b$	

which is usually read, looking at the budget constraint of firms in the first column of Table 8.3, as an *ex post* identity, stating that investment is financed by profits, new loans from banks or by issuing new equities. In our case, assuming instead that investment is financed by issuing new equities, and that the supply of equities matches demand

$$\Pi = -\Delta D \tag{14}$$

So that, if households' demand for new bank deposits is zero, $\Delta D = 0$, firms' receipts from sales are sufficient to pay back the initial loan *plus* interests, as in our previous example in Table 8.1. If, on the contrary, households increase their end-of-period stock of deposits, firms will have a positive end-of-period debt with the banking sector.

In this model, loans create deposits, in the sense that in this credit economy money is injected into the system by an initial loan made from banks to firms, and the liquidity transferred from firms to households will generate a stock of deposits which is always equal, at any instant of the production period, to the outstanding stock of loans. But deposits determine loans at the end of the period, since if households decide to keep their savings in the form of bank deposits, rather than purchasing equities, firms will remain indebted towards banks by an amount which is exactly equal to households' desired holdings of bank deposits. In our approach, deposits determine loans in a way which is entirely different from the 'conventional' view, where the single bank is allowed to lend money only when it has collected deposits from households. As Graziani (2003) and other circuitists note, while this is true for the single bank, it cannot be true for the banking system as a whole.

In our view, by neglecting a proper representation of the accounting of their model, most circuitists fail to see that interest payments on loans constitute a source of income for banks which will be used in a way consistent with the model. Graziani comes very close to making this point. When analyzing the payment of interests on loans he first states that 'if the only liquidity in existence originates from bank loans, the firms, by selling commodities and issuing securities, will at best get back the money they have initially spent. This means that firms will be able at best to repay the principal but not the interest on the loans granted them by banks.'[13] But immediately afterwards he states 'The interest payments that the banks receive from firms are partly used to cover current costs (such as wages and salaries to employees), and partly are net profits to be used for purchasing real goods'.[14] Therefore, interest payments made from firms to banks imply a further monetary payment from banks (or bank owners) to firms for purchasing goods. The payment of interest implies that banks acquire part of firms' production, but does not imply that interest is paid 'in kind.' Graziani does not pursue his own point to its conclusions, as we have suggested in our simple model, and when presenting formal models in his latest contribution he neglects net bank profits when specifying either disposable income or demand for equities.

8.4 Some further results

8.4.1 On banks' behavior

Our result about the end of period stock of firms' debt changes if we modify our assumption about banks' behavior, so that demand for equities from banks is given by bank liquidity, for example, profits *plus* the increase in banks' deposits.[15] Looking again at banks' budget constraint in Table 8.3, we can verify that this assumption implies that the end-of-period stock of loans will always be zero. If this is the case, at the end of the production period firms will always be able to pay back the initial loan plus interests, and money disappears entirely – wealth is cumulated only in the form of equities.

8.4.2 On households' behavior

In our simple model, we implicitly adopted that consumption and savings decisions are based on current income. However, the only possible rationale for an increase in households' holdings of bank deposits is given by an increase in future consumption. If this is the case, consistency would require that current consumption decisions be based both on current income and on past cumulated savings. This would alleviate the finance problem for firms, since in each period they will recover at least part of the liquidity which was 'missing' in previous periods of production.

Moreover, we believe that even when modeling a single production period, it should be assumed an initial stock of wealth for some sectors, such as land or 'capital' owned by firms, or 'gold.' By providing loans to firms, banks will therefore be able to appropriate either part of the current production of goods, or part of the existing stock of wealth.

Using a single period of production may be appropriate to outline the basic principles of the TMC, but proper models for monetary economies should be developed in a dynamic context.

8.4.3 A post-Keynesian version

It would be reasonably simple to modify our model along post-Keynesian lines, splitting the households sector into wage earners, who spend all of their income, and firms' owners, who have a positive propensity to save. Results would not change as far as the paradox of profits is concerned, provided that interest payments on bank deposits, and banks' distributed profits, are properly taken into account in determining households disposable income.

8.4.4 TMC, Say's Law and the Keynesian approach

At a first look, the TMC outlined here may resemble the neoclassical approach, in which savings decisions to determine investment, rather than the Keynesian approach of effective demand, in which investment decisions determine the level of output. As shown in our accounting in Tables 8.2 and 8.3, investment needs to be financed by issuing equities, and demand for equities ultimately arises from savings, so it may seem that saving decisions ultimately determine investment.

Even though we consistently used the assumption that supply equals demand, we believe TMC to be compatible with a Keynesian approach – assuming that firms have excess capacity, an increase in investment will stimulate an equal increase in the production of capital goods. This will in turn require an increase in the wage bill for the capital goods sector, and an equivalent increase in loans demanded by this sector. The increase in the wage bill will stimulate production in the consumption goods sector, following the standard multiplier effect. TMC is thus entirely Keynesian in spirit, but stresses that increases in production, generated by a rise in effective demand, may be constrained by credit rationing, if firms pay real wages in advance.

8.5 A two-sector model

To enrich our discussion of investment and the determination of profits in the TMC, we now move to a neo-Kaleckian approach, according to the taxonomy proposed by Parguez (2004). Namely, we split firms into a sector producing consumption goods, and a sector producing investment goods. We begin our analysis following the model in Rochon (2005), namely that firms do not issue equities, and finance investment only through profits, but we modify Rochon's model to treat interest payments on loans consistently as in our simpler model.

Model accounting is now summarized in Table 8.4 for flows, and Table 8.5 shows the corresponding allocation of savings to financial assets and physical capital. To make our analysis as close as possible to that in Rochon (2005), let us assume first that firms do not issue equities, and that banks distribute all of their profits. Households' savings will therefore take the form of an increase in the stock of banks deposits.

If banks distribute all of their profits ($\Pi b = 0$), distributed profits will be given by row and column 5 in Table 8.3:

$$Fb = r{\cdot}Lc + r{\cdot}Li \qquad (15)$$

Assuming that wage earners and bank owners have the same propensity to save we can consolidate rows 3 and 4, and the corresponding columns, to obtain demand for consumption goods:

$$C = Wc + Wi + Fb - Sh \qquad (16)$$

Profits in the consumption and investment sector will be given by rows and columns 1 and 2, respectively:

$$\Pi c = C - r{\cdot}Lc - Wc \qquad (17)$$

$$\Pi i = Ic + Ii - r{\cdot}Li - Wi \qquad (18)$$

Table 8.4 Social accounting matrix two sector Model 2: A two sectors model

	Firms		**Households**		**Banks**	**Capital account**	**Total**
	Cons. goods	**Inv. goods**	**Wage earners**	**Bank owners**			
1. Cons. goods			C				C
2. Inv. goods						$Ic + Ii$	I
3. Wage earners	Wc	Wi					W
4. Bank owners					Fb		Yhb
5. Banks	$r{\cdot}Lc$	$r{\cdot}Li$					Yb
6. Capital account	Πc	Πi	Sh		Πb		Sav
			Yh				
Total	Yc	Yi			Yb	I	

Table 8.5 Flow of funds for Model 2

	Firms		Households	Banks	Total
	Cons. goods	**Inv. goods**			
Deposits			$+\Delta D$	$-\Delta D$	0
Loans	$-\Delta Lc$	$-\Delta Li$		$+\Delta L$	0
Equities	$-\Delta Ec$	$-\Delta Ei$	$+\Delta Eh$	$+\Delta Eb$	0
Capital	$+Ic$	$+Ii$			$+I$
Total	Πc	Πi	Sh	Πb	

Using (15) and (16) in (17) we obtain

$$\Pi c = Wi + r \cdot Li - Sh \tag{19}$$

The hypothesis in Rochon that firms investment is given by profits implies

$$Ic = \Pi c \tag{20}$$

$$Ii = \Pi i \tag{21}$$

Using (19) and (20) in (18) we get

$$\Pi i = -Sh + Ii \tag{22}$$

If households spend all of their income ($Sh = 0$), at the end of the production period firms in the consumer goods sector will recover enough liquidity to pay back the initial loan plus interests, and will have positive profits to cover for investment. Demand for capital goods from this sector will have a value exactly equal to costs of production in the investment goods sector, which will be able to pay back its initial loan. However, comparing (21) and (22) it becomes apparent that investment in the capital goods sector remains undetermined – the assumption that firms in this sector invest all of their profits is inappropriate, since profits in this sector are ultimately given by investment in the same sector, so that the equations hold for any level of investment. We must drop equation (21), and keep investment in this sector as exogenous, to determine profits in this sector.

$$Ii = Ii^* \tag{21'}$$

If households' saving is positive, profits in the consumer goods sector will be lower by an amount equal to saving, and profits will however be positive as long as

$$Sh < Wi + r \cdot Li.$$

Sales of investment goods will be lower, and the capital goods sector will not be able to recover enough liquidity to reimburse the initial loan. At the end of the production period the increase in the stock of banks' deposits will equal the increase in the outstanding debt of firms, as in our simpler model.

Let us now allow firms to issue equities to finance investment. Equations (20) and (21′)[16] need to be changed into

$$Ic = \prod c + \Delta Ec \tag{20'}$$

$$\Delta Ei = Ii^* \tag{21''}$$

We may also assume that banks distribute only a share γ of their profits, and cumulate wealth by acquiring equities. We will have

$$Fb = \gamma \cdot (r \cdot Lc + r \cdot Li) \tag{15'}$$

$$\Delta Eb = (1 - \gamma) \cdot (r \cdot Lc + r \cdot Li) \tag{23}$$

The model may now be closed with appropriate assumptions on households' and banks' demand for financial assets, given their relative rate of return.

It remains true, as in our simpler model, that, if households' demand for banks' deposits increases, firms will not recover the initial loan plus interests from sales in the goods or the financial market, unless we modify our equation (23) for banks' behavior, allowing banks to convert any increase in deposits to an increase in their demand for equities.

A more complex model including a central bank and the government sector, which we believe to be entirely compatible with this approach, can be developed along the lines in Zezza and Dos Santos (2004), where it is shown that the major features of the TCM approach, and in particular the endogeneity of money, are maintained.

8.5 Conclusions

In this chapter, we have addressed some puzzles in the Monetary Theory of Production, or Monetary Circuit, namely the determination of aggregate profits within a single period of production when firms have to pay interests on an initial bank loan.

We have shown that the 'profit paradox' disappears when bankers' income arising from interest payments is treated consistently as a source of either demand for goods or demand for financial equities issued by another sector. Our assumption is required for the consistent modeling of the banking sector – if interest payments are obtained, they must be used before the end of the financial period, and this in turn implies that the overall time period for the circuit, which starts when the initial loan is made, and ends when the loan is paid back, is longer than the production period.

We have examined the implications of our approach to TMC – a first major point is that, if households have a positive demand for bank deposits, this implies that consumption and saving decisions must depend on cumulated wealth, and that the analysis of a single production period becomes inappropriate. We also showed how the TMC approach may be reconciled with Keynesian and Kaldorian approaches, and we have shown the similarities with the stock-flow approach adopted by, among others, Godley. In particular, while Godley focuses on the end-of-period stock of loans outstanding, the TMC focuses on the beginning-of-the-period initial finance, but the two approaches are entirely compatible.

We have finally extended our results to a two-sector model, showing that some hypothesis on investment decisions proposed in the TMC literature may be inappropriate.

We hope our contribution will help the development of robust Post-Keynesian models compatible with the TMC approach.

Notes

1. See Graziani (2003).
2. Proceedings are in Fontana and Realfonzo (2005). Arena and Salvadori (2004) is the volume of the proceedings from a previous conference in honor of Graziani.
3. Godley (1996).
4. See Graziani (2003) for a discussion of the differences among a barter economy, a credit economy and a monetary economy.
5. '...there is a gap in (historical) time between production and sales which generates a systemic need for finance' (Godley 2004, p. 127).
6. In the TMC, money is created when a loan is made, and it is destroyed when the loan is paid back. Keen (2010) argues that a different characterization

can be used through a 'revolving fund' where money created by banks is kept, without money destruction. In our view, this approach does not change the functioning of the circuit substantially.

7. I am grateful to Anwar Shaikh for several discussions on this issue.
8. Marc Lavoie pointed out to me – in a comment to a previous draft of this paper – that the same topics we are discussing were present in Lavoie (1987).
9. See Forges-Davanzati, Pacella and Realfonzo (2011), pp. 8–9.
10. See Forges-Davanzati, Pacella and Realfonzo (2011), p. 8, equation [2].
11. Lavoie (2004) has pursued this point. Lavoie (2004) has pursued this point. Cavalieri (2004), adopting a point of view critical of the circuitists approach, states that 'In a circuit approach the possibility of using a stock-flow monetary framework appears problematic' (p. 7).
12. If we assume that households' demand for bank deposits is positive, households obtain an additional source of income from interest payments on deposits. Such payments will reduce banks' profits by the same amount, so that changes in the interest rate on deposits in this simple model will affect the distribution of final demand between consumption and investment goods, but will not alter the value of liquidity that firms can recover by selling either consumer goods or equities.
13. See Graziani (2003), p. 118.
14. Ibid.
15. I am grateful to Marcello Messori for addressing this point in a comment on a previous draft. Messori notes that, if banks are able to obtain goods or equities in exchange for money created by opening a line of credit, they may also create money to acquire any level of equities they desire to hold. In our view, addressing this point properly would require extending our model to define in detail how the market price of equities is determined. We simply note that, in our simpler approach, if we assume that firms finance their investment decisions by obtaining credit from banks, it does not matter whether credit is obtained by opening a line of credit on firms' deposits, or by selling equities to banks, but the amount of money created at the beginning of the circuit should depend on firms' decisions, which may or may not be met by adequate supply of funds from banks, but we don't see how banks can pump more money into the system in excess of the amount which is demanded from firms.
16. We still need to keep investment in the capital goods sector to be exogenous: if we revert to equation (21) investment and profits in this sector will still be undetermined with the addition of equities.

References

Accoce, J.-V. and T. Mouakil (2007) 'The Monetary Circuit Approach: A Stock-flow Consistent Model,' in E. Hein and A. Truger (eds) *Money, Distribution and Economic Policy: Alternatives to Orthodox Macroeconomics* (Cheltenham: Edward Elgar), pp. 66–96.

Arena, R. and N. Salvadori (2004) *Money, Credit and the Role of the State* (Aldershot: Ashgate).

Bruun, C. and C. Heyn-Johnsen (2009) 'The Paradox of Monetary Profits: An Obstacle to Understanding Financial and Economic Crisis?' *Economics Discussion Papers*, no. 2009-52, http://www.economics-ejournal.org/economics/discussionpapers/2009-52.

Cavalieri, D. (1994) 'La teoria monetaria della produzione di Keynes e i teorici del circuito: a proposito di un libro di Augusto Graziani,' *Studi Economici* 49(54): 133–52.

Cavalieri, D. (2004) 'On Some Equilibrium and Disequilibrium Theories of Endogenous Money: A Structuralist View,' *History of Economic Ideas* 12(3): 51–83.

Fontana, G. and R. Realfonzo (2005) *The Monetary Theory of Production: Tradition and Perspectives* (London: Palgrave Macmillan).

Forges-Davanzati, G., A. Pacella and R. Realfonzo (2009) 'Fiscal Policy in the Monetary Theory of Production: An Alternative to the "New Consensus" Approach,' *Journal of Post Keynesian Economics* 31(4): 605–21.

Forges-Davanzati, G. and R. Patalano (2011) 'The Equilibrium Problem in the Monetary Circuit Approach: A Critical Assessment,' Working paper.

Godley, W. (1996) 'Money, Finance and National Income Determination: An Integrated Approach,' Working Paper No. 167 (Annandale-on-Hudson, NY: Levy Economics Institute of Bard College).

Godley, W. (2004) 'Weaving Cloth from Graziani's Thread: Endogenous Money in a Simple (But Complete) Keynesian Model,' in R. Arena and N. Salvadori (eds) *Money, Credit and the Role of the State: Essays in Honour of Augusto Graziani* (Aldershot: Ashgate), pp. 127–35.

Godley, W. and F. Cripps (1983) *Macroeconomics* (London: Fontana).

Godley, W. and M. Lavoie (2007) *Monetary Economics: An Integrated Approach to Credit, Money, Income, Production and Wealth* (Basingstoke, UK: Palgrave Macmillan).

Graziani, A. (2003) *The Monetary Theory of Production* (Cambridge: Cambridge University Press).

Keen, S. (2010) 'Solving the Paradox of Monetary Profits,' *Economics Discussion Papers*, Vol. 4, 2010-31, October, http://dx.doi.org/10.5018/economics-ejournal.ja.2010-31.

Lavoie, M. (1987) 'Monnaie et Production: Une Synthèse de la Théorie du Circuit,' *Économies et Sociétés* 20(9): 65–101.

Lavoie, M. (2004) 'Circuit and Coherent Stock-flow Accounting,' in R. Arena and N. Salvadori (eds) *Money, Credit and the Role of the State* (Aldershot: Ashgate), pp. 134–49.

Messori, M. and A. Zazzaro (2004) 'Monetary Profits Within the Monetary Circuit: Ponzi Finance or "Mors Tua Vita Mea"?', working paper no. 200, Dipartimento di Economia, Università delle Marche.

Parguez, A. (2004) 'The Solution of the Paradox of Profits,' in R. Arena and N. Salvadori (eds) *Money, Credit and the Role of the State* (Aldershot: Ashgate), pp. 255–68.

Rochon, L.-P. (2005) 'The Existence of Monetary Profits Within the Monetary Circuit,' in G. Fontana and R. Realfonzo (eds) *Monetary Theory of Production: Tradition and Perspectives* (Basingstoke: Palgrave Macmillan).

Seccareccia, M. (2003) 'Pricing, Investment and the Financing of Production Within the Framework of the Monetary Circuit: Some Preliminary Evidence,' in L.-P. Rochon and S. Rossi (eds) *Modern Theories of Money: The Nature and Role of Money in Capitalist Economies* (Cheltenham: Edward Elgar), pp. 173–97.

Stone, R. (1966) 'The Social Accounts from a Consumer Point of View,' *Review of Income and Wealth* 12(1): 1–33.

Zezza, G. (2004) 'Some Simple, Consistent Models of the Monetary Circuit,' Working Paper No. 405 (Annandale-on-Hudson, NY: Levy Economics Institute of Bard College).

Zezza, G. and C.H. Dos Santos (2004) 'The Role of Monetary Policy in Post-Keynesian Stock-flow Consistent Macroeconomic Growth Models,' in M. Lavoie and M. Seccareccia (eds) *Central Banking in the Modern World: Alternative Perspectives* (Cheltenham: Edward Elgar), pp. 183–210.

9

The Stock-flow Consistent Approach with Active Financial Markets*

Jo Michell and Jan Toporowski

9.1 Introduction

Wynne Godley is best known for his insightful forecasting using stock-flow consistent models. His insistence that economic stocks and flows should be consistently laid out was also, if less obviously, an insistence that all economic variables are interrelated. Accordingly, production could not be carried out without distributional implications. More importantly, for the theory of a modern credit economy, the financial flows that arise in the process of production and exchange have to be integrated into the model of the economy at large.

Stock-flow consistency has clear implications for economic forecasting. However, it also has very critical implications for econometrics, in its modern sense of deriving theory from statistical data. For, if statistics are themselves the product of a stock-flow consistent taxonomy, then there are no independent variables, but all variables are interdependent (Godley and Lavoie, 2007; Toporowski, 2001). One interpretation of this interdependence could be the New Classical view that an economy is at all times more or less in successive states of general equilibrium, or shifting between them under the impact of various 'shocks,' usually identified with hindsight. In such a situation, forecasting is only possible on the basis of probability distributions derived from the frequency distribution of past 'shocks.'

We argue here that a disequilibrium interpretation is also possible. This could be a Wicksellian cumulative process derived from non-equilibrium transactions in markets over real time. Two situations may

* This chapter draws on discussions that we have had with Jago Penrose and Marc Lavoie. The authors take full responsibility for all remaining errors.

give rise to such a cumulative process. One is capital market inflation, in which the rising values of financial assets give rise to wealth effects behind which lie bank disintermediation and overcapitalization of large corporate businesses. The other situation is overcapitalization itself, a form of liquidity preference in which non-financial firms enter into the business of financial intermediation.

This chapter aims to illustrate the problems of capturing the subtleties of changes in financial structure and firm behavior in a pure stock-flow consistent model, through a discussion of the issues surrounding firms' decisions in financially developed capitalist systems, and in particular, overcapitalization and liquidity management. These concepts emerge from the work of Kalecki, Steindl and Minsky.

By considering these ideas in the context of the constraint of stock-flow consistency, the problems of incorporating financial development, cyclical behavior and heterogeneous agents into a formal stock-flow model are illustrated. Insights are also gained into Kaleckian ideas on the relationship between investment and profits, and, in particular, the financial counterparts to the identities linking these real-sector flows. The exercise also serves to highlight some of the logical implications of firm overcapitalization and liquidity management that emerge when considered in a stock-flow consistent framework.

9.2 Simple 'classical' system

The starting point for the discussion will be a simple system in which firms borrow in order to invest in new capital, all saving takes place in the household sector, and the only form of financial assets are bank deposits and loans. This system is shown in Table 9.1.

Following Godley and Lavoie (2007), the table shows a 'transactions flow matrix' – a specification of all the potential real and financial flows in the model economy. This is essentially an abstract representation of the accounts published as the 'flow of funds' in many countries. In the matrix, positive values represent sources of funds while negative values represent uses of funds. For each sector, total sources and uses of funds must be equal, implying that columns must sum to zero. Likewise, the constraint that all flows must 'go somewhere' implies that all rows must also sum to zero – all liabilities issued must appear as assets elsewhere in the system, and all spending in the real sector must be matched by expenditure. The firm and bank sectors are split into a current account and a capital account. This allows for the explicit inclusion into the matrix of profits and investment flows.

Table 9.1 'Classical' case: investment funded by bank loans – no profits in firm sector

	Households	Firms (cur)	Firms (cap)	Banks (cur)	Banks (cur)	Total
Consumption	$-C$	$+C$				0
Investment		$+I$	$-I$			0
GDP		$[Y]$				
Wages	$+W$	$-W$				0
Firm Profits						0
Bank Profits				$-S_b$	$+S_b$	0
Deposit interest	$+r_D \cdot D_{(-1)}$			$-r_D \cdot D_{(-1)}$		0
Loan interest		$-r_L \cdot L_{(-1)}$		$+r_L \cdot L_{(-1)}$		0
Net fin. balance	$[S_h]$	[0]	$[-I]$	[0]	$[S_b]$	0
Chge in Deposits	$-\Delta D$				$+\Delta D$	0
Chge in Loans			$+\Delta L$		$-\Delta L$	0
Total	0	0	0	0	0	0

It should be stressed that stock-flow consistent models, in the form presented by Godley and Lavoie, contain two broad 'layers' of constraints that define the structure of the model. The first such layer is that imposed by the system of accounting matrices that defines the configuration of stocks, flows, and – in more complex models – asset revaluations that define the broad structure of the model, particularly the financial system. As this set of constraints takes the form of a set of pure of accounting relationships, no assumptions about the causality of the system can be included in, or inferred from, a model of this type. Assumptions on the causality underlying the functioning of the economic system are then introduced by the careful construction of a set of behavioral equations that fit together in such a way as to ensure that the stock-flow constraints cannot be breached. It is thus the case that a wide range of behavioral models can be constructed on the basis of a given set of stock-flow accounting relations. Rather than constructing a fully specified behavioral model, this chapter focuses on a sequence of stock-flow accounting relationships. This allows for consideration of both the problems of modeling financial development – which is here captured through a series of modification to the set of stock-flow relationships – and of the potential for interesting behaviors that are problematic to capture in a fully specified algebraic model.

Returning to the matrix, the zero totals that enforce stock-flow consistency allow for one equation to be obtained from each row and column of the system. In the matrix shown above, the rows are trivial and can thus be omitted, giving the following system of equations. It should be noted that this system of equations is over-determined: any one equation in the system is implied by the other three.

$$W + r_D \cdot D_{(-1)} = C + \Delta D \tag{1}$$

$$C + I = W + r_L \cdot L_{(-1)} \tag{2}$$

$$I = \Delta L \tag{3}$$

$$\Delta D + r_L \cdot L_{(-1)} = \Delta L + r_D \cdot D_{(-1)} \tag{4}$$

(See Table 9.1 for definitions of terms.)

This system bears at least a passing resemblance to a classical system of perfect competition – firms do not make any profits so all revenue is returned to households in the form of wages or interest payments. The system differs from a classical model, however, in the fact that no restrictions are imposed on the division of household income between these two flows. In particular, there is no requirement that the marginal productivity of factors of production determines the distribution of household incomes between interest and wage incomes.[1]

The assumption of zero entrepreneurial profits means that firms have only one option for the financing of investment – to increase their financial liabilities by obtaining fresh bank loans. In any period, the total spent on investment will be exactly the same as the net volume of new loans extended by the banking system – thus the total outstanding stock of bank loans will at any point in time equal the total spent on investment up until that point in time.

An entry is included in the matrix for bank profits. This allows for the possible existence of a margin between the rates of interest on bank loans and deposits. However, before examining the implications of the inclusion of banking profits in the model, we consider the simpler case in which banks are assumed to operate costlessly and without profits. This assumption requires that lending and deposit rates must be equal and therefore – if we put aside the possibility of non-performing loans for the time being – that the total volume of loans outstanding must, at any given point in time, equal the total volume of deposits held by households. The volume of deposits will, in the absence of bank profits, therefore also be equal to the total amount spent on investment up until that point.

If the system were constrained to operate according to marginalist principles, in any given period banks would lend to firms up until the point at which the expected returns on new investment were equal to the rate of interest on loans. This rate of interest would also be that which was just enough to bring forth the quantity of additional deposits needed to finance this additional investment. This is the standard neoclassical view in which 'deposits finance investment.'

The alternative view is that in which bank lending leads deposits. This version originates with Withers (1920), and is subsequently found in both Keynes (1936, chapter 7) and Hayek (1933) and is emphasized by post-Keynesians such as Chick (1986). In this version of the story, economic expansion is led by the decisions of banks and firms. Banks extend loans to the firms sector which invests, using the additional deposits created by the banking system to purchase capital goods from other firms. Receipts for firms are increased by the extra spending, and, in the current model, must therefore accrue as additional wages to households.

Any successful decision to undertake investment by firms will thus result in an increase in the level of deposits held by households as the financial counterpart to saving, as well as expanding the banks' balance sheet. This will then give rise to increased claims on future output in the form of deposit interest. Additional interest payable by firms will be offset by additional interest received on deposits (Toporowski, 2010). But these will be held by households since, by assumption here, firms have no net liquidity or saving. If the investment undertaken increases output, this will be realized through these interest payments as well as potentially lower prices or higher wages. Conversely, if investment is unsuccessful, households will have claims on output in the form of interest payments that firms are unable to meet unless wages are lowered or prices increased.

The preceding discussion highlights some of the potential pitfalls of reasoning in terms of systems of money flows. All of the equations that can be derived from the matrix are *ex post* identities. One must be extremely careful about the hazards of introducing implicit assumptions about causation into any conclusions drawn about the workings of the system. For example, the previous discussion demonstrated that, with all other entries in the matrix held constant and assuming zero banking profits, in order to have an increased level of spending on investment, there must be an equivalent increase in the level of loans and deposits in the system. This is a very different proposition to the statement that firms are able to automatically increase the level of investment, and therefore output, as long as they are able to gain access to bank loans. The identities of the matrix are equally compatible with the reverse causation: because a higher level of household deposits requires higher investment, the system could be read as showing that higher household saving will result in higher investment. This, of course, is the view that was refuted by Keynes in his 'paradox of thrift.' The key point is that the intentions of units at the micro level do not necessarily translate into the equivalent intersectoral flows at the macro level. The transactions matrix can only illustrate at the macro level the various potential logical outcomes of the flow system, regardless of whether these outcomes are compatible with the intentions and expectations of the agents that give rise to them.

Before introducing the first modification to the matrix, let us consider the implications of dropping the assumption that banks make zero profits. If a margin between lending and deposit rates is introduced, while retaining the assumption that the banking system operates with no costs such as wages, the only option is for the rate of accumulation of loans and deposits to diverge by an equal rate. Thus, if the rate of interest set on loans is above that set on deposits, the volume of loans outstanding will expand faster than the volume of household deposits. The net worth of the banking system will thus increase – assets are expanding faster than liabilities. A process of this sort will result in households 'owning' less than the total capital stock, as the volume of deposits held by households will be less than the total spent on investment. A positive spread between deposit and lending rates could also be used as a strategy by the banking system in an attempt to avoid crisis if firms are unable to meet their interest payments and consequently default on their loans – leaving banks with liabilities they cannot meet in the form of deposit interest.

There is one final possibility allowable by the current configuration of the matrix: that the rate of deposit interest is set *above* the loan rate. Consider the case in which the entire firms sector has defaulted on its debts, and no further loans are being issued: $\Delta L = r_L \cdot L_{(-1)} = 0$. Firms then have no outgoings other than wages and no receipts other than consumption spending, meaning these two flows must be equal. Banks could then continue to pay their interest obligations by continuing to credit household deposits with additional deposits. A situation of this type is clearly not sustainable indefinitely since it would require the banking sector to issue to each other assets to correspond to the growing deposits of households.

9.3 Profits in the firms sector

If we remove the assumption that the profits of the firms sector are zero, as shown in Table 9.2, it becomes possible for firms to be in a position in

Table 9.2 Retained earnings – not all receipts 'recycled' through the banking sector

	Households	Firms (cur)	Firms (cap)	Banks	Total
Consumption	$-C$	$+C$			0
Investment		$+I$	$-I$		0
GDP		$[Y]$			
Wages	$+W$	$-W$			0
Profits		$-S_f$	$+S_f$		0
Deposit interest	$+r_D \cdot D_{(-1)}$			$-r_D \cdot D_{(-1)}$	0
Loan interest		$-r_L \cdot L_{(-1)}$		$+r_L \cdot L_{(-1)}$	0
Net fin. balance	$[S_h]$	[0]	$[S_f - I]$	[0]	
Change in Deposits	$-\Delta D$			$+\Delta D$	0
Change in Loans			$+\Delta L$	$-\Delta L$	0
Total	0	0	0	0	0

which revenues are not all returned to households in the form of wages and interest payments.[2] This reduces the firms sector's reliance on bank loans to finance investment. By using earnings to finance investment, firms are able to 'short-circuit' the banking system thus avoiding the need to pay interest on loans taken out to finance investment. This may then have second-round effects in that the increase in net revenues in future periods may also be diverted to further investment rather than spent on consumption by the household sector.

How can we get from a situation such as that shown in the previous matrix, in which all income is returned to households in the form of wages and interest, to a situation in which firms are able to 'recycle' revenues back into investment? The only way that firms can 'directly' divert a portion of current income to investment – rather than this occurring via the banking system – is for outgoings to be reduced relative to receipts. In the current configuration of the model this implies a reduction in either wages or interest payments relative to total income. Viewed in neoclassical terms, this implies that the model has departed from a world of perfect competition, with firms able to exert some degree of monopoly power, allowing for a mark-up between costs and prices.

In the previous matrix, the possibility of 'forced saving' existed through banks extending loans to firms. Investment could thus take place and would result in deposits accruing to households as the counterpart to loan-financed investment. With the possibility of a mark-up on prices over costs, firm's profits become another mechanism by which saving, and thus investment, can be 'forced' into the system. The advantage to firms in this case is that new investment can now take place without a corresponding increase in liabilities on their balance sheets. In the extreme case, in which all new investment is financed out of profits, all investment results in an increase in net worth for the firms sector with no increase in liabilities.

The difference between this case and the previous one in which all new investment is financed through bank lending occurs purely in the financial sector – exactly the same level of consumption and increase in the capital stock could take place in each of the two scenarios. Adjustments of the price of consumption goods relative to wages thus allows for a range of financial sector outcomes that are compatible with a single set of real-sector flow magnitudes.

This matrix may be utilized to shed some light on the well-known Kalecki–Steindl profit reflux equation. This can be obtained by extracting the *net financial balance* row from the matrix, and rearranging to give

$$S_f = I - S_h \tag{5}$$

The usual interpretation of this identity is that an increase in household saving – or the failure of it to decrease in the face of a drop in investment – will reduce the retained profits of firms. Furthermore, the only variable over which firms have direct influence is investment. Thus, investment is seen as the source of profits at the aggregate level, with a higher level of investment resulting in a higher level of firm's profits, and thus an increase in the financial assets of firms: 'If additional investment is financed by bank credit, the spending of the amounts in question will cause equal amounts of saved profits to accumulate as bank deposits (Kalecki, 1954, p. 50).

In this configuration of the model, another possibility is shown. If firms are assumed at this stage not to hold financial assets such as bank deposits, firms' net income after interest and dividends must be used to pay off the loans used to finance investment. Thus, if profits increase to a level greater than the amount spent on investment, the balance sheet of the banking system will contract as repayment of debts cancels both deposits and loans. The contraction of household deposits is a necessary counterpart to the negative financial balance that must be run by the sector in order that firm profits can exceed investment. Conversely, a lower level of profit implies higher household saving in the form of bank deposits, and hence greater firm indebtedness. Without the inclusion of a government or external sector, the worst possible position for the firms sector is just to break even: $S_f = 0$ and $S_h = I$. By expanding the model to include a government sector and external sector, and allowing firms to borrow to cover operating losses as well as investment, the full version of the Kalecki–Steindl equation[3] could be incorporated. The inclusion of these sectors results in the possibility of the firms sector operating at a loss and hence being forced to incur increased debt if the government surplus and current account deficit combine with household saving to exceed investment.

9.4 Excess capital

The next modification we make to the flow model is to allow the holding of bank deposits by firms, as shown in Table 9.3. With this change comes a much broader range of possible ways in which the configuration of assets and liabilities in the system can evolve. By introducing the possibility that firms may choose to hold financial assets rather than engage in productive investment, the potential for overcapitalization of the firms sector arises.

Overcapitalization refers to the 'holding of financial liabilities in excess of those needed to undertake production' (Toporowski, 2008). This is obviously not possible in the previous stages of the model in which the only uses of funds available to firms are the payment of wages, and investment in capital goods. This changes once firms have the opportunity to accumulate funds in the form of bank deposits – as long as a firm has both financial assets and liabilities on its balance sheet it is, by the above definition, holding excess capital.

Table 9.3 Simple overcapitalization: excess capital held in the form of deposits

	Households	Firms (cur)	Firms (cap)	Banks	Total
Consumption	$-C$	$+C$			0
Investment		$+I$	$-I$		0
GDP		$[Y]$			
Wages	$+W$	$-W$			0
Profits		$-S_f$	$+S_f$		0
Deposit interest	$+r_D \cdot D_{h(-1)}$	$+r_D \cdot D_{f(-1)}$		$-r_D \cdot D_{(-1)}$	0
Loan interest		$-r_L \cdot L_{(-1)}$		$+r_L \cdot L_{(-1)}$	0
Net fin. balance	$[S_h]$	[0]	$[S_f - I]$	[0]	
Change in Deposits	$-\Delta D_h$		$-\Delta D_f$	$+\Delta D$	0
Change in Loans			$+\Delta L$	$-\Delta L$	0
Total	0	0	0	0	0

What are the implications of the holdings of excess capital by firms? This depends in part on the way in which this capital is accumulated. It is argued by (Toporowski, 2008, p. 8) that

> ...it may be supposed that since saving equals investment, it is not possible for firms to hold excess capital, except as net debt issued by either households, the government, or the foreign sector. This is true if it is assumed that all production is, and has only ever been, undertaken by capitalistic firms.

In this view, if we take as given that our model represents a system of capitalistic production, that is production using capital equipment, the only sector that could issue this net debt is the household sector. Thus, as a consequence of the household sector consuming in excess of its income, it would emit liabilities the counterpart of which would be financial assets held by the firms sector. The problem with this is that in order for the firms sector to be overcapitalized, it must have issued financial liabilities in order to finance its purchase of financial assets. Who then will hold these financial liabilities as assets? If these assets are held by households, these then would offset household liabilities, resulting in a neutral net financial position, rather than a position of net issuance of debt.

There is another alternative suggested by the current configuration of the model. The possibility of the household sector being in a negative net financial position is excluded by the assumption that households are unable to issue any financial liabilities. However, the firms sector as a whole may now hold excess capital simply by having both loans and deposits on its balance sheet. How would such a situation arise? Consider the two following extreme cases in which the total stock of deposits that are the counterpart to loan-financed investment end up on respectively on the balance sheets of households, in the first instance, and firms in the second.

The standard 'sectoral deficits' story, in which a surplus in the household sector finances investment in the corporate sector via the banking system, is as follows: banks create loans and deposits simultaneously by crediting the accounts of firms at the same time as issuing new loans. This money is used to finance new investment. The additional receipts for firms from selling capital goods, over and above that received as the result of household spending on consumption, is returned to households in the form of wages, by transferring deposits from the accounts of firms to the accounts of households. As wages total an amount greater than that spent on consumption, the household sector has unspent deposits at the end of period equal to the amount spent on investment, and to the volume of new loans created. Thus, each period, $S_h = \Delta D_h = \Delta L$ and $S_f = 0$.

This is entirely compatible with the classical theory: in subsequent periods, the additional output that results from new investment will accrue as interest, via the banking system, to the household sector, allowing for increased consumption. Neoclassical theory assumes that all prices, and the rate of interest, will adjust such that the amount of investment undertaken by firms will be of exactly the amount that will give a return equal to the amount of saving desired by households.

Consider now the alternative wherein instead of firms paying out in wages (and interest, in periods other than the initial one) an amount equal to total receipts, they are able to pay wages and interest such that $C = W + r_D \cdot D_{h(-1)}$ – wages and interest payments on deposits exactly cover the amount spent on consumption. If households were to spend the same amount on consumption as in the previous example, they will now exhaust all of their income and see no change in the level of deposits held. Firms, on the other hand, will have an excess of income over outgoings equivalent to the amount spent on investment, which will be returned as deposits.

Note that the *real sector* outcome in each of the two scenarios is identical: a proportion $I/(C + I)$ of total output is directed to investment, which is by definition equal to saving. The differences between the two cases lie in the configuration of financial assets and liabilities at the end of the period. This 'accounting' difference is significant, as the owners of deposits will receive interest payments on their 'lending', while issuers of liabilities in the form of loans must pay interest.

In the first of the two cases, the final configuration of deposits and liabilities represents net lending from the household sector to the firms sector. The investment undertaken by firms must thus generate increased output in future periods of an amount great enough to cover the interest liabilities resulting from this lending. In the second case of 'overcapitalization,' there has been no intersectoral net lending – the increase in deposits held by the firms sector is equal to the increase in loans it holds. Thus, the cost of borrowing to the firms sector as a whole is in this case proportional to the margin between the loan and deposit rates of interest, rather than the absolute value of the loan rate of interest, as is usually assumed in discussion of the effect on investment of changes in the rate of interest (Toporowski, 2010). The per-period cost of additional excess capital financed from bank lending is thus the following:

$$\Delta L(r_L - r_D)$$

Toporowski describes the situation where investment continues to be financed as in this way, with further investment in subsequent periods also financed out of bank lending:

> What happens if firms finance their investment entirely through debt? After a number of years, firms will end up with a stock of debt that is exactly equal to the sum of their expenditures on capital formation over those years. In addition... all firms will have deposited into their banks retained profits exactly equal to the amount that the firms have spent on capital formation. The banking system will have deposit liabilities to firms that exactly equal to the amount that the banks have advanced to firms to pay for that capital formation. The firms sector as a whole will have debts equal to the capital equipment that has been purchased over the years. But those debts will be exactly hedged (for the capitalist firms as a whole) by cash deposits in the banking system. If the financing structure of all firms corresponds to some representative 'average' firm, then the financing of every firm will be perfectly hedged with bank deposits. (Toporowski, 2010, pp. 2–3)

There is another possibility: once firms have undertaken investment financed in the way shown in Table 9.3, at the start of the subsequent period the firms sector will be holding deposits equal to the total expenditure in the current period. Firms thus only *need* to expand the liability side of their balance sheet in subsequent periods if they wish to invest a greater amount than in the current period – or if they wish to increase their level of excess capital. This would be equivalent to a switch to financing through retained profits.

In either the case of 'complete overcapitalization,' in which firms end up with a stock of debt and deposits matched by the total spent on investment, or the case of 'marginal overcapitalization,' in which the stock of debt is incrementally increased as desired investment exceeds the stock of retained profits, the rate of interest – and thus the balance sheet of the firms sector – behave in a quite different way to that of standard marginalist theory. As previously noted, it is the *margin* between the lending and deposit rates faced by firms that represents the cost of overcapitalization – and in this example, real investment.[4] Thus, the standard view of the relationship between the investment decisions of firms and the conduct of interest rate policy by the central bank – higher bank rate will, *ceteris paribus*, induce lower investment – may not hold unless a higher bank rate in some way results in a wider spread between lending and deposit rates.[5] Similarly, if the central bank were to operate in such a way as to attempt to restrict the availability of loans through quantitative measures, textbook theory would argue that the reduced availability of credit and the associated interest rate rises should ensure that only more potentially profitable investments would be undertaken. However, if the spread between lending and deposit rates does not widen, the cost of investment will not rise. The distribution of credit among firms may in this case be determined by factors other than expected returns on investment. In practice, credit restrictions would increase the margin between deposit and lending rates.

If we assume for the time being that all deposits will be held by firms and not households, what factors will determine the level of overcapitalization of firms – what proportion of the total spent on investment will be held as deposits funded by equivalent outstanding loans?[6] Liquidity preference due to uncertainty about the future is one obvious answer to this question. Another possibility is that the banking system may in some way induce the firms sector to hold excess liquidity, through monopoly power over firms or by forcing firms to borrow for longer periods than required.

It is at this point that some limitations of the accounting identities come into focus. Firstly, just from inspection of the transactions matrix, there does not appear to be any direct connection between real investment and the financial assets and liabilities of the firms sector. Given any initial set of valid values for the matrix, spending on investment can be increased by any amount – without violating any of the identities implied by the matrix – as long as profits are increased by the same amount. However, we know that an increase in investment cannot take place without a prior expansion of lending by banks to the firms sector – even if all this additional spending remains within the firms sector as retained profits. It is, of course, possible that firms will borrow from banks to undertake investment, and then in the same period use the retained earnings to repay the bank loans, thus resulting in a set of net transactions that show only an increase in profits and investment.

A second issue, and one that to which we will return later, is the problem of the level of disaggregation in the model. By examining the money flows into and out of a number of sectors of the economy, the dynamics of changes within each of those sectors is obscured from view. There are many ways in which this could mask important economic behavior. One possibility relates to variations in the financing structure of businesses within the firms sector – although in the overcapitalization case it appears that the firms sector as a whole is fully hedged against its liabilities as deposits circulate within the sector as a whole and do not end up in the hands of households, it is possible that a redistribution of assets and liabilities is taking place within the sector. For example, it is possible that larger firms are more profitable than smaller firms, due to monopoly pricing for example. This would mean smaller firms requiring a higher level of loan finance to undertake investment, while large firms are able to invest using retained earnings. In this case, some part of the deposits that are the counterpart to the loans used to finance investment end up not on the balance sheets of the small firms that took out the loans, but on those of the larger monopolist firms. This type of effect could be incorporated into the model by splitting the firms sector into large and small firms. However, each additional division of the system in this way increases, by a significant margin, the complexity of any fully specified behavioural model built upon the matrix. Furthermore, the intrasectoral flow dynamics may be more subtle than can be captured by a simple two-way division: there may a gradation of financing structures as firms increase in size, or different financing structures depending on the type of industry in which the firm operates. In particular, financing of investment by means of retained profits would result in increases in fixed capital assets, but with no change in the loan liabilities of firms. There would be an increase or decrease in wage revenue and profits depending on whether there was an increase or decrease in investment. But there would be no change in the financial balances of the firms sector as a whole.

9.5 Equity issuance

The final development that will be discussed is the inclusion of equities as an asset class. In most models, equity issuance is seen as an alternative way for firms to obtain access to investment funds in the form of the savings of other sectors – primarily the household sector – often channeled via institutional intermediaries such as pension funds. The issuance of equity allows for the expansion of investment without the concomitant expansion of debt liabilities.

Much of the recent literature on 'financialization' tends to focus on issues of 'shareholder value' – models are constructed which examine the effects on growth of the way in which firms allocate earnings between real investment and dividend payouts, with increasing shareholder power resulting in a focus on short-term profits at the expense of longer-term investment.[7]

It is argued here that there are important aspects of firm behavior that are overlooked in these models. These relate to both firms' decisions on the structure of liabilities issued, and to the decisions of firms on the allocation of funds between real and financial assets. It is argued by Toporowski (2000) that, rather than issuing equity for the purposes of financing new investment in real assets, those firms that have access to the capital markets use them to maintain internal liquidity by raising cash against previous investment projects. Equity issuance is thus used as a mechanism to maintain a state of overcapitalization following the depletion of internal funds by spending on investment projects. Furthermore, when faced with a situation of rising prices in the equities markets, it may become profitable for overcapitalized firms to allocate excess capital to financial assets in preference to engaging in real investment.

Table 9.4 shows the transactions matrix used in the previous examples, modified to include a new class of financial assets in the form of equities. The number of equities issued is represented by e, the price is represented by p, and the dividend payout per-share by d. Two additional financial flows are thus shown in the transactions matrix: the

Table 9.4 Speculative overcapitalization: firms hold excess capital as financial securities

	Households	**Firms (cur)**	**Firms (cap)**	**Banks**	**Total**
Consumption	$-C$	$+C$			0
Investment		$+I$	$-I$		0
GDP		$[Y]$			
Wages	$+W$	$-W$			0
Profits		$-S_f$	$+S_f$		0
Deposit interest	$+r_D \cdot D_{h(-1)}$	$+r_D \cdot D_{f(-1)}$		$-r_D \cdot D_{(-1)}$	0
Loan interest		$-r_L \cdot L_{(-1)}$		$+r_L \cdot L_{(-1)}$	0
Dividend payments	$+d \cdot e_{h(-1)}$	$-d \cdot e_{h(-1)}$			0
Net fin. balance	$[S_h]$	[0]	$[S_f - I]$	[0]	
Change in Deposits	$-\Delta D_h$		$-\Delta D_f$	$+\Delta D$	0
Change in Loans			$+\Delta L$	$-\Delta L$	0
Change in Equity issuance	$-\Delta e_h \cdot p_e$		$+\Delta e_h \cdot p_e$		0
Total	0	0	0	0	0

change in equity holdings by the household sector, and the dividend payout based on holdings in the previous period.

It was argued in the previous section that the cost to the firms sector of holding liquidity in the form of deposits depends on the level of profitability of firms, or equivalently the level of household saving – if firms do not turn a profit then any liquidity held by the firms sector must be borrowed from the banking sector, with the margin between deposit and lending rates as the cost of this liquidity. Note that this liquidity is not borrowed from the household sector – both the loans and deposits that are 'created' with new bank lending appear on the balance sheets of firms.

Once firms gain access to the capital markets, the issuance of equity provides an alternative to debt as a way of maintaining a state of over-capitalization. By issuing fresh equity, firms can replenish their stocks of liquidity, using the returns on previous investment to fund the dividend payments that they become liable for with the issuance of new stock. The issue of new equity, purchased by households, transfers bank deposits from households (or other firms) to firms issuing equity.

The introduction of equities as an asset class also allows for the consideration of capital gains – something that presents problems in the context of a flow-of-funds analysis, as the prices of equities can change without resulting in any intersectoral flows.[8]

Broadly speaking, there are two reasons why the prices of equities would change in the absence of any new issuance of shares. The first is the appearance of some new piece of information on the prospective returns from real investment. If there is a rise in the expected level of dividend payments, money flows will arise as a result of funds being reallocated between bank deposits and securities in the portfolios of households. Any rise in retained profits, in the form of increased firms' bank deposits, would reinforce the expectation of a higher dividend and increase the potential value of equity. The second possibility arises from the fact that, once a rise in the prices of shares has taken place, the expectation of further rises in share prices and thus the prospect of capital gains for the owners of equity may cause further inflows into these assets. In turn, this inflow of funds causes prices to rise, validating the judgment of those astute enough to have seen them coming.

In the case of equity-financed investment, there would be a reduction in the bank deposits of the households (or firms) buying new equity. However, there would then be a corresponding increase in the bank deposits of firms as a result of the investment expenditure. Accordingly, on the balance sheet of the firms sector, the new equity liabilities would be balanced by bank deposits. In addition, of course, firm balance sheets would also show further increases on the asset side in the form of new fixed capital equipment.

As always, in a closed flow-of-funds system, a flow into a class of assets cannot happen in isolation – all flows must originate somewhere. If all equity is initially held by households, how can household buying of equity in response to some exogenous event cause a rise in share prices? Again the problem of aggregation in a stock-flow model shows itself – what is required is that some subdivision of the household sector is willing to purchase equities at a price higher than that which was paid by the current holders. There is thus a redistribution of the ownership of equity within the household sector, accompanied by a rise in the prices of shares. There must also be a corresponding intra-sectoral flow in the opposite direction representing the payment for the newly purchased shares. This is likely to take the form of a redistribution of bank deposits to offset the change in equity holdings.

If it is assumed that all purchases of equity in the secondary markets by households are undertaken using bank deposits as payment, there is thus a limit to the extent to which price inflation in the capital markets can take place, set by the total stock of deposits in the household system – eventually the distribution of equities and deposits within the household sector will take on a configuration such that no further redistribution and price rises are possible, without further deposits becoming available to the household sector to use as means of payment.

Although, at first glance, the impression given by the matrix is that households are the only sector which holds equities, we may also consider the situation wherein newly issued equities are purchased by other firms within the corporate sector – in this situation there will be a reallocation of deposits *within* the firms sector and an increase in both the holding and issuance of equities within the sector. However, none of these changes will result in an intersectoral flow of funds, and thus an entry on the transactions matrix. A change in the relative wealth of the household and firms sectors is possible without any entry appearing on the flow matrix, in both the case of a redistribution of equities within the household sector and within the firms sector. The only changes that will be visible in the current schema are those which involve a change in the total holdings of equities by households.

What are the consequences of the holding of equities by the firms sector? In a setting of rising prices in equity markets, overcapitalized firms face a trade-off in how to allocate excess capital between real investment, deposits and equities – it is possible that the expected capital gains on equities will be great enough to offset the cost of overcapitalization (Toporowski, 2008). The conditions under which this will be the case depends initially on the historical profitability of firms, that is to what extent the financial assets corresponding to previous investment have accrued on the balance sheets of households or firms, and upon whether equity was initially purchased by households or firms. We can examine each combination of cases in turn.

Consider first the case wherein firms collectively have no retained profits, so that the deposits that correspond to real saving and investment are all held in the household sector, so $S_h = I = D_h = L$. Now, as argued before, if they wish to overcapitalize, the cost to firms will be the margin between lending and deposit rates, as any deposits held by the firms sector will have to be obtained through bank lending. If firms now begin to issue equity as a way of raising further capital, these equities may be purchased either by households, or by other firms.

Again the two 'edge cases' are of interest: if all equity is bought by households, the result is a flow of deposits from households to firms as payment. Firms are thus able to increase the liquidity of their balance sheets without recourse to further bank borrowing. The cost of this excess capital is now the margin between the dividends paid out on the equity held by households, and the rate of interest paid on the deposits of firms. Now consider a further development whereby at some subsequent point, in response to a rise in equity prices, firms choose to purchase stocks on the assumption that they will make capital gains. If all equity is bought back from the household sector, the balance sheets of all sectors are identical to how they were before equity was issued, except that some subset of the firms sector now holds the equity of some other subset of the firms sector. The cost to the firms sector of this form of overcapitalization is nil at the aggregate level – all dividends paid out remain within the firms sector. The final balance sheet position of each of the three sectors in this case is shown in Table 9.5.

Alternatively, as equity is initially issued, firms may purchase it directly from each other. In the case under discussion where all deposits are held by households as the counterpart to loan-funded investment, firms will only be able to purchase equities by obtaining fresh liquidity in the form of further loans from the banking system. The deposits created as the counterpart to these loans will remain within the firms sector, as firms purchase shares from one another. Not all firms will necessarily increase their liabilities – some firms may only issue fresh equity, as a way of increasing liquidity or paying back previous loans,

Table 9.5 Sectoral balance sheet: saving in household sector, equity initially bought by households

	Households	Firms	Bank
Physical Capital		$+K$	
Deposits	$+D$		$-D$
Loans		$-L$	$+L$
Equities		$-e \cdot p$	
		$+e \cdot p$	
Total (Net Worth)	D	$K-L$	0

while some take on fresh debt in order to buy equities. Some firms may both issue new equity and purchase stocks, meaning they are able to hold equities without incurring further debt. The total level of debt in the firms sector will thus depend upon the extent to which firms that issue new equity choose to use newly available liquidity to pay off loans. In the case that no loans are paid off, there will have been an increase in both loans and deposits in the firms sector by exactly the amount that was raised by issuing equity. The cost to the firms sector as a whole of this new asset and liability structure will thus be the amount raised by equity issuance multiplied by the margin between deposit and lending rates, $e \cdot p \cdot (r_L - r_D)$. The final sectoral balance sheets for this case are shown in Table 9.6. In this balance sheet, those magnitudes greater than the total amount spent on real investment are marked with an asterisk: for example, the volume of loans outstanding is greater than the amount spent on real investment in this case, since firms have used loans both to finance real investment and to purchase equities.

Now consider a third case in which the financial saving that is the counterpart to real investment has accrued to firms as profits, and the household sector holds no financial assets. In this case, if firms begin to issue equity, it is not possible for the household sector to purchase the shares as they hold no savings. Thus the only possibility is for firms to buy the stock of other firms. As this takes place, there is once again no intersectoral flow of funds since the deposits used by firms to buy stock are transferred to other firms. The additional costs to the firms sector as a whole in holding additional capital in the form of equities is thus once again zero in this case. The balance sheet for this case is shown in Table 9.7.

There are thus three potential 'edge case' configurations of firm overcapitalization through the ownership of equity: two that originate with the situation in which real investment was originally financed by

Table 9.6 Sectoral balance sheet: saving in household sector, equity initially bought by firms

	Households	Firms	Bank
Physical Capital		$+K$	
Deposits	$+D_h$	$+D_f$	$-D^*$
Loans		$-L^*$	$+L^*$
Equities		$-e \cdot p$	
		$+e \cdot p$	
Total (Net Worth)	D_h	$K-(L^*-D_f)$	0

Table 9.7 Sectoral balance sheet: saving in firm sector, equity initially bought by firms

	Households	Firms	Bank
Physical Capital		$+K$	
Deposits		$+D$	$-D$
Loans		$-L$	$+L$
Equities		$-e \cdot p$	
		$+e \cdot p$	
Total (Net Worth)	0	K	0

a sectoral surplus in the household sector, and one in which retained earnings allowed firms to invest without incurring any net financial liabilities. The balance sheets of these three possible cases are shown in Tables 9.5, 9.6 and 9.7. In each of the three cases, the combination of the net worth of each sector, and the cost to the firms sector of holding excess capital in the form of equity, is different.

There exists finally the possibility of a process of capital market inflation (Toporowski 2000, Part I). This would correspond to an increase in the value of equity held by households, through insurance and pension fund intermediaries. In the firms sector, the increase in equity liabilities would be matched by a reduction in firms' borrowing from banks and/or an increase in bank deposits. In the case of an increase in bank deposits, this would correspond to the case of firm overcapitalization described above. Reduced bank borrowing by firms, or an increase in firms' bank deposits, means an increase in banks' overall net liabilities to the firms sector. In the balance sheet of the banking system, the increase in net liabilities to firms is then balanced by higher borrowing of households, which could be secured against their equity holdings, but could just as easily be secured against other assets, such as residential property.

9.6 Concluding remarks

This chapter has examined, under the conditions imposed by adhering to stock-flow consistency, the possible evolution of a highly simplified, idealized system of sectoral financial accounts. The focus has been upon financial development, and, specifically, the changing ways in which firms finance their investment as financial development progresses. A stylized progression from funding investment via bank lending, through to financing from retained earnings and finally to equity issuance, overcapitalization and financial speculation are introduced.

The various possible balance sheet structures that arise as a consequence of different paths of the financing of investment in real assets and speculative financial positions result in differing levels of financial fragility for the firms sector. In particular, the Kalecki–Steindl result that household saving increases firms' indebtedness, and hence financial fragility, is demonstrated in a simple stock-flow framework. However, the consequences of overcapitalization in particular depend on subsequent movements in capital markets and firms' investment decisions. For example, firms may borrow to buy equities within the firms sector, pushing up the price of equities, resulting in increased liquidity in the firms sector as well as higher balance-sheet wealth. This in turn may spur investment, increasing firm profitability, thus *ex post* validating the increase in share prices (Minsky, 1986 [2008], Chapter 8). Alternatively, if firms push up share prices through redistributing deposits among themselves in preference to real investment, taking on additional loan liabilities in the process – as in Table 9.6 – the potential exists for crisis when interest liabilities cannot be covered from operating profits and capital gains. The liquidity of capital markets is thus vital to the ability of firms to realize capital gains, while the internal liquidity of firms may be an important determinant of their ability to gain access to further bank lending.

Although the development of the financial system, and thus of the financing structures of firms within that system, is presented here as a linear process, in a real economic system the evolution of firms' balance sheets will be conditioned both by the level of overall financial development, and by the current position in the business cycle. It is this cyclical perspective in particular that is largely missing in the current crop of 'stock-flow consistent' models. Minsky's ([1975] 2008) critique of Chapter 17 of the General Theory was that at the crucial point in Keynes' analysis, he reverted to a marginalist conception of investment – rather than the cyclical perspective that can be detected in the rest of the book. This critique is also applicable in some respects to these stock-flow models. Although they are based around the balance sheets of the various sectors of the economy, and incorporate detailed financial structure – thus considering explicitly the evolution of assets and liabilities and their associated money flows – the method by which the models are employed to draw conclusions about the workings of the economic system is in fact very close to that of neoclassical dynamic-stochastic general equilibrium models, such as that of Woodford (2003). This method utilized is to first locate the steady-state equilibrium of the model, and then use computer simulations to examine the behaviour of the system when some exogenous shock is applied to the system – with the system eventually returning to equilibrium.

A final conclusion may therefore be that stock-flow consistent models need to incorporate more explicitly the type of financially driven cyclical behavior, emphasized by Minsky, and development as a process of disruption to the normal circular flow as described by Schumpeter:

> ... development in our sense is a distinct phenomenon, entirely foreign to what may be observed in the circular flow or in the tendency towards equilibrium. It is the spontaneous and discontinuous change in the channels of the flow, disturbance of equilibrium, which forever alters and displaces the equilibrium state previously existing. (Schumpeter 1934)

Notes

1. The system is also has a similarity to the Wicksell's (1936) 'Pure Credit Economy', although in Wicksell's system the finance for investment is provided not by surpluses in the household sector but by 'capitalists'. This finance is lent via the banking system to a distinct class of 'entrepreneurs' who use these borrowed funds to finance investment in working capital.
2. We have also reintroduced the assumption that banks make zero profit, which allows us to simplify the matrix by removing the distinction between the current and capital accounts of the banking system.
3. $S_f = I - S_h + (G - T) + (X - M)$.
4. We have assumed zero profits in the banking system for the sake of simplicity, which rules out a spread between lending and deposit rates. However, if we were to instead assume that all banking sector profits are returned to households, the difference between investment that results in households holding deposits, and investment that results in firms holding deposits is clear: in the former, the cost to firms of investment is $I{\cdot}r_L$, whereas in the latter case it is $I{\cdot}(r_L - r_D)$.

5. The current model would need to be extended to include a central bank as a separate sector in order to consider the implementation of monetary policy in detail.
6. It is of course possible that the degree of overcapitalization will *exceed* the level of investment: despite investment spending returning to firms as deposits, firms may borrow more than is required to finance investment, and hold the excess as deposits.
7. For example, Hein (2008), van Treeck (2008), Stockhammer (2004).
8. Godley and Lavoie utilize an explicit 'revaluation matrix' in their models to keep track of the changes that arise due to movements in asset prices.

References

Chick, V. (1986) 'The Evolution of the Banking System and the Theory of Saving, Investment and Interest,' *Economies et Sociétés* 3(8–9): 111–26.

Godley, W. and M. Lavoie (2007) *Monetary Economics: An Integrated Approach to Credit, Money, Income, Production and Wealth* (Basingstoke, UK: Palgrave Macmillan).

Hayek, F.A. (1933 [1966]) *Monetary Theory and the Trade Cycle* (New York, NY: Augustus M. Kelley).

Hein, E. (2008) '"Financialisation" in a Comparative Static, Stock-flow Consistent Post-Kaleckian Distribution and Growth Model,' Working Paper No. 21 (Düsseldorf, Germany: IMK at the Hans Boeckler Foundation, Macroeconomic Policy Institute).

Kalecki, M. (1954) *Theory of Economic Dynamics An Essay on Cyclical and Long-Run Changes in Capitalist Economy* (London: George Allen and Unwin).

Keynes, J.M. (1936) *The General Theory of Employment, Interest, and Money* (London: Macmillan Publishing Company).

Minsky, H.P. (1975 [2008]) *John Maynard Keynes* (New York: Columbia University Press) republished in D.B. Papadimitriou and L.R. Wray (eds) *Hyman P. Minsky's John Maynard Keynes* (New York: McGraw-Hill).

Minsky, H.P. (1986 [2008]) *Stabilizing an Unstable Economy* (New Haven, CT: Yale University Press) republished in D.B. Papadimitriou and L.R. Wray (eds) *Hyman P. Minsky's Stabilizing an Unstable Economy* (New York: McGraw-Hill).

Schumpeter, J. (1934) *The Theory of Economic Development* (Cambridge, MA: Harvard University Press).

Stockhammer, E. (2004) 'Financialization and the Slowdown of Accumulation,' *Cambridge Journal of Economics* 28(5): 719–41.

Toporowski, J. (2000) *The End of Finance: The Theory of Capital Market Inflation, Financial Derivatives and Pension Fund Capitalism* (London: Routledge).

Toporowski, J. (2001) 'European Destiny and Macroeconomic Responsibility in the Financial Systems of Germany and the UK: A Balance Sheet Approach,' in S. Frowen and F. McHugh (eds) *Financial Competition, Risk and Accountability, British and German Experiences* (London: Palgrave).

Toporowski, J. (2008) 'Excess Capital and Liquidity Management,' Working Paper No. 549 (Annandale-on-Hudson, NY: Levy Economics Institute of Bard College).

Toporowski, J. (2010) 'Corporate Liquidity and Financial Fragility,' paper presented at the Boeckler Foundation Macroeconomics Conference, Berlin.
van Treeck, T. (2008) 'A Synthetic, Stock-flow Consistent Macroeconomic Model of "Financialisation",' *Cambridge Journal of Economics* 33(3): 467–93.
Wicksell, K. (1936) *Interest and Prices: A Study of the Causes Regulating the Vale of Money* (London, UK: Macmillan).
Withers, H. (1920) *The Meaning of Money* (New York: E.P. Dutton and Company).
Woodford, M. (2003) *Interest and Prices: Foundations of a Theory of Monetary Policy* (Princeton, NJ: Princeton University Press).

10
Financial Integration and Stabilization in a Monetary Union Without or With Bank Rationing

Vincent Duwicquet and Jacques Mazier

10.1 Introduction

In a monetary union like the euro zone adjustments facing asymmetric evolutions are more difficult due to fixed intra-European exchange rates. Since 1999, divergences in the evolution of different European economies have been more important than generally expected. The slowdown observed after 2001 has been unequal across the countries. The slow growth of the large continental countries, especially Germany, has contrasted with the better performances of smaller and more peripheral countries like Finland or Ireland and Spain which were led by a housing bubble. Divergences regarding inflation have also been significant. The financial crisis of 2007–08 didn't hurt all the countries in the same way. Southern European economies have been clearly more touched and the Greek crisis in 2010 has been a threat for the whole euro area. By contrast, Germany, although deeply hurt by the world recession, managed to recover strongly. Such an environment has brought to the fore traditional questions related to monetary union, that is, the nature of adjustment mechanisms and the difficulties due to asymmetric evolutions.

Adjustments mechanisms are defined in a broad sense as mechanisms which permit a country, after a shock, to return to the initial situation or, possibly, to full employment. They vary in nature.

Relative wage and price flexibility had been proposed from the start by single currency instigators and are still proposed in order to take place, at least partially, of exchange rate adjustments. Actually these mechanisms allow only a very slow and partial return to equilibrium with an important cost in terms of growth and employment and with large differences between countries, due to strong structural specificities (Mazier and Saglio, 2008). It is illusory to hope that more flexibility in the products and labor markets, obtained through 'structural reforms', will improve these adjustment mechanisms.

Labor mobility is another potential adjustment mechanism, but it remains limited in the EU. Even in the case of the US, interregional migrations follow a rather long-term dynamics which is not reversible in the short term and cannot be regarded as adjustment factors on a large scale (Mazier et al., 2002, 2007).

Fiscal policy can play a more active role in a federal state like the US, but has no equivalent in the European case. According to rather old evaluations, the stabilization coefficient of the US federal budget would range between 15 per cent and 28 per cent (Pisani-Ferry et al., 1992; Goodhart and Smith, 1993). This question, theoretical in the European case because of the lack of a federal budget, has been re-examined since the second part of the 1990s in an enlarged approach, the 'international risk sharing' one.

Well-integrated capital markets, with portfolio diversification and intra-zone credit, would constitute a powerful adjustment mechanism, examined in detail by the 'international risk-sharing' approach (Asdrubali et al., 1996; Asdrubali and Kim, 2004). The stabilization through capital income would be important in the US case (around 30 per cent) and would reflect a deep financial integration with portfolio diversification at the level of the whole American area. The stabilization by federal transfers would be around 15 per cent, close to the results in previous studies. The stabilization by intra-zone credit would also be important (around 20 per cent) but the interpretation of the econometric estimation raises many problems. More generally, the theoretical basis of the whole model and the econometric methodology used can both be criticized, mainly because they are too focused on the consumption–production adjustment and ignore other components, especially investment and firms' revenue. However, these results are used by advocates of a liberal economic policy in the EU to promote deeper financial integration without having to develop a federal budget.

This is why a different approach is adopted in this chapter based on a 'stock-flow consistent' model of a monetary union with two countries along the lines of Godley and Lavoie (2005–06, 2007a, 2007b) and Lavoie (2003). The model describes assets and liabilities of all the agents (firms, households, and government) and analyzes financial integration in a consistent manner. The banking system of the monetary union comprises commercial banks in each country and a single central bank. We distinguish four kinds of assets: monetary assets held by households; bonds issued by each state and held by households of both countries; Treasury bills also issued by each state and held by commercial banks; equities issued by firms of both countries and held by households and firms of both countries. Firms can finance their real and financial investments by non-distributed profit, banking credit, or new equities issued. This stock-flow consistent approach of the monetary union allows a comprehensive analysis of real and financial adjustments through capital income (interests, dividends, and capital gains) and external finance (credit, equities, Treasury bills and bonds). Using two countries of unequal size, it describes relations between one country and the rest of the union.

Different versions of the model are considered:

- a model of financial autarky without foreign financial assets and without intra-zone credit;
- a complete model with foreign assets and intra-zone credit where the degree of financial integration can be more or less developed;
- a model with intra-zone credit, but without foreign assets and intra-zone capital income transfers.

Furthermore banks can supply credit without rationing or with rationing. This rationing may be global by banks from both countries. Alternatively, it may be specific to resident or nonresident banks. Rationing may also concern Treasury bills which banks may buy without restriction or up to a certain limit, forcing the government to adapt its fiscal policy. Last, if interest rates are generally supposed constant and led by the key interest rate of the central bank, they can also become variable when banks are reluctant to finance an increasing deficit. Based on these different versions of the model, a whole set of simulations is used to study adjustments facing asymmetric shocks. By comparison, it is possible to estimate stabilization effects due to foreign capital income and portfolio diversification and to intra-zone credit.

Several results[1] can be underlined.

- Foreign asset holdings have a stabilizing role, but the capital income stabilizing coefficient seems smaller than the one obtained by the 'risk-sharing' approach.
- By contrast, foreign loans (intra-zone credit) have no specific stabilization effects. This is due to the credit mechanism in a monetary union and to the key role played by refinancing by the central bank. Inside a monetary union, domestic credit and foreign credit from another member of the union are of the same type. There is no increase of the stabilization coefficient to expect from development of intra-eurozone credit. This is true without credit rationing or with global credit rationing by domestic and nonresident banks.

- However, when nonresident banks, in contrast to domestic ones, do not ration credit or buy Treasury bills without restriction, intra-zone credit has a stabilization effect.
- But, when interest rates increase due to banks' reluctance to finance more issue of Treasury bills, intra-zone credit from the rest of the union has no more stabilizing effect due to its increasing cost. This can be regarded as an illustration of the last Greek and Irish crisie and as an argument in favor of direct financing by the central bank.

The chapter is organized as follows. A second section presents the main characteristics of the two-country stock-flow model in its basic specification. A third section presents simulations in response to asymmetric supply or demand shocks with the different versions of the model. Stabilization effects of foreign capital income and intra-zone credit, with or without credit rationing, are analyzed. A last section concludes.

10.2 A stock-flow consistent model of two countries in a monetary union

A SFC model with two countries in monetary union allows a consistent description of assets and liabilities and of all the associated real and financial flows. The monetary union is composed of two countries (N and S) with an asymmetry of size. The country S is five times larger than the country N. This configuration facilitates analyzing the adjustment mechanisms of the country N facing the rest of the monetary union. Consequently, it is possible to estimate the stabilization coefficients associated with capital incomes and intra-zone finance.

This model is inspired by Godley and Lavoie (2005–06, 2007a, 2007b) and Lavoie (2003). But it differs in some respects. We introduce asymmetry in size between the two countries. The monetary and financial sector is more developed. Firms accumulate both real and financial capital. They can finance their investments by non-distributed profit, banking credit, or equities. We introduce two commercial banks capable of supplying credit and also, possibly, rationing credit. Households hold banking deposits, bonds, and equities. We keep a similar representation of the central bank and the two governments which issue bonds and Treasury bills. Finally, the model has been calibrated to represent the structure of the European Monetary Union.

Table 10.1 describes the balance sheet in terms of assets (written with a positive sign) and liabilities (written with a negative sign) of each sector: households, firms, government, commercial banks and a single central

Table 10.1 Balance sheet

	Households N	Firms N	State N	Banks N	ECB	Households S	Firms S	State S	Banks S	Total
Capital		$+K^N$					$+K^S$			$+K^N + K^S$
Deposits	$+BD^N$			$-BD^N$		$+BD^S$			$-BD^S$	0
Currency	$+H_h^N$			$+H^N$	$-H$	$+H_h^S$			$+H^S$	0
Credits		$-L^N$		$+L_N^N$					$+L_S^N$	0
				$+L_N^S$			$-L^S$		$+L_S^S$	
Refinancing				$-RF^N$	$+RF^N + RF^S$				$-RF^S$	0
Bonds	$+p_b^N \cdot B_N^N$		$-p_b^N \cdot B^N$			$+p_b^N \cdot B_S^N$				0
	$+p_b^S \cdot B_N^S$					$+p_b^S \cdot B_S^S$		$-p_b^S \cdot B^S$		
Bills			$-BT^N$	$+BT_N^N$					$+BT_S^N$	0
				$+BT_N^S$				$-BT^S$	$+BT_S^S$	
Equities	$+p_e^N \cdot E_{hN}^N$	$+p_e^N \cdot E_{eN}^N$				$+p_e^N \cdot E_{hS}^N$	$+p_e^N \cdot E_{eS}^N$			0
		$-p_e^N \cdot E^N$								
	$+p_e^S \cdot E_{hN}^S$	$+p_e^S \cdot E_{eN}^S$				$+p_e^S \cdot E_{hS}^S$	$+p_e^S \cdot E_{eS}^S$			
							$-p_e^S \cdot E^S$			
Wealth	$-VH^N$	$-V^N$	$-D^N$	$-VB^N$		$-VH^S$	$-V^S$	$-D^S$	$-VB^S$	$-K^N - K^S$
Total	0	0	0	0	0	0	0	0	0	0

bank. The transaction matrix, national accounts in flows, is provided in the Appendix. Beyond fixed capital (K), seven kinds of monetary or financial assets are distinguished:[2] bank deposits (BD) held by households, bonds issued by governments ($p_b.B$) and held by households of both countries, loans (L) supplied by each commercial bank to firms of the two countries, the equities issued by firms ($p_e.E$) and held by households and firms of both countries, Treasury bills issued by each state (BT) and held by commercial banks of both countries, high-powered money (H) held by households (H_h) as well as commercial banks (reserve requirements) and advances supplied by the ECB to commercial banks (RF).

10.2.1 Households

Households exhibit traditional consumption behavior with a wealth effect, taking into account capital gains on equities and bonds held. We specify a constant ratio of wealth to disposable income in the long run. Households' portfolio choice follows the approach developed by Godley (1999) and Tobin (1969), with an arbitrage between cash (H_h), bank deposits (BD), bonds ($p_b \cdot B$) and equities ($p_e \cdot E_h$), depending on the relative rates of return of each asset: r_b for the interest rate on bonds of each country; i_d for the interest rate on bank deposits which is the same in the two countries; r_e for the rate of return on equities in each country. The cash demand follows a simple transaction demand for money. The demand for bank deposits is not written and determined as a residual, using the accounting equation of the households' balance sheet.

10.2.1.1 Households' equations for country N

Consumption

$$C^N = a0^N + a1 \cdot YHS_h^N + a2 \,.\, VH_{-1}^N$$

(VH^N = households' wealth, YHS_h^N = disposable income with capital gains)

Disposable income

$$YD_h^N = W^N + i_d \cdot BD_{-1}^N + B_{N-1}^N + B_{N-1}^S + DIV_{hN}^N + DIV_{hN}^S - T^N$$

$$YHS_h^N = YD_h^N + CG_h^N$$

(YD = disposable income, W = wages, $i_d \,.\, BD_{-1}$ = interests on bank deposits, B_{N-1}^N and B_{N-1}^S = interest on domestic and foreign bonds, DIV_{hN}^N

and DIV^S_{hN} = received dividends on domestic and foreign equities, T = taxes, CG_h = households' capital gains).

Taxes paid by households

$$T^N = \theta.(W^N + i_d \,.\, BD^N_{-1} + B^N_{N-1} + B^S_{N-1} + DIV^N_{hN} + DIV^S_{hN})$$

Households' bonds demand

$$\frac{p_b^N.B_N^N}{VH^N} = v0 + v1\,.\,r_b^N - v2\,.\,r_b^S - v3\,.\,i_d - v4\,.\,r_e^N - v5\,.\,r_e^S$$

$$\frac{p_b^S.B_N^S}{VH^N} = v0 + v1\,.\,r_b^S - v2\,.\,r_b^N - v3\,.\,i_d - v4\,.\,r_e^N - v5\,.\,r_e^S$$

($P^N_b \,.\, B^N_N$ = government N bonds held by country N households, $P^S_b \,.\, B^S_N$ = government S bonds held by country N households, r_b = interest rate on bonds, i_d = interest rate on bank deposits, r_e = rate of return on equities).

Households' equities demand

$$\frac{p_e^N.E_{hN}^N}{VH^N} = v0 - v1\,.\,r_b^N - v2\,.\,r_b^S - v3\,.\,i_d + v4\,.\,r_e^N - v5\,.\,r_e^S$$

$$\frac{p_e^S.E_{hN}^S}{VH^N} = v0 - v1\,.\,r_b^N - v2\,.\,r_b^S - v3\,.\,i_d - v4\,.\,r_e^N + v5\,.\,r_e^S$$

($p^N_e \,.\, E^N_{hN}$ = equities issued by country N firms and held by country N households, $p^S_e \,.\, E^S_{hN}$ = equities issued by country S firms and held by country N households).

Cash demand

$$H^N_h = \lambda_0 \,.\, C^N$$

Households' transaction equilibrium

$$\Delta BD^N = YD^N_h - C^N - p^N_b \,.\, \Delta B^N_N - p^S_b \,.\, \Delta B^S_N - p^N_e \,.\, \Delta E^N_{hN} - p^S_e \,.\, \Delta E^S_{hN} - \Delta H^N_h$$

(BD = bank deposits).

Households' balance sheet

$$VH^N = BD^N + p^N_b \,.\, B^N_N + p^S_b \,.\, B^S_N + p^N_e \,.\, E^N_{hN} + p^S_e \,.\, E^S_{hN} + H^N_h$$

(VH = households' net wealth).

Households' capital gains on equities and bonds held

$$CG_h^N = \Delta p_b^N \,.\, B_{N-1}^N + \Delta p_b^S \,.\, B_{N-1}^S + \Delta p_e^N \,.\, E_{hN-1}^N + \Delta P_e^S \,.\, E_{hN-1}^S$$

Which gives in sum:

$$\begin{aligned}\Delta VH^N &= YD_h^N - C^N + CG_h^N = \textit{households' saving} + \textit{capital gains} \\ &= YHS_h^N - C^N\end{aligned}$$

10.2.2 Firms

Firms have both real and financial accumulation following a post-Keynesian theoretical framework (see Clévenot and Guy 2010; Clévenot et al., 2010 for more developments). Their desired fixed investment (I^d) depends positively on the profit rate $\left(r_f = \dfrac{UP}{K_{-1}}\right)$ and negatively on the debt structure $\left(\dfrac{L}{K_{-1}}\right)$ and the cost of credit (r_l), with a possible positive demand effect. Their financial accumulation, that is, firms' demand for equities ($p_e.E_e$), is mainly related to the rate of return on equities held (r_e) with an arbitrage between domestic and foreign assets and a positive effect of the rate of profit reflecting the global environment. Firms can finance their investments through undistributed profit (*UP*), bank credit, or by issuing equities. New equities issued by firms ($p_e \,.\, \Delta E$) are determined as a percentage of the total real and financial investment, with positive effects of both credit cost and the debt ratio whose respective increases lead firms to issue more equities. The rate of return on equities r_e is determined by dividends and capital gains.

Finally, income distribution is analyzed in a simple way with a constant share of wages. Undistributed profit is determined by a constant rate of saving by firms (s_f). Distributed dividends between shareholders (households and firms of both countries) are related to the held equities structure.

10.2.2.1 Firms' equations for country N

Fixed investment

$$\frac{I^{dN}}{K_{-1}^N} = k0^N + k1 \,.\, r_{f-1}^N + k2 \,.\, \frac{\Delta Y^N}{Y_{-1}^N} - k3 \,.\, \frac{L^N}{K_{-1}^N} - k4 \,.\, r_l$$

(I^d = desired investment, K = fixed capital stock; Y = GDP; r_f = rate of profit $= \dfrac{UP}{K_{-1}}$, UP = undistributed profit, L = loans, r_l = interest rate on loans).

With the identity for capital accumulation

$$K^N = K^N_{-1}\,(1 - \delta) + I^N$$

Financial accumulation (firms' equities demand)

$$\frac{p_e^N \,.\, E_{eN}^N}{(K^N + p_e^N \,.\, E_{eN}^N + p_e^S \,.\, E_{eN}^S)} = f_0 + f_1 \,.\, r_e^N - f_2 \,.\, r_e^S + f_3 \,.\, r_f^N$$

$$\frac{p_e^S \,.\, E_{eN}^S}{(K^N + p_e^N \,.\, E_{eN}^N + p_e^S \,.\, E_{eN}^S)} = f_0 + f_1 \,.\, r_e^S - f_2 \,.\, r_e^N + f_3 \,.\, r_f^N$$

($p_e^N \,.\, E_{eN}^N$ = equities issued by country *N* firms and held by country *N* firms, $p_e^S \,.\, E_{eN}^S$ = equities issued by country *S* firms and held by country *N* firms, $K^N + p_e^N \,.\, E_{eN}^N + p_e^S \,.\, E_{eN}^S$ = total real and financial assets held by country *N* firms, p_e = equities' price, E = number of equities).

New equities issued

$$\frac{p_e^N \,.\, \Delta E^N}{(I^N + p_e^N \,.\, \Delta E_{eN}^N + p_e^S \,.\, \Delta E_{eN}^S)} = g_1 \,.\, r_l + g_2 \,.\left(\frac{L^N}{L^N + p_e^N \,.\, E^N + V^N}\right)_{-1} + g_3$$

($p_e \,.\, \Delta E$ = new issued equities, $I^N + p_e^N \,.\, \Delta E_{eN}^N + p_e^S \,.\, \Delta E_{eN}^S$ = real and financial investment, $\dfrac{L}{L + p_e.E + V}$ = debt ratio in percentage of firms' total liability, $p_e \cdot E + V$ = firms' own funds equal to issued equities + firms' net wealth).

Rate of return on equities

$$r_e^N = \frac{\left(E_{-1}^N \,.\, \Delta p_e^N + DIV^N\right)}{\left(p_e^N \,.\, E^N\right)_{-1}} = \frac{\Delta p_e^N}{p_{e-1}^N} + \frac{DIV^N}{p_e^N \,.\, E_{-1}^N}$$

($E_{-1} \,.\, \Delta p_e$ = capital gains, DIV= distributed dividends).

Firms' flows of funds

$$I^{rN} + p_e^N \,.\, \Delta E_{eN}^N + p_e^S \,.\, \Delta E_{eN}^S = \Delta L^{sN} + UP^N + p_e^N \,.\, \Delta E^N$$

(I^r = restricted investment, ΔL^s = credit supply).

$$I = Min(I^d, I^r)$$

(I = effective investment, I^d = desired fixed investment, I^r = restricted investment).

Firms' balance sheet

$$K^N + p_e^N . E_{eN}^N + p_e^S . E_{eN}^S = L^N + p_e^N . E^N + V^N$$

Wages

$$W^N = \rho . Y^N$$

(W = wages).

Distributed dividends

$$DIV^N = (1 - s_f)\,(Y_{-1}^N - W_{-1}^N - r_l . L_{-2}^N)$$

$$UP^N = s_f \cdot (Y_{-1}^N - W_{-1}^N - r_l . L_{-2}^N)$$

Distribution of dividends

$$DIV_{eN}^N = DIV^N . \left(\frac{E_{eN}^N}{E^N}\right)_{-1}$$

$$DIV_{hN}^N = DIV^N . \left(\frac{E_{hN}^N}{E^N}\right)_{-1}$$

$$DIV_{eS}^N = DIV^N . \left(\frac{E_{eS}^N}{E^N}\right)_{-1}$$

$$DIV_{hS}^N = DIV^N . \left(\frac{E_{hS}^N}{E^N}\right)_{-1}$$

(DIV_{eN}^N, DIV_{hN}^N, DIV_{eS}^N, DIV_{hS}^N = dividends of country N's firms distributed to country N and S firms and households in relation with the number of equities held E_{eN}^N, E_{hN}^N, E_{eS}^N and E_{hS}^N).

10.2.3 Banks

Two regimes can be considered:

- one where firms can get from banks all the credits demanded without restriction; credit demand is determined by the balance of the firms' flow of funds. Investment is equal to the desired investment (Model 1).

- the other with credit rationing; the credit supply of banks depends on the financial fragility of firms represented by two parameters: the rate of profit (r_f) describing the ability of firms to face debt commitments and the debt ratio as a proxy of firms' financial soundness. Credit rationing occurs when credit demand is larger than credit supply. The restricted investment (I^r) is then determined by the different flows of financing: profit, equities and credit rationing from banks (L^S) (Model 2).

To complete, the share between domestic and foreign banks' loans is simply related to the degree of openness of the economy. Reserve requirements in high-powered money represent a fixed share of bank deposits and do not provide interest payments. A highly simplified treatment of interest rates is retained. The interest rate on loans (r_l) is presumed equal to the key interest rate of the central bank (i_b) plus a constant mark-up. To realize profits, banks apply a spread between the key rate and the rate on deposits (i_d). The central bank provides advances (*RF*) to commercial banks to allow the latter to provide the cash that households are asking for. These advances are made at a rate of interest (i_b) which is the key instrument of the monetary policy. They are determined as banks' balance. The central bank pays taxes, equal to its profit, which are shared between the two national governments in relation with each country's size.

10.2.3.1 Country N banks' equations

Credit

$$\Delta L^{sN} = \alpha n1 . r_f - \alpha n2 . \left(\frac{L^N}{K^N}\right)_{-1} + \alpha n3$$

$$\Delta L^{dN} = I^{dN} - UP^N - p_e^N . \Delta E^N + p_e^N . \Delta E_{eN}^N + p_e^S . \Delta E_{eN}^S$$

$$\Delta L^N = min(\Delta L^{dN}, \Delta L^{sN})$$

(ΔL^s = credit supply, ΔL^d = credit demand)

$$\Delta L^N = \Delta L_N^N + \Delta L_S^N$$

$$L_S^N = \left(\frac{X^N}{Y^N}\right).L^N$$

(L_S^N = credit supplied by country *S* banks to country *N* firms; L_N^N = credit supplied by country *N* banks to country *N* firms, $\frac{X}{Y}$ = rate of openness).

Reserves requirements

$$H^N = \varepsilon \, . \, BD^N$$

(H = reserve requirements in high-powered money, BD = bank deposits).

Taxes paid by commercial banks

$$TB^N = \theta_b \, . \, (r_l \, . \, L_{N-1}^N + r_l \, . \, L_{N-1}^S + r \, . \, BT_{N-1}^N + r \, . \, BT_{N-1}^S - i_d \, . \, BD_{-1}^N - i_b \, . \, RF_{-1}^N)$$

Banks' profit

$$PB^N = (1 - \theta_b) \, . \, (r_l \, . \, L_{N-1}^N + r_l \, . \, L_{N-1}^S + r \, . \, BT_{N-1}^N + r \, . \, BT_{N-1}^S - i_d \, . \, BD_{-1}^N - i_b \, . \, RF_{-1}^N)$$

Banks' net wealth

$$\Delta VB^N = PB^N$$

Refinancing

$$\Delta RF^N = \Delta H^N + \Delta L_N^N + \Delta L_N^S + \Delta BT_N^N + \Delta BT_N^S - \Delta BD^N - PB^N$$

(RF = refinancing by the central bank, BT = Treasury bills purchased by commercial banks, BD = bank deposits, PB = banks' profit).

Central bank tax

$$T€B = i_b \, . \, (RF_{-1}^N + RF_{-1}^S)$$

$$T€B^N = T€B . \left(\frac{Y^N}{Y^N + Y^S} \right)$$

($T€B^N$ = tax paid by the central bank to country *N* government).

Central bank money

$$H = H_h^N + H_h^S + H^N + H^S$$

Central bank equilibrium

$$\Delta H = \Delta RF^N + \Delta RF^S$$

(this equation is derived from others).

Interest rates

$$r_l = i_b + m1_b$$

$$i_d = i_b - m2_b$$

$$r = r_l = r_b^N = r_b^S$$

$$p_b^N = \frac{1}{r_b^N}$$

(i_b = key interest rate of the central bank, exogenous, r_l = interest rate on loans, i_d = interest rate on deposits, r = interest rate on Treasury bills, r_b = interest rate on bonds, p_b = bonds price).

In another version resident and nonresident banks have specific behaviors. Credit rationing may come from banks of the small country facing economic constraints while banks of the rest of the union provide credit without restriction (Model 3). Alternatively, credit rationing may come from banks of the rest of the union while banks of the small country do not ration. This case illustrates the diffusion effect of a major bank crisis (Model 3bis). The corresponding equations will be given later on. The case of variable rate of interest will be introduced at the end.

10.2.4 Government

Public finance is described in a simple way with exogenous expenditures and income taxes paid by households, commercial banks and central bank. Treasury bills are purchased by commercial banks without restriction, with the distribution between foreign and domestic bills related to the degree of openness. Interest rates on Treasury bills (r) and on bonds (r_b) are supposed to be equal to interest rates on loans (r_l).

10.2.4.1 Country N government equations

Budget balance

$$\Delta BT^N = G^N + r_n \,.\, BT_{-1}^N + B_{-1}^N - T^N - TB^N - T€B^N - p_b^N \,.\, \Delta B^N$$

(BT = Treasury bills, G = public expenditures exogenous, T = income taxes, TB = tax paid by commercial banks, $T \in B$ = tax paid by the central bank, r = interest rate on Treasury bills, B = interest on bonds, $p_b \, . \, \Delta B$ = new bonds issued by government).

Treasury bills

$$\Delta BT^N = \Delta BT_N^N + \Delta BT_S^N$$

$$BT_S^N = \left(\frac{X^N}{Y^N} \right) . BT^N$$

(BT_S^N = country N Treasury bills held by foreign commercial banks of country S, BT_N^N = country N Treasury bills held by domestic banks).

Bonds held by households

$$\Delta B^N = \Delta B_N^N + \Delta B_S^N$$

(B_S^N = country N bonds held by country S households).

Public debt

$$D^N = -BT^N - p_b^N \cdot B^N$$

In sum we have:

$$VH^N + V^N + VH^S + V^S + D^N + D^S + VB^N + VB^S = K^N + K^S$$

(Total net wealth at the level of the whole monetary union is equal to the total fixed capital; this equation is derived from others).

In another version banks of the small country are reluctant to purchase Treasury bills without restriction. According to the structure of their balance sheet, they ration the Treasury bills and constraint the government to adjust its fiscal policy if nonresident banks do not afford additional financing (Model 4). In a last case variable interest rates are introduced. Banks may tighten the financial conditions and raise the interest rate on Treasury bills, with or without additional financing coming the rest of the union (Model 5). The corresponding equations will also be given later on.

10.2.5 Foreign trade and current account

Foreign trade inside the monetary union depends only on the volume effect, since prices and exchange rates are fixed. The current balance (CUR) is composed of the trade balance, the balance of capital incomes received and paid to the rest of the monetary union, and the exchanges inside the banking system. Commercial banks pay interest to the central bank for their refinancing. But the central bank pays taxes to each government. In case of a deficit incurred by country N, the current balance is financed through three channels: the holding of more assets of country N (bonds, Treasury bills, equities) by country S than the opposite (holding of assets of country S by country N); the channel of credit by banks of country S to firms of country N; the refinancing by the central bank which plays a key role as lender of last resort.

10.2.5.1 Current account equations

Foreign trade

$$log(IM^N) = \mu_0 + \mu_{In} \cdot log(Y^N)$$

$$X^N = IM^S$$

IM = imports, X = exports.

Current balance

$$CUR^N = (X^N - IM^N) + (B^S_{N-1} + r\,.\,BT^S_{N-1} + r_l\,.\,L^S_{N-1} + DIV^S_{hN} + DIV^S_{eN} + T \in B^N) - (B^N_{S-1} + r\,.\,BT^N_{S-1} + rl\,.\,L^N_{S-1} + DIV^N_{hS} + DIV^N_{eS} + i_b \cdot RF^N_{-1})$$

Goods and services equilibrium

$$Y^N = C^N + I^N + G^N + X^N - IM^N$$

In total, the model has 107 equations for 107 endogenous variables. G^N, G^S (public expenditures) and i_b (key interest rate fixed by the central bank) are exogenous.

10.2.6 Calibration

The model can be calibrated using balance sheets and national accounts in flows from Eurostat for the European countries. Two sets of calibration have been used, the first one with an important share of equities (400 per cent of GDP as in France in 2006) which reflects a high degree of financialization. Dividends are larger than interest. The second calibration retains a smaller share of equities (172 per cent of GDP) and a greater role played by credit. The capital–income ratio is also smaller ($\frac{K}{Y}$ = 2 instead of 4), and equities are more held by firms than by households. Lastly, the share of foreign dividends in the total dividends received is kept constant instead of being determined by the structure of equities held. This assumption is more in line with the relative weakness of the capital income received from abroad. Our second calibration can be regarded as more realistic. But, as will be shown, the results of the two calibrations are rather close.

The elasticities in the equations are close to usual estimations. The basic scenarios follow a rate of growth of GDP of 2 per cent and a gross rate of accumulation of 7 per cent and a rate of accumulation net of depreciation of 2 per cent. The table in the Appendix gives the values of the main parameters for calibration.

10.3 Adjustments inside the monetary union and stabilization effects

10.3.1 Methodology

After the presentation of the model's main characteristics, adjustment mechanisms facing supply or demand shocks can be analyzed. They allow a measure of stabilization coefficients, especially for capital incomes coming from the rest of the union and intra-zone finance. In order to identify the stabilization effects specific to each factor, three successive versions of the model will be used:

- The basic version corresponding with financial autarky (Version 1) is without foreign assets and without intra-zone credit; there is no capital income from abroad; the current account is then financed only through refinancing by the central bank to the commercial banks;
- The second version (Version 2) is the most complete case of financial integration with foreign assets and intra-zone credit. Two calibrations are distinguished. In Version 2a residents hold 25 per cent of foreign equities in their portfolio which is close to the observed value; in Version 2b the share of foreign equities is supposed to be higher (80 per cent of the total) which corresponds to a rather unrealistic value, but gives an upper evaluation of the stabilization effects through capital income;
- The third version (Version 3) includes intra-zone credit and Treasury bills, but excludes foreign equities and bonds. Capital incomes from abroad are consequently missing. This version allows an estimation of the stabilization effect of intra-zone credit solely, by comparison with the basic Version 1 of financial autarky.

Table 10.2 Adjustments in a monetary union: the different configurations

Models \ Versions	**Financial autarky**	**Normal financial integration**	**High financial integration**	**Intra-zone credit alone**	**High Intra-zone credit**
Model 1: Without global credit rationing	Model 1.1	Model 1.2a	Model 1.2b	Model 1.3	
Model 2: With global credit rationing	Model 2.1	Model 2.2a	Model 2.2b	Model 2.3	
Model 3: With credit rationing by domestic banks	Model 3.1			Model 3.3a	Model 3.3b
Model 3bis: With credit rationing by nonresident banks	Model 3b is 1			Model 3bis3a	Model 3bis3b
Model 4: Treasury bills rationing	Model 4.1			Model 4.3	
Model 5: Variable interest rate	Model 5.1			Model 5.3	

These three versions will be combined with the five forms of the model which have been presented in the previous section, the Model 1 without global credit rationing, the Model 2 with global credit rationing, the Model 3 with credit rationing by domestic banks or by nonresident banks (Model 3bis), the Model 4 with Treasury bills rationing by domestic banks, the Model 5 with variable rate of interest on Treasury bills.

Table 10.2 sums up the whole set of configurations which will be considered. To simplify, a single shock will be examined in each case, a loss of competitiveness in country N facing the rest of the union.[3]

10.3.2 Adjustments with no credit rationing (Model 1)

Adjustments mechanisms are analyzed through a shock of a loss of competitiveness of country N facing the rest of the union. In the first version of the model there is no credit rationing and firms can get from banks all the demanded credit. Similarly Treasury bills are purchased by commercial banks without restriction. The loss of competitiveness of country N is described by an increase of the import propensity of 1 per cent ($d\mu_{1n} = 0.01$). The GDP of country N decreases to the benefit of the rest of the union (country S). That country's trade deficit and current account deficit increase, inducing a larger foreign debt and payment of interest and dividends to country S. Due to their income's reduction, country N households consume less and demand fewer assets. Country N firms adjust in the same way and pay less dividends, which decreases the equities rate of return of country N and makes equities of country S more attractive. Thanks to the holding of country S assets, capital income of country N households and firms improves with rising dividends distributed by S firms whose profit are increasing. This contributes to sustain the demand and reduces the country N decrease, which leads to a stabilizing effect.

The loss of competitiveness and the foreign debt deteriorate the trade and current balances of country N. After an initial decline the current balance improves slightly more than the trade balance, thanks to the distribution of dividends of country S to country N. But this effect does not last and is quickly compensated by the rise of capital incomes paid to country S in the wake of growing foreign debt.

These adjustment mechanisms through capital incomes and through external finance from country S can be analyzed with the different structures of the model. Figure 10.1 compares the respective declines of GDP in country N after the loss of competitiveness in each of the four structures of the model.

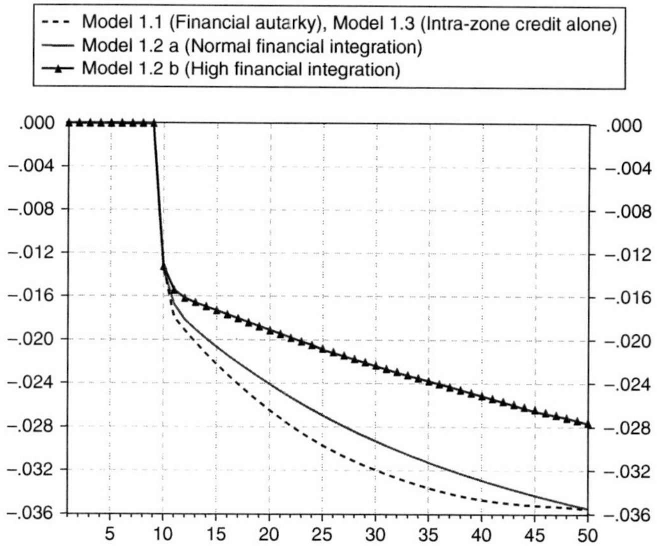

Figure 10.1 Effects on the GDP of a loss of competitiveness in country N without credit rationing

The first result is the identity between financial autarky (Model 1.1 without foreign assets and without intra-zone finance) and the case where there is only foreign finance with intra-zone credit and Treasury bills (Model 1.3). This means that the foreign finance through intra-zone credit or Treasury bills has no specific stabilization effect. As the central bank refinances already the commercial banks, the development of intra-zone credit or Treasury bills has no additional effect in the face of a shock. In a monetary union there is no difference of nature between domestic credit and foreign, but intra-zone, credit. The refinancing by the central bank plays in the same way.

The comparison between financial autarky (Model 1.1) and the two cases of complete financial integration (Model 1.2a and 1.2b) with foreign assets and capital income is interesting. The decline of the GDP is clearly less pronounced in Model 1.2b where the share of foreign assets in total assets is high (and even very high). This means that capital incomes indeed have a stabilization effect. However, in Model 1.2a, where the share of foreign assets is more limited (and more realistic), the dampening of the shock is reduced, but significant in the short to medium term.

In the long run there is a reversal, characterized by a stabilization that becomes more important in the basic model without foreign assets. This is explained by the more sustained growth which can be obtained in country S when capital income is kept at home instead of being distributed to country N. This stronger growth of country S is sufficient in the long run to sustain the country N growth through more exports from country N to country S. But this is only a long-term effect.

A stabilization coefficient can be calculated by measuring the gap between financial autarky and the other models. For Model 1.1, the relative decline of the GDP after the shock (at period 10) can be written at period 13: $\frac{(\text{Yn after the shock} - \text{Yn before the shock})}{\text{Yn before the shock}} = -2.05\%$.

For Model 1.2-a, we get: $\frac{(\text{Yn after the shock} - \text{Yn before the shock})}{\text{Yn before the shock}} = -1.91\%$.

The gap between the two models is obtained by the ratio of the relative decrease of the GDP:

$$\frac{\textit{Model}\ 1.2a}{\textit{Model}\ 1.1} = \frac{-1.91\%}{-2.05\%} = 93.4\%$$

which is equivalent to a stabilization coefficient of 6.6 per cent. Table 10.3 gives different stabilization coefficients measured with the same method at three periods and for the three models examined.

The stabilization by capital incomes (according to Model 1.2a) would be 6.6 per cent, which is small. For Model 1.2b the stabilization would be around 19 per cent for the period 13. This is obviously higher, but corresponds to an unrealistic hypothesis as already indicated. The underlying idea is simple: the more country N agents hold country S assets, the more will capital incomes from country S to country N have an adjustment effect, as the country S benefits of a recovery thanks to its gain of competitiveness and distributes more dividends.

Complementarily, the diffusion effects of a negative shock in a monetary union can be analyzed and related to the degree of financial integration. More precisely, the impact of a financial crisis in the rest of the union (country S) will be simulated successively by a fall of the rate of accumulation and of the equities' prices. A decrease of the rate of accumulation in the rest of the union diffuses to the country N. The higher the financial integration is, the more the diffusion effect is marked. Figure 10.2 gives the effect on the GDP of country N. In financial autarky (Model 1.1) the country N is less touched. By contrast, with a high degree of financial integration (Model 1.2b) the negative impact is more important, due to the reduction of capital income coming from the rest of the union. The simulation also confirms that intra-zone credit alone has no impact on the diffusion mechanisms (Model 1.3). The negative values of the stabilization coefficients, computed in the same way as before, illustrate also the negative diffusion effects due to financial integration (Table 10.4).

Similarly, the simulation of a negative shock on the stock exchange in the rest of the union (country S) underlines the importance of diffusion effects in a monetary union with financial integration. A decrease of equities' prices in country S has a strong negative impact on the GDP of country N, as is illustrated by Figure 10.3. In financial autarky (Model 1.1),

Table 10.3 Stabilization coefficients after a loss of competitiveness without credit rationing (shock in t=10)

	t=13	t=15	t=20
Model 1.2a Normal financial integration	6.6%	7.5%	9.0%
Model 1.2b High financial integration	19.0%	22.5%	27.8%
Model 1.3 Intra-zone credit alone	0.0%	0.0%	0.0%

Source: Author's estimation.

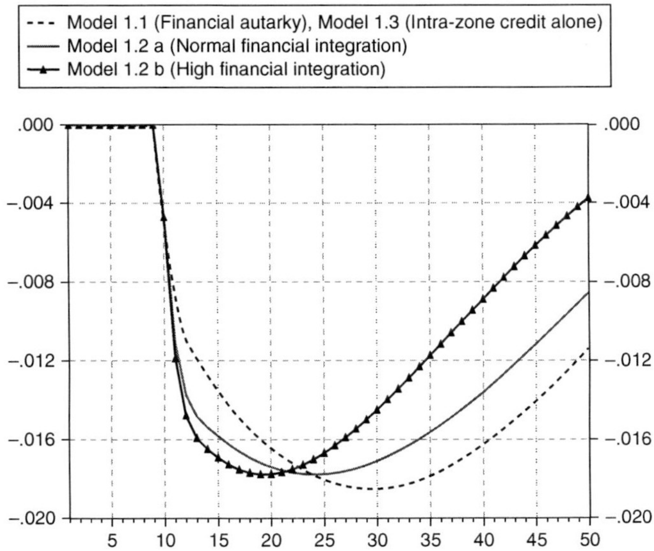

Figure 10.2 Effect on country N GDP of a decrease of the rate of accumulation in the rest of the union (country S) equivalent to –1 per cent of GDP

Table 10.4 Stabilization coefficients after a decrease of the rate of accumulation and a decrease of equities' prices in the rest of the union (country S)

Decrease of the rate of accumulation in country S (equivalent to –1 per cent of GDP)			
	t=13	t=15	t=20
Model 1.2a Normal financial integration	−23.0%	−17.0%	−5.8%
Model 1.2b High financial integration	−32.4%	−25.1%	−8.0%
Model 1.3 Intra-zone credit alone	0.0%	0.0%	0.0%
Decrease of equities' prices in country S (–2 per cent)			
	t=13	t=15	t=20
Model 1.2a Normal financial integration	−58.4%	−76.7%	−118.6%
Model 1.2b High financial integration	−142.0%	−168.1%	−216.3%
Model 1.3 Intra-zone credit alone	0.0%	0.0%	0.0%

the shock's diffusion goes only through the foreign trade and remains limited. With normal financial integration (Model 1.2a) the shock is also transmitted through assets portfolios and capital losses of country N firms and households. The negative impact on GDP is even more important in

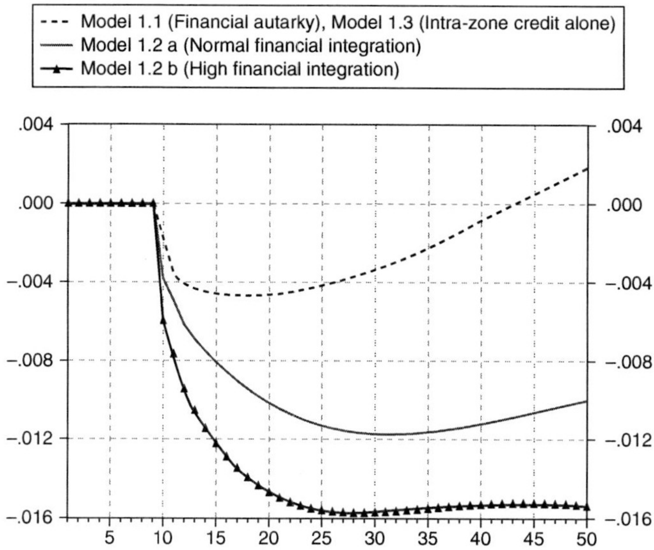

Figure 10.3 Effect of a fall of country S equities' prices (–2 per cent) on GDP of country N

the case of high financial integration (Model 1.2b). As before, intra-zone credit alone has no impact on diffusion effects (Model 1.3). The stabilization coefficients illustrate the amplitude of these effects in the case of normal or high financial integration (Table 10.4).

10.3.3 Adjustment with global credit rationing (model 2)

In Model 2 there is a global credit rationing and country N firms cannot obtain from banks all of the credit they demand. Therefore their investment is constrained by the total flow of available finance which depends specially of the credit supplied by banks. Like previously, adjustment mechanisms are analysed through a loss of competitiveness in country N facing the rest of the union. The loss of competitiveness induces an increase of country N imports and a decline of production and profit. Firms demand more credit but are rationed by banks of both countries.[4] Results are different according to the various versions of the model (Figure 10.4).

As previously, there is no stabilizing effect by the intra-zone credit. Model 2.1 (financial autarky) and Model 2.3 (with only intra-zone credit) give the same results. By contrast, financial integration (via the

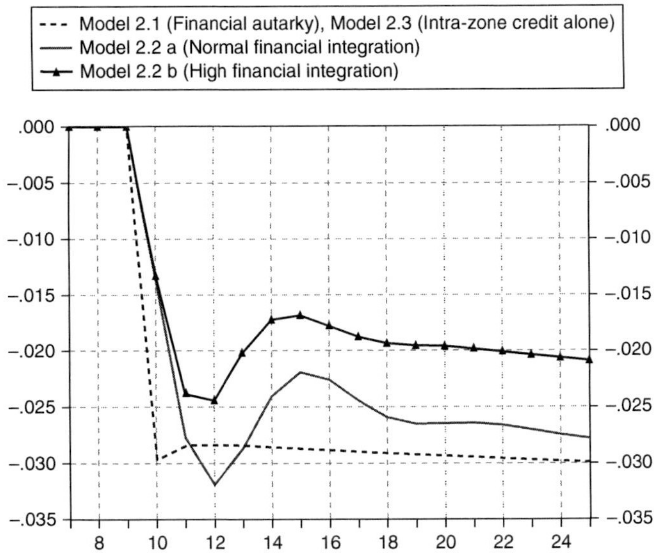

Figure 10.4 Effect of a loss of country N competitiveness on GDP of country N with global credit rationing

Table 10.5 Stabilization coefficients after a loss of country N competitiveness with global credit rationing

	t=13	t=15	t=20
Model 2.2a Normal financial integration	−0.9%	23.7%	9.8%
Model 2.2b High financial integration	29.0%	41.4%	33.2%
Model 2.3 Intra-zone credit alone	0.0%	0.0%	0.0%

stock market) has a stabilizing effect in the event of global rationing of enterprises. This stabilization effect is all the more marked as financial integration is important (Models 2.2a and 2.2b).

The year of the shock, higher financial integration allows country N companies of not being rationed. In the short term, the comparison of Models 2.1 (financial autarky) and 2.2a (financial integration) may be noticed. The decline of GDP is larger the year of the shock in Model 1 (financial autarky). But in t + 1, GDP rebounds in financial autarky. Indeed, as banks do not give the credit requested by companies, the credit crunch forces companies to reduce their investments. In addition, firms issue fewer shares following the decline of private income (the loss of competitiveness reduces the income of private agents who therefore require fewer shares). Firms pay lower dividends and thereby restore their profit. This temporary adjustment in period t +1 allows companies to invest more. In Model 2.2a, credit rationing occurs in t +1 after the shock of the loss of competitiveness. As in autarky, credit rationing forces companies to invest less. However, as country S holds a part (25 per cent) of the country N shares, the demand of shares depends partly of country S economic activity.

At first the GDP of country S is stimulated by the trade shock, as country N imports more goods from country S. But in a second time, banks ration country N and the GDP decline reduces the country S exports and thus its income. The investment financing becomes more difficult than in autarky where demand of action does not depend on country S income. After period 13 GDP is recovering in Model 2.2a through the restoration of profit rate and rising demand of shares from the companies. In Model 2.2b, there is a stronger stabilization of GDP. The first shock (increase of exports S) allows the country N to benefit from the feedback effects of higher income of country S. The issue of shares decreases less than in the other two models, limiting the decline in investment. After the rationing of country N banks, GDP recovers as in Model 2.2a. The negative effect on output is mitigated by the fact that banks do not ration credit to periods 14 and 15. The external financing through shares can relax the financing constraint imposed by country N banks.

10.3.4 Adjustment with credit rationing by domestic banks (Model 3)

We now assume that only domestic banks ration credit. Banks from the rest of the union do not ration and a smoothing effect of asymmetric shocks may be obtained through this channel. In order to measure this stabilization effect, Version 3 of the model (with only intra-zone credit and without other foreign assets) is slightly modified. We first assume that the domestic banks of country N ration credit of country N firms and do not finance the rest of the union. The variation of the credit supply of domestic banks of country N is supposed constant.

$$\Delta CRED^{N} = \Delta CRED^{sN} = \Delta CRED^{sN}_{N} = \eta 0$$

$$\Delta CRED^{N}_{S} = 0$$

Banks of the rest of the union (country S) supply credit without rationing to firms of country S ($CRED^{dS}_{S}$) and of country N ($CRED^{dS}_{N}$).

Consequently, they supply credits requested by country N firms for financing their investments (ΔL^{dN}).

$$CRED^{dS} = CRED_S^{dS} + CRED_N^{dS}$$

$$\Delta L^{dN} = I^{dN} - UP^N - p_e^N . \Delta E^N + p_e^N . \Delta E_{eN}^N + p_e^S . \Delta E_{eN}^S$$

$$\Delta L^{dN} = \Delta CRED_N^{dN} + \Delta CRED_N^{dS}$$

$$\Delta L^N = \Delta CRED_N^{sN} + \Delta CRED_N^{dS} = \eta 0 + \Delta CRED_N^{dS}$$

Country N firms are financed both by domestic credit ($CRED_N^{sN}$) and credit from the rest of the union ($CRED_N^{dS}$). The share of foreign credit is simply linked to the degree of openness.

$$CRED_N^{dS} = \left(\frac{X^N}{Y^N}\right) . L^{dN}$$

In the standard version of the model (Model 3.3a) this share of foreign credit is stable around 25 per cent, close to the observed data. In another version (Model 3.3b) a higher level of intra-zone credit (75 per cent) is introduced in order to appreciate the effect of a deeper integration.[5]

Finally, in this Model 3 with credit rationing by domestic banks, firms are constrained at domestic level, but not vis-à-vis the rest of the union. Banks of the rest of the union (country S) do not ration country N firms, which may constitute an adjustment mechanism facing asymmetric shocks. The identity between Model 3.1 (financial autarky) and Model 3.3 (with intra-zone credit), which was observed in the previous cases, will not prevail.

Adjustment mechanisms are analyzed once again in the case of a loss of competitiveness in country N. The increase of country N imports has a negative impact on production. The situation in autarky (Model 3.1) is similar to the one studied in case of overall rationing on country N firms (Model 2.1). Firms of country N have domestic credit as the sole source of bank financing. Credit rationing by domestic banks leads to a stronger recession than in the case where companies can underwrite loans abroad from the rest of the union (Model 3.3a and 3.3b). Figure 10.5 illustrates this evolution. In the short term, the stabilization by external borrowing is around 9 per cent in case of a moderate, but realistic, degree of intra-zone credit (Model 3.3a). In Model 3.3b (with a higher degree of intra-zone credit), stabilization of production via the intra-zone credit is 22 per cent (Table 10.6). However, in the long term a reversal between the three models can be observed.

The decline of GDP in the financial autarky case is less important in the long run than in the case where companies can obtain finance from the rest of the union. This reversal is primarily a consequence of the credit dynamics. Initially the credit to country N firms increases in Models 3.3a and 3.3b, allowing companies to invest more, compared with the case of financial autarky. But in the long run, the decline of consumption pulls down production and corporate profit. The investment declines more sharply, reducing demand for loans (desired by companies). In autarky, where rationing is constant, the economy is more stable over the long term.

10.3.5 Adjustment with credit rationing by nonresident banks (Model 3 bis)

A higher intra-zone integration of credit may also be a vehicle for the diffusion of negative shocks inside the monetary union. We consider the case of country N firms facing credit rationing by nonresident

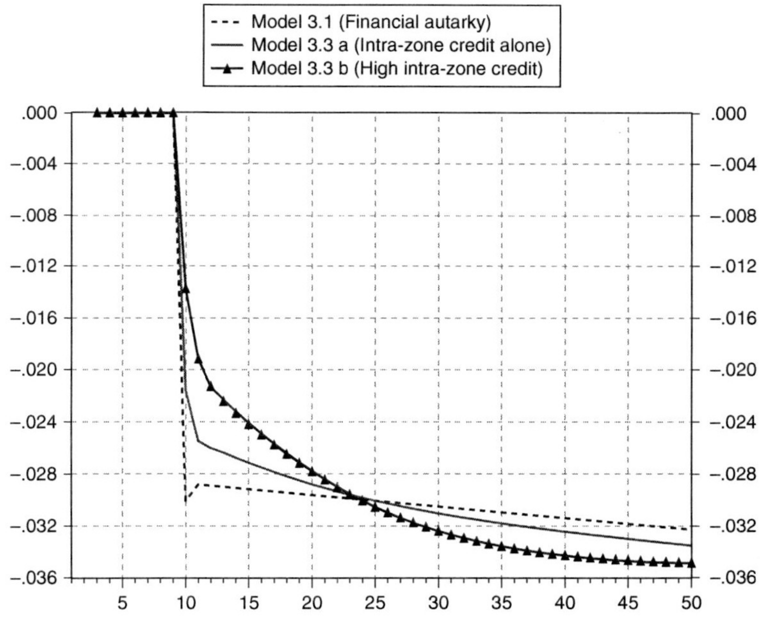

Figure 10.5 Effect of a loss of country N competitiveness on GDP of country N with credit rationing by domestic banks

Table 10.6 Stabilization coefficients after a loss of competitiveness in country N with credit rationing by domestic banks

	t=13	t=15	t=20
Model 3.3a Intra-zone credit alone	8.6%	6.7%	2.9%
Model 3.3b High intra-zone credit	22.1%	16.8%	16.6%

banks of the rest of the union (country S) in order to estimate contagion effects on the production of country N. We assume now that country N banks do not ration country N firms and supply all the credits requested ($\Delta CRED^{dN}_{N}$). For sake of simplicity we also assume that they do not finance country S firms ($\Delta CRED^{N}_{S} = 0$).

The banks of the rest of the union (country S) ration their credit supply ($\Delta CRED^{sS} = \lambda_s$) which is shared between country S firms ($\Delta CRED^{sS}_{S}$) and country N firms ($\Delta CRED^{sS}_{N}$). $\Delta CRED^{sS} = \Delta CRED^{sS}_{S} + \Delta CRED^{sS}_{N}$

Country S firms are completely rationed while country N firms are only rationed by banks of the rest of the union (country S), but can get their requested credits from the domestic banks. The effective distributed credits to country N firms (ΔL^{N}) and to country S firms (ΔL^{S}) are given by the following equations:

$$\Delta L^{N} = \Delta CRED^{dN}_{N} + \Delta CRED^{sS}_{N}$$

$$\Delta L^{S} = \Delta CRED^{sS}_{S}$$

We simulate the impact of a bank crisis in the rest of the union (country S) with a dramatic credit rationing (decrease of λ_s) and we estimate the contagion effect on country N. We compare the case of financial integration with intra-zone credit (Model 3bis.3) with the financial autarky where country N firms do not receive credit from the rest of the union (Model 3bis.1). Figure 10.6 describes the dynamics of GDP of country N following this brutal credit rationing. Logically, in financial autarky the GDP decreases much less than in the case of intra-zone credit. In Model 3bis.3b where the share of intra-zone credit is very high (almost 75 per cent of total loans), the diffusion of the shock of credit rationing from country S to country N is very important.

The coefficients of (de)stabilization are also very high in the short and medium term (Table 10.7). In autarky, country N is only indirectly affected by the rationing of country S's banks through the trade channel. Country S's banks ration firms of their country credit which induces a fall of business investment and production in country S. This sharp

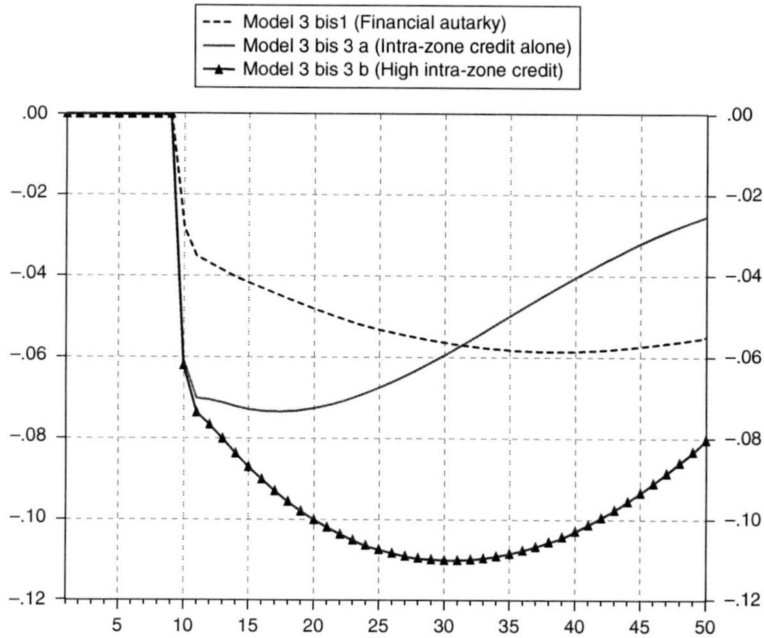

Figure 10.6 Effect of credit rationing by country S banks on the GDP of country N

Table 10.7 Stabilization coefficients in case of credit rationing by country S banks

	t=13	t=15	t=20
Model 3bis3a Intra-zone credit alone	−83.5%	−74.4%	−50.2%
Model 3bis3b High intra-zone credit	−106.1%	−108.2%	−106.7%

drop in income has an impact on foreign trade. Country S imports less, thereby reducing country N's exports. This decline is spread to households and firms and depresses consumption and investment. But the recession in financial autarky is smaller than in case of intra-zone credit. In Model 3bis.3b, where the intra-zone credit is large, the tightening of credit conditions in the country S leads to a strong and long recession in country N. In Model 3bis.3a (average but more realistic degree of intra-zone credit), the country N's GDP is less affected, but the negative impact appears clearly in the short and medium term by comparison with the situation of financial autarky. In the long run, a resumption of GDP can be observed in country N with Model 3bis.3a. This is due to the support given by domestic credit which is not rationed and can compensate in the long run the credit rationing by nonresident banks.

10.3.6 Treasury bills rationing (Model 4)

The Greek and Irish crisis of spring and autumn 2010 highlighted the importance of external financing in a monetary union. The increase in public and external debt was reflected in the financial markets by raising interest rates on the Greek and Irish bonds. In standard SFC models, the issue of government securities is not constrained. State can finance its deficit without restriction. In order to take into account the constraints of financing public deficit, we modify the standard model and introduce rationing on government securities. In addition, we will endogenize the interest rates to assess the impact of debt burden on the economy.

We return to the initial model, where credit is not rationed, but we assume now that government bonds of country N may be rationed by country N banks due to the degradation of the economic situation. The goal here is to compare, in an economy with Treasury bills rationing, the effect of a negative shock on output in a case of financial autarky (Model 4.1) and in the case of intra-zone credit (Model 4.3). Securities issued by country N government and underwritten by country N banks are rationed according to the balance sheet of banks. The following equations describe the Treasury bills issued by country N government (ΔBT^N) and the Treasury bills rationed by country N banks (ΔBT_N^N).

$$\Delta BT^N = G^N + r_n \,.\, BT_{-1}^N + B_{-1}^N - T^N - TB^N - T€B^N - p_b^N \,.\, \Delta B^N$$

$$\Delta BT_N^N = \text{m0} \,.\, (\Delta H^N + \Delta L_N^N)$$

H^N = banks reserves requirement at the central bank
L_N^N = Credits supplied by country N's banks to country N's firms.

In financial autarky, bank rationing implies that the government must adjust its fiscal policy. Assuming that banks are unwilling to finance the entire deficit, the state is forced to cut public expenditures (Model 4.1a). Another alternative would be to raise taxes to increase state revenue. In this case, taxes depend on the banks rationing (Model 4.1b).

$$\Delta G^N = \Delta BT_N^N - r_n \,.\, BT_{-1}^N - B_{-1}^N + T^N + TB^N + T€B^N + p_b^N \,.\, \Delta B^N$$

$$\Delta T^N = G^N + r_n \,.\, BT_{-1}^N + B_{-1}^N - TB^N - T€B^N - p_b^N \,.\, \Delta B^N - \Delta BT_N^N$$

By contrast, if the State can sell its Treasury bills in the rest of the union (country S), the budgetary policy is no longer constrained. Purchase of Treasury bills by banks of country S adjusts the gap between issued securities and securities held by domestic banks:

$$\Delta BT_S^N = \Delta BT^N - \Delta BT_N^N$$

We simulate a loss of competitiveness of country N and compare the damping of the shock in financial autarky (Model 4.1a or 4.1b) and with extra-zone finance (Model 4.3). The worsening trade balance reduces country N's national income. Therefore tax revenues fall and the public deficit becomes larger. The need for government funding increases but banks are rationing the demand for public securities. This Treasury bill rationing forces the state to pursue a restrictive policy which augments the slow down. On the contrary, with extra-zone finance, the funding requirement is met by country S's banks (Model 4.3).

Intra-zone financing of Treasury bills stabilizes part of the shock. In t+3 after the shock, stabilization by external financing is 15 per cent. In the medium term, this stabilization is around 20 per cent. Restrictive fiscal policy in financial autarky amplifies long-term recession. It may be noted that in this case fiscal policy (Model 4.1b) is less costly than the decline of public spending (Model 4.1a). About 3 per cent of the shock can be stabilized by higher taxes compared to a policy of reduced public expenditure (Figure 10.7 and Table 10.8).

10.3.7 Variable interest rate (Model 5)

In addition to the quantitative adjustment of fiscal policy, financial conditions may also worsen. Facing rising public deficit, banks of country N can finance part of the deficit, but at higher rates. The increase of interest rate on government securities is determined by confrontation of the supply of Treasury bills issued by the government of country N to finance the remaining part of its public deficit (ΔBT^N) and the demand of these bills by domestic banks (BT_N^N) and by banks from the rest of the union (BT_S^N). For sake of simplification, the demand of these bills by domestic banks is a simple linear rising function of the rate of interest r_n.

$$BT_N^N = \beta_{1N} * r_n + \beta_{0N}$$

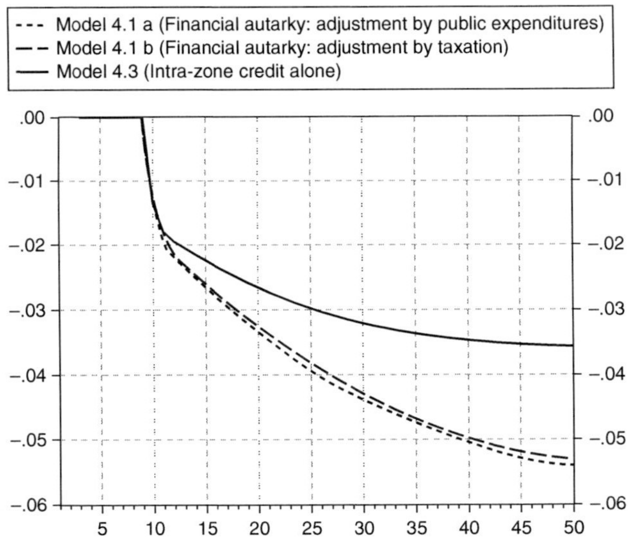

Figure 10.7 Impact of a loss of country N competitiveness on GDP of country N with or without Treasury bills rationing

Table 10.8 Stabilization coefficients after a loss of competitiveness with or without Treasury bills rationing

	t=13	t=15	t=20
Model 4.3 Intra-zone credit alone	14.7%	17.0%	21.1%
Model 4.1b Financial autarky: adjustment by tax	3.5%	3.4%	3.1%

Symmetrically, we assume that the demand of country N Treasury bills N by banks from the rest of the Union (BT^N_S) depends positively of the rate of interest of these bills.

$$BT^N_S = \beta_{1S} * r_n + \beta_{0S}$$

with $\Delta BT^N = \Delta BT^N_N + \Delta BT^N_S$.

Fiscal policy takes into account the interest burden related to external financing (Model 5.3a).

$$G^N = G^N_{baseline} - (r_n * BT^N_{-1})$$

Interest rates on bonds and loans (respectively rb_n and rl_n) are modeled in the same manner as the rates on Treasury bills (r_n). As bond prices represent the inverse of interest rates, the effect of a change in the rate on the bonds will lead to capital gains/losses. But, in order not to overestimate this effect on GDP, we introduce a lag vis-à-vis the rate on government securities (r_n). Therefore, the equation of interest rates on bonds is:

$$rb_n = rb_{n-1} * (1 - a) + a * r_{n-1}$$

rb_n = interest rate on bonds, r_n = interest rate on Treasury bills

Interest rates on loans will be simply supposed equal to the rate on Treasury bills:

$$rl_n = r_n$$

rl_n = interest rate on loans from banks of country N.

As previously, we compare the effect of a loss of competitiveness in country N in the case of financial autarky with endogenous interest rates and restrictive fiscal policy through expenditures cut or increasing taxes (Model 5.1a or 5.1b) and in the case of intra-zone finance, also with rising interest rates (Model 5.3). The evolution of GDP after the shock of competitiveness is illustrated by Figure 10.8. In the short term, in financial autarky domestic banks finance a part of the public deficit, but with higher interest rates which increases the deficit. The government is forced to adopt a restrictive policy which accentuates the slowdown. By contrast, in the short term, external financing can cushion the recession thanks to larger funds which authorizes a less restrictive policy.

But in the medium to long run, a reversal appears. Without external financing the state pursues a more restrictive fiscal policy which reduces the public deficit and makes the state less dependent on financial markets. With intra-zone finance, nonresident banks contribute to finance a larger deficit of country N. But public debt increases continuously and interest rates reach exorbitant levels, generating a cumulative process. The slowdown is accentuated by expenditures cut and the fall of investment which is more marked in Model 5.3.

In financial autarky, the relative decline of GDP is stabilized at –5 per cent in the long term. GDP does not dive as in the model with external financing The shock of competitiveness shows that a crisis may appear because of excessive leverage vis-à-vis the financial markets.

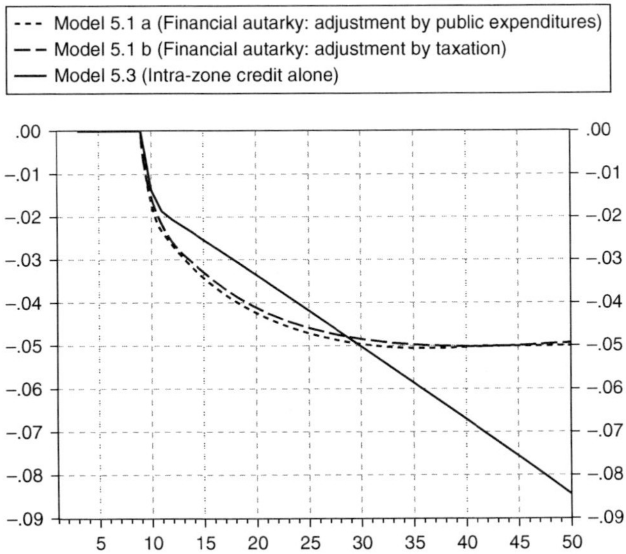

Figure 10.8 Impact of a loss of country N competitiveness on GDP of country N with variable interest rates

Table 10.9 Stabilization coefficients in case of a loss of country N competitiveness with variable interest rates

	t=13	t=15	t=20
Model 5.3 Intra-zone credit alone	24.2%	25.0%	21.4%
Model 5.1b Financial autarky: adjustment by tax	0.8%	1.1%	2.3%

Maintaining funding too costly plunges the economy into a cumulative recession that could lead to payment defaults.

In financial autarky, the relative growth of GDP has stabilized at –5 per cent in the long term. GDP does not fall as in the model with external financing to the extent that the state pursues a more restrictive fiscal policy in the short term which makes it less dependent on financial markets.

Financial openness can finance larger deficits, but the level can reach exorbitant interest rates cut spending and, in particular, private investment (the interest rate on long-term increasing more with external financing, the fall in investment will be higher in the variants of Model 3).

The shock of competitiveness shows that a crisis may appear because of excessive leverage vis-à-vis the financial markets. Maintaining a funding too costly plunges the economy into a cumulative recession that could lead to the payment default.

10.4 Conclusion

An approach based on a 'stock-flow consistent' model of a monetary union with two countries along the lines of Godley and Lavoie has been proposed. The model describes assets and liabilities of all the agents and analyses financial integration in a consistent manner. Using different versions of the model, a whole set of simulations has been realized to study adjustments facing asymmetric shocks. Several results have been obtained.

Foreign asset holdings have a stabilizing role, but the capital income stabilizing coefficient seems smaller than the one obtained by the 'risk-sharing' approach. By contrast, foreign loans (intra-zone credit) have no specific stabilization effects. This is due to the credit mechanism in a monetary union and to the key role played by refinancing by the central bank. Inside a monetary union, domestic credit and foreign credit from another member of the union are of the same type. There is no increase of the stabilization coefficient to expect from development of intra-eurozone credit. This is true without credit rationing or with global credit rationing by domestic and nonresident banks.

However, when nonresident banks, contrary to domestic ones, do not ration credit or buy Treasury bills without restriction, intra-zone credit have a stabilization effect. But when interest rates increase due to banks' reluctance to finance more issue of Treasury bills, intra-zone credit from the rest of the union has no more stabilizing effect due to its increasing cost. This can be regarded as an illustration of the last Greek crisis and as an argument in favor of direct financing by the central bank or by a European Monetary Fund which could be created.

Appendix

Table 10.A.1 Transaction matrix

	COUNTRY N								COUNTRY S						
	Households N	Firms N		Government N	Banks N		Central Bank		Households S	Firms S		Government S	Banks S		Σ
Goods N	$-C^N$	$+Y^N$	$-I^N$	$-G^N$					$-X^N + IM^N$						0
Goods S	$-X^S + IM^S$								$-C^S$	$+Y^S$	$-I^S$	$-G^S$			0
Wages	$+W^N$	$-W^N$							$+W^S$	$-W^S$					0
Interest on loans		$-r_l \,.\, L^N_{-1}$			$+r_l \,.\, L^N_{N-1}$								$+r_l \,.\, L^N_{S-1}$		0
					$+r_l \,.\, L^S_{N-1}$					$-r_l \,.\, L^S_{-1}$			$+r_l \,.\, L^S_{S-1}$		0
Interest on deposits	$+i_d \,.\, BD^N_{-1}$				$-i_d \,.\, BD^N_{-1}$				$-i_d \,.\, BD^S_{-1}$				$-i_d \cdot BD^S_{-1}$		0
Interest on refinancing					$-i_b \cdot RF^N_{-1}$		$-i_b \cdot (RF^N_{-1} + RF^S_{-1})$						$-i_b \cdot RF^S_{-1}$		0
Interest on bonds	$+B^N_{N-1}$			$-B^N_{-1}$					$+B^N_{S-1}$						0
	$+B^S_{N-1}$								$+B^S_{S-1}$			$-B^S_{-1}$			0
Interest on bills				$-r \,.\, BT^N_{-1}$	$+r \,.\, BT^N_{N-1}$								$+r \,.\, BT^N_{S-1}$		0
					$+r \,.\, BT^S_{N-1}$							$-r \,.\, BT^S_{-1}$	$+r \,.\, BT^S_{S-1}$		0
Dividends	$+DIV^N_{hN}$	$+DIV^N_{eN}$ $-DIV^N$							$+DIV^N_{hS}$	$+DIV^N_{eS}$					0
	$+DIV^S_{hN}$	$+DIV^S_{eN}$							$+DIV^S_{hS}$	$+DIV^S_{eS}$ $-DIV^S$					0

(continued)

Table 10.A.1 Continued

	COUNTRY N								COUNTRY S						
	Households N	**Firms N**		**Government N**	**Banks N**		**Central Bank**		**Households S**	**Firms S**		**Government S**	**Banks S**		Σ
Tax	$-T^N$			$+T^N$					$-T^S$			$+T^S$			0
				$+TB^N$	$-TB^N$							$+TB^S$	$-TB^S$		0
				$+T€B^N$			$-T€B$					$+T€B^S$			0
Profit		$-UP^N$	$+UP^N$							$-UP^S$	$+UP^S$				0
					$-PB^N$	$+PB^N$							$-PB^S$	$+PB^S$	0
Deposits	$-\Delta BD^N$					$+\Delta BD^N$			$-\Delta BD^S$					$+\Delta BD^S$	0
Currency	$-\Delta H_h^N$					$-\Delta H^N$		$+\Delta H$	$-\Delta H_h^S$					$-\Delta H^S$	0
Loans			$+\Delta L^N$			$-\Delta L_N^N$								$-\Delta L_S^N$	0
						$-\Delta L_N^S$					$+\Delta L^S$			$-\Delta L_S^S$	0
Refinancing						$+\Delta RF^N$		$-\Delta RF^N$ $-\Delta RF^S$						$+\Delta RF^S$	0
Bonds	$-p_b^N \, . \, \Delta B_N^N$			$+p_b^N \, . \, \Delta B^N$					$-p_b^N \, . \, \Delta B_S^N$						0
	$-p_b^S \, . \, \Delta B_N^S$								$-p_b^S \, . \, \Delta B_S^S$			$+p_b^S \, \Delta B^S$			0
Bills				$+\Delta BT^N$		$-\Delta BT_N^N$								$-\Delta BT_S^N$	0
						$-\Delta BT_N^S$						$+\Delta BT^S$		$-\Delta BT_S^S$	0
Equities	$-p_e^N \, . \, \Delta E_{hN}^N$		$-p_e^N \, . \, \Delta E_{eN}^N$ $+p_e^N \, . \, \Delta E^N$						$-p_e^N \, . \, \Delta E_{hS}^N$		$-p_e^N \, . \, \Delta E_{eS}^N$				0
	$-p_e^S \, . \, \Delta E_{hN}^S$		$-p_e^S \, . \, \Delta E_{eN}^S$						$-p_e^S \, . \, \Delta E_{hS}^S$		$-p_e^S \, . \, \Delta E_{eS}^S$ $+p_e^S \, . \, \Delta E^S$				0
Σ	0	0	0	0	0	0	0	0	0	0	0	0	0	0	0

Table 10.A.2 Main parameters for calibration

Equities	400	Dividends received from foreign	7	Distribution of equities held	
Bonds	23	Interest (Bonds) received from foreign	0.2	Households	50%
Loans	50	Interest (Loans) received from foreign	0.2	Firms	50%
Bills	26	Interest (Bills) received from foreign	0.1	Foreign Dividends determined by detention of foreign equities	
Capital	410	GDP	100		
Elasticities		Propensity to consume a1	0.75	GDP growth	2% per year
		Wealth elasticity a2	0.04		
		Effect of profit rate on investment k1	0.5	Accumulation of capital	7% per year
		Propensity to import mu1	1		

Notes

1. Preliminary results have been already presented in the case where there is no credit rationing (Duwicquet and Mazier, 2010–11).
2. When there are two symbols (N and S), the subscript denotes the country where the asset is held, the superscript the country where the asset is issued. For example, BT_N^S is the bills held by country N and issued by the country S.
3. Results are given with a simplified version of the model where rates of growth of equity prices are exogenous. Consequently, the equations concerning the issue of new equities are taken out.
4. In the baseline, before the shock, credit supply is slightly larger than demand and there is no credit rationing. But, following the shock, production and profit decrease, which worsen firms' financial structure and incites banks to ration credit. For technical reasons bank rationing takes place from the first year of the shock in Model 2.1 and 2.3, but only after one year in Models 2.2a and 2.2b.
5. In the model 3.3b $CRED^{dS}_N = 3.\left(\frac{X^N}{Y^N}\right).L^{dN}$

References

Asdrubali, P. and S. Kim (2004) 'Dynamic Risksharing in the United States and Europe,' *Journal of Monetary Economics* 51(4): 809–36.

Asdrubali, P., B.E. Sorensen and O. Yosha (1996) 'Channels of Inter-State Risk-Sharing: United States 1963–1990,' *Quarterly Journal of Economics* 111(4): 1081–110.

Clévenot M. and Y. Guy (2010a) 'The Distributive Conflict in the "Patrimonial Regime" Through a SFC Model,' in C. Gnos and L.-P. Rochon (eds) *Employment, Growth and Development: A Post-Keynesian Approach* (Cheltenham, UK: Edward Elgar).

Clévenot M., Y. Guy and J. Mazier (2010b) 'Investment and Rate of Profit in a Financial Context: The French Case,' *International Review of Applied Economics* 24(6): 693–714.

Duwicquet, V. and J. Mazier (2010–11) 'Financial Integration and Macroeconomic Adjustments in a Monetary Union,' *Journal of Post Keynesian Economics* 33(2): 333–70.

Godley, W. (1999) 'Money and Credit in a Keynesian Model of Income Determination,' *Cambridge Journal of Economics* 23(4): 393–411.

Godley, W. and M. Lavoie (2007a) 'A Simple Model of Three Economies with Two Currencies: The Eurozone and the USA,' *Cambridge Journal of Economics* 31(1): 1–23.

Godley, W. and M. Lavoie (2007b) *Monetary Economics* (London: Palgrave Macmillan).

Godley, W. and M. Lavoie (2005–06) 'Comprehensive Accounting in Simple Open Economy Macroeconomics with Endogenous Sterilization of Flexible Exchange Rates,' *Journal of Post Keynesian Economics* 28(2): 241–76.

Goodhart, C.A.E. and S. Smith (1993) '"Stabilisation" in The Economics of Community Public Finance,' *European Economy* 5(V): 417–55.

Italianer, A. and J. Pisani-Ferry, J. (1992) 'Systèmes Budgétaires et Amortissement des Chocs Régionaux: Implications pour l'Union Économique et Monétaire,' *Economie internationale* 51(3): 49–69.

Lavoie, M. (2003) 'A Fully Coherent Post-Keynesian Model of the Euro Zone,' in P. Arestis, M. Baddeley and J. McCombie (eds) *Globalisation, Regionalism and Economic Activity* (Cheltenham, UK: Edward Elgar).

Mazier, J. and S. Saglio (2008) 'Interdependency and Adjustments in the European Union,' *International Review of Applied Economics* 22(1): 17–44.

Mazier, J., E.M. Mouhoud, J. Oudinet and S. Saglio (2007) 'Quel Rôle Jouent les Migrations dans le Fonctionnement de l'Union Monétaire?,' in *L'Europe et ses Migrants, Ouverture ou Repli?* (Paris: Harmattan), pp. 151–214.

Mazier J., S. Saglio and J. Oudinet (2002) 'La Flexibilité des Prix Relatifs et la Mobilité du Travail en Union Monétaire: Une Comparaison Europe–Etats-Unis,' *Revue de l'OFCE* 83: 325–88.

Taylor, L. (2004) *Reconstructing Macroeconomics* (Cambridge, MA: Harvard University Press).

Tobin, J. (1969) 'A General Equilibrium Approach to Monetary Theory,' *Journal of Money, Credit and Banking* 1(1): 15–29.

11

Debt-deflation Traps Within Small Open Economies: A Stock-flow Consistent Perspective

Stephen Kinsella and Saed Khalil[1]

11.1 Introduction

The goal of this chapter is to build a stock-flow consistent model to simulate the macroeconomic effects of a small open economy experiencing a debt deflation. After the 2007–10 crisis, many countries are experiencing rapid declines in their price levels, while being overburdened by levels of debt, which constrains their growth (Kinsella and Leddin, 2010; Koo, 2009). This chapter traces out the macroeconomic consequences and recovery options in a two-country model. We assume one country is small, and open to trade, while the other is larger, with trade accounting for a much smaller fraction of its overall economic output.

We simulate the effects of a series of investment shocks on our stock-flow consistent macro model under varying assumptions. We find that debt overhangs take close to a decade to recover from, especially when the small open economy is particularly open to trade, and mechanisms to reduce debt can help speed the economy to a recovery following a debt buildup.

A debt deflation occurs when a fall in the price level raises the real value of nominal debt (Fisher, 1933). This phenomenon can exacerbate the costs of a deflation. Households that find themselves heavily in debt do not continue to consume more at the margin, but rather refrain from investing and consuming out of discretionary income in order to pay down loans more quickly. Domestic consumption and non-autonomous investment in productive capacity, as well as import and export demand, all suffer. The economy contracts as a result of the de-leveraging activities of firms and households, which further deepens the crisis. Combined with increases in government expenditure from automatic stabilizing mechanisms like social welfare payments, the increase in debt-servicing costs can be punitive for small open economies like Ireland, unable to stimulate their economies in a textbook Keynesian (or new-Keynesian) manner.

Tobin (1980, p. 58) describes the debt-deflation problem in stark terms:

> When nominal prices and wages are deflated, debt service is a higher proportion of debtors' incomes, and the reduction or elimination of their margins of equity disqualifies them from further access to credit. Bankruptcies and defaults do likewise, and transmit the distress of debtors to their creditors, threatening the solvency and liquidity of individual lenders and financial institutions.

The issue of stability arises because the relation runs both ways: deflation causes financial distress, and financial distress in turn exacerbates deflation. Negative aggregate price shocks had a significantly negative impact on financial conditions during the Great Depression.

On the debit side of the balance sheet, deflation decreases the purchasing power of the debtor at a time when the economy requires increased levels of consumption and investment, which deepens the downturn, and exacerbates the crisis. The two depressions of the past 150 years – the 1890s and the 1930s – had substantial deflations. Prices fell at up to 15 per cent per annum in the 1890s in the United States. Prices fell over 10 per cent per annum for two years during the Great Depression (DeLong, 1999). In a deflation, even a relatively low nominal rate of interest become a larger real interest rate, forcing a contraction in economic activity.

On the credit side, deflation increases the value of creditors' assets. However, with a large percentage of Irish firms and households over-indebted – unable to service their debts and meet recurring expenses – the increase in uncertainty associated with an increased likelihood of large-scale default (and consequent bad debt write down by public and private banks) outweighs the potential increase in creditors' funds from the deflation.

A higher level of debt finance imposes obligatory interest and principal repayments on firms and households. At the firm level, if a firm buys assets with borrowed money then, under extreme market conditions, it may owe more money than it has and, with reduced cash flow, its expectation of paying off its loans goes down and the firm defaults. If this happens on a sufficiently wide scale, then it can severely stress creditors and cause them to fail. High personal debt also inhibits the formation of new businesses and the expansion of existing small enterprises, since the balance sheet of owners is an important determinant of the ability of a firm to obtain credit. A common defensive reaction of firms that have suffered an adverse income shock is to reduce discretionary expenses, for example, investment, employment, wages, and/or dividend payments. A highly indebted set of firms can more easily fail or go into liquidation under the weight of debt service costs that cannot be met out of current income or cash reserves, increasing unemployment.

At the macroeconomic level, modern monetary systems require relatively stable price levels. Financial institutions and contracts are based on the prescription of reasonable price level stability. There are asymmetric affects of variations in the price level. Unexpected jumps in inflation, say, can in principle provide a temporary stimulus, as wealth is redistributed from creditors to debtors – who include most entrepreneurs. Deflation does the opposite, and in fact undermines the financial stability of many businesses, which undermines the institutional structures upon which successful economies are built (Nell, 2003).

The remainder of this chapter is as follows: Section 11.2 describes several 'channels' through which a debt deflation can operate, then moves on to a description of the model in Section 11.3, a discussion of the results in Section 11.4, and Section 11.5 concludes. An appendix contains the full description of the model.[2]

11.2 Debt-deflation channels: Directions for modeling

The link between financial distress to deflation (and back again) takes place through several channels. Different authors have, naturally, focused on different channels. For our work in modeling debt-deflation, clearly understanding and delineating these channels is important.

Fisher (1933), who originated the modern theory of debt-deflation, argued that borrowers attempting to reduce their burden of debt engage in *distress selling* to raise money for repaying debt. But repayment in aggregate causes a contraction in the money supply, and price level deflation. Fisher's finding was echoed by Kindleberger (1996), who expanded Fisher's analysis to other crises in economic history.

Keynes (1936) argued that a downward spiral of prices (and especially nominal wages) in an economy suffering from substantial unemployment would increase the real interest rate and the burden of servicing debts, and would discourage businesses from beginning new investments, making the liquidity constraint facing the economy worse. Keynes also argued that a fall in nominal (he used the term 'money') prices and wages would indirectly *increase* liquidity in the economy if the central bank maintained the nominal quantity of money, since when prices and wages are lower, the same nominal quantity of money represents relatively more purchasing power, relaxing the liquidity constraint on households and firms.

Keynes held that this roundabout way is the most painful way to create more liquidity in the economy, since the central bank could achieve the same thing by simply increasing the nominal money supply. Keynes held that nominal wage cuts could not bring about a fall in the real wage, because nominal wages are a large part of the costs of production. As nominal wages fall in the economy, all producers find their costs lowered, and competition will force them to lower the prices of goods and services bought by workers in proportion. This movement keeps the real wage constant, and leaves the economy with involuntary unemployment. A downward spiral of money wages and money prices is the last thing an economy suffering from substantial unemployment needs.

A modern Keynesian story for a small open economy like Ireland in a highly globalized international financial system runs like this: periods of persistent consumption growth can foster investment booms and output expansion, which in turn reinforces optimistic outlooks for permanent income and further stimulate consumption demand. So a mild consumption expansion triggered by optimism may turn into prolonged periods of over-expansion, and via a simple multiplier–accelerator process, the economy becomes destabilized. When borrowers have strong incentives to accumulate assets, and lenders are willing to supply credit elastically, endogenous boom–bust cycles can emerge, and such cycles result in excessive investment and over accumulation of capital during the boom and under investment in the slump.

Minsky (1986 [2008]) elaborated and extended Fisher's original concept to incorporate deflation in the asset market. Minsky recognized that distress selling reduces asset prices, causing losses to agents with maturing debts and, importantly, to highly leveraged agents with new debts. This reinforces distress selling, and reduces consumption and investment spending, which deepens deflation. Bernanke (1983) argued that debt-deflation involves widespread bankruptcy, impairing the process of credit intermediation. The resulting credit contraction depresses aggregate demand, thus exacerbating the crisis.

Woodford (2003) has argued that macroeconomic outcomes are largely independent of the performance of the financial system, and, in a bubble, simple wage-cost deflation towards trend is in fact desirable. Von Peter (2004) has emphasized the need for a removal of equilibrium constraints in modeling the current crisis. A stock-flow consistent perspective offers us the ability to produce models that incorporate these insights.

For an economy with an independent monetary policy, the standard policy prescription is for the central bank to credibly commit to being expansionary for a considerable period of time, by keeping interest rates near zero even after the economy has emerged from deflation (Eggertsson and Woodford, 2003). The notion of unstable debt-deflation ultimately relies on reasons why agents try to contain or reduce their indebtedness. Margin requirements can be one such reason. A credit crunch, which interferes with the accommodation necessary for stability, can be another, as discussed by King (1994).

The 'modern' debt-deflation process therefore encompasses falling asset prices, debt repayment difficulties, a reluctance to lend, a financial crisis, the impact on the banks, and the interdependency of the financial system. Recent debt-deflations have been aborted by lender-of-last-resort intervention and government support of the financial system during a crisis.

11.3 Model

Our debt-deflation mechanism is as follows. A macroeconomic shock occurs following a build-up of debt in the form of bills, bonds, and equities, which causes debt liquidation leading to distressed selling. This distressed selling of assets leads to a contraction of deposit currency and of its velocity. The small economy experiences a fall in the level of prices, and a still greater fall in the net worth of businesses. Businesses record falls in their profits. There follows a reduction in output, in trade, and in the employment of labor, leading to pessimism and loss of confidence. (Importantly, consumers and producers may lose or gain confidence at the beginning or the middle of this causal chain.) The decline in prices leads to an increase in debt servicing, and this offsets levels of debt liquidation. The economy experiences hoarding and a further slowing down of the velocity of circulation of money. We see complicated disturbances in the rates of interest on our financial goods. These interactions are summarized in Figure 11.1.

The model itself takes Godley and Lavoie (2007) as its starting point. The stock-flow consistent models they build are based on national income and product accounts and flow of funds accounts. Godley and Lavoie (1999, 2004, 2007) emphasize the dynamic interaction between price formation and functional income distribution. Godley and Lavoie's models are set up in such a way as to facilitate the construction of behavioral macroeconomic models in the tradition of Keynes (1936) and Kalecki (1971). This model building results in aggregate dynamics that can be

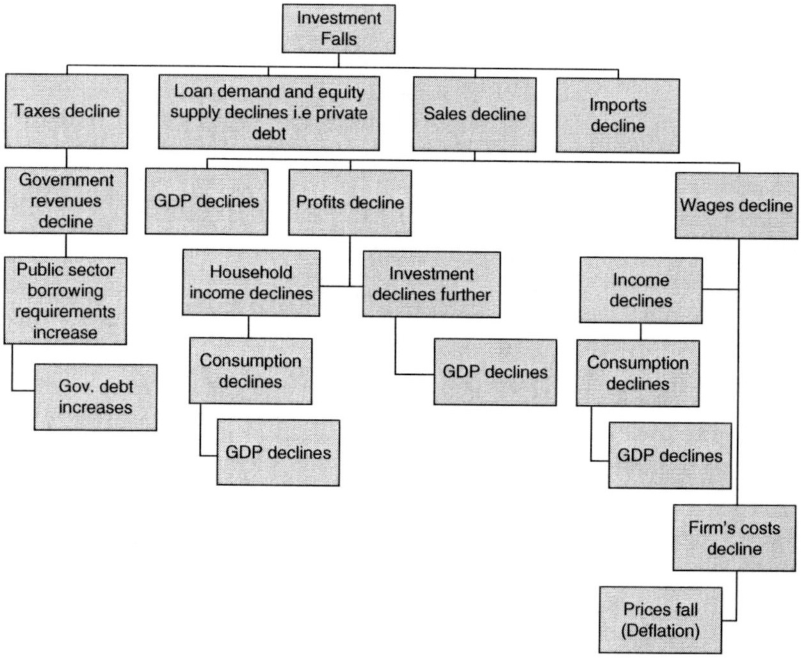

Figure 11.1 Causal structure of the model, following a fall in investment

described as business cycles, that is, the models replicate observed empirical regularities when parameterized. The extended accounting scheme underpinning any aggregate dynamics simulated in a stock-flow consistent model summarizes the transactions taking place within a realistic and modern financial sector that contains securities and financial facilities.

Each model divides the economy into five sectors: firms, households, government, the central bank, and private banks. These sectors are designed in such a way that the income inflows to one sector are outflows from other sectors. The same is true for financial transactions. These flows, when they accumulate over time, as they must in a dynamic context, become stocks; thus, the models are stock flow consistent (Taylor 2004, 2008). Ours is no different, and has five sectors also, which we describe briefly below.

First, let us discuss the balance sheets for this model. Tables 11.1 and 11.2 describe the interactions between different sectors. In reading the tables, the subscript *b* refers to a bank. The subscript *cb* refers to a central bank. The subscript *d* refers to demand. The superscript *e* refers to the expected value or volume. The subscript f denotes firms. The subscript h denotes households. The superscript or subscript i refers to 1 for country one and 2 for country two. The subscript l refers to loans. The subscript m refers to deposits. The superscript T refers to target value or volume. The superscript $z = 1$ for country one and 2 for country 2, such that $z \neq j$. $xr = e$ when $z = 1$ and $1/e$ when $z = 2$.

We assume two countries and five sectors in each country. Country 1 is assumed to be large relative to country 2, in terms of population, trade flows, and overall economic output. The exchange rate, E, mediates between the two nations in the usual way. We assume a floating exchange rate. All assets are in monetary units. Households and firms in this model hold several assets: treasury bills, B, bonds, BL, and equities, e. Subscripts denote countries 1 and 2, respectively. For ease of reading, we sketch the interaction of the five sectors below, and relegate the complete algebraic description of the model to an appendix.

11.3.1 Households

There are many households in this sector, and in the aggregate, we consider the household 'sector'. Households take loans L from the financial sector to finance consumption, as well as consuming out of their wages WB in each period and their savings from past periods V. Disposable income YD is the difference between the value of personal income YP, Taxes, T, and servicing interest r on loans L:

$$YD^i = YP^i - T^i_I - r^i_{l-1} \cdot L^i_{hd-1}$$

Households are assumed to consume the amount c in each period according to

$$c^i = \alpha^i_0 + \alpha^i_1 \cdot (yd^{ei} + nl^i) + \alpha^i_2 \cdot v^i_{-1}$$

Where each α^i represents the propensity to consume, inter alia, from current income and loans nl, and from past income v. In addition to loans, households can hold many types of assets in varying proportions. Households' financial portfolios may consist of domestic and foreign bills B, domestic and foreign bonds BL, deposits M, and equities, e. The balancing equations for the portfolio choice of each household are given in the appendix.

Households are also assumed to own the private banks in the system via (OF), hold cash money, and taking loans from these private banks.

Table 11.1 Balance sheets matrix

	Country 1					Ex. Rate	Country 2					Sum
	Households	Firms	Gov.	C. Bank	Banks		Households	Firms	Gov.	C. Bank	Banks	
Inventories		$+IN^1$				E		$+IN^1$				ΣIN
Fixed Capital		$+K^1$				E		$+K^2$				ΣK
HPM	$+H^1{}_{h\,d}$			$-H^1{}_s$	$+H^1{}_{b\,d}$		$+H^2{}_{h\,d}$			$-H^2{}_s$	$+H^2{}_{b\,d}$	0
Advances				$+A^1{}_s$	$-A^1{}_s$					$+A^2{}_s$	$-A^2{}_s$	0
Household Loans	$-L^1{}_{h\,d}$				$+L^1{}_{h\,s}$		$-L^2{}_{h\,d}$				$+L^2{}_{h\,s}$	0
Firm Loans		$-L^1{}_{f\,d}$			$+L^1{}_{f\,s}$			$-L^1{}_{f\,d}$			$+L^2{}_{f\,s}$	0
Deposits	$+M^1{}_d$				$-M^1{}_s$		$+M^2{}_d$				$-M^2{}_s$	0
Bills¹	$+B^1{}_{h\,1\,d}$		$-B^1{}_s$	$+B^1{}_{cb\,1\,d}$	$+B^1{}_{b\,1\,d}$	E	$+B^1{}_{h\,2\,d}$					0
Bills²	$+B^2{}_{h\,1\,d}$			$+B^2{}_{cb\,1\,d}$		E	$+B^2{}_{h\,2\,d}$		$-B^2{}_s$	$+B^2{}_{cb\,2\,d}$	$+B^2{}_{b\,2\,d}$	0
Bonds¹	$+BL^1{}_{1\,d}.P^1{}_{bl}$		$-BL^1{}_{1\,s}.P^1{}_{bl}$			E	$+BL^1{}_{2\,d}.P^1{}_{bl}$					0
Bonds²	$+BL^2{}_{1\,d}.P^2{}_{bl}$					E	$+BL^2{}_{2\,d}.P^2{}_{bl}$		$-BL^2{}_{2\,s}.P^2{}_{bl}$			0
Firm Equities	$+e^1{}_d.P^1{}_e$	$-e^1{}_s.P^1{}_e$					$+e^2{}_d.P^2{}_e$	$-e^2{}_s.P^2{}_e$				0
Bank Capital	$+OF^1$				$-OF^1$		$+OF^2$				$-OF^2$	0
Reserves				$+R^1$		E				$+R^2$		ΣR
Balance	$-V^1_h$	$-NW^1{}_f$	$-NW^1{}_g$			E	$-V^2{}_h$	$-NW^2{}_f$	$-NW^2{}_g$			$\Sigma K + \Sigma R$
Sum	0	0	0	0	0		0	0	0	0	0	0

Table 11.2 Transactions flows matrix

Country 1	Households	Firms		Government	C. Bank		Banks		Ex. Rate
		Current	Capital		Current	Capital	Current	Capital	
Consumption	$-C^1$	$+C^1$							
G. Expenditure		$+G^1$		$-G^1$					
Investment		$+I^1$	$-I^1$						
Exports		$+X^1$							E
Imports		$-IM^1$							E
Δ Inventories		$+\Delta IN^1$	$-\Delta IN^1$						
Taxes	$-T^1_l$	$-T^1{}_s$		$+T^1$					
Wages	$+WB^1$	$-WB^1$							
Firm profits	$+FD^1_f$	$-F^1{}_f$	$+FU^1{}_f$				$-r^1_{l-1}.NPL^1$		
Bank profits	$+FD^1_b$						$-F^1_b$	$+FU^1_b$	
C. Bank profits				$+F^1_{cb}$	$-F^1_{cb}$				
Interest on									
Advances					$+r^1{}_{a-1}.A^1{}_{s-1}$		$-r^1{}_{a-1}.A^1{}_{d-1}$		
Household loans	$-r^1{}_{l-1}.L^1{}_{h\,d-1}$						$+r^1{}_{l-1}.L^1{}_{h\,s-1}$		
Firm loans		$-r^1{}_{l-1}.L^1{}_{f\,d-1}$					$+r^1{}_{l-1}.L^1{}_{f\,s-1}$		
Deposits	$+r^1{}_{m-1}.M^1{}_{d-1}$						$+r^1{}_{m-1}.M^1{}_{s-1}$		
Bills[1]	$+r^1{}_{b-1}.B^1{}_{h\,1\,d-1}$			$-r^1{}_{b-1}.B^1{}_{s-1}$	$+r^1{}_{b-1}.B^1{}_{cb\,1\,d-1}$		$+r^1{}_{b-1}.B^1{}_{b\,1\,d-1}$		E
Bills[2]	$+r^2{}_{b-1}.B^2{}_{h\,1\,d-1}$				$+r^2{}_{b-1}.B^2{}_{cb\,1\,d-1}$				E

(continued)

Table 11.2 Continued

Country 1	Households	Firms		Government	C. Bank		Banks		Ex. Rate
		Current	Capital		Current	Capital	Current	Capital	
Bonds[1]	$+BL^1_{1\,d-1}$			$-BL^1_{s-1}$					E
Bonds[2]	$+BL^2_{1\,d-1}$								E
Δ Stocks of									
Advances						$-\Delta A^1_s$		$+\Delta A^1_d$	
Household loans	$+\Delta L^1_{h\,d}$							$-\Delta L^1_{h\,s}$	
Firm loans			$+\Delta L^1_{f\,d}$					$-\Delta L^1_{f\,d}$	
HPM	$-\Delta H^1_{h\,d}$					$+\Delta H^1_s$		$-\Delta H^1_{b\,d}$	
Deposits	$-\Delta M^1_d$							$+\Delta M^1_s$	
Bills[1]	$-\Delta B^1_{h\,1\,d}$			$+\Delta B^1_s$		$-\Delta B^1_{cb\,1\,d}$		$-\Delta B^1_{b\,1\,d}$	E
Bills[2]	$-\Delta B^2_{h\,1\,d}$					$-\Delta B^2_{cb\,1\,d}$			E
Bonds[1]	$-\Delta BL^1_{1\,d} \cdot p^1_{bl}$			$+\Delta BL^1_s \cdot p^1_{bl}$					E
Bonds[2]	$-\Delta BL^2_{1\,d} \cdot p^2_{bl}$								E
Equities	$-\Delta e^1_d \cdot p^1_e$		$+\Delta e^1_s \cdot p^1_e$						
Reserves						$-\Delta R^1$			E
Default loans			$+NPL^1$					$-NPL^1$	
Sum	0	0	0	0	0	0	0	0	

Table 11.2 Continued

Country 2	Households	Firms		Government	C. Bank		Banks		Sum
		Current	Capital		Current	Capital	Current	Capital	
Consumption	$-C^2$	$+C^2$							0
G. Expenditure		$+G^2$		$-G^2$					0
Investment		$+I^2$	$-I^2$						0
Exports		$+X^2$							0
Imports		$-IM^2$							0
Δ Inventories		$+\Delta IN^2$	$-\Delta IN^2$						0
Taxes	$-T^2{}_I$	$-T^2{}_s$		$+T^2$					0
Wages	$+WB^2$	$-WB^2$							0
Firm profits	$+FD^2{}_f$	$-F^2{}_f$	$+FU^2{}_f$				$-r^2{}_{l-1}.NPL^2$		0
Bank profits	$+FD^2{}_b$						$-F^2{}_b$	$+FU^2{}_b$	0
C. Bank profits				$+F^2{}_{cb}$	$-F^2{}_{cb}$				0
Interest on									
Advances					$+r^2{}_{a-1}.A^2{}_{s-1}$		$-r^2{}_{a-1}.A^2{}_{d-1}$		0
Household loans	$-r^2{}_{l-1}.L^2{}_{h\,d-1}$						$+r^2{}_{l-1}.L^2{}_{h\,s-1}$		0
Firm loans		$-r^2{}_{l-1}.L^2{}_{f\,d-1}$					$+r^2{}_{l-1}.L^2{}_{f\,s-1}$		0
Deposits	$+r^2{}_{m-1}.M^2{}_{d-1}$						$-r^2{}_{m-1}.M^2{}_{s-1}$		0
Bills[1]	$+r^1{}_{b-1}.B^1{}_{h\,2\,d-1}$								0
Bills[2]	$+r^2{}_{b-1}.B^2{}_{h\,1\,d-1}$			$-r^2{}_{b-1}.B^2{}_{s-1}$	$+r^2{}_{b-1}.B^2{}_{cb\,2\,d-1}$		$+r^2{}_{b-1}.B^2{}_{b\,2\,d-1}$		0
Bonds[1]	$+BL^1{}_{2\,d-1}$								0
Bonds[2]	$+BL^2{}_{2\,d-1}$			$-BL^2{}_{s-1}$					0

(*continued*)

Table 11.2 Continued

Country 2	Households	Firms		Government	C. Bank		Banks		Sum
		Current	Capital		Current	Capital	Current	Capital	
Δ Stocks of									
Advances						$-\Delta A^2{}_s$		$+\Delta A^2{}_d$	0
Household loans	$+\Delta L^1{}_{hd}$							$-\Delta L^2{}_{hs}$	0
Firm loans			$+\Delta L^1{}_{fd}$					$-\Delta L^2{}_{fd}$	0
HPM	$-\Delta H^1{}_{hd}$					$+\Delta H^1{}_s$		$-\Delta H^2{}_{bd}$	0
Deposits	$-\Delta M^1{}_d$							$+\Delta M^2{}_s$	0
Bills[1]	$-\Delta B^1{}_{h2d}$								0
Bills[2]	$-\Delta B^2{}_{h2d}$			$+\Delta B^2{}_s$		$-\Delta B^2{}_{cb2d}$		$-\Delta B^2{}_{b2d}$	0
Bonds[1]	$-\Delta BL^1{}_{2d} \cdot p^1{}_{bl}$								0
Bonds[2]	$-\Delta BL^2{}_{2d} \cdot p^2{}_{bl}$			$+\Delta BL^2{}_s \cdot p^2{}_{bl}$					0
Equities	$-\Delta e^2{}_d \cdot p^2{}_e$		$+\Delta e^2{}_s \cdot p^2{}_e$						0
Reserves						$-\Delta R^2$			0
Default loans			$+NPL^2{}_f$					$-NPL^2$	0
Sum	0	0	0	0	0	0	0	0	0

In addition to using loans the movement of financial assets through the system is assured because both countries trade treasury bills, domestic and foreign bills, domestic and foreign bonds, deposits, and equities, all of which are held by households.

11.3.2 Firms

Each firm *i* in this economy follows a recursive mark-up pricing rule based around their inventory flows, *in*, and unit costs, UC. The firm also takes account of total economic output *y*, sales volume *s*, and import volumes, *im*.

$$in^i = in^i_{-1} + (y^i - s^i + im^i)$$

Firms take loans, *L*, supply equities, *e*, and keep part of profits to cover their inventories *in*, and investment in capital *k*. Inflation in the system is driven by sales price increases p^i_s from period to period via

$$\pi^i = \frac{p^i_s}{p^i_{s-1}} - 1$$

The level of real fixed capital k is a linear function of the growth rate of capital, gr^i_k, such that $k^i = k^i_{-1} \,.\, (1 + gr^i_k)$. The growth rate of capital is determined by the real interest rate on loans *rr* and the rate of capacity utilization *u* by the firm. Each firm *i* sets its wage rate *W* in each period according to

$W^i = W^i_{-1} + \Omega^i_3 \,.\, (\omega^{Ti} \,.\, p^i_{s-1} - W^i_{-1})$, where ω^{Ti} represents the target real wage.

The target wage is given by

$$\omega^{Ti} = \left(\frac{W^i}{p^i_s}\right)^T = \Omega^i_0 + \Omega^i_1.Pr^i + \Omega^i_2\{ER^i + z^i_3.(1 - ER^i) - z^i_4.\,bandT^l + z^i_5.bandB^i\}$$

Here worker productivity *Pr* and the employment rate *ER* largely determine the target real wage, with Tax bands *bandT* and bond funding *bandB* also playing a role. We assume firms default part of their loans, around 5 per cent. Firms also attempt to save out of retained earnings and issue equities, *e*.

11.3.3 Government

As in most stock-flow consistent models, the government 'initiates' the model by introducing some amount of spending, *G*, into the system.

The government in this model supplies bills *B* and bonds *BL* to cover its spending requirements, in addition to levying taxes, *T*. The public sector borrowing requirement of each government *PSBR* is given by

$$PSBR^i = G^i + r^i_{b-1} \cdot B^i_{s-1} + BL^i_{s-1} - (T^i + F^i_{cb})$$

Here the government must service its debts from taxes T and from the profits of the central bank F^i_{cb}. The government's spending is a combination of revenues from taxation, borrowing on the bond market, *B*, and bill issuance *BL*.

11.3.4 Banks

Private banks in this model accept deposits, $H_{b\ d}$ give loans $L_{h\ s}$, take advances A_s, and acquire bills $B_{b\ 1\ d}$. The interest rate on advances and banks' liquidity ratio determines each deposit rate in each bank. Each banks' lending rate depends upon the deposit rate. As mentioned above, all bank capital *OF* is held by households. Profits of banks *Fb* are given by

$$F^i_b = r^i_{l-1} \cdot (L^i_{ns-1} + L^i_{fs-1} - NPL^i_{-1}) - r^i_{a-1} \cdot A^i_{d-1} + r^i_{b-1} \cdot B^i_{b\ d-1} - r^i_{m-1} \cdot M^i_{s-1}$$

Here the nominal interest rate *r* is conditioned on Loans sold to households *Lh* and firms *Lf*, as well as advances to the government *A*, repayments of debt, and the level of deposits in the banks *M*.

Banks have a capital adequacy ratio *CAR* given by

$$CAR^i = \frac{OF^i_b}{L^i_{h\ s} + L^i_{f\ s}}$$

where *OF* is the level of 'own funds' held by the banks.

11.3.5 Central bank

The central bank supplies money endogenously to the system, as well as issuing private banks with liquidity upon demand, *A*. Importantly, each country's central bank can generate off-balance-sheet funds *R* in order to ensure the economy continues to function.

$$F^1_{cb} = r^1_{a-1} \cdot A^1_{s-1} + r^1_{b-1} \cdot B^1_{cb1d-1} + r^2_{b-1} \cdot B^2_{cb1d-1}$$

The central bank's profits *F* are determined by interest payments on advances *A* to private banks, and to the interest earned on bonds issued in previous periods.

We simulate each country for 150 periods.

11.4 Results

11.4.1 Investment shock with a floating exchange rate

First, we simulate the effects of a domestic shock in the smaller country. What happens when investment levels drop by 33 per cent in country 1? The asymmetric effect is picked out in Figures 11.2 and 11.3.

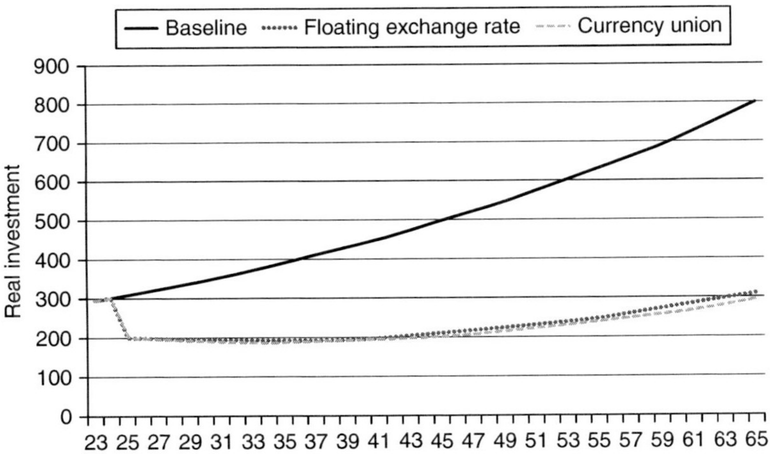

Figure 11.2 Real investment in country 1

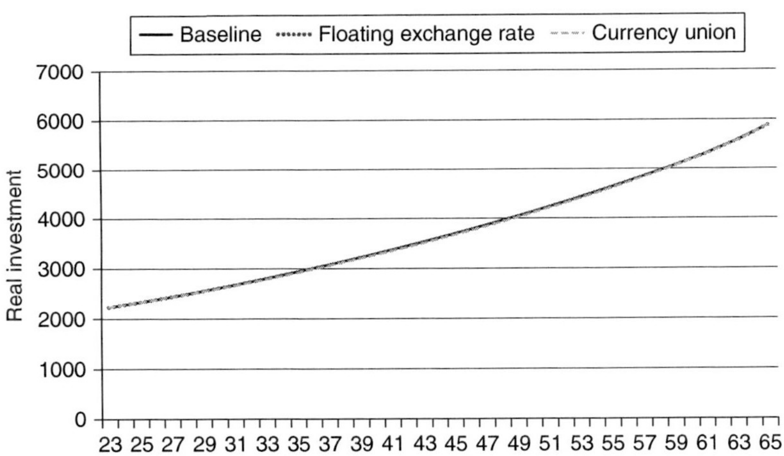

Figure 11.3 Real investment in country 2

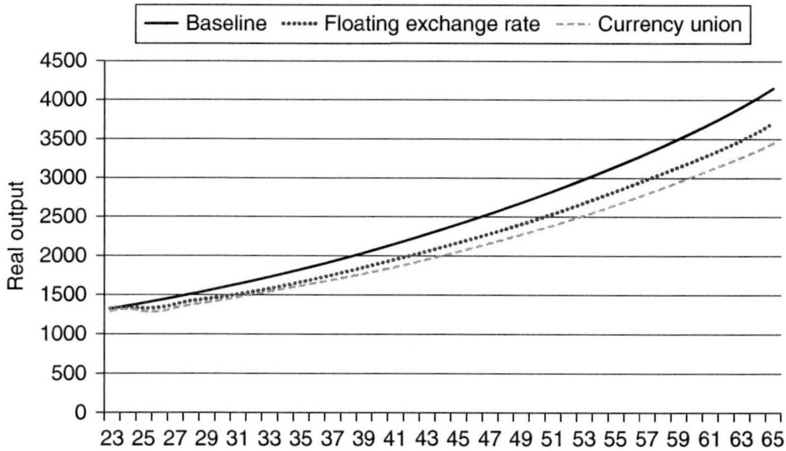

Figure 11.4 Real GDP in country 1

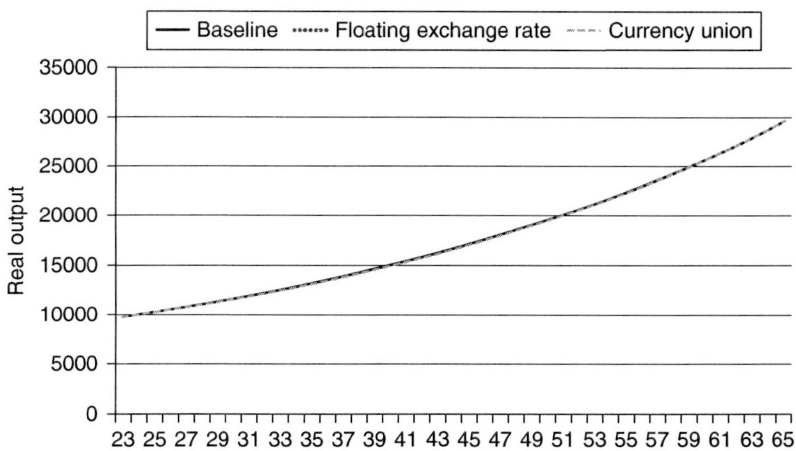

Figure 11.5 Real GDP in country 2

We clearly see investment falling in country 1, while country 2 remains unchanged. Similarly Real GDP is reduced in country 1, and remains increasing in country 2.

Now, to stay afloat, firms begin borrowing from the central bank, and public and private debt ramps up (Figures 11.8 and 11.9). There is a deflation, but it is short lived, as we see in Figure 11.10, because we choose to shock the economy once only. To keep firms and banks afloat,

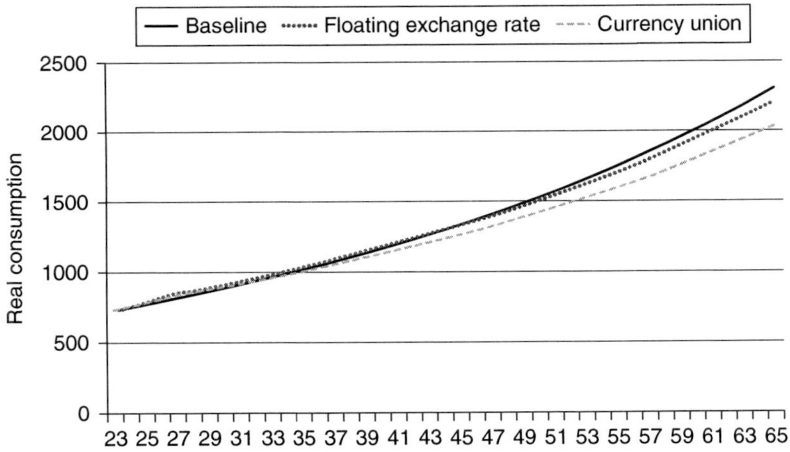

Figure 11.6 Real consumption in country 1

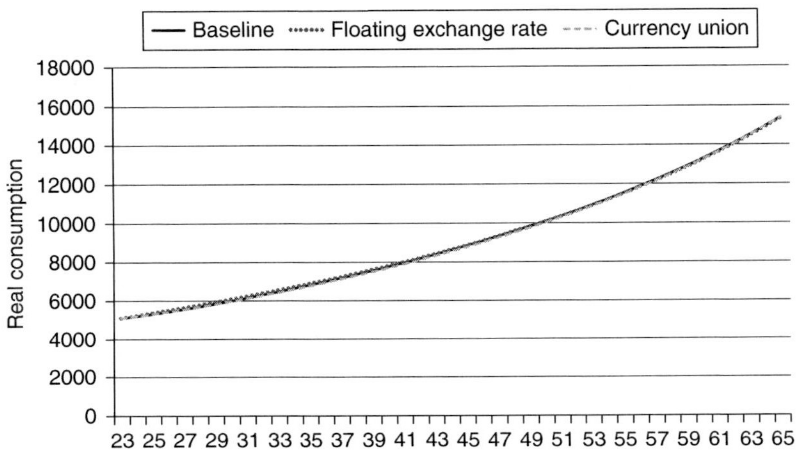

Figure 11.7 Real consumption in country 2

the government in country 1 borrows from abroad, increasing its public sector borrowing requirement substantially, and permanently. The capital account balance moves in opposite directions for each country. Government spending is the anchor in this model, keeping the system from experiencing a decline in overall GDP over time. The circulation of money increases as central banks print money to keep the system going, and Figure 11.11 shows Tobin's Q for country 1 increases linearly, while

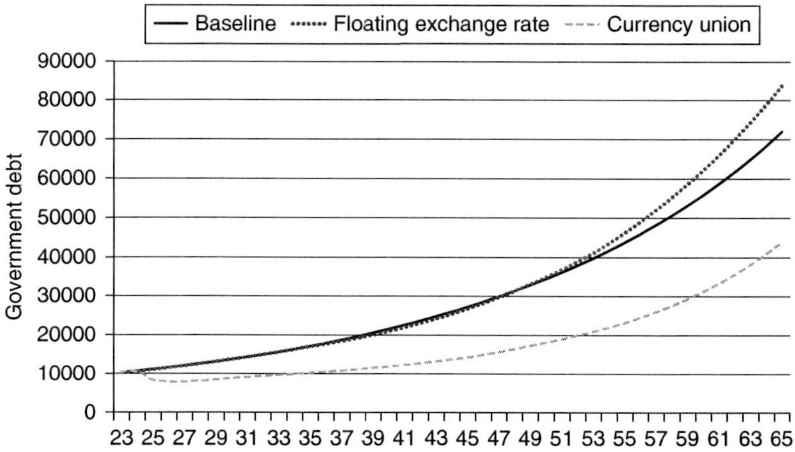

Figure 11.8 Government debt in country 1

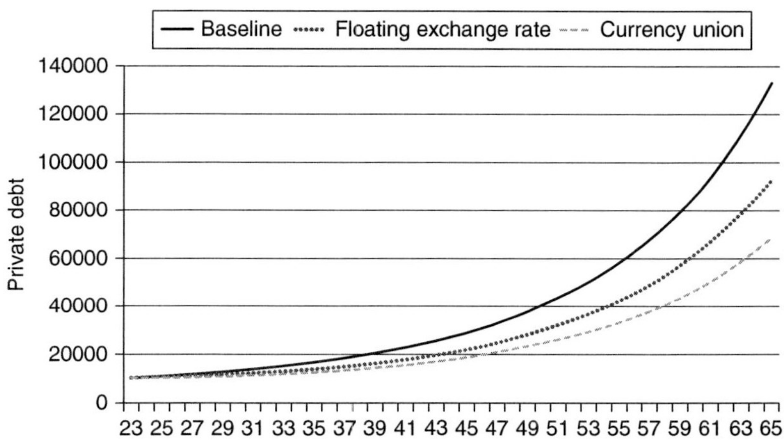

Figure 11.9 Private (firms) debt in country 1

remaining constant in country 2. The exchange rate initially dips, and then returns to normal, as one would expect, as we see in Figure 11.12.

In summary, this model seems quite capable of simulating the effects described in Figure 11.1 above.

Importantly, employment suffers in both economies as a result of the investment drop, but country 2 recovers much more quickly as we see in Figures 11.13 and 11.14.

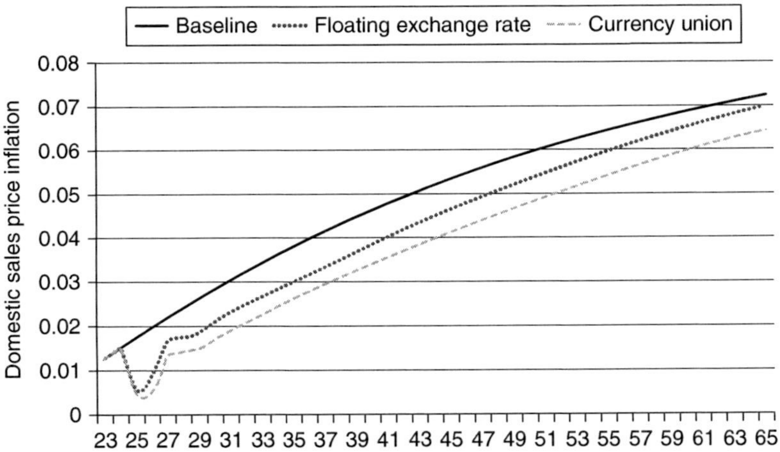

Figure 11.10 Domestic price inflation in country 1

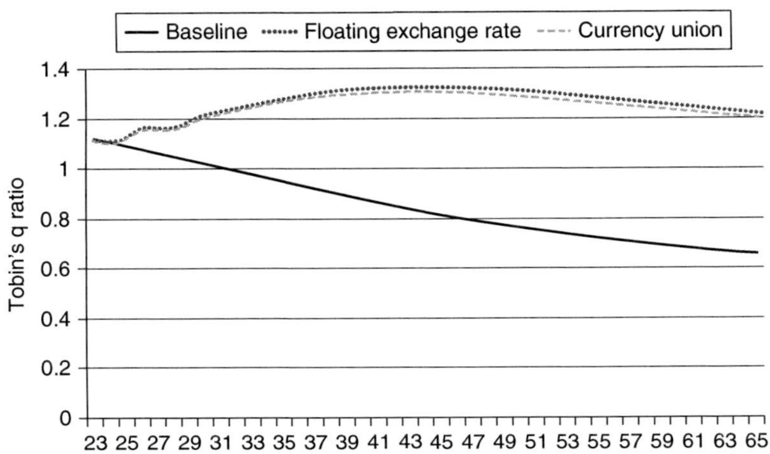

Figure 11.11 Tobin's q ratio for country 1

11.4.2 Investment shock within a currency union

We examine the effects of a currency union formation. We assume an external shock to real investment in country 1 by 33 per cent in period 25 with both our economies inside a currency union. Care must be taken in interpreting the figures, as the debt allocation might be different. The structures of each economy are different from scenario 1 with regard to government and private debt, but of course each country's debt/GDP ratio

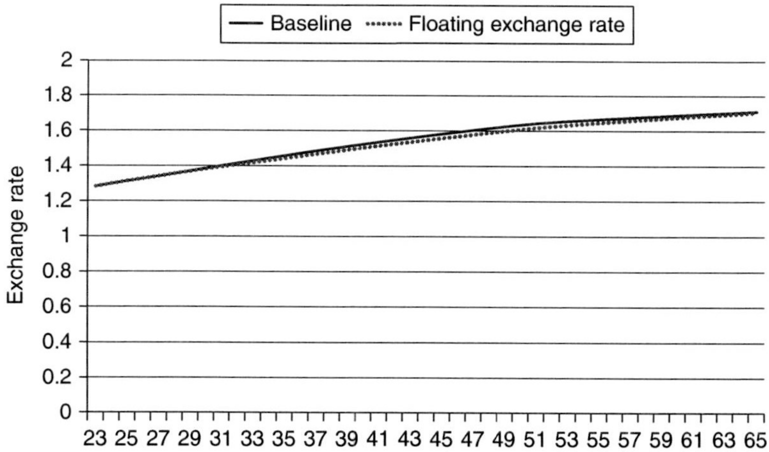

Figure 11.12 Exchange rate

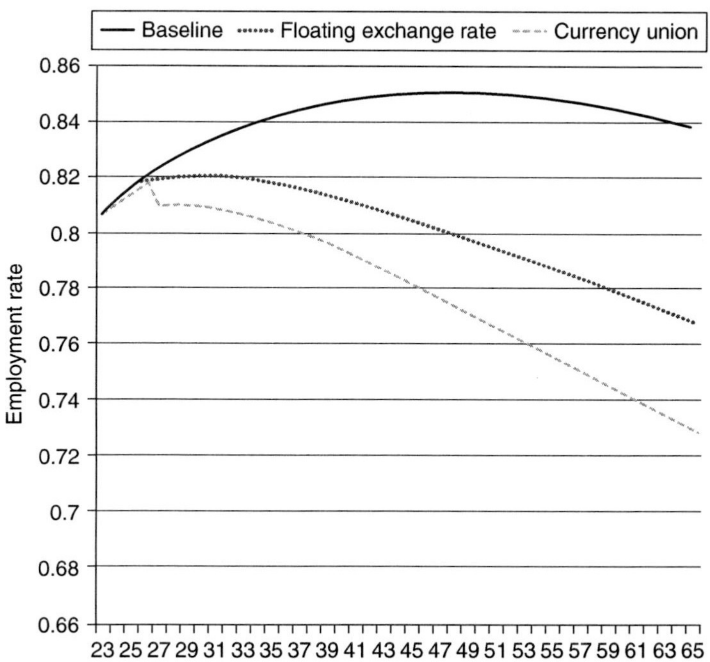

Figure 11.13 Employment rate in the 1st country

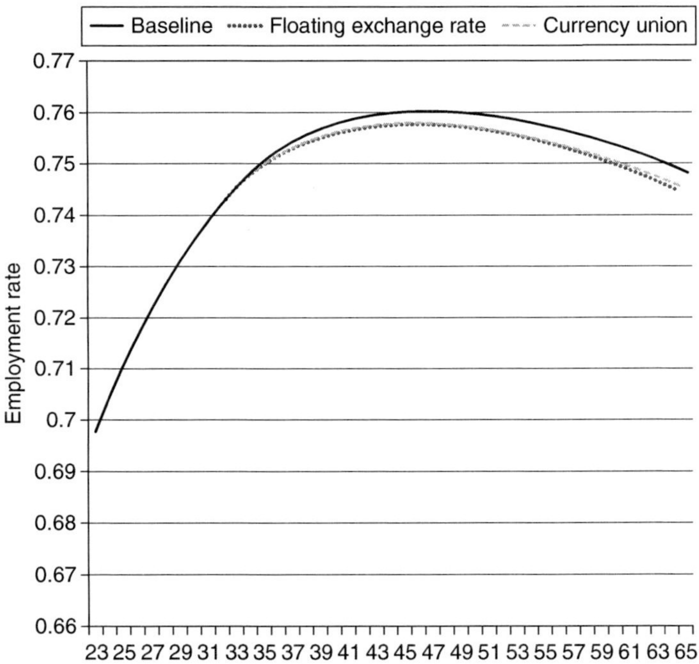

Figure 11.14 Employment rate in the 2nd country

is comparable. We see clearly from these scenarios that the existence of a currency union exacerbates the debt deflation occurring in the small economy, as country 1 experiences a large shock with respect to its sovereign debt levels. The current (and capital) account balance of country 1 also clearly experiences a large shock as shown in Figures 11.15 and 11.16.

11.5 Conclusion

This chapter examines debt deflation within a stock-flow consistent framework. Drawing on the seminal work of Godley and Lavoie (2007). We construct a 2-country stock-flow consistent model, where one small country experiences a large investment shock leading to a debt deflation, as the larger country in turn 'bails out' the smaller country by borrowing from abroad.

We simulate the effects of a series of investment shocks on our stock-flow consistent macro model under varying assumptions. We find that debt overhangs take close to a decade to recover from, especially when the small open economy is particularly open to trade, and mechanisms

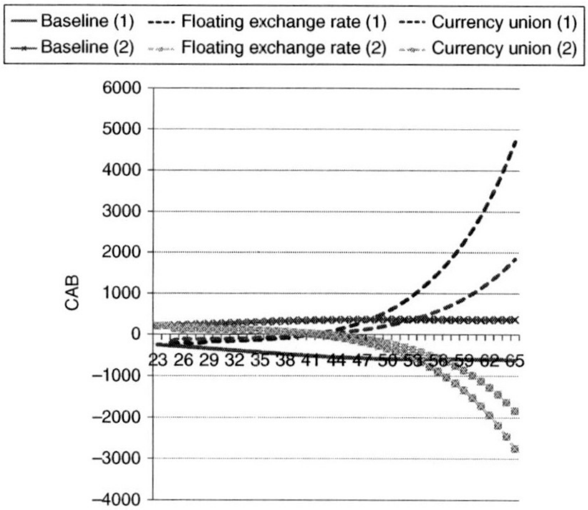

Figure 11.15 Current account balance in both countries

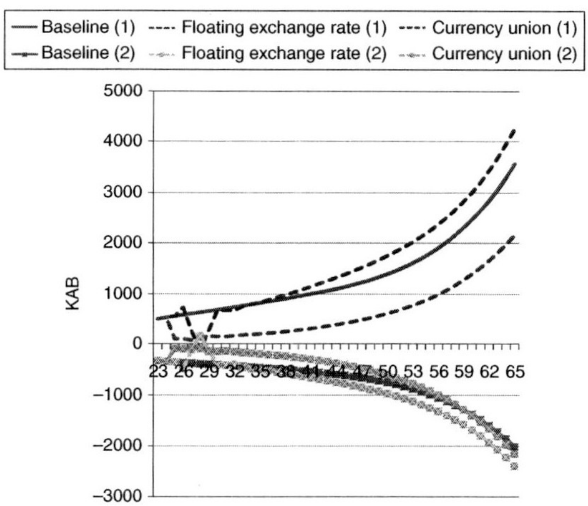

Figure 11.16 Capital account balance in both countries

to reduce debt can help speed the economy to a recovery following a debt build-up.

The government in the smaller country tries to keep government spending high to 'keep the show on the road', and so public sector and private sector borrowing increase.

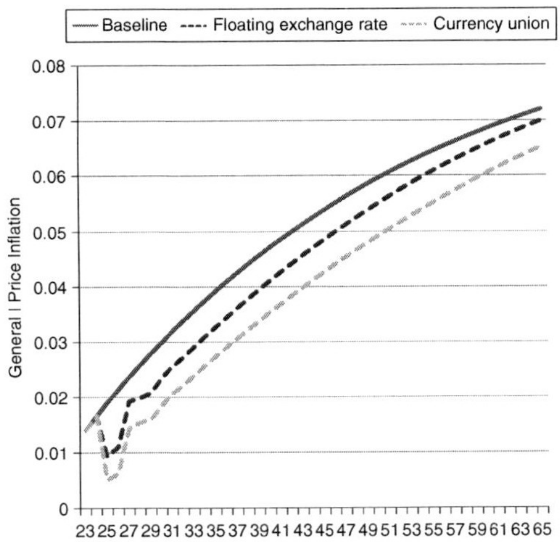

Figure 11.17 General price inflation in country 1

The price level collapses as investment in the real economy drags down aggregate demand. The level of private and government debt increases, as does the cost of debt servicing.

The model simulates an investment shock in the small economy, country 1. We consider a floating exchange regime, and a monetary union. In the case of the monetary union, the investment shock prolongs and extends the debt-deflation of the small open economy.

Future research will concentrate on calibration of stock flow consistent models of this type for small open economies.

Appendix

Production firms equations

$y^i = s^{ei} + \Delta in^{ei} - im^{ei}$

$s^{ei} = \beta^i . s^i + (1 - \beta^i) . s^i_{-1} \, . \, (1 + gr^i_{pr})$

$in^{ei} = in_{-1} + \gamma^i \, . \, (in^{Ti} - in^i_{-1})$

$in^{Ti} = \sigma^{Ti} . s^{ei}$

$im^{ei} = \beta^i . im^i + (1 - \beta^i) . im^{ei}_{-1}$

$in^i = in^i_{-1} + (y^i - s^i + im^i)$

$k^i = k^i_{-1} . (1 + gr^i_k)$

$gr^i_k = gr^i_0 + \gamma^i_u \, . \, u^i - \gamma^i_r \, rr^i_l$

$$u^i = \frac{y^i}{k^i_{-1}}$$

$$rr_l^i = \left\{\frac{(1+r_l^i)}{(1+\pi^i)}\right\} - 1$$

$$\pi^i = \frac{p_s^i}{p_{s-1}^i} - 1$$

$$i^i = (gr_k^i + \delta^i).k_{-1}^i$$

$$s^i = c^i + g^i + i^i + x^i$$

$$S^i = s^i.p_s^i$$

$$IN^i = in^i\ UC^i$$

$$I^i = i^i.p_s^i$$

$$K^i = k^i.p_s^i$$

$$Y^i = s^i.p_s^i + \Delta in^i.UC^i - im^i\ .\ p_m^i$$

$$P_y^i = \frac{Y^i}{y^i}$$

$$\omega^{Ti} = \left(\frac{W^i}{P_s^i}\right)^T = \Omega_0^i + \Omega_1^i.Pr^i + \Omega_2^i\{ER^i + z_3^i.(1 - ER^i) - z_4^i.bandT^i + z_5^i.bandB^i\}$$

$$ER^i = \frac{N_{-1}^i}{N_{fe-1}^i}$$

$$z_3^i = 1 \quad if\ 1 - bandB^i \leq ER^i \leq 1 + bandT^i$$

$$z_4^i = 1 \quad if\ ER^i > 1 + bandT^i$$

$$z_5^i = 1 \quad if\ ER^i < 1 - bandB^i$$

$$W^i = W_{-1}^i + \Omega_3^i.(\omega^{Ti}.p_{s-1}^i - W_{-1}^i)$$

$$Pr^i = pr_{-1}^i.(1 + gr_{pr}^i)$$

$$N^i = N_{-1}^i + \eta^i.(N^{Ti} - N_{-1}^i)$$

$$N^{Ti} = \frac{y^i}{pr^i}$$

$$WB^i = W^i.N^i$$

$$UC^i = \frac{WB^i}{y^i}$$

$$NUC^i = \frac{W^i}{pr^i}$$

$$NHUC^i = (1 - \sigma^{Ni}).NUC^i + \sigma^{Ni}.\ (1 + r_{lN}^i).\ NUC_{-1}^i$$

$$P_s^i = (1 + \varphi^i).NHUC^i$$

$$F_f^i = S^i - IM^i + \Delta IN^i - T_s^i - WB^i - r_{l-1}^i.L_{fd-1}^i$$

$$FD_f^i = \psi_D^i.F_{f-1}^i$$

$$FU_f^i = F_f^i - FD_f^i - r_{l-1}^i.(L_{fd-1}^i - IN_{-1}^i) + r_{l-1}^i.NPL_f^i$$

$$L_{fd}^i = L_{fd-1}^i + I^i + \Delta IN^i - FU_f^i - \Delta e_s^i.p_e^i - NPL_f^i$$

$$NPL_f^i = npl_f^i.L_{fd-1}^i$$

$$e_s^i = e_{s-1}^i + (1 - \psi_U^i).\frac{I_{-1}^i}{p_e^i}$$

$$r_k^i = \frac{FD_f^i}{(e_{s-1}^i . p_{e-1}^i)}$$

$$PE^i = \frac{p_e^i}{\left(\dfrac{F_f^i}{e_{s-1}^i}\right)}$$

$$q^i = \frac{(e_s^i . p_e^i + L_{f\,d}^i)}{(K^i + IN^i)}$$

Trade equations

$$P_x^1 = v_0^1 + v_1^1.E + v_2^1.P_y^1 + v_3^1.P_y^2$$
$$P_m^1 = v_0^1 + v_1^1.E + v_2^1.P_y^1 + v_3^1.P_y^2$$
$$P_x^2 = P_m^1.E$$
$$P_m^2 = P_x^1.E$$
$$E = \frac{B_{h1s}^2}{B_{h1d}^2}$$
$$x^1 = \varepsilon_0 - \varepsilon_1.(P_{m-1}^2 - P_{y-1}^2) + \varepsilon_2.y^2$$
$$im^1 = \mu_0 - \mu_1.(P_{m-1}^1 - P_{y-1}^1) + \mu_2.y^1$$
$$im^2 = x^1$$
$$x^2 = im^1$$
$$CAB^1 = X^1 - IM^1 + r_{b-1}^2.B_{h1d-1}^2 + r_{b-1}^2.B_{cb1d-1}^2 - r_{b-1}^1.B_{h2s-1}^1$$
$$CAB^2 = X^2 - IM^2 + r_{b-1}^1.B_{h2d-1}^1 - r_{b-1}^2.B_{h1s-1}^2 - r_{b-1}^2.B_{cb1s-1}^2$$
$$KAB^1 = \Delta B_{h2s}^1 - \Delta B_{h1d}^2 - \Delta B_{cb1d}^2$$
$$KAB^2 = \Delta B_{h1s}^2 + \Delta B_{cb1s}^2 - \Delta B_{h2d}^1$$

Households equations

$$YP^i = WB^i + FD_f^i + FD_b^i + r_{m-1}^i.M_{d-1}^i + r_{b-1}^i.B_{hid-1}^i + r_{b-1}^z.B_{hid-1}^z + BL_{id-1}^i + BL_{id-1}^z$$
$$YD^i = YP^i - T_l^i - r_{l-1}^i.L_{hd-1}^i$$
$$yd^i = \frac{yD^i}{P_s^i} - \pi^i \frac{V_{-1}^i}{P_s^i}$$
$$c^i = \alpha_0^i + \alpha_1^i.(yd^{ei} + nl^i) + \alpha_2^i.v_{-1}^i$$
$$yd^{ei} = \varepsilon_2^i.yd_{-1}^i + (1 - \varepsilon_2^i).yd_{-1}^{ei}$$
$$\Delta V^i = YD^i - C^i$$
$$GL^i = n_l^i.YP^i$$
$$\eta_l^i = \eta_0^i + \eta_r^i.rr_l^i$$
$$NL^i = GL^i - REP^i$$
$$REP^i = \delta_{rep}^i.L_{hd-1}^i$$
$$L_{hd}^i = L_{hd-1}^i + NL^i$$

$$nl^i = \frac{NL^i}{p^i_{ds}}$$

$$BUR^i = \frac{(REP^i + r^i_{l-1}.L^i_{h\,d-1})}{YP^i}$$

$$C^i = c^i.P^i_s$$

$$v^i = \frac{V^i}{P^i_s}$$

$$H^i_{hd} = \lambda^i_c.C^i$$

$$V^i_{fma} = V^i - H^i_{hd} - L^i_{hd} - OF^i$$

$$\frac{M^i_d}{V^i_{fma}} = \lambda^i_{10} + \lambda^i_{11}.r^i_m + \lambda^i_{12}.r^i_b + \lambda^i_{13}.(r^z_b + d(xr)) + \lambda^i_{14}.r^i_{bl} + \lambda^i_{15}.(r^z_{bl} + d(xr)) + \lambda^i_{16}.r^i_k$$

$$\frac{B^i_{h\,i\,d}}{V^i_{fma}} = \lambda^i_{20} + \lambda^i_{21}.r^i_m + \lambda^i_{22}.r^i_b + \lambda^i_{23}.(r^z_b + d(xr)) + \lambda^i_{24}.r^i_{bl} + \lambda^i_{25}.(r^z_{bl} + d(xr)) + \lambda^i_{16}.r^i_k$$

$$\frac{p^i_{bl}.BL^i_{i\,d}}{V^i_{fma}} = \lambda^i_{40} + \lambda^i_{41}.r^i_m + \lambda^i_{42}.r^i_b + \lambda^i_{43}.(r^z_b + d(xr)) + \lambda^i_{44}.r^i_{bl} + \lambda^i_{45}.(r^z_{bl} + d(xr)) + \lambda^i_{16}.r^i_k$$

$$\frac{xr.p^z_{bl}.BL^z_{i\,d}}{V^i_{fma}} = \lambda^i_{50} + \lambda^i_{51}.r^i_m + \lambda^i_{52}.r^i_b + \lambda^i_{53}.(r^z_b + d(xr)) + \lambda^i_{54}.r^i_{bl} + \lambda^i_{55}.(r^z_{bl} + d(xr)) + \lambda^i_{16}.r^i_k$$

$$\frac{p^i_e.e^i_d}{V^i_{fma}} = \lambda^i_{60} + \lambda^i_{61}.r^i_m + \lambda^i_{62}.r^i_b + \lambda^i_{63}.(r^z_b + d(xr)) + \lambda^i_{64}.r^i_{bl} + \lambda^i_{65}.(r^z_{bl} + d(xr)) + \lambda^i_{66}.r^i_k$$

$$\frac{B^z_{h\,i\,d}}{V^i_{fma}} = \lambda^i_{30} + \lambda^i_{31}.r^i_m + \lambda^i_{32}.r^i_b + \lambda^i_{33}.(r^z_b + d(xr)) + \lambda^i_{34}.r^i_{bl} + \lambda^i_{35}.(r^z_{bl} + d(xr)) + \lambda^i_{16}.r^i_k$$

$$e^i_d = e^i_s$$

Government equations

$$G^i = g^i.P^i_s$$

$$g^i = g^i_{-1}.(1 + gr^i_g)$$

$$T^i_s = \tau^i_s.S^i$$

$$T^i_l = \theta^i.YP^i$$

$$T^i = T^i_s + T^i_l$$

$$B^i_{his} = B^i_{hid}$$

$$B^i_{hzs} = B^i_{hzd}.xr$$

$$BL^i_s = BL^i_{i\,s} + BL^i_{z\,s}$$

$$BL^i_{i\,s} = BL^i_{i\,d}$$

$$BL^i_{z\,s} + BL^i_{z\,d}.xr$$

$$B^i_{b\,s} = B^i_{b\,d}$$

$$B^1_{cb\,1\,s} = B^1_{cb\,1\,d}$$

$$B^2_{cb\,2\,s} = B^2_{cb\,2\,d}$$

$$B^2_{cb\,1\,d} = constant$$

$$B^2_{cb1\,s} = B^2_{cb1\,d}.xr$$

$$PSBR^i = G^i + r^i_{b-1}.B^i_{s-1} + BL^i_{s-1} - (T^1 + F^1_{cb})$$
$$\Delta(B^1_s) = PSBR^1 - \Delta BL^i_s.p^i_{bl}$$
$$GD^i = B^i_{h\,i\,s} + B^i_{h\,z\,s} + BL^i_s + H^i_s$$

Central bank equations

$$\Delta H^1_s = \Delta A^1_s + \Delta B^1_{cb\,1\,d} + \Delta B^2_{cb\,1\,d} + \Delta R^1$$
$$\Delta B^2_{cb\,2\,d} = \Delta H^2_s - \Delta A^1_s - \Delta R^2$$
$$H^2_s = H^2_{h\,s} + H^2_{b\,s}$$
$$F^1_{cb} = r^1_{a-1}.A^1_{s-1} + r^1_{b-1}.B^1_{cb\,1\,d-1} + r^2_{b-1}.B^2_{cb\,1\,d-1}$$
$$F^2_{cb} = r^2_{a-1}.A^2_{s-1} + r^2_{b-1}.B^2_{cb\,2\,d-1}$$
$$H^1_{b\,s} = H^1_s - H^1_{h\,s}$$
$$H^2_{b\,s} = H^2_{b\,d}$$
$$H^i_{h\,s} = H^i_{h\,d}$$
$$B^1_{cb\,1\,d} = B^1_s - B^1_{h\,1\,s} + B^1_{b\,s} - B^1_{h\,2\,s}$$
$$B^2_{h\,1\,s} = B^2_s - B^2_{h\,2\,s} - B^2_{b\,s} - B^2_{cb\,2\,d} - B^2_{cb\,1\,s}$$
$$r^i_b = constant$$
$$r^i_a = \varsigma^i.r^i_b$$
$$r^i_{bl} = r^i_b + add^i_{BL}$$
$$p^i_{bl} = \frac{1}{r^i_{bl}}$$

Private banks equations

$$H^i_{b\,d} = \rho^i.M^i_s$$
$$M^i_s = M^i_d$$
$$L^i_{h\,s-1} = L^i_{h\,d-1}$$
$$L^i_{f\,s-1} = L^i_{f\,d-1}$$
$$F^i_b = r^i_{l-1}.(L^i_{h\,s-1} + L^i_{f\,s-1} - NPL^i_{-1}) - r^i_{a-1}.A^i_{d-1} + r^i_{b-1}.B^i_{b\,d-1} - r^i_{m-1}.M^i_{s-1}$$
$$FD^i_b = \lambda^i_b.F^i_{b-1}$$
$$FU^i_b = F^i_b - FD^i_b$$
$$\Delta OF^i_b = FU^i_b - NPL^i$$
$$r^i_l = r^i_m + add^i_1$$
$$CAR^i = \frac{OF^i_b}{L^i_{h\,s} + L^i_{f\,s}}$$
$$A^i_d = \{bot^i.M^i_s - B^i_{b\,d\,n}\}.\ z^i_1$$
$$z^i_1 = 1 \quad iff\ BLR^i_N < bot^i$$
$$B^i_{b\,d\,N} = M^i_s - H^i_{b\,d} - L^i_{h\,d} - L^i_{f\,d} + OF^i_b$$
$$BLR^i_N = \frac{B^i_{b\,d\,N}}{M^i_s}$$
$$BLR^i = \frac{B^i_{b\,d}}{M^i_s}$$

$$\Delta r^i_m = \xi^i_m(z^i_1 - z^i_z)$$
$$r^i_m = r^i_{m-1} + \Delta r^i_m + \xi^i_b.\Delta r^i_a$$
$$z^i_1 = 1 \quad iff\, BLR^i_N < bot^i$$
$$z^i_2 = 1 \quad iff\, BLR^i_N > top^i$$
$$B^i_{b\,d} = A^i_d + M^i_s - H^i_{b\,d} - L^i_{h\,d} - L^i_{f\,d} + OF^i_b$$

The subscript *b* refers to a bank.
The subscript *cb* refers to a central bank.
The subscript *d* refers to demand.
The superscript *e* refers to the expected value or volume.
The subscript *f* = firms.
The subscript *h* = households.
The superscript or subscript *i* = 1 for country one and 2 for country two.
The subscript *l* refers loans.
The subscript *m* refers deposits.
The superscript *T* refers target value or volume.
The superscript z = 1 for country one and 2 for country 2, such that z ≠ j.
xr = *e* when *z* =1 and 1/*e* when *z* = 2.

A	Advances
B	Government treasury bills
BL	Government bonds (number)
BLR	Bank liquidity ratio
BLR_N	Notional bank liquidity ratio
BUR	Households debt burden
C	Nominal consumption
C	Real consumption
CAB	Current account balance
CAR	Capital adequacy ratio
E	Exchange rate, how much units of the first country currency per one unit of the first country currency.
e	Firms equities (number)
ER	Employment rate
F	Profits
FD	Dividends
FU	Returned earnings
G	Nominal government expenditure
g	Real government expenditure
GD	Government debt
GL	Households gross loans
gr_g	Government expenditure growth rate
gr_k	Capital growth rate
gr_pr	Productivity growth rate
H	High powered money
HC	Hestoric cost
I	Nominal investment
I	Real investment
IM	Value of imports

im	Volume of imports
IN	Value of inventories
in	Volume of inventories
K	Nominal fixed capital
k	Real fixed capital
KAB	Capital account balance
L	Loans
M	Bank deposits
N	Number of employees
N_{fe}	Number of employees in a full employment level
$NHUC$	Normal historic unit cost
NL	Value of new loans
nl	Real value of new loans
NPL	Value of non-performing loans
npl	Ratio of NPL as a share of total loans demand
NUC	Normal unit cost
OF	Own funds of banks
ω^T	Real wages
P_{bl}	Government bond price
P_e	Equity price
P_m	Import prices
P_s	Sales prices
P_x	Export prices
P_y	GDP deflator
PE	Price earning ratio
φ	Price mark-up
π	Price inflation
pr	Workers' productivity
$PSBR$	Public sector borrowing requirement
q	Tobin's q ratio
R	Reserves
r_b	Treasury bills interest rate
r_{bl}	Bonds interest rate
r_k	Dividend yield of firms
r_l	Loans interest rate
r_m	Deposits interest rate
REP	Households loans repayments
rr_l	Real interest rate on loans
S	Nominal sales
s	Real sales
T	Taxes
T_s	Firms taxes (sales tax)
T_I	Households taxes (income tax)
U	Capacity utilization
UC	Unit cost
V	Nominal wealth
V_{fma}	Financial market asset wealth
v	Real wealth
W	Wage rate

WB	Wage bill
X	Value of exports
x	Volume of exports
Y	Nominal output or GDP
y	Real GDP
YD	Nominal disposable income
yd	Real disposable income
YP	Value of personal income

Notes

1. To appear in a volume honoring the late Wynne Godley, edited by Dimitri B. Papadimitriou and Gennaro Zezza. Thanks to Dimitri Papadimitriou for spearheading this project, and to Wynne Godley for his years of encouragement in macroeconomic modeling. It almost goes without saying this chapter is dedicated to Wynne for the intellectual vista he opened up together with his coauthors. The usual disclaimer applies.
2. This model was built and simulated in *EViews*. The software is available from the authors upon request.

References

Bernanke, B. (1983) 'Non-Monetary Effects of the Financial Crisis in Propagation of the Great Depression,' *American Economic Review* 73(3): 257–76.

Blecker, R.A. (2002) 'Distribution, Demand, and Growth in Neo-Kaleckian Macro-Models,' in M. Setterfield (ed.) *The Economics of Demand-led Growth: Challenging the Supply-Side Vision of the Long Run* (Cheltenham, UK: Edward Elgar), pp. 129–52.

DeLong, J.B. (1999) 'Should We Fear Deflation?,' *Brookings Papers on Economic Activity* 1(1): 225–52.

Eggertsson, G.B. and M. Woodford (2003) 'The Zero Bound on Interest Rates and Optimal Monetary Policy,' *Brookings Papers on Economic Activity* (1): 139–233.

Fisher, I. (1933) 'The Debt-deflation Theory of Great Depressions,' *Econometrica* 1(4): 337–57.

Godley, W. (1999) 'Seven Unsustainable Processes: Medium-Term Prospects and Policies for the United States and the World,' Levy Economics Institute, Strategic Analysis.

Godley, W. (1999) 'Money and Credit in a Keynesian Model of Income Determination,' *Cambridge Journal of Economics* 23(2): 393–411.

Godley, W. and M. Lavoie (2005–06) 'Comprehensive Accounting in Simple Open Economy Macroeconomics with Endogenous Sterilization or Fixed Exchange Rates,' *Journal of Post Keynesian Economics* 28(2): 241–76.

Godley, W. and M. Lavoie (2007) *Monetary Economics: An Integrated Approach to Credit, Money, Income, Production and Wealth* (London, UK: Palgrave Macmillan).

Kalecki, M. (1971) *Selected Essays on the Dynamics of the Capitalist Economy* (London, UK: Cambridge University Press).

Keynes, J.M. (1936) *The General Theory of Employment, Interest, and Money* (London, UK: Cambridge University Press).
Kindleberger, C. (1996) *Manias, Panics and Crashes: A History of Financial Crises* (New York: NY: John Wiley and Sons).
King, M. (1994) 'Debt-deflation: Theory and Evidence,' *European Economic Review* 38(3–4): 419–45.
Kinsella, S. and A. Leddin (2010) *Understanding Ireland's Economic Crisis: Prospects for Recovery* (Dublin: Blackhall Press).
Koo, R. (2009) *The Holy Grail of Macroeconomics: Lessons from Japan's Great Recession* (Singapore: John Wiley and Sons).
Minsky, H.P. (1986 [2008]) *Stabilizing an Unstable Economy* (New Haven, CT: Yale University Press) republished in D.B. Papadimitriou and L.R. Wray (eds) *Hyman P. Minsky's Stabilizing an Unstable Economy* (New York: McGraw-Hill).
Nell, E.J. (2003) 'Nominal Money, Real Money and Stabilization,' in S. Bell and E.J. Nell (eds), *The State, the Market and the Euro: Chartalism verus Metallism in the Theory of Money*. Cheltenham, UK: Edward Elgar.
Taylor, L (2004) *Reconstructing Macroeconomics: Structuralist Proposals and Critiques of the Mainstream*. Cambridge, MA: Harvard University Press.
Taylor, L. (2008) 'A Foxy Hedgehog: Wynne Godley and Macroeconomic Modelling,' *Cambridge Journal of Economics* 32: 639–63.
Taylor, L. and S. O'Connell (1985) 'A Minsky Crisis,' *Quarterly Journal of Economics* 100 (Supplement): 871–85.
Tobin, J. (1980) Asset *Accumulation and Economic Activity* (Oxford, UK: Basil Blackwell).
von Peter, G. (2004) 'Asset Prices and Banking Distress: A Macroeonomic Approach,' Working Paper 167 (Basel, Switzerland: Bank for International Settlements).
Woodford, M. (2003) *Interest and Prices: Foundations of a Theory of Monetary Policy* (New York: Princeton University Press).

12
A Debate with Wynne Godley on the Neutrality of Fiscal Policy

*Edwin Le Heron**

This chapter stems from a controversy I had with Wynne Godley in 2006. I met him during a lecture at the University of Paris XIII a few years earlier. I was very impressed. To our astonishment, Wynne Godley began his speech in perfect French, which is a quality increasingly rare in Anglo-Saxon intellectuals today. Apologizing even for some of his blunders, he explained that he had been an oboist in the orchestra of the Paris Opera after the Second World War. Godley's conference was a lesson in macroeconomics. From simple relationships in a stock-flow consistent (SFC) model and statistics, he explained with great accuracy the position of the United States and the European Union at the time. Everything became clear. The character gave off a great kindness and calm, but showed great determination. Then I took him back to his hotel and we had a very interesting discussion on the University of Cambridge in the 1960s and 1970s. He was like a living encyclopedia, telling stories about all these characters that I had only studied in books: Joan Robinson, Piero Sraffa, and so on. It was difficult to leave and I decided to build a SFC model that would combine the main elements from my doctoral thesis of 1984. And Wynne Godley, with Marc Lavoie (2007), provided me with the framework to model my theoretical ideas.

A few months later, I sent him my SFC model with a complex private bank sector introducing more realistic features, introducing notably the borrower's and the lender's risks issued from the Minskyan approach (1975). He encouraged me to continue. I wanted to experiment with a shock in central bank monetary policy, that is, an increase or decrease

* My grateful thanks to Nick Parsons (University of Cardiff) and Leslie Redmond.

in the key rate. Then I asked him a simple question to which I had no obvious answer.

Monetary policy was exogenous to be able to experiment with monetary shocks. On the other hand, the behavior of private agents was endogenous to analyze their reaction. But in my model, fiscal policy was also endogenous, developing a counter-cyclical effect of the traditional Keynesian policies. Therefore, how could one measure the real impact of monetary policy, given that fiscal policy would react to mitigate this impact? My question was: how to neutralize fiscal policy with the aim of measuring only the effects of monetary policy?

For post-Keynesians (PK), talk about neutrality or neutralization of fiscal policy does not just happen, because they develop an active fiscal policy in the framework of the policy mix.

In the first part, we present various assumptions of the neutrality or neutralization of fiscal policy. In the second part, we make a short presentation of our SFC-PK model before developing in the third part experiments with monetary policy shock for our different hypotheses of the neutralization of fiscal policy. Finally, we seek to answer the question.

12.1 Various hypotheses to neutralize fiscal policy

The post-Keynesian idea is that the economic policy is a mix of monetary and fiscal policies seeking to find a certain rate of economic growth usually compatible with full employment. Neutrality must be understood in terms of general economic policy (policy mix of monetary and fiscal policies) and not at the level of fiscal or monetary policies alone. As post-Keynesians believe that fiscal policy is active and develop a policy mix, how can fiscal policy be neutralized to measure the effects of monetary policy? How can one set fiscal policy to measure only the effects of a monetary policy shock in a post-Keynesian model? What may be the definition of a 'neutralized' fiscal policy in a post-Keynesian sense, that is, without any Ricardian consumers or strict fiscal rules? Four hypotheses can be made, which could correspond to the PK approach. And we add two hypotheses, which respect two orthodox definitions of the neutrality.

12.1.1 Hypothesis 1: Independent central bank or *ceteris paribus*

The first hypothesis (H1) is to change nothing. We keep the same model of fiscal policy, which leads to the steady state. It is a kind of ceteris paribus assumption. Fiscal policy reacted to the shock of monetary policy under the same terms as before the shock. This hypothesis is consistent with the current independence of central banks. With this independence, the central bank changes the monetary policy without coordination with the government's fiscal policy. It will react, as it would respond to any economic shock. With H1, fiscal policy is neither neutral nor neutralized. It continues to be counter-cyclical. We maintain the same function of government's response to changes in monetary policy. The original definition of fiscal policy is essential to understanding the evolution of the economic situation and thus the impact of monetary policy.

We assume that public expenditure is growing at the same rate as the national income. When we solve the model, this assumption makes it easier to find a steady state. Public expenditure seems to be pro-cyclical, because public expenditure falls with GDP. But the final effect of fiscal policy is measured by government deficit. Public earnings (taxes) are proportional to income and hence vary in line with public expenditure. But with a contractionary monetary policy and its higher interest rate, the financial costs of the national debt, and then the fiscal deficit, increase. The global impact is linked (inversely) to the key interest rate. With *H1*, the economy has a self-stabilizing tendency due to the fiscal policies, though the fiscal effect comes through the effects of the interest rate on the government deficit.

12.1.2 Hypothesis 2: Fiscal deficit targeting rule

The second hypothesis (*H2*) corresponds to a change in the response function of fiscal policy. We consider that the neutralization of fiscal policy passes through the stabilization of the deficit at the corresponding steady state. So faced with a monetary policy shock, the government will stabilize the deficit. The ratio of government deficit to GDP (*DG/Y*) remains constant. Fiscal policy will be neither more nor less active than before, if we consider that the main action of fiscal policy comes through changes in the government deficit: higher for economic recovery, lower to slow down the economy. A balanced budget is not necessary, as we stabilize the *DG/Y* ratio at the steady state, which was positive in our model. *H2* is a 'fiscal deficit targeting rule' such as the Maastricht Treaty seeks to promote with its rule of balancing the budget or its ratio of a maximum deficit of 3 per cent. Since Haavelmo, we know that a balanced budget is not neutral since it changes income distribution. The monetary policy shock will change the interest rate, and hence the cost of debt. We get the same result in a deficit on income transfers such as banks (who receive interest) and companies (who receive public expenditure), which is not neutral in our model. Therefore to stabilize the *DG/Y* ratio does not imply neutrality of fiscal policy, but the neutralization of government policy following the logic of Keynesian policy through the government deficit.

12.1.3 Hypothesis 3: Fiscal debt targeting rule

The third hypothesis (*H3*) is a fiscal targeting rule as in the previous one, but we stabilize the public debt ratio, that is to say, the government debt to GDP (*B/Y*). The rule *H3* is in stock and not in flow (*H2*). Fiscal policy will be neither more nor less active than before, if we consider that the main action of fiscal policy comes through changes in the government debt. In each pair of variables [growth rate, interest rate] match a specific fiscal deficit and public debt. Following a change in the key interest rate, the growth rate changes. If the monetary policy shock is permanent, a new steady state will be found. If the shock is transitory, the path to reach the steady state will differ according to the previous three hypotheses. We let vary the ratios of deficit and debt (*H1*), then only the debt ratio (constant fiscal deficit ratio) (*H2*) and finally only the deficit ratio (constant debt ratio) (*H3*). We find this 'fiscal debt targeting rule' in terms of stock in the Maastricht Treaty, with a maximum debt ratio (*B/Y*) of 60 per cent.

12.1.4 Hypothesis 4: the Wynne Godley proposal

The fourth hypothesis (*H4*) is the proposal made by Wynne Godley in his email (20 July 2006): 'I think there is a general answer to the question. Whenever you have a growth steady state (or a stationary one) it can be considered to exhibit a neutral fiscal stance. So if you retain that fiscal stance, you by definition exhibit the effect of changing monetary policy.'

Following the Wynne Godley proposal, it would be good to model the growth rate of public expenditure as a constant parameter during the monetary policy shock. The growth rate of public expenditure becomes exogenous. In line with Godley, we call the fiscal policy 'passive' ('active') if the growth rate of public expenditure is larger (smaller) than the steady-state growth rate of public expenditure. Neutral fiscal policy corresponds to the growth rate of public expenditure, and more generally the fiscal stance, adequate to the steady state.

12.1.5 Hypothesis 5: Ricardian equivalence

We develop two assumptions that correspond to the orthodox framework. The orthodox definition starts its analysis by stating a 'neutrality' result for fiscal policy which is due to David Ricardo (1817 [1951]), and whose formal illustration is due to Robert Barro (1974). The Ricardian proposition can be expressed in the following way: given a sequence of government expenditures, it is irrelevant for households if such expenditures are financed by levying current taxes, or by raising current debt and levying higher taxes in the future. In other words, the choice of fiscal policy (debt or taxes) to finance expenditures is 'neutral' on households' consumption allocations. Households' consumption spending changes to neutralize the fiscal policy.

The hypothesis (*H5*) is the orthodox approach of the Ricardian equivalence developed by Barro. This time we assume that households neutralize fiscal policy by changing their consumption levels inversely to the amount of variation in the government deficit. With rational expectations, households neutralize fiscal policy. Starting from the steady state considered as equilibrium in the neoclassical framework, the increase in demand from the public deficit is offset by an equivalent reduction in household consumption. Monetary policy is seen as seeking only price stability. Since money is considered neutral (money is not a source of fluctuations in real economic activity), monetary policy needs not to be neutralized. In the case of Ricardian equivalence, neutral fiscal policy should respect a rule. 'The New Keynesian literature on the desirable design of macroeconomic policies concludes that operational policy rules should not be a source of non-fundamental fluctuations in economic activity, implying that the induced rational expectations equilibrium should be at least locally unique' (Leith and von Thadden, 2006).

Monetary policy rules have been analyzed in great analytical detail. But there is no similarly rich literature on the appropriate use of fiscal instruments. This asymmetric treatment is adequate in many commonly used models in which fiscal policy acts through variations in lump-sum taxes in an environment of Ricardian equivalence.[1] In line with the logic spelled out in Leeper (1991), the joint design problem of monetary and fiscal policymaking then essentially reduces to two separable problems which can be recursively addressed. First, isolated from fiscal aspects, there are monetary aspects, as witnessed by the large literature on the Taylor principle, which typically establishes conditions for local equilibrium determinacy solely in terms of monetary policy parameters. Second, if the monetary dynamics are determinate, there is no 'active' role for fiscal policy, that is, the determinacy feature remains preserved if government debt dynamics evolve 'passively' in a stable manner. Bi and Kumhof add (2009): 'Taylor is one of the very few recent examples that analyses a feasible, practice fiscal policy rule. In his case the budget surplus depends on the output gap. But Taylor argues that such a rule is unnecessary, and in fact undesirable, because the Fed has been very successful at stabilizing the business cycle and would only suffer from having to forecast the fiscal stance.'

If, however, the dynamic system without fiscal policy exhibits one degree of indeterminacy, then potentially unstable debt dynamics are needed to restore equilibrium determinacy, consistent with Leeper's notion of 'active' fiscal policy[2] or, alternatively, with the view of the 'fiscal theory of the price level' expressed in Sims (1994) and Woodford (1994, 2003). If defined in this way, a passive fiscal policy ensures under Ricardian equivalence that government debt dynamics per se are not explosive, while under an active rule locally stable debt dynamics require the adjustment of some other variable, like a change in the price level. There are so many New Keynesian rules today, that it is certainly better to just present their framework. More, as we model neither the general price level, nor the potential output or the NAIRU in our SFC-PK model,[3] we cannot develop Leeper's framework.

This logic needs to be modified in an environment, which departs from Ricardian equivalence, implying that equilibrium dynamics are driven by a genuine interaction of monetary and fiscal policy. This is the case with the more traditional and simplest rule of the *Treasury view*.

12.1.6 Hypothesis 6: the Treasury view

Hypothesis (*H6*) corresponds to what Keynes called the *Treasury view*. Under this traditional neoclassical approach of public finance, monetary policy stabilizes the general level of prices and fiscal policy maintains a balanced budget. Then fiscal balance is always sought, leading ultimately to a debt-free government. Fiscal policy will be amended to implement a strict neutrality of the Treasury, complying with the strict rule of balanced public finances. This strict rule in fiscal policy adds a shock to the monetary policy shock and we analyze the effects on the steady state.

12.2 A short presentation of the stock-flow consistent model

To simplify the chapter, we used our first SFC-PK model that was published in *Metroeconomica*. It is the paper that we discussed with Wynne Godley in 2006. You will find a complete presentation of the model in Le Heron and Mouakil (2008). We present only the most specific and the new features of the model with five sectors: government, firms, households, private banks and central bank. The full model (Appendix) contains 61 equations.

All production must be financed. However, current production is financed by the working capital of entrepreneurs (retained earnings) and by contracted revolving funds granted by banks at the current rate of interest. These two factors constitute a shock absorber to possible monetary rationing by banks. We are limiting our study to the effects that a change in the key interest rate might have on new financing for investment and growth of production. Let us proceed to examine the supply of finances by banks (ΔF), which refers to the new flow of money (as opposed to the existing stock of money (D)). Also, there is a stock of money demand equal to transaction, precautionary and speculative motives, whereas the finance demand (ΔF_D) represents the new flow of financing required by firms (finance motive). Assuming a closed economy, this flow of demand for money can be satisfied by banks, either by the stock markets or by credit. At the end of the period, net financing demand (ΔF_D) can be constrained by net money supply from banks (ΔF) (granted financing – paid off financing). ΔF determines monetary creation in the period. Like Minsky (1975), we introduce the borrower's and the lender's risks.

The national income (Y) adds household consumption (C), investment of firms (I) and public expenditure (G). The rate of growth of national income is gr_y. In this model, the expected value of any variable for the current period (represented with the superscript a) depends on its value from the previous period plus an error correction mechanism where (θ) represents the speed of adjustment in expectations.

$$Y = C + I + G \tag{1}$$

$$gr_y = \Delta Y / Y_{-1} \tag{2}$$

$$gr_y^a = gr_{y-1} + \theta\,(gr_{y-1} - gr_{y-1}^a) \tag{3}$$

12.2.1 Fiscal policy of the government

Government expenditures are only final sales of consumption goods. The government finances any deficit by issuing bills, so that the supply of Treasury bills (B) in the economy is identical to the stock of government debt. In other words, it is given by the pre-existing stock of debt plus its current deficit (DG). We assume that private banks give limitless credit to government at the long-term rate of interest (i_l).

Hypothesis 1: Independent central bank or ceteris paribus

To obtain the steady state, we assume a stabilizing effect of fiscal policy. With *H1*, we do not change the equations of the fiscal policy of the government after the monetary policy shock. Public expenditure (G) is always growing at the same rate of expected growth rate (gr_y^a) as the national income (Y). Tax revenue is proportional to income and hence varies in line with the public expenditure. With state debt, the global impact is linked to the key interest rate and, then, to monetary policy. The final effect of the fiscal policy is measured by the government deficit (DG). Our economy has a self-stabilizing tendency due to fiscal policy. With the independent central bank, monetary policy changes without coordination with the government. This is the reason for conserving the same equations after the shock.

$$G = G_{-1} . (1 + gr_y^a) \tag{H1-4}$$

$$DG = G + (i_{b-1} . B_{-1}) - T - P_{cb} \tag{H1-5}$$

$$\Delta B = DG \tag{H1-6}$$

For the following hypotheses, we change the equations during the monetary policy shock. So we always start from the same steady state.

Hypothesis 2: Fiscal deficit targeting rule

We stabilize the fiscal deficit ratio (DG/Y_{-1}) at the steady state, which is positive in our model. It is a fiscal rule.

$$G = DG - (i_{b-1} . B_{-1}) + T + P_{cb} \tag{H2-4}$$

$$DG = r_{DG} . Y_{-1} \quad \text{with } r_{DG} = DG/Y_{-1} = \text{constant} \tag{H2-5}$$

$$\Delta B = DG \tag{H2-6}$$

Hypothesis 3: Fiscal debt targeting rule

H3 is a fiscal targeting rule as in the previous hypothesis, but we stabilize the public debt ratio (B/Y_{-1}). The rule *H3* is in stock and not in flow (*H2*).

$$G = DG - (i_{b-1} . B_{-1}) + T + P_{cb} \tag{H3-4}$$

$$DG = \Delta B \quad \text{(H3-5)}$$

$$B = r_B \,.\, Y_{-1} \quad \text{with } r_B = B/Y_{-1} = \text{constant} \quad \text{(H3-6)}$$

Hypothesis 4: Wynne Godley proposal

The growth rate of public expenditure becomes exogenous and corresponds to the previous steady state.

$$G = G_{-1}.\, (1 + gr_G) \quad \text{with } gr_G = \Delta G/G_{-1} \text{ from the steady state} \quad \text{(H4-4)}$$

$$DG = G + (i_{b-1} \,.\, B_{-1}) - T - P_{cb} \quad \text{(H4-5)}$$

$$\Delta B = DG \quad \text{(H4-6)}$$

Hypothesis 5: Ricardian equivalence

The equations 4, 5 and 6 are the same as those in *H1*, but we change the consumption function of households, which neutralizes the changes in fiscal deficit:

$$G = G-1.\, (1 + gr_y{}^a) \quad \text{(H5-4)}$$

$$DG = G + (i_{b-1} \,.\, B_{-1}) - T - P_{cb} \quad \text{(H5-5)}$$

$$\Delta B = DG \quad \text{(H5-6)}$$

$$C = \alpha_1 \,.\, Y^a_w + \alpha_2 \,.\, Y^a_v + \alpha_3 \,.\, D_{-1} - DGH \quad \text{With } \alpha_i\text{: constant} \quad \text{(H5-7)}$$

$$DGH = \Delta DG \quad \text{(H5-8)}$$

Hypothesis 6: the Treasury view

With the *Treasury view*, we implement a strict fiscal rule of balanced budget, leading to debt-free government.

$$G = DG - (i_{b-1} \,.\, B_{-1}) + T + P_{cb} \quad \text{(H2-4)}$$

$$DG = r_{DG} \,.\, Y_{-1} \quad \text{with } r_{DG} = 0 \quad \text{(H2-5)}$$

$$\Delta B = DG\ (= 0) \quad \text{(H2-6)}$$

The government collects taxes from households (T_H) on wages and from firms (T_F) on distributed profits.

$$T = T_H + T_F \tag{9}$$

$$T_H = \tau_h \,.\, W_{-1} \quad \text{With } \tau_h\text{: constant} \tag{10}$$

$$T_F = \tau_f \,.\, P^d_{-1} \quad \text{With } \tau_f\text{: constant} \tag{11}$$

12.2.2 Investment of firms

The investment function is the most important one in a growth model. The stock of capital (K) increases with the flow of net investment (I) that is financed by the total of external funds from commercial banks (ΔF) and by the internal funds of firms. The self-financing of firms corresponds to the retained earnings (P^u) minus the capital losses of firms (CG). The capital losses of firms are also the capital gains of banks, measured by the capital losses on equities (CG_e) and on fixed rate bonds (CG_{of}). Firms issue equities (E), bonds with fixed rates of interest (OF) and commercial papers (CP), and borrow money from banks (variable rate) (L) to finance investments.

In our model, we focus on the difference between effective investment (I) and the desired investment of firms (I_D). The banks accept to finance totally or in part the latter according their lender's risk (LR). A rationing in investment financing can exist ($I < I_D$). The desired rate of accumulation (gr_{kD}) is a function of an exogenous state of confidence (γ_0), the capacity utilization rate (u) and of the borrower's risk, which is measured by the rate of cash flow (r_{cf}) and by the financial condition index (FCI). The rate of cash flow is the ratio of retained earnings to capital and the financial condition index captures the sensitivity of investment to the level of indebtedness, to the long-term interest rate, to the short-term interest rate and to the financial capitalization ratio. The lender's risk and the borrower's risk come from Minsky's analysis.

$$I_D = gr_{kD} \,.\, K{-}1 \tag{12}$$

$$gr_{kD} = \gamma_0 + (\gamma_1 \cdot r_{cf-1}) + (\gamma_2 \cdot u_{-1}) - (\gamma_3 \cdot FCI_{-1}) \quad \text{With } \gamma_i\text{: constant} \tag{13}$$

where the rate of capacity utilization is defined as the ratio of output to full capacity output (Y_{fc}). The capital-to-full capacity ratio (σ) is defined as a constant. Distributed dividends (P^d) are a fraction of profits realized in the previous period and are shared between government (T_F) and banks (P^{dB}).

$$r_{cf} = P^u/K_{-1} \tag{14}$$

$$u = Y/Y_{fc} \tag{15}$$

$$Y_{fc} = K_{-1} \cdot \sigma \quad \text{With } \sigma\text{: constant} \tag{16}$$

$$FCI = (\mu f_1 \cdot i_1 \cdot (L+OF)/K) + (\mu f_2 \cdot i_{cb} \cdot CP/K) - (\mu f_3 \cdot E/Y) \quad \text{With } \mu f_i\text{: constants} \tag{17}$$

$$P^d = (1 - s_f) \, . \, P_{-1} \quad \text{With } s_f\text{: constant} \tag{18}$$

12.2.3 Consumption of households

We assume that households determine their consumption expenditure (C) on the basis of their expected disposable income and their wealth from the previous period that consist entirely of bank deposits. Following the Kaleckian tradition, wages are mostly consumed while financial income is largely devoted to saving ($\alpha_1 > \alpha_2$). The financial behavior of households is simplified and they hold only a banking deposit account. Y^a_w is the expected disposable income of workers, Y^a_v the expected disposable financial income and each (α_i) is a propensity to consume. The consumption decision determines the amount (ΔD) that households will save out of their disposable income (Y_h), except in the Ricardian equivalence (see H5-4) where households take account of the variations in fiscal deficit.

$$C = \alpha_1 . Y^a_w + \alpha_2 \, . \, Y^a_v + \alpha_3 \, . \, D_{-1} \quad \text{With } \alpha_i\text{: constant} \tag{19}$$

12.2.4 Financing by private banks

Firms' financing is fundamental in a monetary economy of production. Firms begin by being self-financed then turn to external finance (ΔF_D). We try to introduce more realistic features in the banking system.[4] Banks only finance projects they consider profitable, but confidence in their judgment is variable and can justify various strategies. Banks examine firms' productive and financial expectations and also their financial structure. This investigation is made according to their confidence in the state of long-term expectations of yields on capital assets, influencing what Keynes referred to as 'animal spirits'. After the study of expected production and of the demand for financing that integrates the firm's borrowing risk, bankers can refuse to finance. The state of confidence of banks summarizes these factors. A monetary constraint issued from banks can be happen $[F < F_D]$. In the model, banks do not make loans to households.

Banks experience a lender's risk (LR) when underwriting finance and creating money. The lender's risk is the sum of three fundamental risks: risk of default, risk of liquidity and market risk. Fluctuations in capital asset prices modify their value and explain capital risk – which is very high for equities (E) and fixed-yield bonds (OF). For the fixed-yield bonds, capital risk is inversely proportional to interest rates. The risk to income mainly concerns the highly uncertain dividends of equities and the variable yield of loans. Finally, monetary policy involves a money market risk when fluctuations in the money interest rates occur.

In equations (22, 26), the lender's risk (LR) is measured by the gap of the current leverage ratio with a conventional leverage ratio. The higher the current indebtedness of firms ($(CP + OF + L)/K$) is over accepted indebtedness, the higher the lender's risk is. The accepted indebtedness is conventional, but this conventional indebtedness can increase during a boom and decrease during a crisis. We also introduce Tobin's q ratio and the cost of indebtedness. Tobin's q ratio is measured by the financial value of the firms over the capital (K). The financial value is the value of the equities on the market ($e \cdot p_e$). The market risk is taken into account by the expected capital gains on equities (CG^a_e) and on fixed-yield bonds (CG^a_{of}), but also by the central bank interest rate. The capital losses of firms are also the capital gains of banks.

When the lender's risk is at a maximum ($LR = 1$), commercial banks refuse to finance the net investment of firms: $\Delta F = 0$. Desired investment (I_D) faces a serious finance rationing. The flow of net investment is only financed by self-funding, that is the retained earnings (P^u), minus the capital losses of firms. If the lender's risk is null ($LR = 0$), desired investment is fully financed: $\Delta F = \Delta F_D$. This is the post-Keynesian 'horizontalist' case.

$$\Delta F = \Delta F^d \cdot (1 - LR) \quad \text{With } 0 \leq LR \leq 1 \tag{20}$$

$$\Delta F_D = I_D - P^U + CG \tag{21}$$

$$LR = \gamma_4 + a_1 \cdot (lev_{-1} - lev_c) - (b_1 \cdot q) + (c_1 \cdot i_{cb}) \quad \text{With } \gamma_4, a_1, b_1, c_1 \text{ et } lev_c\text{: constant} \tag{22}$$

$$lev = (CP + OF + L) \,/\, K \tag{23}$$

$$q = e \cdot p_e \,/\, K \tag{24}$$

We follow the methodology developed by Godley and Lavoie (2007) and inspired by Tobin (1958) to define the portfolio behavior of banks. Banks can hold four different assets: bonds (with fixed rates of interest) ($OF = of \,.\, p_{of}$), equities ($E = e \,.\, p_e$), loans at variable long-term interest rates (L) and commercial paper (CP) at short-term interest rates:

While central banks fix the short-term rates, private banks' liquidity preference determines banking rates (short-, medium- and long-term interest rates). Significant rates for growth and financing (loan) are the long-term interest rates (i_l). The link between short-term and long-term interest rates is complex. Macroeconomic banking interest rates are the production costs of money plus a risk premium. The first element corresponds to functioning costs (wages, investment, immobilization); payment costs for monetary liabilities (subjected to the firms' competition for households' savings) and the cost of high-powered money determined by the central bank; and to a rate of margin (χ) corresponding to standard profits of banks. The production costs of money are equal to i_{cb} plus a relatively constant mark up (χ).

Risk premiums are not constant because they are the fruits of the banks' liquidity preference. Risk premiums cover the lender's risk (*lr*). In the model, we use the same lender's risk as the one seen previously (equation 19). But with the different coefficients, *lr* can be negative and reduces the mark-up. Therefore the long-term interest rate becomes endogenous and the spread between i_{cb} and i_l is not constant. We introduce an endogenous curve of the interest rates. Banks apply a spread (χ_3) between the key rate and the rate on deposits in order to make a profit.

$$i_l = i_{cb} + lr + \chi_1 \quad \text{With } \chi_1\text{: constant } \chi_1 > \chi_2 \tag{25}$$

$$lr = \gamma_5 + a_2 \,.\, (lev_{-1} - lev_c) - (b_2 \,.\, q) \quad \text{With } \gamma_5, a_2, b_2, lev_c \text{ constant} \tag{26}$$

$$i_{cp} = i_{cb} + \chi_2 \quad \text{With } \chi_2\text{: constant } \chi_1 > \chi_2 \tag{27}$$

$$i_d = i_{cb} - \chi_3$$

Economic activity also depends on the animal spirits of banks. Finance scarcity can only be the consequence of a deliberate choice. 'Desired scarcity' of financing is the sign of banks' liquidity preference. From an optimal structure of their balance sheet, we can measure the profits of commercial banks (P_b) obtained by monetary financing:

$$\begin{aligned} P_b \equiv\; & i_{b-1} \,.\, B_{-1} + i_{l-1} \,.\, L_{-1} + i_{cp-1} \,.\, CP_{-1} + i_{of} \,.\, of_{-1} \\ & + p^{dB} - i_{d-1} \,.\, D_{-1} - i_{cb-1} \,.\, REF_{-1} \end{aligned} \tag{28}$$

12.2.5 Monetary policy of central bank

The central bank has neither operating costs nor net worth and pays all its profits to the government. Following the theory of endogenous money, we assume that the central bank is fully accommodating. First, the central bank fixes the key rate of interest (i_{cb}) according to its monetary policy and second it provides whatever advances (*REF*) are demanded by banks at this rate. Monetary authorities determine exogenously the key rate on the money market (i_{cb}). The exogenous key rate allows us to make monetary policy shocks.

12.3 Experiments with a monetary policy shock and six hypotheses on fiscal policy

Having found a steady state, we conduct experiments by modifying the key rate of the monetary policy. Heterodox economists do not easily accept the notion of a steady state. We use it only as an analytical tool but we recognize that such a theoretical construction is never reached in practice because parameters and exogenous variables are actually changing all the time. That is why, when making a simulation, it is important to differentiate between the initial effects of some change (in the early periods of the dynamic response) and the terminal effects (in the steady state). These terminal effects will eventually arise as long as the structure of the model is left unchanged, although we know that this is unlikely. However, the final steady state, that is to say after the shock, is not the same as the initial steady state. There is no long-term predetermined equilibrium. This only signifies a kind of resilience in the economy. In real life and despite shocks, capitalist economies are not submitted to a full instability in the long term.

Two kinds of shocks will be made. First, we implement a zero interest rate policy (ZIRP) through a permanent shock. The key rate decreased from 2 per cent to 0 per cent. Second, we implement a temporary shock with a higher key rate during four years (from 2 per cent to 3 per cent the first year, from 3 per cent to 4 per cent the second and the third years and from 4 to 3 per cent the fourth year). The first policy provides a permanent stimulus to the economy, while the latter will temporarily slow it down.

We present the effects of both monetary policies on the most important variables in diagrams. Every hypothesis has a corresponding color. We group four hypotheses (*H1*, *H2*, *H3* and *H4*) in a first diagram, as they are reasonably close to the post-Keynesian approach. The impact of monetary policies will be fairly close. In a second diagram, we add the two hypotheses (*H5* and *H6*) corresponding to the neoclassical approach. The lines corresponding to the six hypotheses are:

- *H1*: the independent central bank:
- *H2*: the 'fiscal deficit targeting' rule:
- *H3*: the 'fiscal debt targeting' rule:
- *H4*: the Wynne Godley proposal:
- *H5*: Ricardian equivalence:
- *H6*: the *Treasury view*:

Of course, the calibration of the economy is not indifferent to results. The fiscal stance at the steady state is close to the situation of the current crisis in many countries. The fiscal debt ratio is 60 per cent, the fiscal deficit is 10 per cent, but the rate of growth is clearly positive.

12.3.1 A permanent zero interest rate policy

With the lower key interest rate (ZIRP), the new steady state corresponds to higher growth rates for the assumptions close to the post-Keynesian approach (*H1, H2* and *H3*). The exception is the proposal of Wynne Godley (*H4*). Indeed, his definition of neutralization is the return (in the medium term) to the previous steady state. With *H4*, fiscal policy neutralizes the impact of monetary policy. Fiscal policy is countercyclical and can be considered neutral because it corresponds neither to acceleration nor to slowdown in growth. Rather than to separate the effects of each policy (monetary and fiscal), the post-Keynesians reflect the policy mix. The best result in terms of growth is the 'fiscal debt targeting rule' behind the 'fiscal deficit targeting rule' (Figure 12.1a). Stabilizing the debt can be obtained with a larger deficit because economic recovery and zero key rates make the debt repayment easily sustainable. Even if the debt is contracted at a positive long-term interest rate. The original policy (*H1*) involves a slight acceleration of growth.

On the other hand, the two orthodox proposals lead to a slower growth rate than the previous steady state, in spite of the very accommodating monetary policy (Figure 12.1b). With Ricardian equivalence (*H5*), households counterbalance changes in fiscal deficit. But the strict financial orthodoxy implemented by the *Treasury view* involves a strong recession that appears disastrous. This drop in the growth rate is largely compounded by the importance of the fiscal stance in the previous steady state. However, this corresponds to policies implemented in Ireland or Portugal today. To represent these countries, we should raise more sharply the risk premium on long-term interest rate ($lr + \chi 1$).

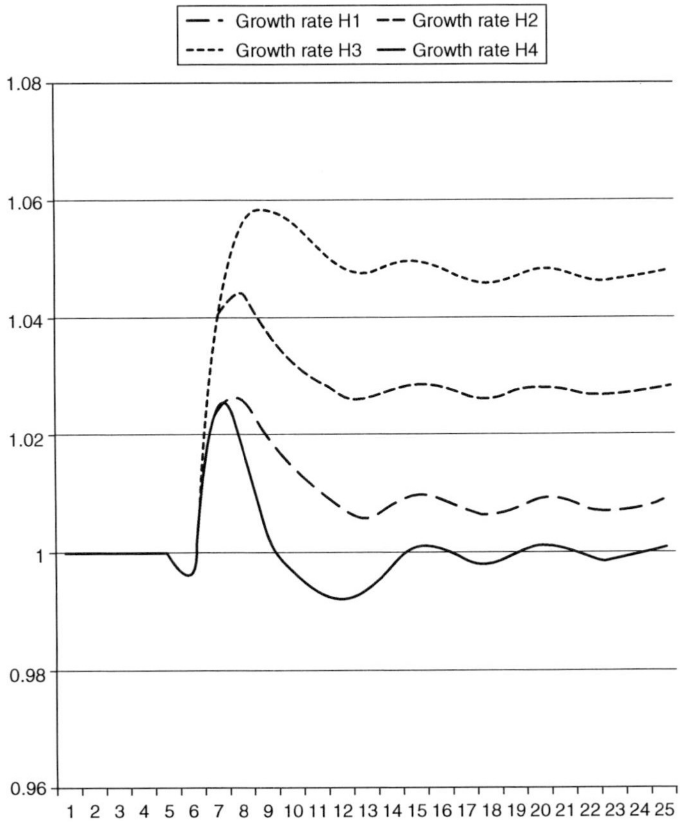

Figure 12.1a Effects on the growth rate of the economy

Business cycles reappear with the end of the counter-cyclical policies (*H6*). More than half of economic growth is lost.

The zero interest rate and fiscal debt reduction make firm debts easier. They increased in all cases except with the rule of stabilization of public debt (*H3*) (Figure 12.2a). Obviously the massive fiscal debt reduction, imposed by the *Treasury view*, transfers this large indebtedness to the firm sector, which becomes very vulnerable to a rise in interest rates (Figure 12.2b). Only the 'fiscal debt targeting rule' (*H3*) allows an increase in the fiscal deficit owing to the very low cost of debt. The other assumptions (except *H2* and *H6* obviously) involve a similarly weak decline in the fiscal deficit (Figures 12.3a and 12.3b), which explains the decreasing public debt ratio (Figure 12.4a). Paradoxically, the Ricardian consumer entails an increase in the public debt ratio. The government seeks to compensate

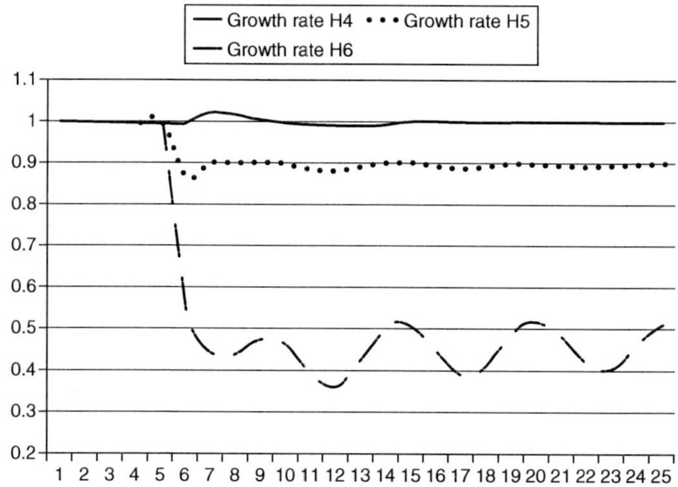

Figure 12.1b Effects on the growth rate of the economy

the household reduction in consumption (Figure 12.4a and 12.4b). Obviously, the consumption decreases with Ricardian consumer and is growing strongly with declining public economic activity according the *Treasury view* (Figures 12.6a and 12.6b). Improved financial conditions and higher growth rate reduce the lender's risk, which explains the drop in monetary rationing (Figures 12.5a and 12.5b).

12.3.2 A temporary shock with higher key interest rate

This time, the monetary policy shock is temporary and in the opposite direction than in the previous example. Regarding the two orthodox policies, the neutralization of fiscal policy by the Ricardian consumer (H5) and the implementation of a strict financial orthodoxy according to the Treasury view (H6), have a much greater influence than the single monetary policy shock. Therefore, the observed trends for the different variables are virtually identical regardless of the monetary policy (Figures 12.7b, 12.8b, 12.9b, 12.10b, 12.11b and 12.12b). We focused on the first four hypotheses.

As the shock is temporary, the growth rate comes back in the four cases to the steady state. As before, *H3* is more sensitive to the monetary policy than are the other hypotheses, in particular the Wynne Godley proposal (*H4*) (Figure 12.7a). Only the 'fiscal debt targeting rule' (*H3*) causes an increase in the indebtedness of firms (Figure 12.8a) and a decrease in the fiscal deficit ratio (Figure 12.9a). With the temporary rising key rate, which implies a higher cost of debt, the ratio of fiscal

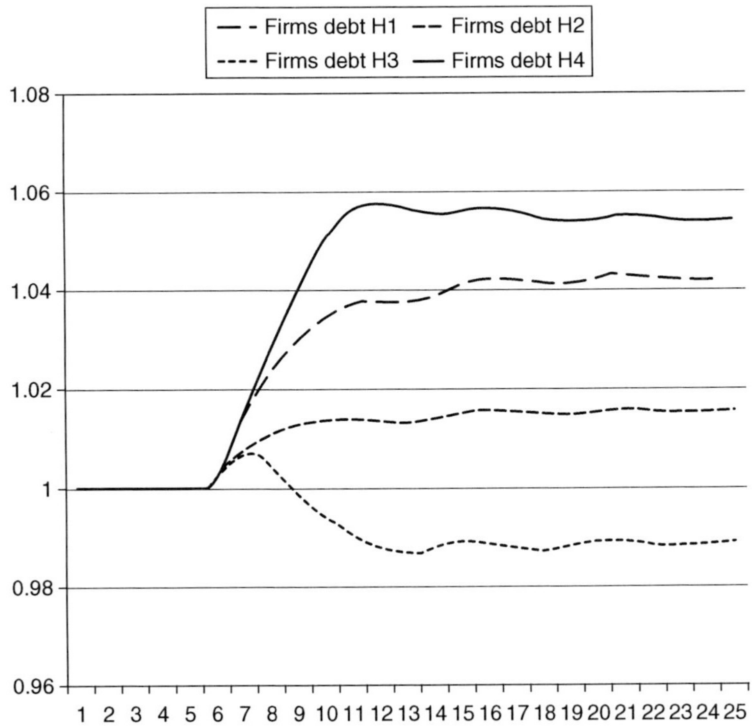

Figure 12.2a Effects on the firms' debt ratio

debt increases (except for *H3* obviously, Figure 12.10a). The rise in credit rationing explains that we observe (except for *H3*), that is, lower firm indebtedness by enhancing the impact of slower growth (Figure 12.11a). Consumption replaces investment (Figure 12.12a).

12.4 Conclusion

Now we can answer the original question. Since Keynes and Haavelmo, post-Keynesians know that fiscal policy is never neutral, even with a balanced budget. The transmission channels are numerous. The impact on income distribution and the injection of income by the fiscal deficit are two channels among the most important. The fiscal stance corresponding to the steady state also plays a role. Fiscal policy is never neutral and we cannot neutralize all the transmission channels at once. We have also seen in our simulations that the debt burden (stock issued from the past) plays an important role, especially in the case of changing

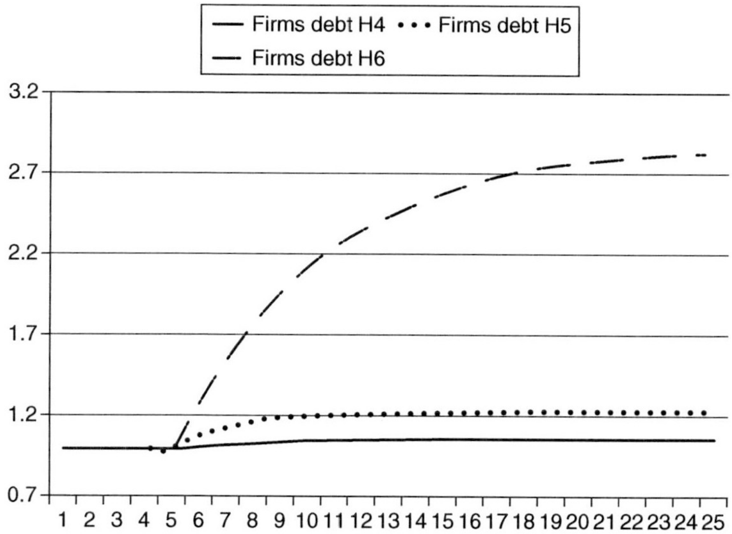

Figure 12.2b Effects on the firms' debt ratio

interest rates. In addition, to analyze the monetary policy independently of fiscal policy does not match the post-Keynesian framework, which prefers the resolution of a policy mix. The independence given to central banks has unfortunately not eliminated the problem of coordination between different policies. Instead, our model shows the fundamental importance of a coordinated joint resolution of monetary, fiscal and income policy. Keeping the same model to analyze monetary policy is not a bad solution. But we must keep in mind that the fiscal stance continues to act and fiscal policy is therefore not neutral.

The post-Keynesian idea is that the economic policy is a mix of monetary and fiscal policies seeking to find a certain rate of economic growth usually compatible with full employment. Neutrality must be understood in terms of general economic policy and not at the level of one policy. Post-Keynesians believe that fiscal policy is always active; to measure only the effects of monetary policy is simply an illusion. With the proposal of Wynne Godley, fiscal policy neutralizes the impact of monetary policy. Fiscal policy is counter-cyclical and can be considered neutral because it corresponds nor to acceleration, neither to slowdown in growth. Wynne Godley's proposal is the best post-Keynesian answer.

The final conclusion is that fiscal policy rules notably advocated by orthodox economists will always make more damage than the alleged problems arising from these policies.

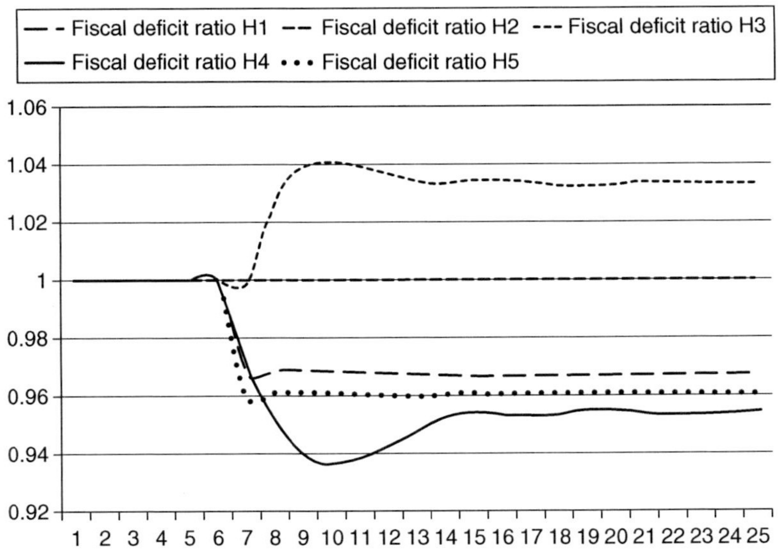

Figure 12.3a Effects on the fiscal deficit ratio

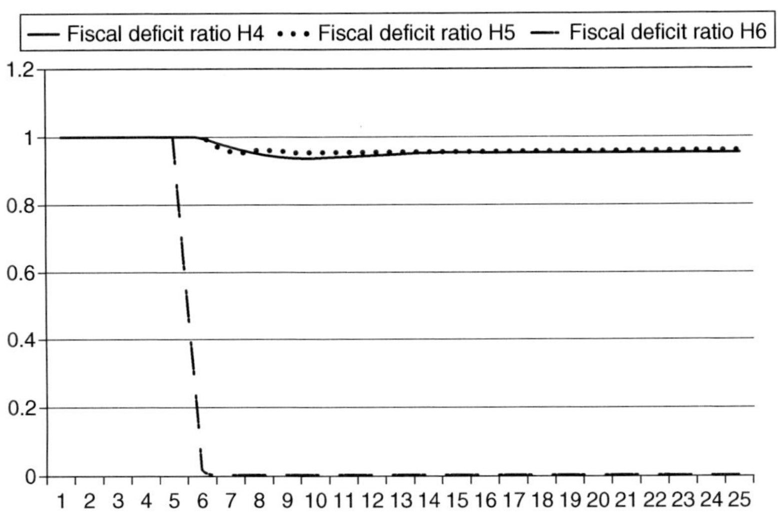

Figure 12.3b Effects on the fiscal deficit ratio

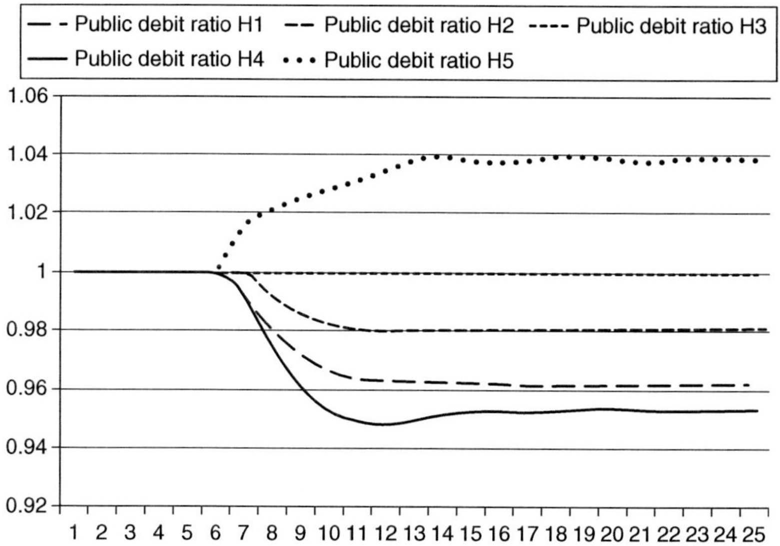

Figure 12.4a Effects on the public debt ratio

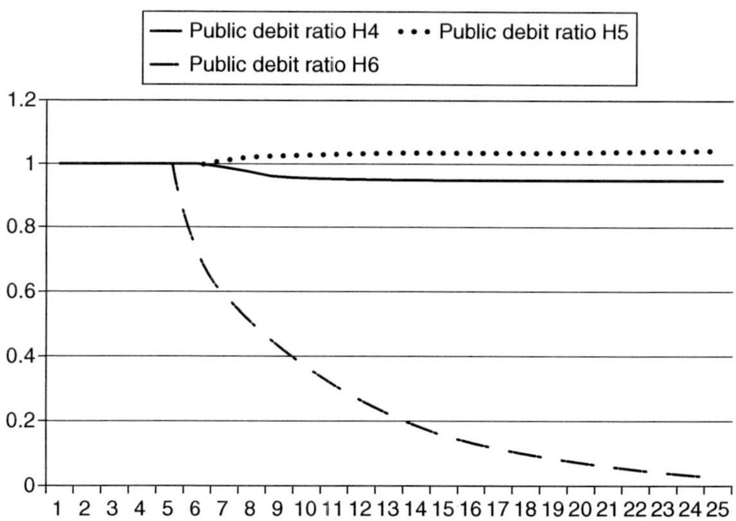

Figure 12.4b Effects on the public debt ratio

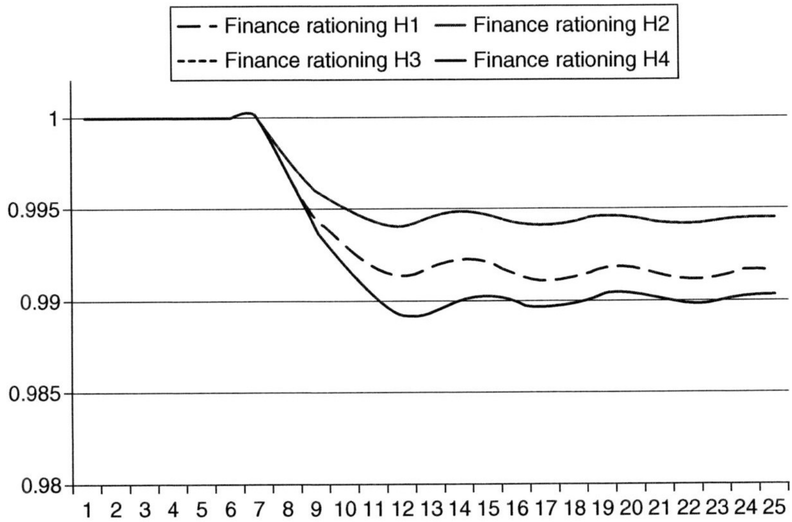

Figure 12.5a Effects on the finance rationing

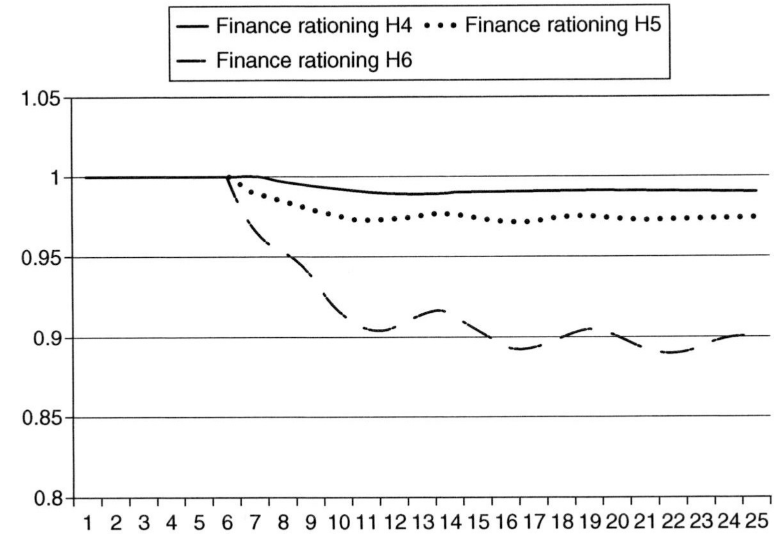

Figure 12.5b Effects on the finance rationing

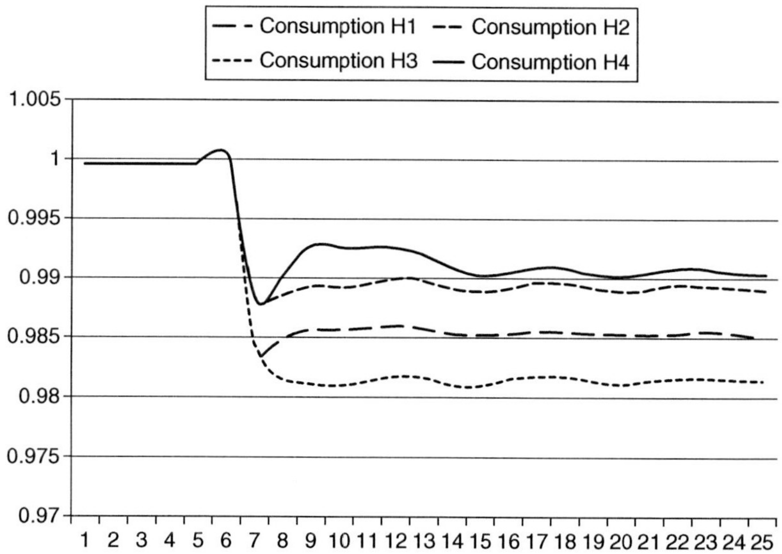

Figure 12.6a Effects on the consumption

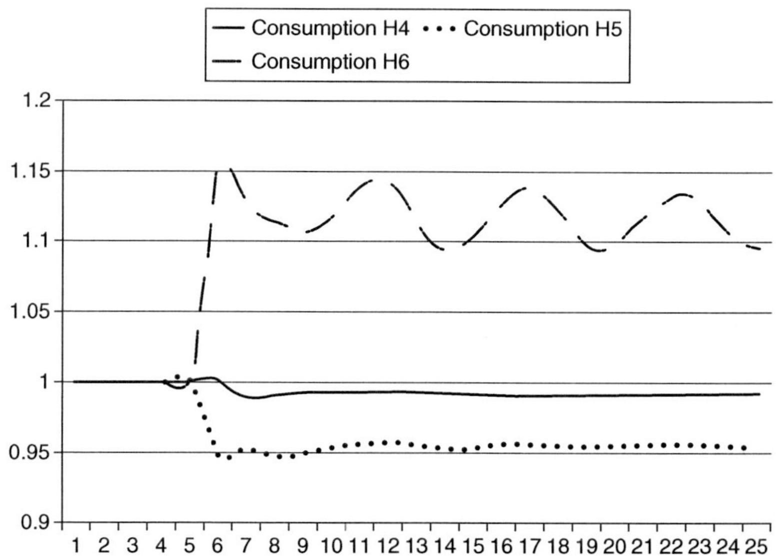

Figure 12.6b Effects on the consumption

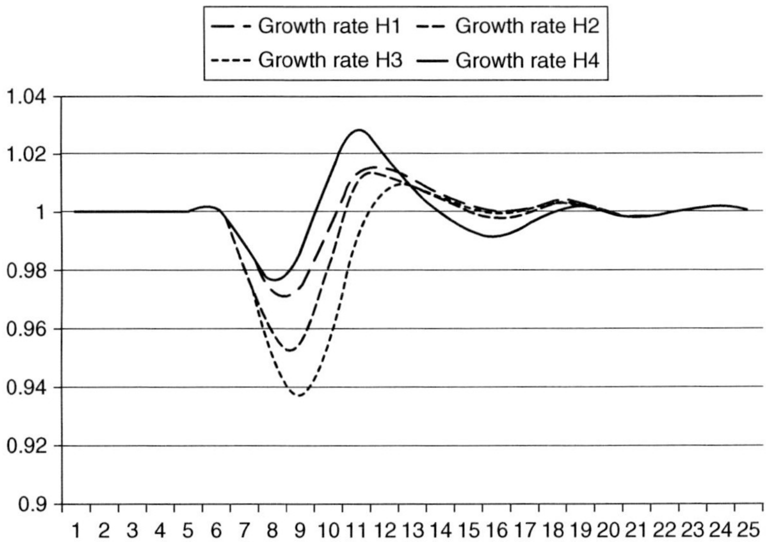

Figure 12.7a Effects on the growth rate of the economy

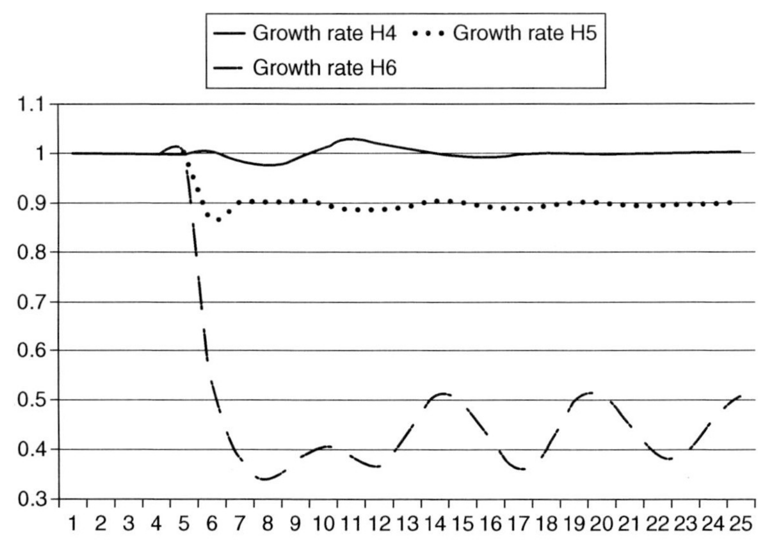

Figure 12.7b Effects on the growth rate of the economy

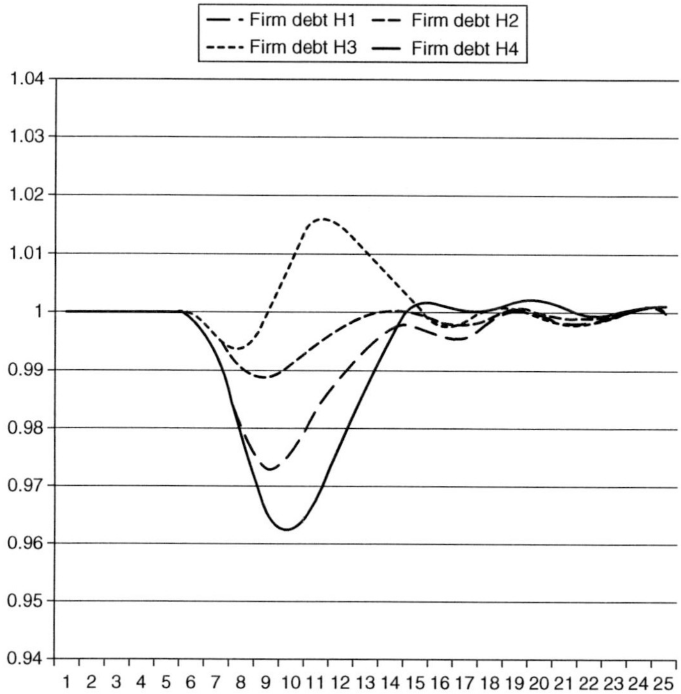

Figure 12.8a Effects on the firms' debt ratio

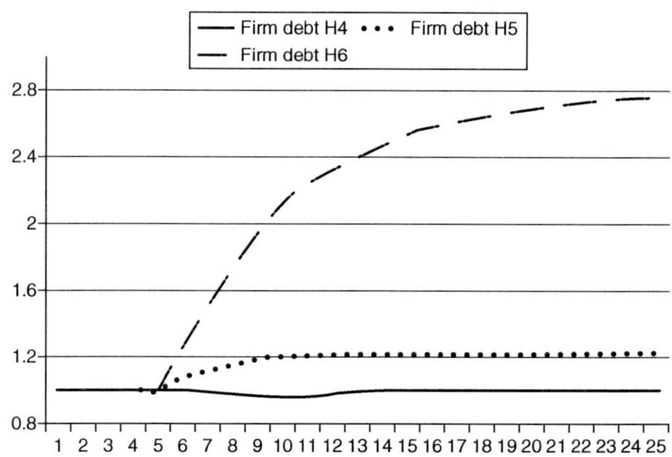

Figure 12.8b Effects on the firms' debt ratio

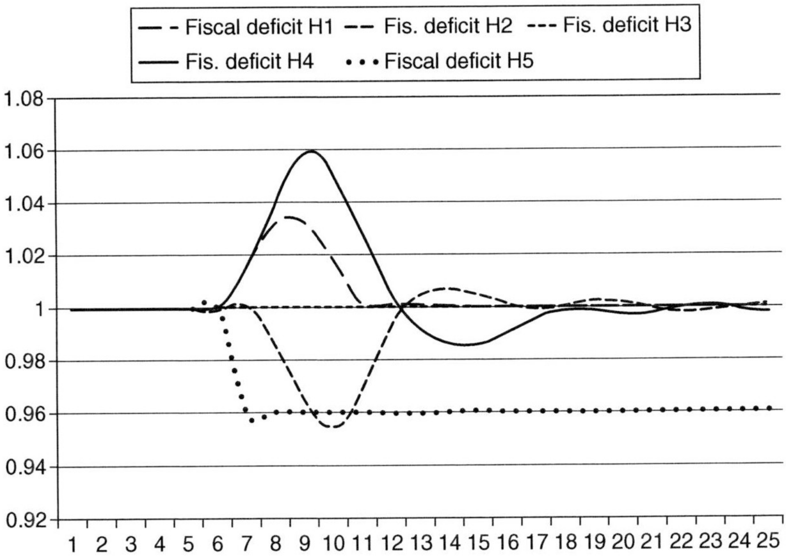

Figure 12.9a Effects on the fiscal deficit ratio

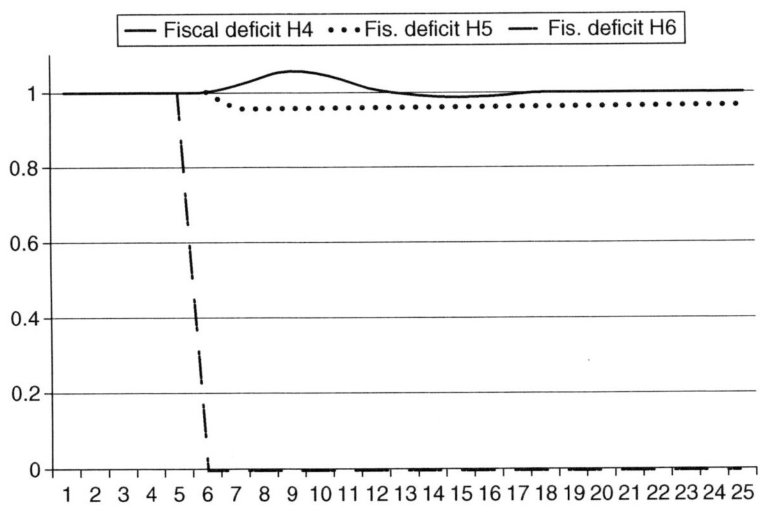

Figure 12.9b Effects on the fiscal deficit ratio

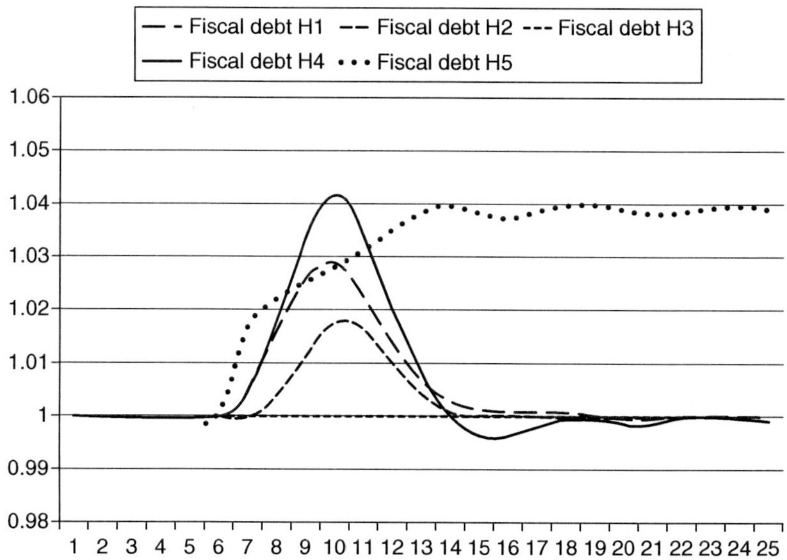

Figure 12.10a Effects on the public debt ratio

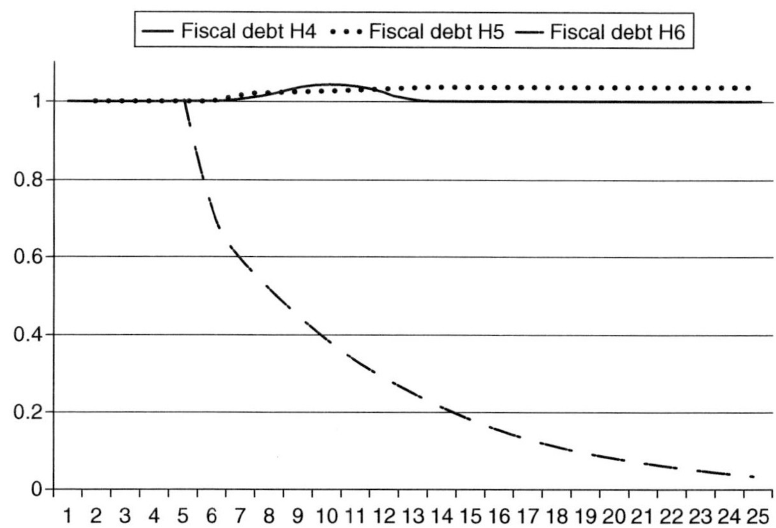

Figure 12.10b Effects on the public debt ratio

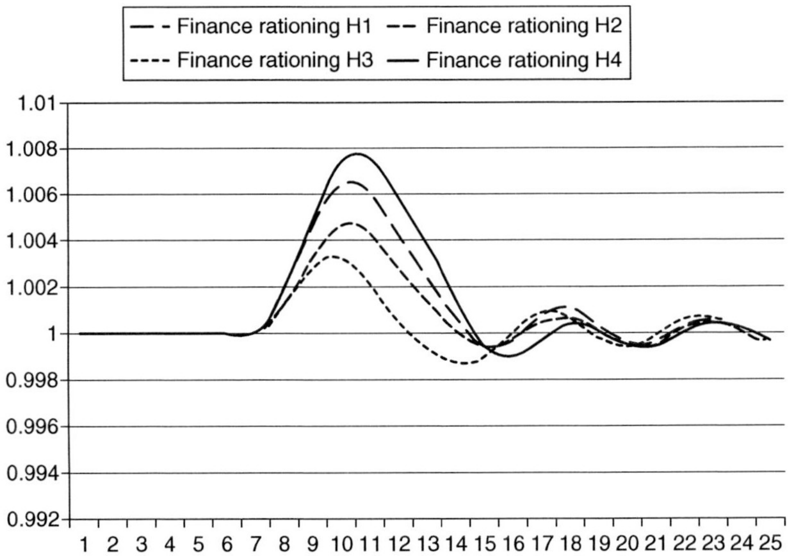

Figure 12.11a Effects on the finance rationing

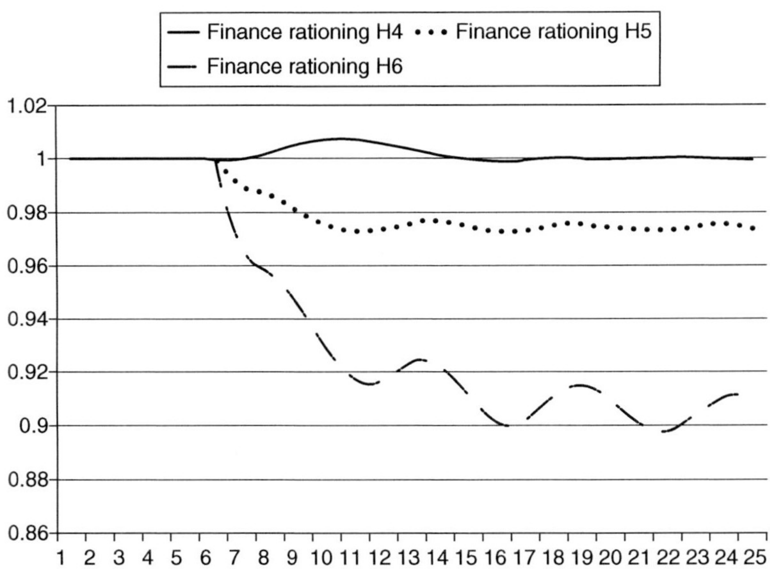

Figure 12.11b Effects on the finance rationing

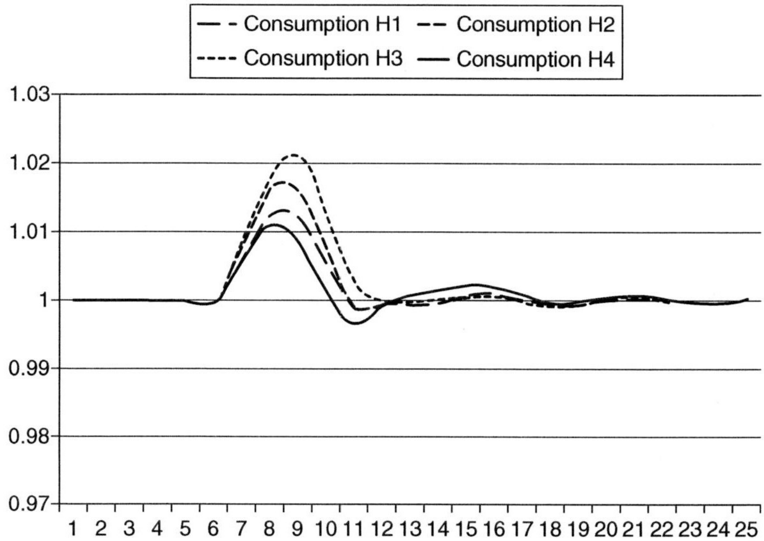

Figure 12.12a Effects on the consumption

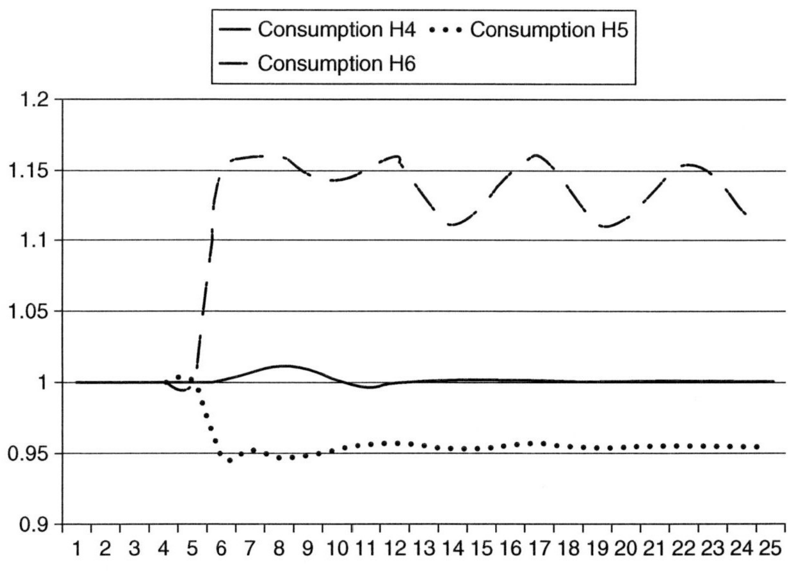

Figure 12.12b Effects on the consumption

Appendix

The complete model for the steady state

Equation	Parameters	Description
(1) $gr_y = \Delta Y / Y_{-1}$		Growth rate of national income
(2) $gr_y^a = gr_{y-1} + \theta\,(gr_{y-1} - gr_{y-1}^a)$		Expected growth rate
(3) $Y = C + I + G$		National income
(4) $T = T_H + T_F$		Taxes
(5) $T_H = \tau_h \,.\, W_{-1}$	With τ_h: constant	Taxes on households
(6) $T_F = \tau_f \,.\, P_{-1}^d$	With τ_f: constant	Taxes on firms
(7) $G = G_{-1} \,.\, (1 + gr_{y\,-1})$		Government expenditure
(8) $DG = G + i_{b-1} - B_{-1} - T - P_{cb}$		Government deficit
(9-i)[5] $B \equiv B_{-1} + DG$		Treasury bills
(10) $i_b = i_1$		Interest rate on treasury bills
(11) $K = K_{-1} + I$		Stock of capital
(12-ii) $I \equiv \Delta F + P^u - CG$		Net investment
(13) $CG \equiv CG_e + CG_{of}$		Capital gains of banks
(14) $I_D = gr_{kD} \,.\, K-1$		Investment demand
(15) $gr_{kD} = \gamma_0 + \gamma_1 \,.\, r_{cf-1} + \gamma_2 \,.\, u_{-1} - \gamma_3 \,.\, FCI_{\,-1}$	With γ_i: constant	Desired growth in stock of capital
(16) $r_{cf} = P^u / K_{-1}$		Ratio of cash flow
(17) $u = Y / Y_{fc}$		Capacity utilization rate
(18) $Y_{fc} = K_{-1} \,.\, \sigma$	With σ: constant	Output of full capacity
(19) $FCI = \mu_1 \cdot i_1 \cdot (L+OF)/K + \mu_2 - i_{cb} \,.\, CP/K - \mu_3 - E/Y$	With μ_i: constant	Financial Condition Index
(20) $W = Y / (1 + \rho)$	With ρ: constant	Wages
(21-iii) $P \equiv Y - W - i_{l-1} \,.\, L_{-1} - i_{cp-1} \,.\, CP_{-1} - i_{of} \,.\, of_{-1}$		Firms profits
(22) $P^d = (1 - s_f) \,.\, P_{-1}$	With s_f: constant	Distributed profits
(23) $P^{dB} = P^d - T_F$		Distributed profits to banks
(24-iv) $P^u \equiv P - P^d$		Undistributed profits
(25) $e = e_{-1} \,.\, (1 + gr_Y^a)$		Number of equities

(continued)

Appendix (Continued)

	Equation	Condition	Description
(26)	$C = \alpha_1 . Y_w^a + \alpha_2 . Y_v^a + \alpha_3 - D_{-1}$	With α_i: constant	Consumption
(27)	$Y_w^a = Y_{w-1} + \theta_h . (Y_{w-1} - Y_{w-1}^a)$	With θ_h: constant	Expected disposable income of workers
(28)	$Y_v^a = Y_{v-1} + \theta_h . (Y_{v-1} - Y_{v-1}^a)$		Expected disposable financial income
(29)	$Y_w = W - T_H$		Disposable income of workers
(30)	$Y_v = i_{d-1} . D_{-1}$		Disposable financial income
(31)	$Y_h = Y_w + Y_v$		Disposable income of households
(32-v)	$D \equiv D_{-1} + Y_h - C$		Bank deposits
(33)	$\Delta F = \Delta F_D . (1 - LR)$	With $0 \leq LR \leq 1$	External finance
(34)	$LR = a_1 . (lev_{-1} - lev_c) - b_1 . q_{-1} + c_1 . i_{cb}$	With a_1, b_1, c_1 and lev_c: constants	Lender's risk
(35)	$lev = (CP + OF + L) / K$		Leverage ratio
(36)	$q = e . p_e / K$		Tobin's q ratio
(37)	$F_D = F_{-1} + I_D - P^U + CG$		External finance demand
(38)	$OF = (\lambda_{10} + \lambda_{11} . r_{of}^a - \lambda_{12} . r_e^a - \lambda_{13} . i_1 - \lambda_{14} . i_{cp}) . F$		Bonds (Fixed rate)
(39)	$E = (\lambda_{20} - \lambda_{21} . r_{of}^a + \lambda_{22} . r_e^a - \lambda_{23} . i_1 - \lambda_{24} . i_{cp}) . F$		Equities
(40)	$L = (\lambda_{30} - \lambda_{31} . r_{of}^a - \lambda_{32} . r_e^a + \lambda_{33} . i_1 - \lambda_{34} . i_{cp}) . F$		Loans (variable long-term rate)
(41)	$CP = F - OF - E - L$		Commercial paper
(42)	$r_{of}^a = i_{of} + CG_{of}^a / OF_{-1}$	With i_{of} : constant	Expected yield of bonds
(43)	$CG_{of}^a = CG_{of-1} + \theta_b . (CG_{of-1} - CG_{of-1}^a)$		Expected capital gains on bonds
(44)	$CG_{of} = \Delta p_{of} . of_{-1}$		Capital gains on bonds
(45)	$of = OF / p_{of}$		Number of bonds
(46)	$p_{of} = p_{of-1} (1 + i_{of}) / (1 + i_1)$		Price of fixed rate bonds
(47)	$r_e^a = (P^{dBa} + CG_e^a) / E_{-1}$		Expected return on equities
(48)	$P^{dBa} = P_{-1}^{dB} + \theta_b . (P_{-1}^{dB} - P_{-1}^{dBa})$		Expected distributed profits
(49)	$CG_e^a = CG_{e-1} + \theta_b . (CG_{e-1} - CG_{e-1}^a)$		Expected capital gains on equities
(50)	$CGe = \Delta p_e . e_{-1}$		Capital gains on equities

Equation	Comment	Description
(51) $p_e = E / e$		Price of equities
(52) $i_l = i_{cb} + lr + \chi_1$	With χ_1: constant	Interest rate on loans
(53) $lr = a_2 \cdot (lev_{-1} - lev_c) - b_2 \cdot q_{-1}$	With a_2, b_2: constants	Lender's risk for LT interest rate
(54) $i_{cp} = i_{cb} + \chi_2$	With χ_2: constant	Interest rate on commercial paper
(55) $i_d = i_{cb} - \chi_3$		Interest rate on deposits
(56-vi) $P_b \equiv i_{b-1} . B_{-1} + i_{l-1} . L_{-1} + i_{cp-1} . CP_{-1} + i_{of} . of_{-1} + P^{dB} - i_{d-1} . D_{-1} - i_{cb-1} . REF_{-1}$		Banks profits
(57) $H = \eta . D$		High-powered money
(58-vii) $P_{cb} \equiv i_{cb-1} . REF_{-1}$		Central bank profits
(59-viii) $REF \equiv REF_{-1} + \Delta H + \Delta B + \Delta F - CG - P_b - \Delta D$		Reserve requirements
(60) $i_{cb} = i_{cb0}$	With i_{cb0}: constant	Central bank key interest rate

Missing equation: (61-ix) $REF \equiv H$

Notes

1. For this analysis of New Keynesian literature on 'active' and 'passive' monetary and fiscal policies, on non-Ricardian consumers and on Leeper's framework, see Leeper (1991), Leith and von Thadden (2006) and Guillard (2004).
2. In line with Leeper (1991), if the unique fiscal instrument is the lump-sum tax rate, we call the fiscal policy 'passive' ('active') if the feedback coefficient of taxes on debt is larger (smaller) than the steady state real interest rate.
3. For a SFC-PK model that includes the price level with a New Keynesian Phillips Curve, see Le Heron (2008b).
4. See Godley, (1999) and Godley and Lavoie, (2006).
5. When we use an accounting identity, we add a Roman numeral. A feature of SFC models is that if there are M columns and N non ordinary rows in the transactions matrix, then there are only (M + N – 1) independent accounting identities in the model. Due to this principle, highly similar to Walras' Law, one equation must be kept out; we shall use exactly eight accounting identities in the model. The missing identity (61-ix) is the one relative to the capital account of the central bank. Of course, this accounting identity must hold invariably. When we solve the model, we have to verify that the numbers issued from simulations respect the missing identity.

References

Barro, R. (1974) 'Are Government Bonds Net Wealth?,' *Journal of Political Economy* 82: 1095–117.

Bi, H. and M. Kumhof (2009) 'Jointly Optimal Monetary and Fiscal Policy Rules Under Borrowing Constraints,' IMF Working Paper 286 (Washington, DC: International Monetary Fund).

Godley, W. (1999) 'Money and Credit in a Keynesian Model of Income Determination,' *Cambridge Journal of Economics* 23(4): 393–411.

Godley, W. and M. Lavoie (2007) *Monetary Economics: An Integrated Approach to Credit, Money, Income, Production and Wealth* (London: Palgrave Macmillan).

Guillard, M. (2004) 'Politique Monétaire et Fiscale dans un Monde Non Ricardien: Une Théorie Fiscale de l'Inflation,' Working Paper 28 September (Paris: Centre National de la Recherche Scientifique).

Lavoie, M. and W. Godley (2006) 'Features of a Realistic Banking System within a Post-Keynesian Stock-flow Consistent Model,' in M. Setterfield (ed.) *Complexity, Endogenous Money and Macroeconomic Theory* (Cheltenham, UK: Edward Elgar), pp. 251–68.

Leeper, E. (1991) 'Equilibria Under "Active" and "Passive" Monetary and Fiscal Policy,' *Journal of Monetary Economics* 27: 129–47.

Le Heron, E. (2008) 'Fiscal and Monetary Policies in a Keynesian Stock-Flow Consistent Model,' in J. Creel and M. Sawyer (eds) *Current Thinking on Fiscal Policy* (London: Palgrave Macmillan), pp. 145–75.

Le Heron, E. and T. Mouakil (2008) 'A Post Keynesian Stock-Flow Consistent Model for the Dynamic Analysis of Monetary Policy Shock on Banking Behavior,' *Metroeconomica* 59(3): 405–40.

Leith, C. and L. von Thadden (2006) 'Monetary and Fiscal Policy Interactions in a New Keynesian Model with Capital Accumulation and Non-Ricardian Consumers,' Working Paper No. 649 (Frankfurt: European Central Bank).

Minsky, H.P. (1975 [2008]) *John Maynard Keynes* (New York: Columbia University Press) republished in D.B. Papadimitriou and L.R. Wray (eds) *Hyman P. Minsky's John Maynard Keynes* (New York: McGraw-Hill).

Ricardo, D. (1817 [1951]) *Principles of Political Economy and Taxation*, vol. 1, in P. Sraffa (ed.) *The Works and Correspondence of David Ricardo*, 10 vols (1951–55) (Cambridge: Cambridge University Press).

Sims, C. (1994) 'A Simple Model for Study of the Determination of the Price Level and the Interactions of Monetary and Fiscal Policy,' *Economic Theory* 4: 381–99.

Taylor, J.B. (1993) 'Discretion versus Policy Rules in Practice,' Carnegie-Rochester Conference Series on Public Policy, 39: 195–214.

Taylor, J.B. (2000) 'Reassessing Discretionary Fiscal Policy,' *Journal of Economic Perspectives* 14(3): 21–36.

Tobin, J. (1958) 'Liquidity Preference as Behavior Towards Risk,' *Review of Economic Studies* 67: 65–86.

Woodford, M. (1994) 'Monetary Policy and Price Level Determinacy in Cash-in-Advance Economy,' *Economic Theory* 4: 345–80.

Woodford, M. (2003) *Interest and Prices: Foundations of a Theory of Monetary Policy* (Princeton, NJ: Princeton University Press).

13
The Effectiveness of Fiscal Policy in the Levy Institute's Stock-flow Model

Philip Arestis and Malcolm Sawyer

13.1 Introduction

There has been a major shift within macroeconomic policy over the past three decades or so, in terms of the relative importance given to monetary policy and to fiscal policy. The former is gaining considerably in importance, while the latter is being so much downgraded that it is rarely discussed at least in academic circles these days. There are, of course, exceptions to this general statement. The onset of the 'great recession' prompted governments to initiate fiscal measures that avoided another 'great depression'. However, that was rather short-lived. It is now the case that a number of governments have resumed their hostility to fiscal policy as a stabilization instrument. In Arestis and Sawyer (1998, 2003a, 2004), we critically examined the significance of this shift in terms of monetary policy, which led us to question the effectiveness of interest rates now being used as the main instrument of monetary policy. In the same paper, but also in Arestis and Sawyer (2003b, 2006, 2010), we explored the role of fiscal policy, and argued that in the 'new consensus in macroeconomics' within which macroeconomics in general and monetary policy in particular is generally discussed, there is barely any mention of fiscal policy.[1] We strongly suggested there that fiscal policy should be reinstated, and concluded that fiscal policy remains a potent tool for offsetting major changes in the level of aggregate demand. This chapter aims to consider further those particular conclusions, by concentrating on the stock-flow Levy model.[2]

The Levy model has been designed to facilitate the construction of scenarios, and we use that model in this chapter for the construction of scenarios arising from specified fiscal expansions. It differs in that sense from many other econometric models, which are generally designed to provide short-term forecasts. The Levy model has undergone changes over the years. For example, versions with complicated structural relationships for inflation, wage and labor market have been constructed. The version utilized for the purposes of this chapter has an incomplete account of the channels of monetary policy (for example, via the exchange rate), and an incomplete link amongst a number of variables (such as wages and inflation), and was designed to deal with periods of negligible rates of inflation. In what follows in this chapter we utilize this version of the model, which is by no means fully completed.

We begin in section 13.2 by discussing the Levy model's stock-flow consistency aspects, before we provide a summary of its bare essentials in section 13.3. We then consider fiscal policy within this framework in section 13.4, providing quantitative estimates of fiscal policy multipliers in this model. In the final section, section 13.5, we summarize the argument and conclude.

13.2 The stock-flow consistency of the model

The model under investigation belongs to that category of models that take explicitly into consideration the stock implications that relate to debt and asset accumulation of the flow behavior. Lavoie and Godley (2001–02) argue that 'The stock-flow monetary accounting framework provides ... an alternative... foundation... that is based essentially on [a number of] principles... the accounting must be right. All stocks and flows must have counterparts somewhere in the rest of the economy. The watertight stock flow accounting imposes system constraints that have qualitative implications. This is not a matter of logical coherence; it also feeds into the intrinsic dynamics of the model' (p. 131; words in square brackets added). It is, thus, paramount that an adequate accounting framework is present to provide a 'system-wide' logical requirement, relevant to the issue under scrutiny. This would ensure that flows necessarily change stocks, which influence future flows, thereby establishing the dynamics of the system. Further requirements of such a framework to satisfy two sets of constraints are the following. The first is the 'sectoral budget' constraint, that in each accounting period economic agents are constrained by what is available at the beginning of the period; and the second is the 'adding-up' constraint, that the whole is equal to its parts and that combinations of stocks and flows obey certain identities.

The model is thereby more sensitive to changes in theoretical assumptions and accounting definitions, than in other models precisely because of these constraints. This makes the study of the model's dynamics particularly interesting in that the constraints that are required to satisfy the identities and accounting definitions of the model, may give results that are not necessarily expected from standard theoretical assumptions. And yet, explicit recognition of stock-flow relationships imply, by their very construction, a dynamic approach to modeling, contrary to the more conventional, Keynesian IS/LM models, which are predicated on static short-run equilibrium analysis. Indeed, and as Turnovsky (1977) puts it, the stock-flow models 'necessarily impose a dynamic structure on the macroeconomic system, even if all the underlying relationships are static' (p. xi). Tobin (1982) is also explicit on this issue. He argues that 'a model of short-run determination of macroeconomic activity must be regarded as referring to a slice of time, whether thick or paper thin, and as embedded in a dynamic process in which flows alter shocks, which in turn condition subsequent flows' (p. 189). 'Past stocks affect current flows and current flows affect current stocks, which affect future flows. Not only is this dynamic element of enormous importance, but also that the accounting framework in place, has no "black holes" and in which every flow comes from somewhere and goes somewhere' (Godley, 1996, p. 7). In this regard, the model is unique in terms of its macroeconomic reasoning, and also in terms of its logical coherence (Tobin, 1980, 1982; Godley and Shaikh, 2002; Lavoie and Godley, 2001–02; Godley and Lavoie, 2007a, 2007b).[3]

A further important facet of this type of models follows Solow's (1983) suggestion that the construction of stock-flow models is essentially an attempt to 'complete' Keynes' (1936) General Theory. This is so in view of 'the largest theoretical gap in the model of the General Theory' which 'was its relative neglect of stock concepts, stock equilibrium and stock-flow relations. It may have been a necessary simplification for Keynes to slice the time so thin that the stock of capital goods, for instance, can be treated as constant even while net investment is systematically positive or negative. But those slices soon add up to a slab, across which stock differences are perceptible. Besides, it is important to get the stock-flow relationships right; and since flow behaviour is often related to stocks, empirical models cannot be restricted to the shortest of the short runs' (p. 164).[4]

It would be instructive to compare this approach with that of a more mainstream perspective.[5] Clearly the latter does not pay any attention to stock-flow issues, which may be rather surprising. This is so since it follows from what has been described so far, that authors of a mainstream persuasion have acknowledged the importance of stock-flow issues (additional examples include Christ, 1967, 1968; Turnovsky, 1977; Buiter, 1980, 1983). However, this paradox may be explained by referring to an important assumption of the mainstream approach. This relates to the 'perfect foresight' assumption, not unrelated to the rational expectations assumption, which had been used by mainstream analysis well before the emergence and acceptance of the rational expectations assumption. Foley (1975) demonstrates that under this assumption the distinction between stock and flow equilibria in asset markets is of no consequence. The main reason of this result becomes apparent once the distinction between 'stock' equilibrium, at the beginning of the period, and 'flow' equilibrium, at the end of the period, is made. The end-of-period equilibrium equates instantaneous flow demands for assets with instantaneous flow supply. Stock equilibrium 'equates an instantaneous demand to hold the stock of an asset with an instantaneous supply' (Foley, 1975, p. 315). Although these equilibria have very different qualitative properties, under 'perfect foresight' or 'rational expectations' they are indistinguishable.[6]

The Levy stock-flow model also differs substantially from the more recently developed Dynamic Stochastic General Equilibrium (DGSE) models. The Levy stock-flow model does not share the basic assumptions of this type of models, which rely on the 'representative' agent, who is assumed to optimize intertemporally a utility function based on consumption today and consumption in the future, in a perfectly rational manner. This agent is a fully trustworthy 'representative' agent that would never default under the usual transversality conditions, an assumption that precludes the incorporation of money and a financial sector in these models. Under such assumptions fiscal policy is downgraded and monetary policy is upgraded; the latter is presumed to target inflation to be met through manipulation of the rate of interest under the further assumption of inflation being a monetary phenomenon and price stability the only objective of economic policy (see Arestis, 2009b, for a critique of these assumptions). These are all assumptions that are fully bypassed by the Levy stock-flow model.

Another important difference is the way econometric models are constructed. The conventional approach is to build up a macroeconomic model from its constituent components, such as consumption, investment, wages, inflation and so on. This 'bottom-up' approach can lead to overlooking relevant macroeconomic relationships and to not ensuring that all stocks and flows are accounted for (in effect that one person's asset disposal is another asset acquisition). The Levy approach is a more 'top-down' approach, which begins with a complete set of watertight accounting framework where all stocks and flows are explicitly accounted for and modeled. With the accounting framework in place, the behavior of the constituent components can then be addressed. The Levy approach is, thus, a microeconomic-macroeconomic one in which the behavior of economic variables is modeled and the macroeconomic relationships between economic variables ensured.

These ideas are employed in the construction of the stock-flow consistent Levy model. In order to make sure that 'this model has the merit of consistency, the accounting being watertight in the sense that everything comes from somewhere and goes somewhere, while all financial balances have precise counterparts in changes in stock variables' (Godley, 1999b, p. 23), Table 13.1 describes the accounting structure of the model (see, also, Godley and Lavoie, 2007a). It uses a double entry matrix so that every flow can be seen as a transaction involving at least two sectors. In this way, and as the quote above from Godley (1996, p. 7) makes clear, there are no 'black holes' in the sense that every flow comes from somewhere and goes somewhere. There are four sectors to consider: the private sector, comprising persons and companies, both industrial and commercial companies; the financial sector, which includes banks and other financial institutions; the government sector, including both state and federal governments; and the foreign sector that comprises non-residents, be they companies, persons or governments.

There are crucial and vital assumptions made, which are worth summarizing and commenting on. To begin with, the version of the model utilized for the purposes of this chapter, is a 'pure' demand model, with supply constraints being absent. Additional important assumptions can be summarized as follows. The private sector comprises of households and firms, but does not include financial entities, other than certain aspects of the banking sector. In this sense, it would be best labeled as 'non-financial private sector.' Lumping households and firms is permissible; Matthew and Minford (1980) defend this aggregation by suggesting that 'we do no violation to the theory in lumping firms with households, since we regard them both as obeying similar principles of asset disposition. Earlier work, along similar lines to ours ... was highly disaggregated and perhaps for this reason may have proved hard to use for policy analysis' (p. 645). Furthermore, prices and wages are assumed to be exogenously determined. In terms of the financial sector, the assets of the banks consist of credit extended to firms (so that their income is the interest they receive on credit extended); their liabilities are the stock of liquid assets (SLA_b). The rate of interest on loans is a

Table 13.1 Flow matrix

Sector Transactions	**Private sector**		**Financial sector**	**Government sector**	**Foreign sector**	**E**
	Income and expenditure	**Production expenditure**				
Private expenditure*	– PE	+ PE				0
Government expenditure on goods and services		+ G		– G		0
Exports		+ X			– X	0
Imports		– Q			+ Q	0
Accounting memo GDP = PE + G + X – Q						
Income from abroad	+ GDP_f				– GDP_f	0
Direct taxes	– DT			+ DT		0
Indirect taxes		– IT		+ IT		0
Unemployment benefits	+ UB			– UB		0
Interest payments	+ R.GD (–1)			– R.GD (– 1)		0
Social security contributions	– SSC			+ SSC		0
Other government transfers	+ OGTR			– OGTR		0
Transfers to non-US residents	– TRFP			– TRFG	+ TRF	0
Accounting memo PYD = GDP + GDP_f – DT – IT + UB + R.GD (–1) – SCC + OGTR – TRF						
Uses and sources of funds	+ NAFAP			– PSBR	– CA	0
Flow of personal credit	+ ΔPC		– ΔPC			0
Change in stock of Liquid assets	– ΔSLA		+ ΔSLA_b	+ ΔGD**	+ ΔSLA_f	0
E	0	0	0	0	0	0

Notes:
* This includes expenditures by financial institutions, which is assumed to be negligible.
** ΔGD includes changes in high power money (ΔH).

mark-up over the interest rate stipulated by the financial authorities, and banks are willing to supply whatever loans are demanded at that rate of interest. This means that the rate of interest on credit extended is treated as exogenous, in that it is a constant mark-up over the given interest rate of the financial authorities. Banks provide loans to firms passively on the security of inventories, and they do not have retained earnings. Consequently, disposable income is by definition personal disposal income (PYD). In terms of the government sector, it is assumed that government debt consists of perpetuities only, that is, bonds that pay a fixed amount of money per period; they can be of either short-term or long-term duration. It is also assumed that government deficit and credit to banks are financed by high powered money and government debt.

The first four entries in Table 13.1 comprise GDP (Gross Domestic Product), with the rest of the symbols having their usual meanings, where PE is total private expenditure (consumption plus investment), G is government expenditure, X is exports and Q is imports. The next eight entries portray the components of Personal Disposal Income (PYD) where again the symbols are familiar. Thus, GDP_f is income from abroad, DT is direct taxes, IT indirect taxes, UB is unemployment benefits, SSC is social security contributions, OGTR is other government transfers, R.GD(−1) is interest payments (R is the bond rate, GD is government debt and the minus unity in brackets denotes one period lag), and TRF is transfers to non-US residents which is the sum of TRFP (that part of TRF emanating from the private sector) and TRFG (that part of TRF emanating from the government sector).

The final three entries portray the uses and sources of funds. If any sector has a financial surplus, in that income exceeds expenditure, then it has to either acquire additional financial assets or pay off outstanding debts to the other sectors. Consequently, the Net Acquisition of Financial assets by the Private sector (NAFAP) is equal to its financial surplus, and, therefore, it can be defined as the difference between PYD and PE.[7] It is also equal to the sum of ΔGD and CA (current account of the balance of payments). In the event that NAFAP changes are small, the changes in government financial position would be reflected in changes in the financial position of the foreign sector of a similar magnitude, that is changes in CA.[8] In terms of the sources of funds, NAFAP is equal to the sum of positive ΔPC (the flow of personal credit) and the negative of ΔSLA (changes in the stock of liquid assets; these are non-interest bearing bank liabilities). Finally from the last entry, ΔSLA is the sum of two elements: ΔSLA_b (ΔSLA of the banking system) and ΔSLA_f

(ΔSLA of the foreign sector). All the entries sum to zero both horizontally and vertically.

It is important, under the conditions described in this section, to introduce a new concept instead of the traditional concept of equilibrium. The reason is simple enough, 'the tendency of the system as a whole is governed by stock-flow norms rather than ... equilibrium (or disequilibrium) conditions postulated by neoclassical theory' (Godley, 1999a, p. 396). So that when the system is shocked it goes through a number of changes required by the stock/flow interactions. When these dynamic changes are completed, the system comes to a 'steady-state' position, either in its growth or stationary sense (depending on the assumptions made about the exogenous variables). The concept of equilibrium employed for the purposes of studying this model is rather different from that of the more widely used concept of 'equilibrium'.

13.3 Model description

The model comprises 56 equations, seven of which are estimated equations (two of the estimated equations are non-linear), the rest being identities (37 of them) and calibrated behavioral equations (12 of them). An important distinguishing feature of the model is that it contains a very small number of behavioral relationships. The reason is simple enough and relies on human behavior and its varied characteristics, so that the objective is to 'establish principles which capitalize on adding-up constraints so as to confine behavioural processes to a relatively small number of variables, each of which can then be the object of empirical study. The smaller the number of behavioural variables which govern how the system *must* function in the view of the logical constraints, the more powerful will be our theory as a model of organizing and interpreting data' (Godley and Cripps, 1983, p. 18).

It follows from this theoretical position that the level of aggregation in the Levy model is an open issue. However, the approach to the model has a strong preference for aggregating 'the private sector as a whole'. An additional argument for this aggregation is that consumption is essentially determined by disposable income, and investment is also essentially determined by the disposable income of companies (that is, retained earnings), so that aggregation retains the influence of disposable income on expenditure. This is strengthened by the observation that 'given the well-known difficulty of modeling the corporate sector there is an advantage in aggregation provided the overall relationship is empirically robust' (Cripps and Godley, 1976, p. 336). This observation is based on the argument that the interaction between the personal sector and the company sector in determining their expenditure decisions is extremely complex. Any attempt to isolate them may not provide satisfactory predictions of consumption and investment. It is for these reasons that there is one relationship that describes the expenditure behavior of the whole personal sector, labeled below as 'private expenditure', that is the sum of consumption and investment. Another important dimension of the Levy model is the treatment of the 'financial side' of the economy. Agents' financial decisions, including bank and household portfolio decisions as well as firm investment decisions, along with the consequences of these decisions are treated exogenous.

We may begin summarizing the model with the standard income identity (the symbols are as above; where new symbols are introduced they are immediately defined):[9]

$$GDP = PE + G + X - Q \tag{1}$$

where G is treated as exogenous.

$$PE = PE(PYD, SLA, \Delta PC, SMP, HP) \tag{2}$$

where SMP is the stock market prices, and HP is housing prices, both treated as exogenous variables. An important assumption made is that since all asset transactions (durable goods, equities and land, including housing) are confined to the private sector, they do not affect the budget constraints of the private sector as a whole or of the private sector or, indeed, of the rest of the world.

We proceed to discuss the determinants of the variables that appear in equations (1) and (2), beginning with PYD.

$$\begin{aligned} PYD = {} & GDP + GDP_f - DT - IT + UB + R.GD(-1) \\ & - SSC + OGTR - TRF \end{aligned} \tag{3}$$

where OGTR and TRF (that is, the sum of transfers from the private sector and the government sector to non-US residents) are treated as exogenous. The rate of interest (R) is also treated exogenously determined, on the explicit assumption that the government acts to control the rate of interest on bonds.

$$SLA = SLA_b + SLA_f = SLA(-1) + NAFAP \tag{4}$$

where NAFAP is as in Table 13.1, and in equation (5):

$$\text{NAFAP} = \text{PYD} - \text{PE} = \Delta\text{GD} + \text{CA} = \text{PSBR} + \text{CA} \tag{5}$$

where PSBR is the public sector borrowing requirement, defined as:

$$\text{PSBR} = \text{G} - \text{DT} - \text{IT} + \text{UB} + \text{R.GD}(-1) - \text{SSC} + \text{OGTR} + \text{TRFG} \tag{6}$$

and CA as in (7):

$$\text{CA} = (\text{X} - \text{Q}) + \text{GDP}_f + \text{TRF} \tag{7}$$

We may also write:

$$\text{GDP}_f = \text{R}_f.\text{SLA}_f \tag{8}$$

where R_f is foreign interest rate (treated as exogenous), and SLA_f is the stock of liquid assets of the foreign sector, so that:

$$\text{SLA}_f = \text{SLA}_f\,(-1) + \text{CA} \tag{9}$$

A few simple relationships follow:

$$\text{UB} = \text{UB(U)} \tag{10}$$

where U is the level of unemployment, determined in equation (11) by GDP:

$$\text{U} = \text{U(GDP)} \tag{11}$$

Next, the government budget constraint is written in its familiar form:

$$\Delta\text{GD} = \text{G} - \text{T} + \text{R.GD}(-1) - \Delta\text{H} + \text{OGTR} \tag{12}$$

where T = DT + IT, i.e. total taxes, ΔH stands for changes in higher power money (treated as exogenous), and GD is measured at the end of each quarter.

$$\text{T} = \text{T(GDP)} \tag{13}$$

$$\text{SSC} = \text{SSC(GDP)} \tag{14}$$

Finally, the two variables that comprise the trade balance are endogenized as shown immediately below:

$$X = X(GDP_w, ER, RPX) \tag{15}$$

where GDP_w is world GDP, ER is (real) exchange rate, and RPX is the relative price of exports, with all three variables assumed to be exogenous.

$$Q = Q(GDP, ER, RPQ) \tag{16}$$

where RPQ is the relative price of imports, assumed to be exogenous.

A final comment, which is of particular relevance to the following section and to the policy implications of the model, is the interaction between NAFAP and PE. Recall that PE may be re-written as PE = dPYD + Z, where Z includes all the variables other than PYD in (2). It follows from (5) that NAFAP = (1−d)PYD – Z, where d is the long-run marginal propensity to spend out of disposable income, thought to be equal to unity. Consequently, to the extent that the impact of Z on NAFAP is small and predictable, changes in NAFAP would be small and predictable. It follows from (5) that changes in GD reflect changes in CA. Fiscal policy measures that are accompanied by changes in GD would then have serious implications in that CA would be substantially affected. Furthermore, re-writing PYD = GDP – T + OTH, where OTH is other variables in PYD, and substituting from (1) for GDP, we have: PYD = PE + G + X – Q – T, and substituting in (5) we derive: NAFAP = (G – T) + (X – Q), or NAFAP + (T − G) = (X – Q). This, of course, can be written in 'changes' to give us: Δ(NAFAP) + Δ(T – G) = Δ(X – Q). If Δ(NAFAP) is equal to zero, the result follows that changes in the budget surplus are accompanied by equal ex post changes in the balance-of-payments surplus (which echoes the 'twin deficit' hypothesis).

This, however, is not a conclusion of the Levy model for three reasons. The first is that while changes in NAFAP may have been small at particular times and places, it is not universally so as the experience of the USA and the UK during the 1990s indicates, and specifically in the context of the US economy at the present time changes in NAFAP cannot be assumed to be small. The second is that the budget surplus is an endogenous component in view of the endogeneity of the T element, see equation (12) above; as such, it cannot be under the direct control of the authorities. The third is that even if the budget surplus were exogenous, there would still be the problem of a two-way causation, in which case it cannot be inferred that Δ(T – G) causes Δ(X – Q). We may instead think of conducting policy experiments using the variables that are exogenous. The government expenditure element is such a variable. We turn our attention to this exercise in the session that follows.

13.4 Economic policy dynamic multipliers

We examine in this section two types of economic policy dynamic multipliers – fiscal policy multipliers and monetary policy multipliers; in one case we report multipliers which might be viewed as both fiscal and monetary dynamic multipliers when a change in government expenditure is financed through printing high-powered money. Table 13.2 provides a summary of the exercises undertaken for the purposes of this chapter, and the figures plot the multipliers through time as indicated therein. The model is shocked by increasing government expenditure by $10 billion and by changing the rate of interest by 1 per cent. We report the difference between the simulated and baseline GDP values divided by the increase in the value of the policy instrument (that is change in government expenditure). Figures labeled as 13.1a and 13.1b report similar exercises for CA and PSBR respectively.

Table 13.2 cites the results obtained in terms of the impact multipliers, that is, the first-period impact, and the long-run multipliers, that is the value of the multipliers when the system is at rest, as this term was defined earlier in the text. Three types of exercise have been undertaken: increase in government expenditure financed through borrowing; increase in government expenditure financed through taxation; a mixed fiscal and monetary policy whereby the increase in government

Table 13.2 Dynamic multipliers

Type of change **Change in G and R**	**GDP**	
	Impact multiplier	**Long-run multiplier**
$10 billion increase in G financed by borrowing (ΔGD)	1.46	2.28
$10 billion increase in G financed by government receipts (ΔT)	0.57	0.58
$10 billion increase in G finaced by printing new high power money (ΔHP)	1.46	0.44

expenditure is financed through printing high-powered money. A brief summary of the results provided is that fiscal policy can be effective in influencing economic activity. By contrast, monetary policy in the form of a change in high-powered money is not very effective. When high powered money is allowed to increase the impact on the level of economic activity in the long run is rather small.

We begin discussion of these results with government expenditure multipliers. In a general way, changes in government expenditure potentially have a long-run effect on real output, which in turn has a direct effect on the level of unemployment. In this model, there is no equation for inflation, and hence there is no route through which the level of (or changes in) aggregate demand can impact on the rate of inflation. There are, though, within the model potential crowding-out effects of a change in government expenditure, and these depend heavily on the manner in which government expenditure change is financed. We discuss this possibility in what follows, but we can summarize the potential crowding-out effects as follows: whenever government expenditure increase implies increase in taxes this provides an avenue through which crowding out can occur. Another significant route whereby crowding out can occur is the so-called external crowding out through imports. An interesting case is also the possibility of crowding in, particularly in the case of monetary policy. An increase in the rate of interest affects 'interest income' which has a positive impact on the level of economic activity.

The case of financing an increase in government expenditure through borrowing is portrayed in Figure 13.1. It is clear that the impact multiplier is quite substantial in the first period, but subsequent crowding-out effects, emanating possibly from private sector expenditure, are not strong enough to restrict the positive impact. The increase in government expenditure and associated increase in GDP and PE increase GD and NAFAP. All these outcomes are very expansionary. Ultimately, some increase in imports restricts the increase in GDP and produces the long-run multiplier at the steady state of 2.28. It is worth noting that this value of long-run dynamic multiplier is quite high compared to the findings of many other studies on fiscal multipliers.

Given the importance of the CA and PSBR in the model, and as indicated above, we show the results of similar exercises for CA and PSBR in Figures 13.1a and 13.1b. The plots in these figures are not surprising and confirm the model's properties: that a deficit in both CA and PSBR should be expected. The behavior of CA is dominated by that of imports. With exports treated as exogenously determined, a deficit is

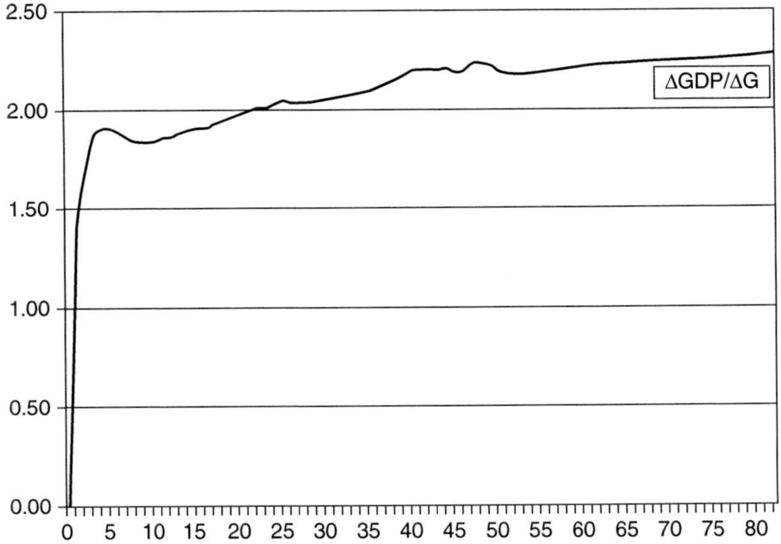

Figure 13.1 Impact of increase in government expenditure on GDP financed by borrowing

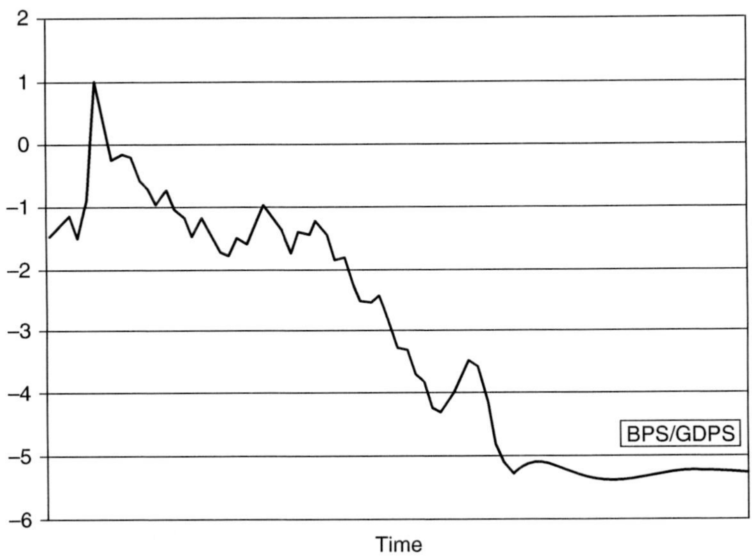

Figure 13.1a Ratio of simulated balance of payments and GDP (bond-financed case)

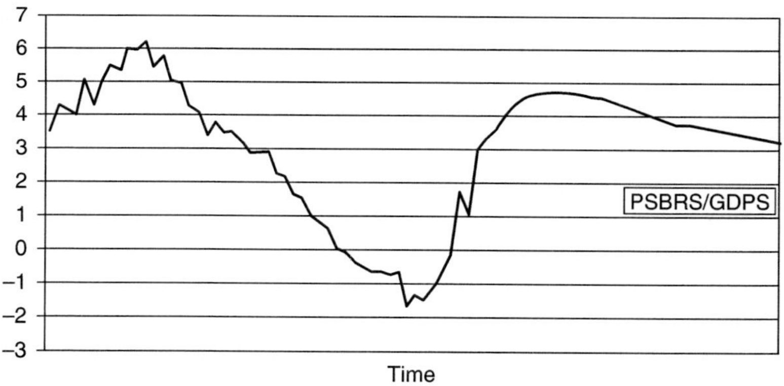

Figure 13.1b Ratio of simulated PSBR and GDP (bond-financed case)

inevitable. The behavior of the PSBR is, of course, dominated by the increase in government expenditure, but also by government receipts, social security contributions, and unemployment benefits, themselves being endogenously determined by the level of economic activity; it is also affected by interest rate receipts, which change substantially given the nature of the exercise. The government expenditure variable, along with the rest of the variables that enter the PSBR equation, are treated as exogenously determined. The point made above about ex-post changes in the current account and changes in the PSBR is confirmed by these results.

Figure 13.2 depicts the case of an increase in government expenditure that is financed by increases in government receipts. The dynamic multipliers in this case, both impact and long-run multipliers, are significantly lower than in the case of those just examined. This is not surprising given that the effects of the increase in government expenditure are to a large extent outweighed by the simultaneous increase in taxes with opposite effects. The initial positive impact on the level of economic activity is not strong enough to outweigh the initial positive effects. The next two exercises introduce monetary policy elements.

Figure 13.3 is a mixture of fiscal and monetary policy elements, while Figure 13.4 is pure monetary policy. If we deal with Figure 13.3 first, the exercise depicted in this figure shows what happens in the Levy stock-flow model when government expenditure increase is financed through increases in high-powered money. The impact multiplier is unsurprisingly the same as in the case of Figure 13.1. The long-run multiplier is, however, significantly lower at 0.44. The reason is that the combined

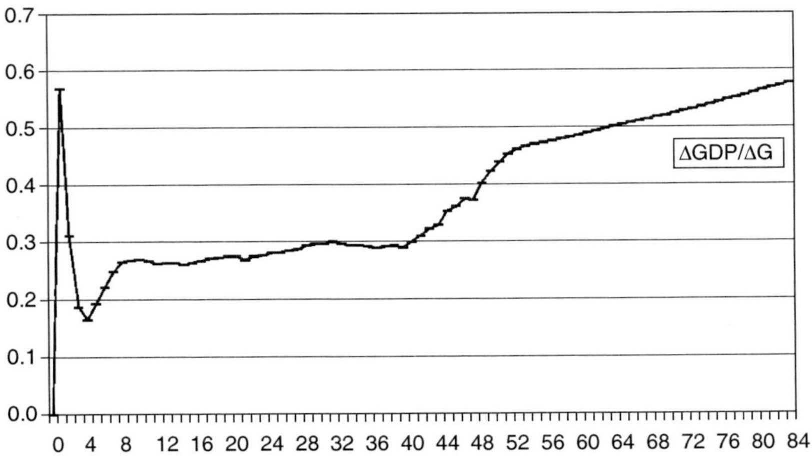

Figure 13.2 Impact of increase in government expenditure on GDP financed by government receipts

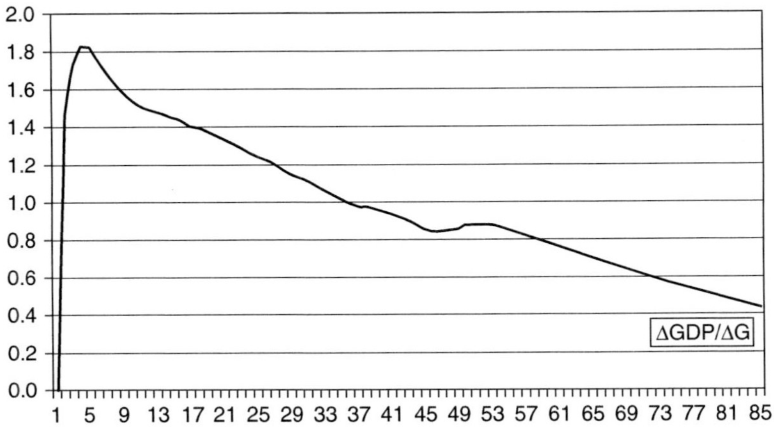

Figure 13.3 Impact of increase in government expenditure on GDP financed by printing new high power money

impact of the increase in government expenditure and in high-powered money and the subsequent increase in taxes reduces GD, see equation (11), which, through its negative impact on PYD, see equation (3), acts as a sort of crowding-out effect. This combined effect ultimately gives a

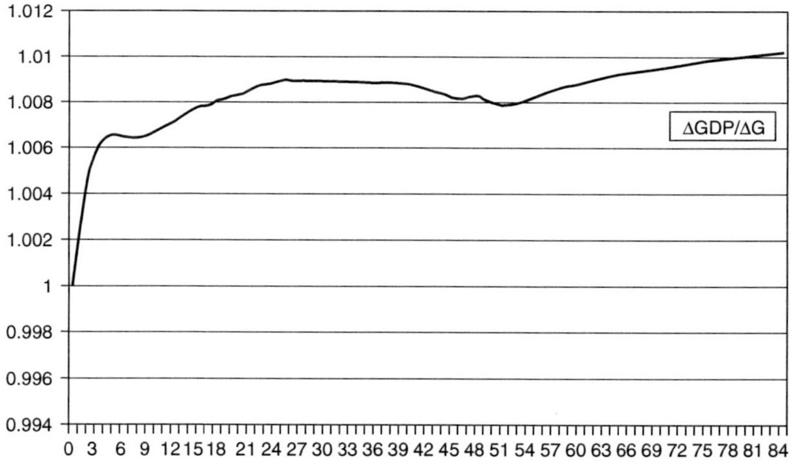

Figure 13.4 Impact of increase in the rate of interest on GDP

low long-run multiplier, which surprisingly is the lowest of all long-run multipliers depicted in Table 13.2.

The results we have just reported are different from what one might expect from the analysis of the 'new consensus macroeconomics', where fiscal policy is substantially downgraded (see, for example, Bernanke et al., 1999; see, also, Arestis, 2009a). But as one might recognize the 'new consensus' type of models may be thought of as unrealistic, simply because of all effects emanating from stock variables and 'interest income' are completely absent. However, a number of people have argued that these effects may be important. For example, Fair (2000) argues that that these effects are actually very important in view of the fact that 'households hold a large amount of short term securities of firms and the government, and when short-term interest rates change, the interest revenue of households change' (pp. 28–9). The results of this chapter are also substantially different from other work where estimates of fiscal multipliers are reported (see Hemmings et al., 2002, for a good representative sample). The fundamental difference is that fiscal multipliers from the Levy model are larger than those reported therein.

This last result, along with the other results reported above, confirm our conclusions elsewhere (Arestis and Sawyer, 2003a, 2003b, 2004, 2006, 2010, are good examples), that fiscal policy has a predictable and effective impact on the level of economic activity as this is proxied by the level of GDP. The inevitable overall conclusion is clear enough: fiscal policy ought to be reinstated.

13.5 Summary and conclusions

The focus of this chapter is on the effectiveness of fiscal policy within the stock-flow Levy model of the US economy. We have attempted in the first instance to explain the importance of the stock-flow consistency aspects of the model and concluded that this is an important, if not the most important, aspect of the model. Other facets of the model have also been highlighted. This enabled us to summarize the essentials of the model before we conducted a number of economic policy exercises.

Three policy exercises have been conducted: two fiscal policy exercises, and one described as a mixture of fiscal and monetary policies. The overall conclusion from these exercises is that fiscal policy is a powerful instrument of economic policy. This is a result that is weakened when fiscal policy is combined with some form of monetary policy (see Figure 13.3). These empirical results lead us to the overall conclusion that the recent economic policy practice of downgrading fiscal policy and upgrading monetary policy is completely the wrong way round. It is the case that fiscal policy remains a powerful instrument of regulating the level of aggregate demand. We have demonstrated this result at the more theoretical level in a series of papers (Arestis and Sawyer, 2003a, 2003b, 2004, 2006, 2010), and this chapter has reached the same conclusion, drawing on the empirics of the stock-flow Levy model. We may, therefore, conclude, in the same manner suggested by Godley and McCarthy (1998), that 'an expansionary fiscal policy is a necessary condition for growth in the long term, reasserting an old Keynesian principle that sustained expansion requires continuously growing exogenous injections to the flow of income' (p. 39).

Notes

1. With the implication, presumably, that fiscal policy does not matter, whereas the focus is on monetary policy and the use of interest rate policy to target inflation.
2. The Levy model has been developed by a group of researchers at the Levy Economics Institute of Bard College (see, for example, Godley, 1996, 1999a, 1999b; Godley and Shaikh, 2002; Godley and Lavoie, 2007a, 2007b). It is closely related to the 'New Cambridge' model developed in the 1970s and 1980s at Cambridge University (see, for example, Cripps and Godley, 1983;

Godley and Cripps, 1983). For an excellent summary and insightful analysis of these models, including a great deal of background material and an assessment of them, see Dos Santos (2003). We are extremely grateful to Claudio Dos Santos and Gennaro Zezza, both from the Levy Economics Institute, for helpful discussions and enormous help especially on the more technical aspects of the Levy model. The usual disclaimer does, of course, apply.

3. A comprehensive summary of these views, and a great deal more details and analysis of the stock/flow models and their implications, can be found in Dos Santos (2003).
4. Tobin (1982) puts it in equally strong terms, 'a model whose solution generates flows but completely ignores their consequences may be suspected of missing phenomena important even in a relatively short run, and therefore of giving incomplete or even misleading analyses' (p. 188).
5. A more mainstream perspective is taken as one that does not concern itself with stock-flow issues.
6. See, also, Dos Santos (2003) for an elaboration of the Foley (1975) proof that under 'perfect foresight' the distinction between flows and stocks does not really matter.
7. Transfers of assets/liabilities within the personal sector do not change NAFAP. If the private sector as a whole is to change NAFAP, say increase it, then it must increase its holdings of assets or reduce its liabilities, to either the government or to the overseas sector. It also follows that a net acquisition of financial assets or a financial surplus of one sector, must be met by a financial deficit in at least one other sector.
8. It is true, though, that the Levy model does not contain such an assumption. It was more prevalent in the older type of models, such as in Cripps and Godley (1983) and Godley and Cripps (1983). See below for a fuller discussion on the importance of the assumption discussed in the text.
9. The reader is reminded that this is only an objective summary of the Levy model. Full details of the latter can be obtained upon request from the Levy Economics Institute.

References

Arestis, P. (2009a) 'Fiscal Policy Within the "New Consensus Macroeconomics" Framework,' in J. Creel and M. Sawyer (eds) *Current Thinking on Fiscal Policy* (Basingstoke, UK: Palgrave Macmillan).

Arestis, P. (2009b) 'New Consensus Macroeconomics and Keynesian Critique,' in E. Hein, T. Niechoj and E. Stockhammer (eds) *Macroeconomic Policies on Shaky Foundations: Wither Mainstream Macroeconomics?* (Marburg, Germany: Metropolis-Verlag).

Arestis, P. and M. Sawyer (1998) 'Keynesian Policies for the New Millennium,' *Economic Journal* 108(1): 181–95.

Arestis, P. and M. Sawyer (2003a) 'On the Effectiveness of Monetary Policy and of Fiscal Policy,' Working Paper No. 369 (Annandale-on-Hudson, NY: Levy Economics Institute of Bard College).

Arestis, P. and M. Sawyer (2003b) 'Reinstating Fiscal Policy,' *Journal of Post Keynesian Economics* 26(1): 4–25.

Arestis, P. and M. Sawyer (2004) 'On the Effectiveness of Monetary Policy and of Fiscal Policy,' *Review of Social Economy* 62(4): 441–63.

Arestis, P. and M. Sawyer (2006) 'Fiscal Policy Matters,' *Public Finance* 54(3–4): 131–53.

Arestis, P. and M. Sawyer (2010) 'The Return of Fiscal Policy,' *Journal of Post Keynesian Economics* 32(3): 327–46.

Bernanke, B.S., M. Gertler and S. Gilchrist (1999) 'The Financial Accelerator in a Quantitative Business Cycle Framework,' in J. Taylor and M. Woodford (eds) *The Handbook of Macroeconomics*, Volume 1 (Amsterdam: North-Holland).

Buiter, W. (1980) 'Walras' Law and All That: Budget Constraints and Balance Sheet Constraints in Period Models and Continuous Time Models,' *International Economic Review* (February): 1–16.

Buiter, W. (1983) 'Measurement of the Public Sector Deficit and its Implications for Policy Evaluation and Design,' *IMF Staff Papers* (June).

Christ, C. (1967) 'A Short-Run Aggregate Demand Model of the Interdependence and Effects of Monetary and Fiscal Policies with Keynesian and Classical Interest Elasticities,' *American Economic Review*, Papers and Proceedings, 57: 434–43.

Christ, C. (1968) 'A Simple Macroeconomic Model with a Government Budget Restraint,' *Journal of Political Economy* 76(1): 53–67.

Cripps, F. and Godley, W. (1976) 'A Formal Analysis of the Cambridge Economics Policy Group Model,' *Economica*, 43(172), 335–48.

Dos Santos, C.H. (2003) *Three Essays in Stock-Flow Consistent Macroeconomic Modeling*, PhD Thesis, New School University, Graduate Faculty of Political and Social Science (Department of Economics).

Fair, R. (2000) 'Structural Macroeconomic Modeling and the Modern View of Macroeconomics,' mimeo.

Foley, D. (1975) 'On Two Specifications of Asset Equilibrium in Macroeconomic Models,' *Journal of Political Economy* 83(2): 303–24.

Godley, W. (1996) 'Money, Finance and National Income Determination: An Integrated Approach,' Working Paper No. 167 (Annandale-on-Hudson, NY: Levy Economics Institute of Bard College).

Godley, W. (1999a) 'Money and Credit in a Keynesian Model of Income Determination,' *Cambridge Journal of Economics* 23(4): 393–411.

Godley, W. (1999b) 'Seven Unsustainable Processes: Medium-Term Prospects and Policies for the United States and the World,' Special Report, Levy Economics Institute of Bard College.

Godley, W. and F. Cripps (1983) *Macroeconomics* (Oxford, UK: Oxford University Press).

Godley, W. and M. Lavoie (2007a) 'Fiscal Policy in a Stock-flow Consistent (SFC) Model,' *Journal of Post Keynesian Economics* 30(1): 79–100.

Godley, W. and M. Lavoie (2007b) *Monetary Economics: An Integrated Approach to Credit, Money, Income, Production and Wealth* (Basingstoke, UK: Palgrave Macmillan).

Godley, W. and G. McCarthy (1998) 'Fiscal Policy will Matter,' *Challenge* 41(1): 38–54.

Godley, W. and A. Shaikh (2002) 'An Important Inconsistency at the Heart of the Standard Macroeconomic Model,' *Journal of Post Keynesian Economics* 24(3), 423–42.

Hemmings, R., M. Kell and S. Mahfouz (2002) 'The Effectiveness of Fiscal Policy in Stimulating Economic Activity: A Review of the Literature,' IMF Working Paper 02/208 (Washington DC: International Monetary Fund).
Keynes, J.M. (1936) *The General Theory of Employment, Interest, and Money* (London, UK: Macmillan Publishing Company).
Lavoie, M. and W. Godley (2001–02) 'Kaleckian Growth Models and in a Stock and Flow Monetary Framework,' *Journal of Post Keynesian Economics* 24(2): 277–311.
Matthew, K. and P. Minford (1980) 'Private Sector Expenditure and Financial Asset Accumulation in the UK,' *Journal of Money, Credit and Banking* 12(4): 644–53.
Solow, R. (1983) 'Comments on Godley,' in G. Worswick and J. Trevithick (eds) *Keynes and the Modern World* (Cambridge, UK: Cambridge University Press).
Tobin, J. (1980) *Asset Accumulation and Economic Activity* (Chicago, USA: University of Chicago Press).
Tobin, J. (1982) 'Money and Finance in the Macroeconomic Process', *Journal of Money, Credit and Banking* 14(2): 171–204.
Turnovsky, S. (1977) *Macroeconomic Analysis and Stabilization Policy* (Cambridge, UK: Cambridge University Press).

14
Of Unsustainable Processes and the US Dollar

Jörg Bibow

14.1 Introduction

I first met Wynne Godley in early 1993, as a first-year PhD student at Cambridge University. In the Lent term, as part of the M Phil program's macroeconomics paper, Wynne offered a series of eight lectures entitled 'Critique of orthodox macroeconomic theory'. As Wynne was to retire from Cambridge University at the end of the academic year, these were his final lectures at the university where he had been since 1970. In his lectures, Wynne introduced his students to stock-flow consistent (SFC) macro modeling.

Despite his Keynesian fame and quite distinctive aura, I found Wynne very approachable and came to know him as a warm and generous person. Our first long one-to-one meeting followed his reading of a draft of my 'finance motive' paper (Bibow, 1995, 2009). Returning from London after a meeting with the 'wise men' panel, he invited me to see him in his rooms at King's College. This became the first long and intense discussion on macroeconomics I had the benefit of having with Wynne, and I suppose it was also the start of our friendship. I seem to recall that we espoused the inconsistencies and follies of the standard IS-LM approach, to easily agree on the superiority of James Tobin's pioneering work on stock-flow modeling (as developed in Tobin's 'Nobel' lecture and his book *Asset Accumulation and Economic Activity: Reflections on Contemporary Macroeconomic Theory*). I had been familiar with Tobin's work before coming to Cambridge and argued that the Keynes of the General Theory was no doubt thinking in terms of a SFC model. Wynne said more than once that he was 'really impressed' with my finance motive draft, which he thought was unearthing a very important point about Keynes' monetary thought and the role of banks in it, but he urged me, also more than once, that I had to start formulating my ideas by using mathematical models (following SFC techniques).

I guess I must have disappointed him in not following his urgings in this direction. But there was never any doubt that our macroeconomic souls had met that day at King's. I think that Wynne later became aware that even while I was rarely writing down equations or running computer simulations myself at the time, I had a stock-flow consistent model operating in the back of my mind. I remember that on the first occasion that he invited his group of M Phil students to his rooms at King's on an evening to go through some of his model simulations I may have somewhat 'shocked' him in this respect. He had briefly introduced the modeling approach (a model of some 30–40 equations) he was using in those simulations earlier that day in class. In that evening session he was then presenting some results of his simulations showing how a model economy could be seen to go off track when the interaction of stocks and flows was captured consistently. The point was to illustrate examples of explosive behavior that would not appear to arise in standard stock-flow-inconsistent modeling exercises. When he had finished his presentation he invited his students to venture what was going on, which is when I came to 'shock' him by immediately offering my explanation of the seen explosive outcomes, emphasizing an insufficient liquidity provision as the underlying force. Wynne approached me with a look of disbelief on his face. He explained that it had taken him several months to get this issue straight in his mind by use of extensive model simulations, and that it was simply impossible that I could give him the right answer just like that. I guess I must have earned his respect that evening. As I was working on my finance motive paper and was doing a lot of thinking about endogenous money and bank behavior at the time, this surely must have helped me to intuitively grasp what was going on in his model.

I submitted my PhD thesis in September 1995. Following my one-year temporary lectureship at Cambridge, I returned to Hamburg, Germany, in 1996. As earlier at Cambridge, Wynne also later helped me in landing a one-year research scholarship at the Levy Institute in 2000–01. A welcome break from the Economics Department at Hamburg, I spent a wonderful and productive year at the Levy, including lots of interaction with Wynne. My family, including my wife Claudia and our two small kids, would meet Wynne and Kitty quite frequently, either at their house in Rhinebeck or at ours (rather, Randy Wray's) in Red Hook. Even physically, Wynne was still quite fit at the time, in his mid-seventies still enjoying a good game of squash.

Wynne's research at the Levy at the time of my stint there focused on the Institute's 'Strategic Analysis' series that had started with his 'Seven unsustainable processes' paper of January 1999 (Godley 1999a). I was familiar with his SFC modeling approach since his lectures at Cambridge, the substance of which he had meanwhile refined in a number of publications leading up to his 1999 *CJE* paper (Godley 1999b). Arguably, it was at the Levy Institute where Wynne's SFC macro modeling approach to applied research came to full fruition with the Strategic Analysis series.[1]

Section 14.2 reviews Wynne's evolving assessments of 'unsustainable processes' underway in the US and global economies since that time, in an attempt to distill his key insights as to sustainability of US internal trends in this period. Section 14.3 then turns to Wynne's analyses, focusing on the sustainability of external imbalances. Section 14.4 highlights the international role of the US dollar and introduces the concept of 'dollar leveraging'. I will argue that Wynne's arguments and concerns regarding the risk of explosive external trends may need to be qualified when due account is taken of the dollar's international role and dollar leveraging. Section 14.5 further explores the issue why US trade deficits may be needed as a global growth engine under conditions of unfettered global finance and ventures some thoughts on the future of the dollar. Section 14.6 concludes.

14.2 Godley on the sustainability of US internal trends

Wynne Godley's whole point about SFC macro modeling is that without proper accounting for the fact that – over historical time – 'flows change stocks' while stocks, that is, balance sheets, in turn, condition future financing and spending flows, one would be at risk of overlooking unsustainable processes that may be underway in seemingly healthy economies. For any individual economic unit the gap between income and expenditure has its systematic reflection in a changing balance sheet position, which will then condition future financing options and spending decisions. For the economy as a whole too the financial structures resulting from actions undertaken by interdependent units need to be properly accounted for to get a true sense of the economic situation and likely future developments.

Finance is largely missing from standard macroeconomic models since, for the economy as a whole, financial assets and liabilities appear to be a 'wash'. By contrast, Hyman Minsky's analytical framework highlights that financial (cash-flow) structures embodied in balance sheet positions may be far from benignly canceling out in the aggregate, but lead to fragility and crisis instead. While coming from a direct line of (New) Cambridge Keynesian pedigree of strong Kaldorian flavor, Wynne Godley followed Hyman Minsky as the Levy Institute's Distinguished Scholar and much enlightened the policy relevance of his predecessor's financial instability hypothesis. Starting from sets of transactions (flow) and balance sheet (stock) matrices Wynne Godley's contribution was to develop mathematical representations of these accounting relationships that could be rendered operational for simulating major economic trends while explicitly and coherently tracing their financial underpinnings.

For policy purposes such as the Levy Institute's Strategic Analysis Wynne favored disaggregation by sector in line with the main macroeconomic aggregates. Starting from the national income identity $Y = PX + G + X - M$ and deducting taxes and transfers from both sides and rearranging yields sectoral 'financial balances' that must add up to zero: $0 = [Y-T-PX] - [G-T] - [X-M]$.

The three major 'financial balances' for the private, public and foreign sectors, based on the national income identity, provide the core of Godley's macroeconomic analysis of the drivers of growth. The CFC modeling structures pioneered by Godley also capture financial intermediation, portfolio choice, and valuation effects, greatly enriching the Keynesian/Minskyan picture of financial complexity. By contrast, standard mainstream approaches used for policy purposes either ignore stock-flow connections or simply abstract from the whole finance issue in the first place by assuming some representative-agent economy that dynamically optimizes over some lifetime income/budget constraint. Both approaches are rather useless for purposes of serious economic analysis. Projections made by the Congressional Budget Office (CBO) are of the former type and provide the benchmark and target for Godley's analysis of 'seven unsustainable processes' diagnosed for the US economy at the end of the last millennium.

Recognizing 'that the US economy may well enjoy another good year or two' Godley (1999b, p. 3) highlights that the three financial balances followed highly unusual trends since the early 1990s. He takes fundamental issue with optimistic 'Goldilocks' views that were highly popular at the time, observing that 'during the last seven years a persistently restrictive fiscal policy has coincided with sluggish net export demand, so rapid growth could come about only as a result of a spectacular rise in private expenditure relative to income. This rise has driven the private surplus into deficit on an unprecedented scale. ... [In contrast to

CBO projections that implicitly assume a continuation of these trends Godley argues that] these negative forces [that is, restrictive fiscal policy and sluggish net export demand] cannot forever be more than offset by increasingly extravagant private spending, creating an ever-rising excess of expenditure over income' (p. 3).

Therefore, and much in contrast to Goldilocks views implicitly extrapolating ongoing sectoral trends, it seemed clear to Godley that for growth to be sustained in the medium term either fiscal policy and/or net export demand would need to turn around sufficiently by the time the foreseeable break in private spending was to occur. This section reviews Godley's take on the domestic situation and the issue of fiscal policy adjustment, while the subsequent section will turn to the external part of the argument.

Stressing that the private sector financial balance had reached a record deficit of over 5 per cent of GDP by early 1999, Godley (1999b) further disaggregates the private sector into personal and corporate subsectors. He concludes that the behavior of corporations during the 1990s was rather normal over the course of the cycle while the behavior of the personal sector was truly exceptional: 'It is the excess of personal consumption and housing investment over personal disposable income that is now much larger than ever before' (p. 8). Rising asset prices and net worth were seen as the source of the spending boom by many observers. Godley debunks popular illusions about 'wealth effects', pointing out that 'a rise in the value of a person's house may result in more expenditure by that person, but the house itself cannot be spent'. Capital gains as such cannot sponsor spending. Spending presupposes liquidity. Apart from running down existing money balances liquidity may be secured either by net realizations of assets (by the sector as a whole) or by net borrowing from other sectors. He acknowledges that share buy-backs and net purchases of US stocks by foreigners were part of the story but stresses rising borrowing from the financial sector as the main source of liquidity. As to the strategic prospects over the next five to 15 years he concludes that 'the growth in net lending to the private sector and the growth *in the growth rate* of the real money supply [as the bank credit counterpart] cannot continue for an extended period. Moreover, if, *per impossibile*, the growth in net lending and the growth in the money supply growth were to continue for another eight years, the implied indebtedness of the private sector would then be so extremely large that a sensational day of reckoning could then be at hand' (p. 11). Eight years later, Godley's Cassandra-like prophecy of sensational doom was proven sensationally right. But an important break occurred earlier in

2001, prompting both a decisive shift in macroeconomic policy stance as well as further insightful commentaries by Wynne Godley.

It seemed clear to Godley from the outset that monetary policy could bring no lasting relief to the underlying imbalances resulting from unsustainable sectoral trends. In his view, 'further relaxation of monetary policy could not sustain the expansion, except temporarily and perversely by giving a new lease on life to the stock market boom' (Godley 1999b, p. 4). Instead, a fundamental shift in fiscal stance was required, the magnitude of which would also be conditional on trade performance. In 'As the implosion begins ...?' of July 2001 Godley (2001a) offers some ballpark numbers, as usual, taking full employment CBO budget forecasts for 2006 as his benchmark. His projection assumes a return of the private financial balance to zero and an unchanged value of the dollar. He concludes:

> With a zero private balance and a 6 per cent balance of payments deficit, there would, by the rules of accounting logic, have to be a general government deficit equal to 6 per cent of GDP. As the CBO is predicting a budget *surplus* of almost 2 per cent of GDP based on the same output and inflation assumptions, the startling implication is that to make our story come true, there would have to be a further fiscal relaxation equal to 8 per cent of GDP in 2006 – roughly $700 billion at today's values. The famous twin deficits last seen in the 1980s would have returned with a vengeance! The magnitudes we adumbrate are enormous, but not really surprising. We are postulating a radical rebalancing in the structure of demand, the scale of which is straightforwardly implied by the extent to which the financial balances are out of kilter at the present time. After all, the private balance is at least 8 percentage points (of GDP) below what used to be normal. (p. 11)

These arguments and estimates were corroborated in October 2001, by which time the US economy had officially entered recession. Godley (2001b) proclaims that 'the United States should now be prepared for one of the deepest and most intractable recessions of the post-World War II period, with no natural process of recovery in prospect unless a large and complex reorientation of policy occurs both here and in the rest of the world' (p. 1). He regrets that the only policy response by that time consisted in aggressive interest rate cuts: 'Mortgage rates have fallen to a relatively low level, which may be why mortgage lending was so high in the second quarter. While this is perhaps the clearest example of interest rate cuts stimulating demand, it is doubtful whether the stimulus will be more than temporary, since in order to be durable the net flow of credit would have to continue expanding. It is doubtful, too, whether this is a stimulus of the right kind, since by adding to households' indebtedness it adds also to their vulnerability' (p. 3). He repeats that a sustainable recovery requires both a shift in fiscal stance and improved trade performance. And in April 2002 Godley and Izurieta (2002, p. 4) estimate a relaxation in fiscal stance of $260 and $300 billion for 2002 and 2003, respectively (2.5–3 per cent of GDP). While welcoming this policy change, they point out that contemporary CBO projections for 2003 and later years imply a renewed deterioration in the private sector financial balance and rising private indebtedness.

In 'The US Economy: A Changing Strategic Predicament', the Strategic Analysis issue of March 2003, Godley focuses squarely on what he identifies as 'the new strategic problem' that will be the subject of the next section, namely: the soaring US current account deficit. Regarding domestic developments, Godley criticizes the Fed's comforting assessment of households' financial position emphasizing that low interest rates have kept the burden of debt service at tolerable levels. Spotting the rising role of 'mortgage equity withdrawals' early on in the game, Godley explains: 'We have no quarrel with the Fed's assessment of the present position, but personal expenditure cannot be financed forever by a growing flow of net lending – that is, by a continuing rise *in the rise* in debt. The drastic fall in interest rates and the extreme ease with which equity in houses can now be 'cashed out' have given a new lease on life to personal expenditure. But a rise of net lending cannot, by its very nature, be an abiding motor for growth of the economy; it can continue for a long time, but it cannot continue forever. Equity can be cashed out only as so long as it exists; the process is a once-and-for-all affair' (Godley 2003, p. 6). Accordingly, in 'Why net exports must now be the motor for US growth', the Strategic Analysis issue of August 2004, Godley (2004, p. 5) judges that 'it seems unlikely that personal borrowing at a rate that is now supplementing disposable income to the tune of 13 per cent will continue much longer, particularly if interest rates continue to rise. Consequently, we expect personal net saving, currently 6 percentage points below its historic average, to rise significantly through the projection period [that is, by the end of 2008].'

As the Fed continued tightening until May 2006, it turned out that Godley underestimated the stamina of the personal sector debt binge, though not by much. The Strategic Analysis issue of September 2005 elaborates on the role of house prices and the value of real estate owned by the personal sector relative to disposable income as the key driving force behind households' borrowing and spending behavior at the time. Godley et al. (2005) reject the Fed's debt burden figures as implying still tolerable levels, arguing that averages would hide that heavily indebted families have become highly vulnerable to negative economic shocks, including a fall in house prices. House prices are diagnosed to be at a late stage of a classic bubble: 'Lending and house prices have both been rising rapidly in a self-reinforcing process' (p. 8). All that would be needed for the bubble to burst is for the rate of growth in debt to slow down toward that of income, with net lending to the private sector judged to be 'close to its peak' (p. 11). It is worthwhile to quote at length from this housing market assessment made in September 2005:

> A further reason for believing that the rise in net lending to the US personal sector, and even its present level, cannot be sustained for much longer is that the whole process has been fed by institutional changes, which are now running their course. Most loans are now negotiated by independent mortgage brokers, who are very lightly regulated. The mortgages they supply are packaged and sold to investment banks and others, including foreign investors, in the form of mortgage-backed securities. By selling off these mortgages, the lenders divest themselves of all risk but they then need to find a further outlet for their activities if they are to remain profitable. There is evidence that in the scramble to lend more money there has been a progressive decline in underwriting standards, manifested in the absurdly easy terms for borrowing money. An increasing proportion of mortgages are of the (misnamed) 'interest-only' variety, which in effect allows negative amortization to take place for the first five to seven years, after which the sum of interest payments and (positive) amortization rises sharply. At the same time, loan-to-value ratios have been rising to ridiculous levels. ... We are influenced in reaching this conclusion that the present position is unstable by the fact that the rise in lending has so far been fed by a *process* (the progressive easing of underwriting standards) that must have nearly run its course. And this conclusion is reinforced by evidence that a new kind of speculative behavior by buyers has invaded the housing market: people are buying second homes, and even buildings that do not yet exist, in the expectation of making the kind of quick profit once reserved for financial assets. In short, we are witnessing a classic bubble. (p. 8)

The housing bubble duly started to unravel in the following year. Referring to the 'collapse in the subprime mortgage market' and the 'multifaceted implosion of the housing market', in 'The US Economy: What's Next?', the Strategic Analysis of April 2007, Godley et al. (2007a, pp. 1–2) therefore dismiss the CBO budget projections of January 2007 year as 'wildly implausible if viewed as predictions.' The following Strategic Analysis issue of November 2007 titled 'The US Economy: Is There a Way out of the Woods?' is particularly interesting both for placing a high probability for a recession in 2008 and for how this pessimistic scenario was rationalized. Exceptionally, Godley et al. (2007b) explain that it would not be 'sensible on the present occasion [to concentrate entirely on medium-term, strategic developments] because of likely adverse developments in the very short term as a result of the credit crunch that would be ridiculous to ignore' (p. 5). The expectation that the bursting of the housing bubble was going to cause a credit crunch therefore provides the starting point of the Strategic Analysis: 'We are going to assume that the overall effects on the economy at large will largely depend on the extent to which net lending to the private sector is reduced through the unwillingness, or inability, of borrowers to borrow and lenders to lend' (p. 6). The next step is to estimate the impact of the credit crunch on private spending. And the final step is to estimate the impact on GDP growth, with assumptions about net exports and fiscal policy added that rely on predictions made by the CBO, *The Economist*, and the IMF. Regarding net exports Godley et al. (2007b) observe that there has been a large improvement which 'seems likely to continue' and which they attribute to the depreciation of the dollar and the unusually rapid growth of world trade. Assuming a favorable external environment seemed to justify the following not overly pessimistic credit crunch scenario: 'The entirely new feature of this projection relative to our earlier estimates is that there is an improvement in net exports such that the balance of payments approaches zero by 2010, to a considerable extent sustaining aggregate demand. Nevertheless, under the "credit crunch" assumption, the fall in private expenditure is so large that the economy will enter a recession next year' (p. 7). Their recommendation therefore is for 'a relaxation of fiscal policy large enough to add perhaps 2 per cent of GDP to the budget deficit. Moreover, should the slowdown in the economy over the next two to three years come to seem intolerable, we would support a relaxation having the same scale, and perhaps duration, as that which occurred around 2001' (p. 8).

The final Strategic Analysis that bears Wynne Godley's name on it, the issue of December 2008 published at the peak of the global crisis and titled 'Prospects for the United States and the World: A crisis that conventional remedies cannot resolve', is very gloomy indeed, concluding that 'even with the application of almost inconceivably large fiscal stimuli [$760 billion or 5.3 per cent of GDP in the 'extreme case'], output will not increase enough to prevent unemployment from continuing to rise through the next two years' (Godley et al. 2008, p. 4). The US authorities had run out of options as 'US fiscal policy alone will not eliminate the imbalances' but would 'bring back a large and growing external imbalance, which will keep world growth on an unsustainable path' (p. 4). Godley et al. (2008) attest a 'need for concerted action' and recall that since the start of the series in 1999 the Strategic Analysis reports have 'emphasized that, in the United States, sustained growth with full employment would eventually require both fiscal expansion and a rapid acceleration in net export demand' (p. 5). A required dollar depreciation of over 25 per cent is hinted at to stimulate US net exports sufficiently, but the report concludes rather glumly 'it is inconceivable that such a large rebalancing could occur without a drastic change in the institutions responsible for running the world economy – a change that would involve placing far less than total reliance on market forces' (p. 5).

In conclusion, one cannot other but be impressed with Wynne Godley's remarkable gift of vigilant observation regarding trends under way in the US economy since the 1990s. The accuracy of his strategic assessments, and even regarding cyclical forces around the times of the dot.com bust and the later housing bust, is truly outstanding. Surely no less remarkable are the hilariously flawed contemporary analyses and forecasts made by other (mainstream) economists, policymakers and institutions such as the CBO that are the targets of Godley's acute criticisms. The next section turns to the external part in Godley's analysis of unsustainable processes and imbalances.

14.3 Godley on the sustainability of US external trends

In fact, Godley's first Levy Institute publications on US economic trends focus squarely on the US's external position (see Godley 1995a, b). In particular, Godley expresses alarm about the 40-percentage-point deterioration in the US net external position since 1970, turning the world's largest creditor into the world's largest debtor; with the external balance sheet deterioration approximately corresponding to cumulative current account deficits during this period. He notes, however, that despite its net debtor position since 1989 the US's net factor income held up surprisingly well for some more years, turning negative only by 1994. Godley attributes this finding to exceptionally low earnings on direct investments in the US. He believes that net factor income is bound to deteriorate further and, by augmenting the rising trade deficit, would put the US's external position on an explosive, that is, unsustainable, path that would also risk undermining the US dollar's status as reserve currency. Producing a range of scenarios based on extrapolating contemporary trends Godley concludes that 'if the US trade deficit remains around its present level for a few more years it will generate an exploding growth in overseas indebtedness which will imperatively demand correction at some stage. ... While the internal (budget) and external deficits are obviously not "twins", they are related to one another in a way which makes it impossible to eliminate one without eliminating the other. ... It is a pre-condition for reducing the budget deficit without generating a depression that US exports rise substantially relative to import penetration' (Godley 1995, p. 2).

Discussing various competing views on the US's external imbalance Godley refutes the 'saving [either private and/or public] is too low' argument of the US current account deficit arguing that 'the only causal relationship linking the balances (given trade propensities) operates through changes in the level of output at home and abroad ... [so that a rise in US saving, either private and/or public] would bring about an improvement in the external deficit only because either would induce a fall in total demand and output, with lower imports as a consequence' (Godley 1995b, p. 21). Furthermore, Godley also rejects the benign interpretation of a self-correcting external imbalance based on the idea that foreign capital inflows into the US would create productive assets that become the source of future export earnings. In his view, the US trade deficit is caused by decisions of US residents to 'purchase imported rather than domestically produced goods and by the relative weakness of US exporting industries' (Godley 1995b, p. 23). Accordingly, he recommends expenditure-switching rather than expenditure-reducing policies to address the external imbalance, but notes that due to changes in the international order orderly dollar devaluation was no longer a readily available policy instrument. As a way out Godley suggests considering the use of non-selective (aggregate) import controls, as allowed under GATT Article 12 (and equally in their reformed price-based WTO version) in order to safeguard a country's external financial position and balance of payments.

It seems fair to say that these assessments of 1995 largely anticipate the essence of the external part of Godley's argument in 'seven unsustainable processes' and subsequently. Introducing his concept of 'quasi-interest rates' calculated as factor income flows over foreign assets and liabilities Godley (1999b; and similarly Godley 2001a,b, with Izurieta) points out that US assets earn a lower rate of return than liabilities as far as financial investments are concerned, with both assets and liabilities tracking the interest rate on US Treasury bills. Following data revisions the US's net factor income balance had remained positive until 1999, which Godley again attributes to a sizeable return differential in the US's favor on account of direct investments.

In 2003, Godley reveals additional insights concerning the key causes behind global imbalances pointing out the US's 'new strategic problem'. Concerning the prospects for (non-US) world growth Godley argues that 'with Japan mired in a seemingly endless stagnation and Europe the victim of perverse rules governing fiscal policy; countries in the rest of the world, not only Japan and China but also nations in Southeast Asia and Latin America, all have an urgent need to expand their exports, and many of them will be prepared to shade their prices in order to raise their shares of the large, open, and well-organized market for manufactures in the United States' (Godley 2003, p. 3). And in the same paper Godley also clarifies that his key concern regarding the US's growing external deficit is about the 'hemorrhage from aggregate demand' that the trade deficit entails rather than the external financing needs that come along with it: 'Deficits in the balance of payments are usually feared because they have to be financed by external borrowing that may not be forthcoming on acceptable terms and because foreign debts have to be serviced. The argument put forward here is an entirely different one: that the developing balance of payments deficit is going to act as a formidable drag on demand' (Godley 2003, p. 7). Such a drag on demand would need to be offset by either private spending or fiscal policy to achieve full employment in the US.

The title of the Strategic Analysis issue of August 2004 'Why Net Exports must Now be the Motor for US Growth' captures what Godley by that time came to see as truly a matter of utmost urgency. In fact, the scenarios for the period until 2009 shown in this report reveal some rather striking implications. In particular, after remarking that 'the "U turn" in fiscal policy that occurred in 2000–04 makes one a bit cynical, remembering all the hype surrounding the budget surpluses achieved in the Clinton years', Godley et al. (2004, p. 5) point out that should another occasion for a massive fiscal rescue of the economy arise, both public as external debt would be sent 'hurtling towards 100 per cent of GDP'. Allowing the private sector to continue to become overstretched would risk crisis down the road and the very need for such a fiscal rescue. Hence, in order to forestall this projected outcome, the US had to turn net exports from a persistent drag on GDP growth into 'the motor for US GDP growth'.

There was only one problem though: the rest of the world might not want to comply. According to Godley et al. (2004, pp. 6–7) 'during the last few years, the non-US world has become heavily dependent on the increasing US deficit as a motor for growth. In order to protect their "low" rates of exchange, foreign countries, notably Japan and China, have accumulated enormous foreign exchange reserves. In our view there is no inherent constraint on the continuation of this process. Nor is there any reason to suppose, in particular, that the accumulation of reserves by foreign central banks generates an uncontrollable increase in their stock of domestic money. On the contrary, if surplus countries are happy to exchange goods and services, not for imports but for what Martin Wolf of the *Financial Times* once called "expensive pieces of paper," a mutual process whereby surplus countries purchase reserve assets that deficit countries are happy to sell can be entirely self-contained.' (A footnote appears here referring to Godley and Lavoie 2004 on the sustainability of 'sterilization'.)

Godley et al. (2005) essentially repeat the aforementioned argument, highlighting that conventional models fail to capture the global situation at hand as in contrast to other countries the US – issuing the global reserve currency – is not running out of reserves. This arrangement is both convenient in granting the US the 'unusual position of being able to consume 6 per cent more resources than she produces without suffering any inflationary pressures' (p. 10), but also inconvenient because 'there is nothing the United States can do [to bring about the needed rebalancing] on her own without resorting to unconventional measures' [such as using Article 12 import controls; p. 10].

As already indicated in section 14.3 above, Godley then briefly turned slightly more optimistic in late 2007, pointing out the 'exciting, if still rather remote, possibility that, once the forthcoming financial turmoil has been worked through, the United States could be set on a path of balanced growth combined with full employment' (Godley et al. 2007, p. 8). Based on the assumption that the impending US recession could be contained by a fiscal stimulus 'large enough to add perhaps 2 per cent of GDP to the budget deficit' (p. 8) while net exports would continue to boost US GDP growth (driven by both dollar depreciation as well as unusually rapid growth of world trade), Godley's optimism proved short-lived.[2]

As the US recession turned into the Great Recession and full-blown global crisis, Godley's final pronouncement on the matter became one of gloom and despair, re-emphasizing that 'US fiscal policy alone will not eliminate the imbalances' and that dollar devaluation significantly larger than 25 per cent were needed (Godley et al. 2008, pp. 4–5).

Back in 1995 Godley had argued that global imbalances have 'arisen because there is no significant international regulation of the system as a whole. Inherent flaws have developed in the system of international production, trade, and payments as that system has expanded and become increasingly deregulated. All the difficulties that exist, or that are foreshadowed in this brief, would be best resolved by energetic international cooperation, of which there is at present little sign' (Godley (1995b). In December 2008 he concluded that it was 'inconceivable that such a large rebalancing could occur without a drastic change in the institutions responsible for running the world economy – a change that would involve placing far less than total reliance on market forces' (Godley et al. 2008, p. 5).

In conclusion, from the start global imbalances featured prominently in Godley's assessments of the US economy. While endorsing the U-turn in US fiscal policy in 2001–04 prompted by the dot.com bust that had ended the Goldilocks boom, starting in 2003, Godley emphasized with rising urgency that net exports could not remain a drag on US GDP growth forever and that a large dollar devaluation would be needed at some point to deliver the needed turnaround in net exports; and preferably before the private sector would once again become so overstretched as to trigger another round of fiscal relaxation that he feared would propel US public debt toward 100 per cent of GDP and beyond. Godley's analyses were not only coherent and convincing at the time but also proven right in due course to a depressingly large extent. In one regard, however, namely the foreseen deterioration in the US's net international investment position and net factor income balance – outcomes have so far defied Godley's fears. The next section addresses this paradox and challenge to Godley's powerful analysis.

14.4 The US dollar and the sustainability of 'global imbalances'

Figure 14.1 shows the evolution of the US current account balance since 1960. Over the period that is the focus of Godley's analysis of unsustainable processes the current account is seen deteriorating sharply from a balanced position in 1991 to a deficit of close to 6 per cent of GDP at its

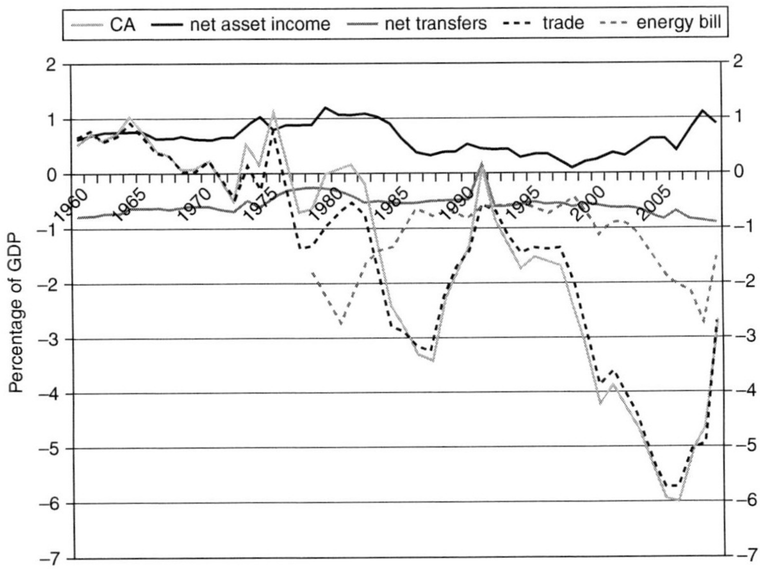

Figure 14.1 US current account shows positive net investment income
Source: Bureau of Economic Analysis.

peak in 2006. The somewhat puzzling fact is that this deterioration in the current account balance is exclusively driven by the trade balance while net factor income (dominated by net asset income) has actually remained *positive* despite the US's *negative* net foreign asset position that had emerged in the late 1980s; even rising again from an interim low point in the late 1990s. It is clear from his observations over the years that Godley was much puzzled by this finding (his puzzlement probably not helped by the fact that contemporary estimates at times suggested that the balance was finally tipping against the US, only to be revised a little later showing the opposite). As mentioned above in section 14.4, Godley identified a significant income yield advantage in the direct investment category as the factor that explained the positive net factor balance of the US. And yet he continued to believe that the net factor income balance would tip against the US in the medium term and potentially become an explosive force behind the US current account deficit and international debtor position.

It seems to me that, while considering the composition of *gross* external assets and liabilities and acknowledging the dollar's reserve currency role in his assessments to some degree, Godley failed to fully comprehend the power of what I dubbed 'dollar leveraging' (Bibow 2010a) in explaining the above paradox concerning US's net factor income balance. Also,

Godley started from a set of assumptions that may not be appropriate for the issuer of the world's reserve currency, assuming that the interest rate on the debt exceeds GDP growth by a sizeable margin, so that debt sustainability would require a primary surplus (see Godley 1995a, b).[3]

A suitably adapted version of Domar's (1944, 1951) approach to debt sustainability may be applied here. In principle, if an economy grew at a constant rate, g, while running a persistent current account deficit as a share of GDP, ca, year after year, then its net international investment position relative to GDP, $niip$, will gradually approach a constant of size: ca/g.

$$niip = ca/g \tag{1}$$

A basic relationship thus exists between the current account and net international investment position (as shares of GDP) and the GDP growth rate. For instance, if a 6 per cent steady-state growth rate of nominal GDP were assumed, a NIIP of (negative) 100 per cent of GDP would imply a maximum 'sustainable' current account deficit of 6 per cent of GDP (sustainable in the sense of a nondeteriorating NIIP as a share of GDP). Similarly, a NIIP of (negative) 50 per cent of GDP would be compatible with a persistent current account deficit of 3 per cent of GDP.

Splitting the current account balance into the primary (or trade) balance, nx, and the (net factor) income balance, ib, and turning to the 'tax rate' required to service the external debt, or, rather the ratio of GDP toward which the income balance on the current account will converge in steady state, this is found to be equal to the value of: $i \,.\, ca/g$, where i is the rate of interest rate paid on the external debt (for simplicity assumed to be tax-exempt and equal to the rate paid on public debt).

$$ib = i \,.\, ca/g \tag{2}$$

Expressed dynamically, equation (3) shows the interest–growth differential as the key driver behind external debt dynamics (as Godley highlights)

$$\partial niip/\partial t = nx + (i-g)niip \tag{3}$$

Setting $\partial niip/\partial t$ equal to zero gives an inverse relation between the interest-growth differential and the sustainable primary (trade) balance seen in equation (4).

$$-nx = (i-g)niip \tag{4}$$

The point is that, given the international role of the US dollar and US Treasury securities, Godley's assumption of a sizeable positive interest-growth differential may not be justified. Beyond the nonnegligible contribution of non-interest bearing greenbacks (used in financing the international cocaine trade), Treasury debt securities feature prominently in US foreign liabilities. While certainly interest bearing, historically, the average interest rate paid on Treasury debt stayed below US nominal GDP growth most of the time (Bibow 2010). In fact, with German, Japanese, and Swiss Treasury securities as the only competitors (of limited weight) out there, low-yielding US Treasuries face high demands by international investors for reasons of offering top safety and liquidity. Arguably, for as long as the US dollar and US Treasuries enjoy this special global status, a sizeable 'liquidity premium' on US public debt will help to contain the interest burden arising from US external liabilities.

While this factor alone questions the idea of a primary *surplus* as required for sustainability, eventually, even under favorable conditions, the current account balance of a debtor nation such as the US would seem to inevitably become dominated by a negative net factor income balance; 'crowding out' the trade deficit over time. For instance, assuming a NIIP of (negative) 50 per cent of GDP and a *favorable* two-percentage-point interest-growth differential, say 4 per cent interest rate and 6 per cent nominal GDP growth rate, the sustainable current account deficit of 3 per cent of GDP would still end up largely consisting of a negative net factor income balance in steady state (namely, 2 per cent of GDP, leaving room for a sustainable trade deficit of only 1 per cent of GDP).

Explaining the paradox of a positive net factor income balance requires shifting the focus of analysis toward the *gross* assets and liabilities on the US external balance sheet rather than its *net* debtor position. Gross positions are much larger than the US's negative net position. The point is that a country benefiting from an 'income yield advantage' on external assets can partly or fully offset any income drain resulting from its net debtor position by *levering up* its external position: 'dollar leveraging' does the trick!

For instance, assume that a country enjoys a two-percentage-point income yield advantage while running a 3 per cent of GDP current account deficit (implying a steady-state NIIP of minus 50 per cent of GDP and a 2 per cent of GDP negative income balance without dollar leveraging). Under these conditions the negative net asset income arising from the country's net debtor position can be fully offset by buying foreign assets of the equivalent of 100 per cent of GDP. This would require selling additional liabilities to foreigners in the same amount, thereby tripling net debt of 50 per cent of GDP to assume gross debt of 150 per cent of GDP, or a 'leverage factor' of 3. (Figure 14.2 illustrates this case.) Similarly, in case of a four-percentage-point income yield advantage, purchasing foreign assets of the equivalent of 50 per cent of GDP would suffice, implying gross foreign debt of 100 per cent of GDP and a leverage factor of 2. An inverse relationship exists between the two critical variables: income yield advantage, *yd*, and leverage factor, *lf*. The requirement for a sustainable trade balance (that is, stable NIIP ratio) in equation (4) may also be amended accordingly.

$$-nx = (i - g - yd\ .(lf - 1))niip \tag{4}$$

As a matter of fact, starting from assets and liabilities both below 40 per cent of GDP in the late 1980s, when the net position was close to zero, Figure 14.3 exhibits sharply rising foreign assets and liabilities (relative to GDP) since the 1990s, a process of levering up the US's external balance sheet. Following a pause around the time of the dot. com boom and bust, US foreign asset holdings surged even faster since

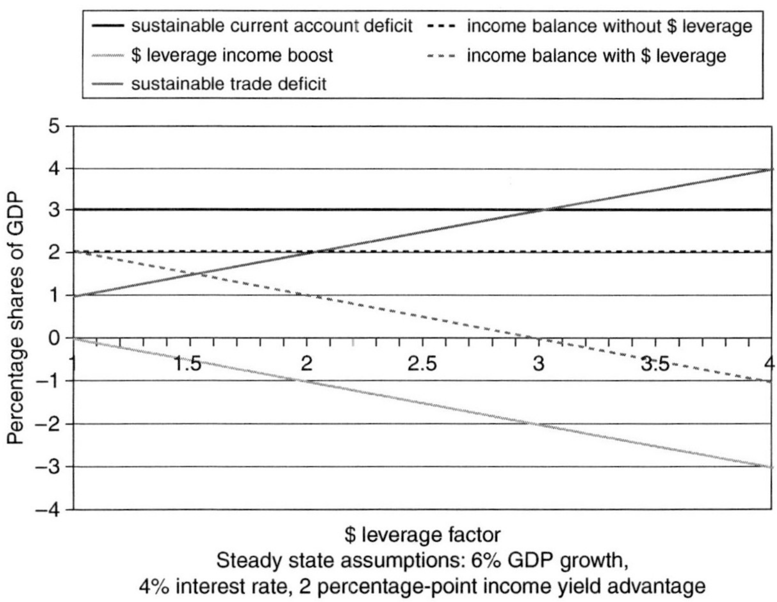

Figure 14.2 Levering the dollar and income yield advantage

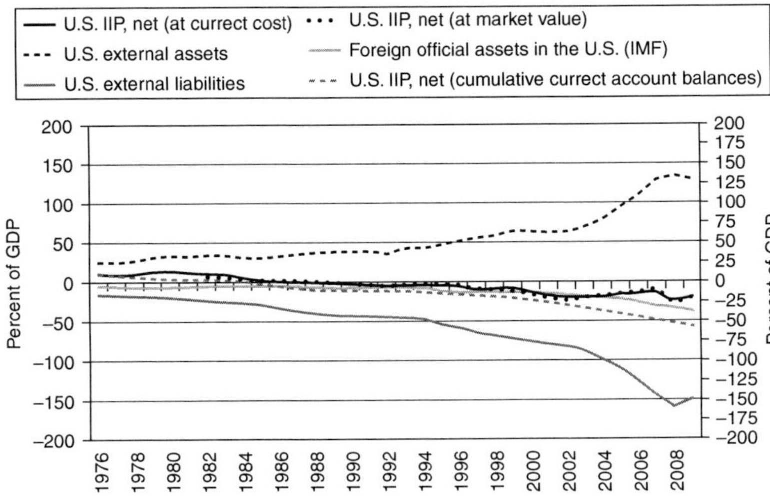

Figure 14.3 US external balance sheet
Source: Bureau of Economic Analysis; IMF COFER database.

2002. In 2007, gross liabilities exceeded the US NIIP by a factor of almost 15! Clearly, given a leverage factor in that order, it actually does not take much of an income yield advantage to keep the US net factor income balance in positive territory. (And the rising share of foreign official assets in the United States among US liabilities since 2001 seen in Figure 14.3 is surely helping too in this regard given the prominence of Treasury debt as official reserves.)

Another part of the paradox identified by Godley may be explained by considering that the US enjoys benefits from the special status of the dollar and Treasuries that consist of more than a plain income yield advantage (as analyzed above and as apparently assumed in Godley's 'quasi-interest rates'). I am referring to the fact is that the US NIIP has stayed surprisingly low and stable below 20 per cent of GDP, even improving strongly between 2004 and 2007 (when estimates of foreign direct investment [FDI] at market value are used), despite huge and soaring current account deficits. This outcome compares rather favorably with a hypothetical NIIP of (negative) 50 per cent of GDP calculated on the basis of cumulative current account balances; hypothetical developments that would accord with Godley's gloomy forecasts.

In their detailed analysis of the US's external balance sheet and related 'exorbitant privilege', Gourinchas and Rey (2005) distinguish a 'return effect,' stemming from higher total returns within each asset class, and a 'composition effect' stemming from an asymmetric balance sheet structure, featuring positive net positions of higher-yielding FDI and portfolio equity holdings and negative net positions of lower-yielding portfolio debt holdings (including US public debt securities, in particular), bank loans, and trade credit. They not only find strong evidence of a sizeable 'excess return' on gross assets over gross liabilities, but also find that 'valuation effects' appear to have played a prominent role in driving a sizeable 'total rate of return advantage' in the US's favor, and in stabilizing the US NIIP too.

Valuation effects, or the capital gains component in the US total rate of return advantage apparently ignored in Godley's quasi-interest rate analysis, can arise from two sources. First, valuation gains arise as market values of US external assets appreciate more (or depreciate less) than market values of US liabilities. Second, valuation gains also arise from dollar depreciation given that US liabilities are largely dollar denominated whereas US assets are predominantly denominated in foreign currencies. Hence dollar depreciation boosts the dollar value of non-dollar assets and asset income (as mentioned, for once, by Godley et al. 2007b).

In conclusion, the insights and findings discussed in this section pose a challenge to Godley's gloomy outlook for trends in the US's external position. The point is that a country facing high international demands for its low-yielding external liabilities may greatly benefit from levering up its external balance sheet. Running a 'long foreign-currency direct investments and portfolio equities, short (low-yielding) dollar debt' balance sheet position may yield a sizeable total rate of return advantage; with any overall income yield advantage boosting the net factor income balance and valuation effects checking the NIIP. By implication, the possibility emerges here that a country in such a position could run sizeable trade deficits for much longer than Godley considered possible. Arguably, while the strategy of leveraging yield differentials is not exclusive to dollar funding, the dollar's role as key reserve currency greatly boosts the demand for low-yielding dollar assets that might potentially find a home in international portfolios, both private and official. The next section therefore offers some thoughts on the international order focusing on 'king dollar' and unfettered global finance.

14.5 Unfettered global finance and 'king dollar'

From the start Godley identified the rebalancing of external trade as one of two main strategic challenges facing the US (the other one being fiscal relaxation). The analysis in the previous section led us to qualify the external strategic predicament. Arguably, for as long as the US dollar and Treasury debt continue to enjoy their special global status, the US may continue to run quite sizeable trade deficits without easily triggering the explosive trends feared by Godley. While theoretically possible, this argument begs at least two important questions though. First, why should the rest of the world wish to run policies that see (and require?) the US running continuous trade deficits? Second, what does the future hold in store for 'king dollar'? Answering these questions requires considering the evolving global order of currency and finance (Bibow 2008, 2009).

The first thing to note is that the dollar's reserve currency status does not seem to require the US to run trade deficits under all conditions. The US actually ran trade (and current account) surpluses until the early 1970s. During this period dollar reserves were supplied at first mainly through Marshall Plan aid and then through US foreign direct investment. It would seem that a global need for a sizeable US trade (and current account) deficit first arose in the early 1980s and then on a more persistent basis since the early 1990s.

The Bretton Woods order of adjustable pegs of 1944 officially established the dollar's role as key reserve currency; although its value was initially tied to gold. Apart from whatever reserves may be provided through multilateral mechanisms managed by the International Monetary Fund (IMF), supplying dollar reserves to the rest of the world requires the US to run a balance of payments deficit of some sort. With only n−1 exchange rates to peg between the n participating countries the system as a whole has one degree of freedom, and as a result the nth country bears the responsibility of acting as currency anchor as well as 'borrower and spender of last resort', as conditions may require. Historically, given the reconstruction boom and catching-up of Western Europe, Japan and other countries, the US's part in the 1950s and 60s was to provide restraint. Serious policy conflicts then emerged in the late 1960s. The Vietnam War and Great Society project turned US restraint into expansion, shifting the US current account balance into deficit in the early 1970s. Around the same time financial liberalization and the growth of euro-dollar markets increasingly undermined monetary control while wage demands began to accelerate around the world. The dollar was taken off gold on August 15, 1971. The ensuing currency market turmoil and economic mal-developments were further aggravated by the oil price shock of 1974.

The US re-emerged as a global leader in the early 1980s as the Reagan fiscal expansion, a surging dollar and soaring US current account deficit pulled the world economy out of the doldrums. The main counterpart countries to the US external deficit were West Germany and Japan. However, as the dollar depreciated following the Plaza Accord and economic growth picked up in surplus countries, the US current account moved back toward balance by the early 1990s. Yet, in important ways the 1980s provided a first run of the global imbalances of the 1990s that caught Godley's attention. The main difference was that in the 1980s the US had large budget deficits apart from its current account deficit: the 'twin deficits' era. By contrast, as Godley highlighted in his highly vigilant analyses, the 1990s saw private sector 'overspending' to a degree that allowed the government budget to even move into surplus as the US current account deficit re-emerged and soared in due course.

The point to highlight then is how exactly US private sector overspending and the corresponding current account deficit actually come about. Mainstream economists fancy the automatic working of market mechanisms is some imaginary full-employment economy. Godley understood that macroeconomic policies in large economies largely determine global economic performance, including global imbalances. On his core concept of the three sectoral financial balances he observed that 'each balance has a life of its own, and it is the level of real output that, with minor qualifications, brings about their equivalence' (Godley et al. 2007b, p. 2). In my own view, ultimately the national authorities' respective degree of tolerance of unemployment is the key factor. Traditionally, given the US's rudimentary welfare system, the US authorities are in no position to tolerate high and rising unemployment. By contrast, in Europe unemployment is *defined* as a structural problem and the macroeconomic authorities largely ignore it. Accordingly, the IMF (2002) accurately diagnosed that the global imbalances of the 1990s originated from diverging growth trends in the main industrialized countries as well as dollar strengthening; a situation that was quite similar to the first half of the 1980s only that in the 1990s first Japan and then Germany (together with the core of Euroland) got stuck in protracted domestic demand stagnation.

Emerging market economies then added to the strains in US labor markets resulting from forces elsewhere in the global economy. The Asian crisis in the late 1990s provoked a sea-change in the behavior of developing countries at large, henceforth making a competitive exchange rate their key policy anchor in their pursuit of export-led growth. The aggregate current account position of the developing world shifted from deficit into surplus in the late 1990s. While a bilateral Sino-American trade imbalance had emerged in the 1990s, China's current account surplus only attained global significance after 2003. How does the US become the key deficit counterpart and global growth engine in all this? Essentially, as the rest of the world becomes ever keener to export and is willing to accumulate dollar reserves to maintain a competitive exchange rate to facilitate their exports, such global (ex-US) behavior sustains dollar strength while strong deflationary forces arrive at the US's shores. As a result, the US authorities feel strong pressures to stimulate domestic demand. Regrettably, as the US authorities also became quite obsessed with fiscal consolidation around that time, the whole burden to provide stimulus to US domestic demand came to rest on the Federal Reserve's shoulders – duly obliging in view of its mandate. The private sector credit and spending bubbles of the 1990s were repeated in the 2000s for the simple reason that monetary policy stimulates private spending through boosting credit and asset prices; helped by financial liberalization easing credit constraints. Against the cheerleaders of Goldilocks dreams Godley warned from early on that this was not a sustainable growth model.

Today, in the aftermath of the global financial crisis and Great Recession, the situation is somewhat different because US monetary policy has lost much of its effectiveness, given that the housing and mortgage market crisis has left the personal sector in deleveraging mode. Fiscal expansion thus became the last resort. But as Godley pointed out correctly years ago, fiscal expansion in the US would tend to bring back the 'twin deficits', which he feared would lead to new unsustainable processes. It is in this particular regard that I qualified Godley's results, arguing that low-yielding Treasury debt and dollar leveraging may grant what I elsewhere dubbed 'Bretton Woods 3' arrangements (see Bibow 2009, 2010a) a longer life span than might at first appear.

There is, however, an important irony that should not be missed: global requirements for the US to act as global borrower and spender of last resort have become so much greater over time as the original Bretton Woods order gave way to 'anything goes' international monetary (non-) order arrangements and global finance was let off the leash. The irony is that 'unfettered global finance seems to have both increased the demand for defensive policies in the rest of the world and the extraction of rent available from meeting that demand' (Bibow 2010a, pp. 25–6). Countries seek safety in relying on a competitive exchange rate and dollar hoarding. Dollar leveraging allows the rent extraction that makes the required US trade deficits sustainable. Outcomes are not equally beneficial for all parties concerned. Unfettered global finance primarily serves the interest of global finance.[4]

To scholars in the tradition of Maynard Keynes and Hyman Minsky it needs no reminder of the fact that unfettered global finance is prone to cause fragility and crisis. The recent crisis certainly provided an illuminating experiment. Underlining the dollar's unchallenged global position, the global financial crisis featured the Federal Reserve acting as 'international lender of last resort' (through currency swap arrangements with foreign central banks that enabled these central banks to provide dollar liquidity in their respective money market centers). Figure 14.4 shows that apart from a shrinking current account deficit source of international dollar liquidity private capital outflows from the US reversed sharply at the peak of the crisis, turning the 'global dollar glut' into a 'global dollar shortage' – a systemic dollar shortage that could only be met by the official US outflows (that is, the Federal Reserve as international lender of last resort; Bibow 2000b).

Concerning king dollar's future, pre-eminence as the world's reserve currency of choice may not last forever. Yet the end of the dollar era does not seem nigh either – for lack of any serious competitor. Except for the establishment of a new monetary order by concerted action, which seems unlikely at this time in view of fundamental policy

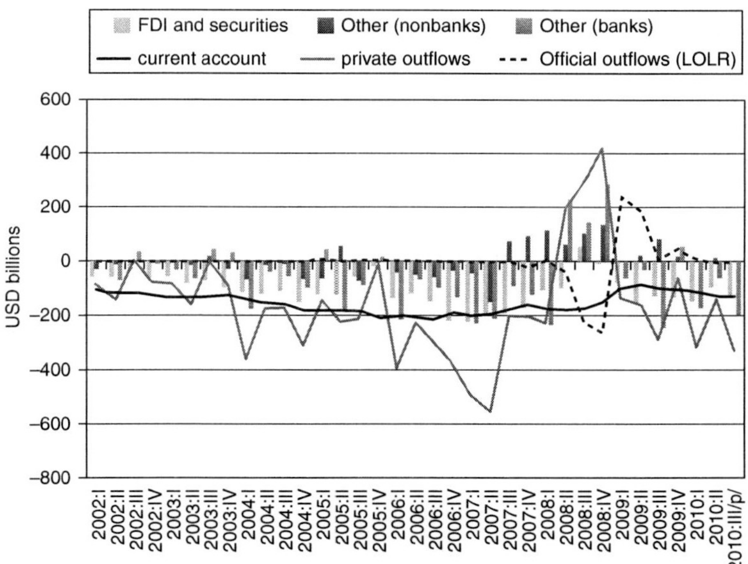

Figure 14.4 New global dollar glut appears on its way
Source: Bureau of Economic Analysis.

conflicts at the G20 level, 'king dollar' will continue to rule and the Federal Reserve will continue to be the 'conductor of the international orchestra' of central banks (Keynes 1930). As Godley noted, this position brings both benefits and challenges. After acting as international lender of last resort, the Federal Reserve, in battling record US unemployment, has unleashed a new global dollar glut and fresh rounds of private capital flow bonanzas headed towards emerging market economies. With 'quantitative easing', dollar leveraging is back too!

How much stress can the global symbiosis withstand then? Private capital outflows from the US tend to weaken the dollar and drive up foreign asset prices. Weakening the dollar would rebalance the US and global economies, while rising foreign asset prices (especially in dollar terms) limit the deterioration in the US's external balance sheet until the rebalancing comes about. Official foreign investors play a crucial role in delaying these adjustments. Whoever wishes to run trade surpluses must provide the finance for such surpluses to continue – or tolerate currency appreciation.

14.6 Conclusions

This chapter revisits Wynne Godley's pioneering work on SFC modeling and its application to US and global economic trends in the Levy Institute's periodic Strategic Analysis reports. Godley has a truly remarkable record at issuing timely warnings of clearly diagnosed unsustainable processes that are underway without appearing on any mainstream radar screens. Faulting mainstream fantasies about the US Goldilocks economy in the late 1990s, Godley's diagnosis of a new private debt bubble based on subprime mortgages in the mid-2000s was equally astute and timely. Arguably, however, with regard to the US's external position, Godley's analysis needs to be qualified. I argued that the dollar's role as reserve currency and the scope for dollar leveraging based on that role open up the possibility of the US acting as global growth engine through continuous trade deficits that are sponsored by public debt (rather than private debt as previously).

Overall, Godley's success rate at identifying coming troubles well ahead of time speak rather well for the SFC modeling methodology that he pioneered and applied in the Levy Institute's Strategic Analysis, despite the fact that the SFC model underlying the Strategic Analysis is still rather rudimentary. The Levy Institute bears a fair share of responsibility in keeping Wynne Godley's legacy alive, a great economist and a good man whom I had the pleasure to know and learn from.

Notes

1. While this contribution focuses on Wynne Godley's intellectual legacy, I should not fail to mention a changing group of collaborators who supported his Strategic Analysis-related research, including: Claudio H. Dos Santos, Edward Chilcote, Greg Hannsgen, Alex Izurieta, Dimitri B. Papadimitriou, Anwar Shaikh, and Gennaro Zezza. Parallel to his applied research proceeded Godley's highly fruitful collaboration with Marc Lavoie that culminated in the textbook *Monetary Economics* in 2007; referred to in an email to the author of 16 February 2007 as 'the product of more than half my life for the last ten years or so.'
2. Wynne did not respond to my email of 12 December 2007 asking, upon reading the latest Strategic Analysis, whether we could 'really trust that the rest of the world has kicked its habit of relying on US growth and will from now on happily stimulate domestic demand sufficiently to pull along a dragging US economy?'
3. Godley (1995a) assumes an interest rate on the debt that exceeds GDP growth by 1.75 percentage points, commenting that 'most people seem to accept, as a "stylized fact", that 2% is a reasonable estimate of this excess under normal conditions' (p. 22, fn. 10).
4. Gourinchas and Rey (2005) find that the US's 'exorbitant privilege' increased strongly in the post-Bretton Woods era, with annual excess returns in US favor estimated at 3.32 per cent for the period 1973–2004.

References

Bibow (1995) '"Some reflections on Keynes" "finance motive" for the demand for money,' *Cambridge Journal of Economics* 19(5): 647–66.

Bibow, J. (2008) 'The International Monetary (Non)Order and the "Global Capital Flows Paradox,"' in E. Hein, P. Spahn, T. Niechoj and A. Truger (eds) *Finance-led Capitalism? Macroeconomic Effects of Changes in the Financial Sector* (Marburg, Germany: Metropolis-Verlag), pp. 219–48 and Working Paper No. 531 (Annandale-on-Hudson, NY: Levy Economics Institute of Bard College).

Bibow, J. (2009) *Keynes on Monetary Policy, Finance and Uncertainty: Liquidity Preference Theory and the Global Financial Crisis* (London: Routledge).

Bibow, J. (2010a) 'Bretton Woods 2 is Dead, Long Live Bretton Woods 3?,' Working Paper No. 597 (Annandale-on-Hudson, NY: Levy Economics Institute of Bard College).

Bibow, J. (2010b) 'Global Imbalances, the US Dollar, and How the Crisis at the Core of Global Finance Spread to "Self-insuring" Emerging Market Economies,' *Intervention – European Journal of Economics and Economic Policies* 7(2): 325–59 and Working Paper No. 591 (Annandale-on-Hudson, NY: Levy Economics Institute of Bard College).

Domar, E.D. (1944) 'The "Burden of the Debt" and the National Income,' *American Economic Review* 34(4): 798–827.

Domar, E.D. (1950) 'The Effect of Foreign Investment on the Balance of Payments,' *American Economic Review* 40(5): 805–26.

Godley, W. (1995a) 'US Foreign Trade, the Budget Deficit and Strategic Policy Problems: A Background Brief,' Working Paper No. 138 (Annandale-on-Hudson, NY: Levy Economics Institute of Bard College).

Godley, W. (1995b) 'A Critical Imbalance in US Trade,' Public Policy Brief No. 23 (Annandale-on-Hudson, NY: Levy Economics Institute of Bard College).

Godley, W. (1996) 'Money, Finance, and National Income Determination,' Working Paper No. 167 (Annandale-on-Hudson, NY: Levy Economics Institute of Bard College).

Godley, W. (1997) 'Macroeconomics without Equilibrium or Disequilibrium,' Working Paper No. 205 (Annandale-on-Hudson, NY: Levy Economics Institute of Bard College).

Godley, W. (1998) 'An Important Inconsistency at the Heart of the Standard Macroeconomic Model,' Working Paper No. 236 (Annandale-on-Hudson, NY: Levy Economics Institute of Bard College).

Godley, W. (1999a) 'Money and Credit in a Keynesian Model of Income Determination,' *Cambridge Journal of Economics* 23: 393–411.

Godley, W. (1999b) 'Seven Unsustainable Processes: Medium-Term Prospects and Policies for the United States and the World,' Special Report, Levy Economics Institute of Bard College.

Godley, W. and A. Izurieta (2001a) 'As the Implosion Begins ...? Prospects and Policies for the US Economy: A Strategic View,' Strategic Analysis (Annandale-on-Hudson, NY: Levy Economics Institute of Bard College).

Godley, W. and Izurieta, A. (2001b) 'The Developing US Recession and Guidelines for Policy,' Strategic Analysis (Annandale-on-Hudson, NY: Levy Economics Institute of Bard College).

Godley, W. and A. Izurieta (2002) 'Strategic Prospects and Policies for the US Economy,' Strategic Analysis (Annandale-on-Hudson, NY: Levy Economics Institute of Bard College).

Godley, W. (2003) 'The US Economy: A Changing Strategic Predicament,' Strategic Analysis (Annandale-on-Hudson, NY: Levy Economics Institute of Bard College).

Godley, W., A. Izurieta and G. Zezza (2004) 'Prospects and Policies for the US Economy: Why Net Exports Must Now Be the Motor for US Growth,' Strategic Analysis (Annandale-on-Hudson, NY: Levy Economics Institute of Bard College).

Godley, W. and M. Lavoie (2004) 'Simple Open Economy Macro with Comprehensive Accounting: A Radical Alternative to the Mundell-Fleming Model,' Working Paper No. 16 (Cambridge, UK: Cambridge Endowment for Research in Finance).

Godley, W., D.B. Papadimitriou, C.H. Dos Santos and G. Zezza (2005) 'The United States and Her Creditors: Can the Symbiosis Last?,' Strategic Analysis (Annandale-on-Hudson, NY: Levy Economics Institute of Bard College).

Godley, W., D.B. Papadimitriou and G. Zezza (2007a) 'The US Economy: What's Next?,' Strategic Analysis (Annandale-on-Hudson, NY: Levy Economics Institute of Bard College).

Godley, W., D.B. Papadimitriou, G. Hannsgen and G. Zezza (2007b) 'The US Economy: Is There a Way Out of the Woods?,' Strategic Analysis (Annandale-on-Hudson, NY: Levy Economics Institute of Bard College).

Godley, W. and M. Lavoie (2007) *Monetary Economics: An Integrated Approach to Credit, Money, Income, Production and Wealth* (Basingstoke, UK: Palgrave Macmillan).

Godley, W., D.B. Papadimitriou and G. Zezza (2008) 'Prospects for the United States and the World: A Crisis that Conventional Remedies Cannot Resolve,'

Strategic Analysis (Annandale-on-Hudson, NY: Levy Economics Institute of Bard College).

Gourinchas, P.O. and H. Rey (2005) 'From World Banker to World Venture Capitalist: US External Adjustment and the Exorbitant Privilege,' Working Paper, No. 11563 (Cambridge, MA: National Bureau of Economic Research (NBER)).

International Monetary Fund (IMF) (2002) *World Economic Outlook* (Washington, DC: International Monetary Fund).

Keynes, J.M. (1930) *A Treatise on Money* (London: Macmillan).

Minsky, H.P. (1975 [2008]) *John Maynard Keynes* (New York: Columbia University Press) republished in D.B. Papadimitriou and L.R. Wray (eds) *Hyman P. Minsky's John Maynard Keynes* (New York: McGraw-Hill).

Minsky, H.P. (1986 [2008]) *Stabilizing an Unstable Economy* (New Haven, CT: Yale University Press) republished in D.B. Papadimitriou and L.R. Wray (eds) *Hyman P. Minsky's Stabilizing an Unstable Economy* (New York: McGraw-Hill).

15

Squaring the Circle in Euro Land? Some Remarks on the Stability Programmes 2010–13

Michael Brecht, Silke Tober, Till van Treeck and Achim Truger

15.1 Introduction

The global economy and the euro area, in particular, face serious challenges in the years ahead. Throughout the year 2010, politicians and financial investors were mainly concerned with the question of whether Greece and other 'deficit countries' should be 'rescued' by the other, seemingly more 'financially responsible' EMU countries in case of solvency problems.

More generally, it is held, from both a global and a European perspective, that the three most important objectives for the years to come are: (1) the reduction of current account imbalances; (2) the reduction of public deficits; and (3) the reduction of unemployment.

This chapter argues that the Stability Programmes (SPs) for the period 2010–13, submitted by the Member States to the European Commission in January/February 2010, will not achieve all three objectives. While we do briefly consider alternative policy recommendations, which necessarily involve some degree of judgment, our main conclusions are essentially derived from assessing the SPs in the light of some very simple accounting identities: Whereas the European Stability and Growth Pact (SGP) focuses exclusively on the government deficit (which should not exceed 3 per cent), we attempt to render explicit the assumptions inherent in the national SPs about overall macroeconomic development in terms of the financial balances of all three sectors in the economy (private, public and foreign). This is essentially an application of Wynne Godley's financial balances approach to the European context.

The chapter proceeds as follows. In the next section, we briefly discuss the importance of each of the three objectives outlined above. In section 15.3, we recall some simple macroeconomic accounting relationships which need to be taken into consideration when attempting to achieve these objectives. Based on this reminder, section 15.4 offers a discussion of how to assess the 'sustainability' of government, private and foreign sector financial balances in the context of the euro area. Section 15.5 looks at the macroeconomic development in the euro area since 1999, and section 15.6 puts the national SPs for 2010–13 in perspective. All data used in the empirical analysis were retrieved from the AMECO database (October 2009), which approximately corresponds to the information available to policymakers when producing the SPs. With this in mind, we show that the latter rely on overly optimistic assumptions about GDP growth and on an improvement of the euro area's current account while implying that current account imbalances within the euro area would remain quite significant. In particular, it seems highly unrealistic (and also undesirable) that private financial balances in countries with current account deficits and high private sector indebtedness fall back to zero or even become negative. By contrast, in countries with a large current account surplus, net private saving is (implicitly) projected to increase further to 8 or 9 per cent of national GDP. We look in some greater depth at the case of Germany, because it is the largest euro area economy and has an extremely large current account surplus. In section 15.7, we then show what would have to happen in each euro area country, in terms of the private financial balances, if we rule out an improvement in the euro area's current account balance vis-à-vis the rest of the world, while maintaining the assumptions about GDP growth and the fiscal consolidation of the national SPs. We argue that the implications for the evolution of private financial balances and the growth contributions of private demand are then even more unrealistic for various countries. In the concluding discussion, we argue that in the absence of a drastic deterioration of private financial balances, the surplus countries will have to accept sustained public deficits over the next years. If our simple analysis is correct, but governments in surplus countries are not prepared to use fiscal policy rather aggressively in the years to come, then it is very likely that the SPs, by focusing on reducing public deficits, will lead to long-lasting stagnation with high levels of unemployment in the euro area.

15.2 The three objectives: reducing current account imbalances, public deficits and unemployment

15.2.1 Reducing current account imbalances

The global imbalances are generally recognized as one of the major macroeconomic distortions leading to the global economic crisis that began in 2008. It is also argued that the reduction of global imbalances is one of the essential preconditions for a sustainable global recovery and for the stabilization of the world economy more generally (for example, Blanchard and Milesi-Ferretti, 2009; Horn et al., 2009; IMF, 2009).

The world's largest deficit countries are the UK, the US, and Spain, with current account deficits of, respectively, 2.7, 5.2, and 10 per cent of national GDP in 2007. The most important surplus countries are China (11 per cent), Germany (7.9 per cent) and Japan (4.8 per cent) (see Figure 15.1).

The euro area as a whole has had only small current account balances with the rest of the world since its creation in 1999. Yet, within the euro area, current account imbalances have become very substantial over the past years (see Table 15.1). Whereas current account surpluses in Germany and in the Netherlands reached about 8 per cent of national GDP by 2007, other countries – such as Greece, Portugal and Spain – ran current account deficits of more than 10 per cent of national GDP. The resulting foreign indebtedness of these countries is one of the main reasons for the speculative attacks against these countries on the financial markets (as apparent in the increasing credit default swap spreads and long-term bond yields, see Figure 15.6).

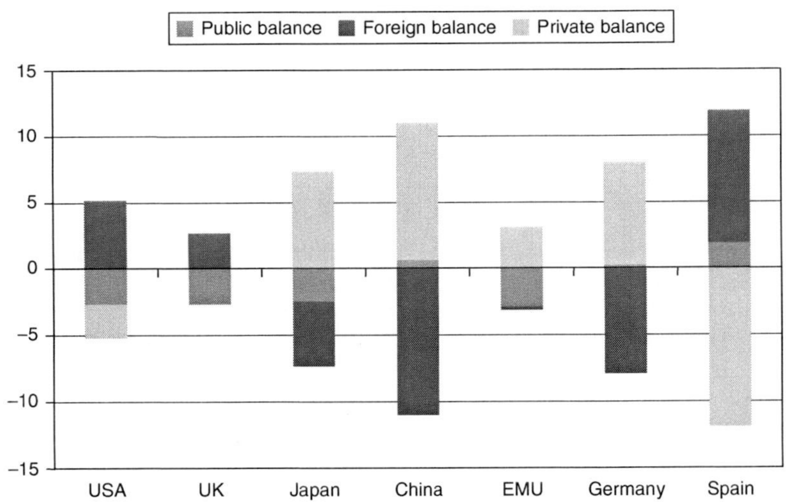

Figure 15.1 Financial balances in selected countries, 2007, in per cent of GDP
Source: AMECO, IMF, authors' calculations.

15.2.2 Reducing public deficits

In 2009 public deficits were higher than the 3 per cent of GDP allowed for by the Stability and Growth Pact (SGP) in all euro area countries except Finland and Luxembourg. In Greece, Ireland and Spain the public deficit even exceeded 10 per cent of GDP, in France and Portugal it was close to 8 per cent of GDP. The euro area average was 6.4 per cent of GDP (see Table 15.2).

The European Commission expects all euro area countries to abide by the 3 per cent limit by 2013. The SGP even states that the Member States should keep their government budget close to balance over the medium term. The public debt–GDP ratio, which has increased steeply during the present crisis from 66.0 per cent in 2007 to 78.2 per cent in 2009 on average (see Figure 15.5), should not exceed 60 per cent of GDP.

In Germany, the so-called 'debt break' rule – written into the Constitution in 2009 – furthermore states that the 'structural' deficit of the federal government must not exceed 0.35 per cent from 2016 onwards. And Germany's regional governments will no longer be allowed to run any structural deficits at all from 2020 onwards.

15.2.3 Reducing unemployment

Unemployment in the euro area has increased significantly since 2007. In Spain, the unemployment rate reached almost 20 per cent in 2009, in Ireland it has more than doubled to 11.7 per cent since 2007, and for most countries it is expected to reach 10 per cent or more in 2010 (see Figure 15.7).

In some countries, and most strikingly in Germany, the rise in unemployment has so far remained relatively moderate. Yet, as part-time work schemes and the reduction of working-time accounts will fade out in the near future, unemployment can be expected to rise in Germany as well, should economic growth remain weak.

As a consequence, in so far as there are links between unemployment and GDP growth, relatively high GDP growth rates will be necessary over the next years to effectively fight unemployment (and, thereby, avoid even more social unrest).

15.3 The interrelatedness of sectoral financial balances: a quick reminder

The following accounting identity holds:

$$\text{Public financial balance} + \text{Private sector financial balance} + \text{Financial balance of the foreign sector} = 0. \quad (1)$$

This simply means that any particular sector in the economy cannot run a surplus, without the remaining two sectors of the economy running a joint deficit of exactly the same magnitude. If one country runs a current account surplus, then at least in one other country the government or the private sector has to run a financing deficit, and so on.

The European debate mainly focuses on public sector balances[1] (and their implications for public debt-to-GDP ratios), and, more recently, also on current account balances[2] (and foreign debt-to-GDP ratios). The national SPs provide projections for the balances of these two sectors. This obviously has immediate implications for the financial balance of the private sector in each country, although these implications are often not discussed explicitly.

Given certain assumptions, the (projected) evolution of the financial balances of the three sectors also has implications for the (projected) growth contributions of the different components of GDP (see Appendix for a more detailed discussion). To see the link between the composition of GDP and sectoral financial balances, simply note that:

$$GDP = C + I + G + X - M, \tag{2}$$

where
C = Private consumption,
I = Private investment,
G = Government expenditures in final goods,
X = Exports,
M = Imports,
and that

$$GNI = GDP + NIA, \tag{3}$$

where
GNI = Gross national income,
NIA = Net income received from abroad.

Gross national income will be used to derive consumption, saving (S) and tax payments to the government net of government transfer payments and subsidies (NT).

$$GNI = C + S + NT, \tag{4}$$

It follows from (3) and (4) that

$$(NT - G) + (S - I) + [(M - X) - NIA] = 0, \tag{5}$$

where (NT – G), (S – I), and [(M – X) – NIA] are the financial balances of the public, private and foreign sectors, respectively.

15.4 When are financial balances 'unsustainable'?

The financial balances of the three sectors necessarily sum to zero. Clearly, any particular sector will only be able to adjust its financial balance in the desired way if one or both of the other two sectors *wish* to adjust their (joint) financial balance by the same amount in the opposite direction. If this is not the case, and the sum of the *desired* balances exceeds, or falls short of, zero, then national income will adjust to bring the *actual* balances in accordance with each other.[3]

When private demand is weak, the private sector financial balance is typically positive and large (or increasing). Clearly, when desired private saving exceeds desired private investment and foreign demand is equally insufficient, that is, (X – M) < (S – I) (*ex ante*), in the absence of government intervention there will be involuntary unemployment as a result of insufficient aggregate demand. In such a case, the government can attempt to reduce unemployment by reducing the public sector financial balance. This is what governments did in the current crisis. Yet, over the medium term such a policy may imply that the government deficit and the public debt-to-GDP ratio eventually increase to what many fear to be 'unsustainable' levels.

There is, as a general proposition, no clear-cut economic criterion which would indicate what 'unsustainable' really means, but the SGP states that it is not sustainable for any country to run government deficits of more than 3 per cent of GDP and to have a public debt-to-GDP ratio of more than 60 per cent[4] (the further stipulation being a balanced government budget over the medium term). In the analysis that follows, we simply take the 3 per cent rule of the SGP as a given to be attained by 2013.

If one believes that public deficits can be 'too large', it follows almost by definition that there are also limits to the extent to which the private sector can be allowed to run a surplus. Clearly, if large current account imbalances – generally also viewed as unsustainable – are to be avoided, then this together with the upper limit for government deficits automatically sets an upper limit for the private surplus.

From this perspective, however, one would certainly have to argue further that private deficits should not become 'too large' either, as this would increase the danger of a solvency crisis. More generally, it would seem that the government financial position cannot be considered 'sustainable'[5] when the private sector financial position is not, as the government would ultimately have to bail out private debtors in a private debt crisis (or drastically increase its deficit to pay for the economic and social costs of such a crisis).[6]

To sum up, once it is argued that the financial balance of any particular sector may be 'unsustainable', this logically implies that the balances of the two other sectors would equally be 'unsustainable' (irrespective of how this is defined).

15.5 Financial balances and macroeconomic development in the euro area, 1999–2009

Figure 15.2 shows the average real growth contributions of the three sectors for selected euro area countries for the period 1999–2007. Looking also at Table 15.1, it can be seen that those countries with relatively strong private demand growth tended to show lower, and sometimes even negative private financial balances.

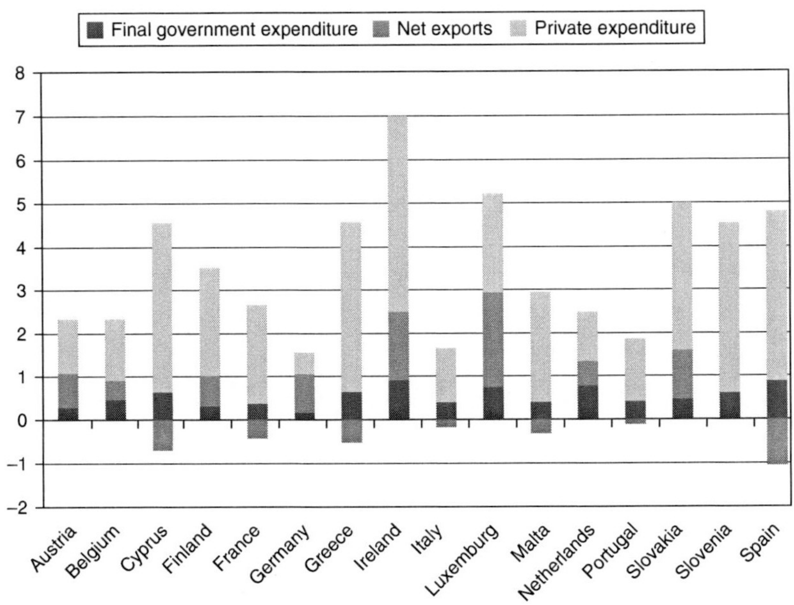

Figure 15.2 Real growth contributions, euro area countries, 1999–2007 average, in percentage points
Source: AMECO, authors' calculations.

Figures 15.3 to 15.5 show the evolution of private and public debt-to-GDP ratios for selected countries since 1999. As indicated by the yields on 10-year government bonds in Figure 15.6, financial markets seem to consider the domestic debt-to-GDP ratios to have attained 'unsustainable' levels in some countries. At the time of writing (March 2010), (rumors about) speculative pressures are focused on countries such as Greece, Ireland, Portugal and Spain. Notice, however, that the public debt-to-GDP ratio used to be significantly lower in Spain or Ireland than, for instance, in Germany. Yet, in both countries public indebtedness has drastically increased during the past two years, as a consequence of rising unemployment and solvency problems in the private sector.

As can be seen from Tables 15.1 and 15.2, private financial balances have increased significantly in all countries from 2007 to 2009. This increase was most pronounced in those countries where private net saving was negative in previous years and private indebtedness was high.

15.6 Assumptions and implications of the national Stability Programmes for 2010–2013

The financial balances for the 16 euro area countries can be written as a system of 16 equations with 48 variables. Moreover, the current account

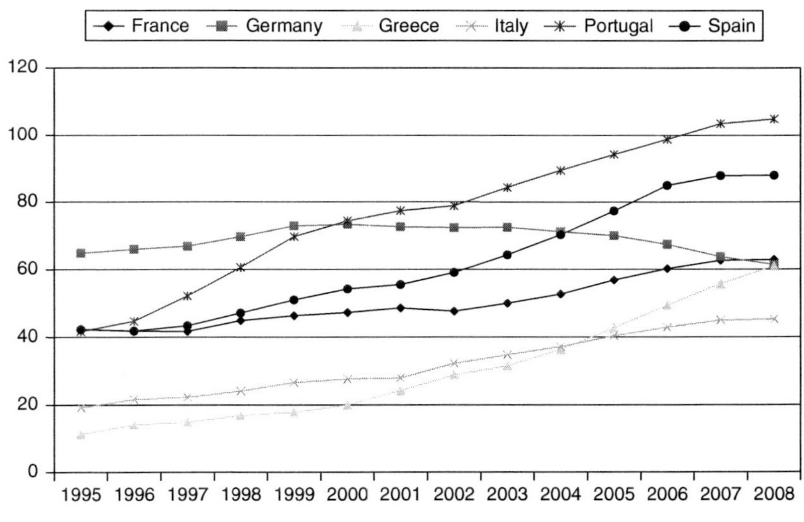

Figure 15.3 Private household debt relative to GDP, selected countries, 1995–2008, in per cent
Source: AMECO, Ecowin, authors' calculations.

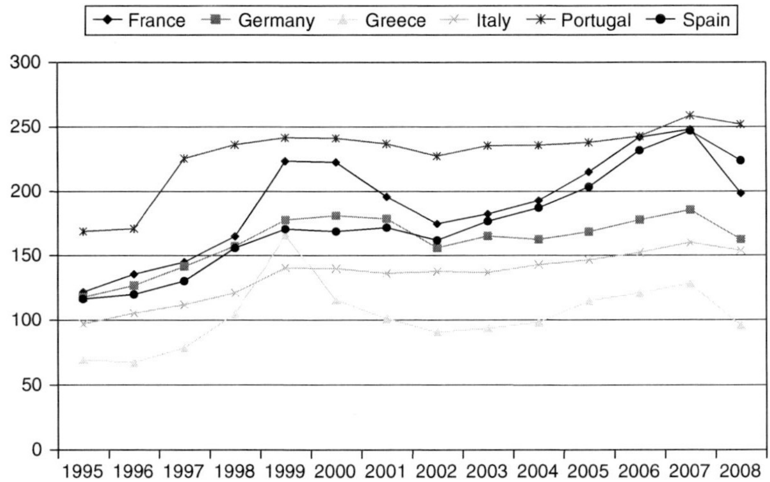

Figure 15.4 Liabilities of non-financial corporations relative to GDP, selected countries, 1995–2008, in per cent
Source: AMECO, Ecowin, authors' calculations.

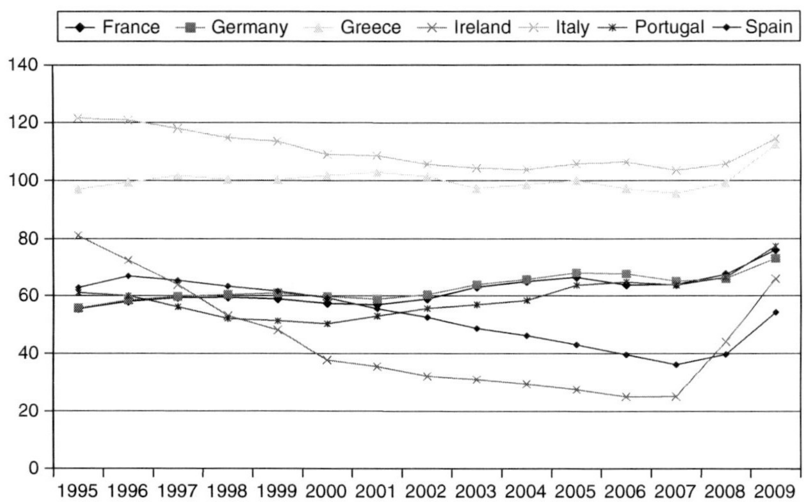

Figure 15.5 General government consolidated debt relative to GDP, selected countries, 1995–2009, in per cent
Source: AMECO, authors' calculations.

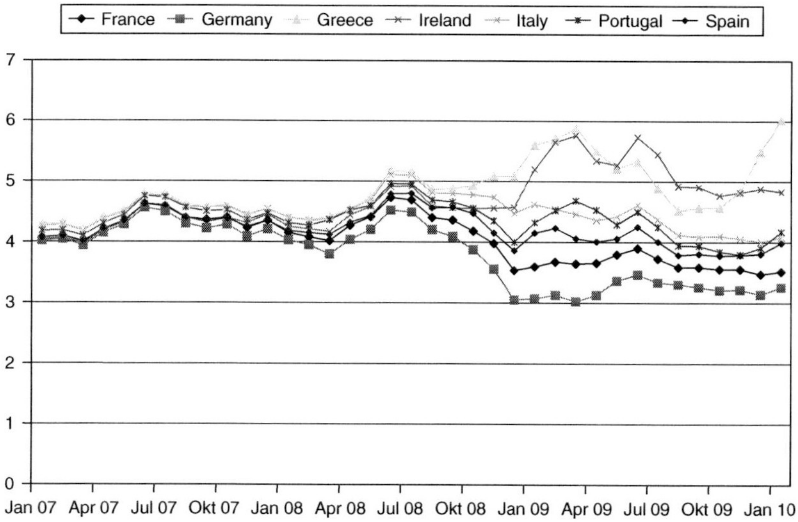

Figure 15.6 10-year government bond yields, selected countries, January 2007–February 2010
Source: ECB, authors' calculations.

balance of the euro area as a whole vis-à-vis the rest of the world is given by the sum of the current account balances of the 16 Member States. Tables 15.1 and 15.2 show this system of equations for the years 2007 and 2009, respectively.

The projected public financial balances and current account balances as a percentage of GDP for 2010–13 are shown in Table 15.3(a). These projections have immediate implications for the financial balances of the private sector in each country and for the financial balance of the rest of the world vis-à-vis the euro area as a whole. Because the Stability Programmes also provide data on projected GDP growth, we can express the financial balances in euros as well as in per cent of GDP. Table 15.3(b) shows the projected real growth contributions and Figure 15.7 the projected unemployment rates for 2010–13 for selected countries. Note that almost all countries expect to reduce – or to at least prevent a further increase in – unemployment compared to 2009. Table 15.4 shows the implications of the Stability Programmes for the financial balances of all sectors for 2013.

First, it should be noted that the assumptions about GDP growth rates appear quite optimistic, given the degree of fiscal consolidation: Already from 2011 onwards, almost all countries expect to grow by

Table 15.1 Financial balances, euro area countries, 2007

	In per cent of GDP			In billions of euros			In per cent of EMU GDP			GDP in billions of euros	
	Public	Foreign	Private	Public	Foreign	Private	Public	Foreign	Private		
Austria	−0.55	−3.36	3.91	−1.50	−9.09	10.59	−0.02	−0.10	0.12	270.78	Austria
Belgium	−0.20	−3.82	4.02	−0.66	−12.79	13.46	−0.01	−0.01	0.02	334.95	Belgium
Cyprus	3.46	12.01	−15.47	0.54	1.87	−2.41	0.01	0.02	−0.03	15.60	Cyprus
Finland	5.23	−4.04	−1.20	9.41	−7.25	−2.15	0.10	−0.08	−0.02	179.66	Finland
France	−2.71	2.27	0.44	−51.32	42.99	8.33	−0.57	0.48	0.09	1894.65	France
Germany	0.20	−7.91	7.71	4.88	−192.13	187.25	0.05	−2.13	2.08	2428.20	Germany
Greece	−3.66	14.73	−11.07	−8.29	33.36	−25.07	−0.09	0.37	−0.28	226.44	Greece
Ireland	0.25	5.34	−5.59	0.47	10.12	−10.60	0.01	0.11	−0.12	189.75	Ireland
Italy	−1.50	1.80	−0.29	−23.23	27.75	−4.52	−2.59	0.31	2.28	1544.92	Italy
Luxemburg	3.68	−9.71	6.03	1.38	−3.64	2.26	0.02	−0.04	0.03	37.46	Luxemburg
Malta	−2.18	6.96	−4.78	−0.12	0.38	−0.26	0.00	0.00	0.00	5.45	Malta
Netherlands	0.19	−8.54	8.35	1.10	−48.55	47.46	0.01	−0.54	0.53	568.66	Netherlands
Portugal	−2.59	9.79	−7.20	−4.22	15.95	−11.74	−0.05	0.18	−0.13	163.05	Portugal
Slovakia	−1.66	4.54	−2.88	−1.02	2.79	−1.77	−0.01	0.03	−0.02	61.50	Slovakia
Slovenia	0.02	4.55	−4.57	0.01	1.57	−1.58	0.00	0.02	−0.02	34.57	Slovenia
Spain	1.91	9.99	−11.89	20.07	105.12	−125.19	0.22	1.17	−1.39	1052.73	Spain
Average/Total	−0.01	2.16	−2.16	−52.50	−31.55	84.05	−2.91	−0.22	3.13	9008.37	Average/Total

Note: The three balances may not sum to zero due to rounding.
Source: AMECO, authors' calculations.

Table 15.2 Financial balances, euro area countries, 2009

	In per cent of GDP			In billions of euros			In per cent of EMU GDP			GDP in billions of euros	
	Public	Foreign	Private	Public	Foreign	Private	Public	Foreign	Private		
Austria	–4.34	–1.42	5.76	–11.96	–3.91	15.88	–0.13	–0.04	0.18	275.54	Austria
Belgium	–5.89	–0.61	6.50	–19.97	–2.08	22.05	–0.22	–0.02	0.24	339.06	Belgium
Cyprus	–3.50	11.64	–8.13	–0.60	2.01	–1.40	–0.01	0.02	–0.02	17.25	Cyprus
Finland	–2.80	–1.06	3.86	–4.92	–1.87	6.79	0.02	–0.02	0.00	175.76	Finland
France	–8.25	2.26	5.99	–160.43	44.01	116.41	–1.78	0.49	1.29	1943.44	France
Germany	–3.36	–3.96	7.32	–80.26	–94.84	175.09	–0.89	–1.05	1.94	2392.05	Germany
Greece	–12.66	8.81	3.85	–30.44	21.18	9.26	–0.34	0.24	0.10	240.43	Greece
Ireland	–12.48	3.14	9.35	–20.50	5.15	15.35	–0.23	0.06	0.17	164.21	Ireland
Italy	–5.27	2.42	2.84	–80.82	37.19	43.63	–0.90	0.41	0.48	1533.80	Italy
Luxemburg	–2.20	–9.39	11.58	–0.82	–3.52	4.35	–0.01	–0.04	0.05	37.53	Luxemburg
Malta	–4.52	3.23	1.29	–0.26	0.18	0.07	0.00	0.00	0.00	5.67	Malta
Netherlands	–4.67	–3.12	7.79	–26.84	–17.91	44.75	–0.30	–0.20	0.50	574.83	Netherlands
Portugal	–7.95	10.21	–2.26	–12.91	16.57	–3.66	–0.14	0.18	–0.04	162.34	Portugal
Slovakia	–6.26	5.81	0.45	–4.15	3.85	0.30	–0.05	0.04	0.00	66.27	Slovakia
Slovenia	–6.34	0.76	5.57	–2.25	0.27	1.98	–0.02	0.00	0.02	35.48	Slovenia
Spain	–11.23	5.36	5.88	–117.83	56.19	61.64	–1.31	0.62	0.68	1049.05	Spain
Average/Total	–6.36	2.13	4.23	–574.97	62.49	512.48	–6.30	0.69	5.61	9012.68	Average/Total

Note: The three balances may not sum to zero due to rounding.
Source: AMECO, authors' calculations.

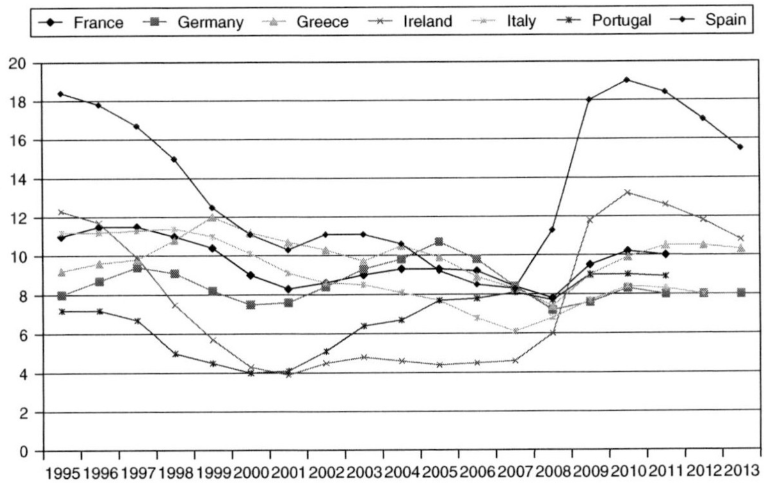

Figure 15.7 Unemployment rate, selected countries, 1999–2013
Source: AMECO, Stability Programmes 2010, authors' calculations. The projections for 2010–13 are based on AMECO estimates for France and Portugal and taken from the Stability Programmes for the other countries.

2 per cent annually in real terms (see Table 15.3(b)), and some even expect to grow much faster. Even more strikingly, the SPs are based on a number of discomforting assumptions that are not always made explicit:

1. The euro area as a whole would improve its current account position by 1.2 percentage points of GDP. This would seem to imply that exporters in the euro area benefit from strong global demand. Hence, if global rebalancing is nonetheless to take place and the large deficit countries, in particular the US and the UK, attempt to reduce their deficits, the EMU SPs increase the pressure on the world's large surplus countries, in particular China and Japan, to stimulate domestic demand and reduce their surpluses.

2. Within the euro area, current account imbalances would persist, although they would be somewhat lower than in 2007. Germany would increase its current account surplus from around 4 per cent of GDP in 2009 to 5.5 per cent in 2013; and the Netherlands would increase their surplus from a bit more than 3 per cent to more than 6 per cent. On the other hand, Greece and Spain would still run deficits of 4 and 3.5 per cent, respectively, with Italy and France continuing to run deficits as well.

Table 15.3 Projections of the Stability Programmes, 2010–13
a) Projected public and foreign financial balances, in per cent of GDP

	Public financial balance				Foreign financial balance			
	2010	2011	2012	2013	2010	2011	2012	2013
Austria	−4.7	−4	−3.3	−2.7	−2.4	−2.7	−2.8	−2.9
Belgium	−4.8	−4.1	−3	−3				
Cyprus	−6.00	−4.50	−3.40	−2.50	11.50	12.20	12.60	12.90
Finland	−3.6	−3	−2.3	−1.9	−1.2	−1.5	−1.8	−2
France	−8.2	−6	−4.6	−3	2.8	2.8	2.7	2.7
Germany	−5.5	−4.5	−3.5	−3	−4.9	−5	−5.5	−5.5
Greece	−8.7	−5.6	−2.8	−2	6.6	5.9	4.9	4
Ireland	−11.6	−10	−7.2	−4.9	0.6	1.2	1.6	1.6
Italy	−5	−3.9	−2.7	−2.7	1.6	1.3	1.3	
Luxemburg	−3.9	−3	−2.1	−1.1				
Malta	−3.9	−2.9	−2.8		3.6	2.2	1.4	
Netherlands	−6.1	−5	−4.5	−3	−5.75	−6.25	−6.25	
Portugal	−8.30	−6.60	−4.60	−2.80	9.30	9.10	8.70	8.3
Slovakia	−5.5	−4.2	−3	−3	3.2	2.7	1.9	
Slovenia	−5.7	−4.2	−3.1	−1.6	0.2	−0.1	−0.6	−0.3
Spain	−9.8	−7.5	−5.3	−3	4.2	3.8	3.6	3.5

b) Projected GDP growth, 2010–13, in percentage points*

	Real growth contribution of domestic demand				Real growth contribution of external balance				Nominal GDP growth			
	2010	2011	2012	2013	2010	2011	2012	2013	2010	2011	2012	2013
Austria	0.7	0.9	1.2	1.4	0.8	0.6	0.7	0.5	2.1	2.9	3.4	3.6
Belgium	1.5	1.5	2		0	0.2	0.2		2.4	3.6	4.1	
Cyprus	0.5	1.5	3	3.2	−1.9	−0.7	−1	−1.1	2.2	3.5	5.1	5.4
Finland	0.1	1.8	2.6	2.3	0.5	0.5	0.9	0.7	1.9	4	5.7	5.2
France	1.4	2.6	2.5	2.4	0	−0.1	0	0	2.5	4	4.3	4.3
Germany	0.6	1.5	1.5	1.5	0.8	0.5	0.5	0.5	2	3	3	3
Greece	−1.63	1.19	1.25	1.8	1.32	0.31	0.65	0.71	1.1	3.4	3.7	4.3
Ireland	−4	2	2.7	2.7	2.4	1.3	1.7	1.5	−2.23	5.58	6.68	6.47
Italy	0.9	1.7	1.9		0.1	0.2	0		2.6	3.8	3.9	
Luxemburg	1.7	2.3	−0.5	−0.3	0.8	0.7	3.3	3.2	3.9	5.4	4.3	4.4
Malta	1.9	2	2.2		−0.8	0.3	0.7		3.5	5	5	
Netherlands	0.25	1.25	1.25		1.25	0.75	0.75		1.5	3	3	
Portugal	0.3	0.4	0.6	1	0.4	0.5	0.7	0.7	1.5	3	3.3	3.8
Slovakia	2	3	3.9		−0.1	1.1	1.5		6	7.4	9	9
Slovenia	−0.3	1.3	3.4	2.8	1.4	1.2	0.3	0.7	1.4	4.6	6	5.7
Spain	−1.4	1.4	2.6	3	1.1	0.4	0.3	0.1	0.2	3.3	4.9	5.2

*Real GDP growth is the sum of the growth contributions of the domestic demand and the external sector balance.
Source: Stability Programmes 2010.

Table 15.4 Financial balances, euro area countries, 2013, according to the Stability Programmes

	In per cent of GDP			In billions of euros			In per cent of EMU GDP			GDP in billions of euros	
	Public	Foreign	Private	Public	Foreign	Private	Public	Foreign	Private		
Austria	–2.70	–2.90	5.60	–8.37	–8.99	17.37	–0.08	–0.09	0.17	310.10	Austria
Belgium	–3.00	–2.00	5.00	–11.69	–7.80	19.49	–0.11	–0.08	0.19	389.79	Belgium
Cyprus	–2.50	12.90	–10.40	–0.51	2.61	–2.10	0.00	0.03	–0.02	20.22	Cyprus
Finland	–1.90	–2.00	3.90	–3.94	–4.14	8.08	–0.04	–0.04	0.08	207.12	Finland
France	–3.00	2.70	0.30	–67.61	60.85	6.76	–0.66	0.59	0.07	2253.70	France
Germany	–3.00	–5.50	8.50	–79.98	–146.64	226.62	–0.78	–1.43	2.21	2666.13	Germany
Greece	–2.00	4.00	–2.00	–5.44	10.87	–5.44	–0.05	0.11	–0.05	271.84	Greece
Ireland	–4.90	1.60	3.30	–9.43	3.08	6.35	–0.09	0.03	0.06	192.53	Ireland
Italy	–2.70	1.30	1.40	–47.61	22.92	24.69	–0.46	0.22	0.24	1763.37	Italy
Luxemburg	–1.10	–7.00	8.10	–0.49	–3.13	3.63	0.00	–0.03	0.04	44.75	Luxemburg
Malta	–2.80	1.40	1.40	–0.19	0.10	0.10	0.00	0.00	0.00	6.79	Malta
Netherlands	–3.00	–6.25	9.25	–19.13	–39.85	58.97	–0.19	–0.39	0.57	637.55	Netherlands
Portugal	–2.80	8.30	–5.50	–5.10	15.10	–10.01	–0.05	0.15	–0.10	181.98	Portugal
Slovakia	–3.00	1.90	1.10	–2.69	1.70	0.99	–0.03	0.02	0.01	89.63	Slovakia
Slovenia	–1.60	–0.30	1.90	–0.67	–0.13	0.80	–0.01	0.00	0.01	42.16	Slovenia
Spain	–3.00	3.50	–0.50	–35.95	41.94	–5.99	–0.35	0.41	–0.06	1198.27	Spain
Average/Total	–2.69	0.73	1.96	–298.80	–51.50	350.30	–2.91	–0.50	3.41	10275.94	Average/Total

Source/Note: Stability Programmes, authors' calculations. When projections end in 2012, we assume that the respective GDP growth rates and financial balances remain unchanged in 2013. We set the current account balances for Belgium and Luxemburg equal to respectively 2 and 7 per cent, which is slightly lower than in recent years.

3. By 2013, private financial balances in the deficit countries would worsen dramatically, in some cases by more than 5 or 6 percentage points (to 0.3 per cent of GDP in France, –2 per cent in Greece, 3.3 per cent in Ireland, 1.4 per cent in Italy, and –0.5 per cent in Spain), while in the surplus countries private net saving would further increase (to 5.6 per cent in Austria, 5 per cent in Belgium, 8.5 per cent in Germany, 9.25 per cent in the Netherlands). The reason is that deficit countries expect GDP growth to be driven – as in the past – by private sector demand, while surplus countries expect GDP growth to be – once again – driven by exports.

In a nutshell: when the SPs are put into context, it becomes clear that their successful implementation implies that the three objectives outlined in section 15.2 would not be simultaneously attained by 2013: government deficits would be brought down to 3 per cent of GDP and GDP growth would be relatively strong (although unemployment would remain very high in many countries). But current account imbalances would remain entrenched, and those countries in which the increase in private indebtedness had been particularly strong during the years prior to the financial crisis (see Figures 15.4 and 15.5) would rely on renewed private demand booms, implying zero or even negative net private saving. The implicit assumptions about private financial balances for 2013 seem particularly heroic for France, Greece, and Ireland. It is quite remarkable that the Stability Programmes expect private financial balances to decline very quickly by 5, 6 or more percentage points of GDP in these countries. By contrast, surplus countries such as Germany and the Netherlands would continue to run private sector surpluses of around 8 or 9 per cent of GDP.

It is equally remarkable that Germany, as the largest economy within the euro area (about one quarter of euro area GDP), plans to continue to run very large current account surpluses. Of course, it may not be an easy task to change the pattern of economic growth immediately. But in the German SP not a single sentence could be found that would indicate that the German authorities perceive the export-led growth strategy as a problem for the stability of the euro area. Instead, it is argued that Germany's 'particularly export-oriented manufacturing sector' will benefit more than other countries from the (expected) 'upturn in global demand', because the German export industry is 'very price competitive (in) international comparison' as a result of 'a long period of market wage moderation' (SP, Germany, p. 20). As more than 40 per cent of Germany's exports go to other euro area countries (and more than 60 per cent to EU Member States), Germany's growth strategy continues to rely heavily on sustained deficits (public or private) in other European countries. Moreover, because non-euro area countries can adjust their price competitiveness vis-à-vis Germany via changes in the nominal exchange rate (while euro area countries obviously cannot), Germany seems to openly advocate bringing current account imbalances within the euro area back to the pre-crisis level.

In fact, despite the strategy of continued export-led growth, the German SP makes very optimistic assumptions about the growth contribution of domestic demand: 1.5 percentage points for 2011–13 is quite large in historical terms. In the period 1999–2007 the average joint growth contribution of the government and private sectors was 0.65 percentage points (0.88 when inventories are not included), the average growth contribution of private demand was 0.49 percentage points (0.73 without inventories), and only in three years (1999, 2000, 2006) was it higher than 1 percentage point. It is furthermore clear that the real growth contribution of government expenditure will not be much larger than 0.1 percentage points as a result of the fiscal consolidation plan and thus lower than before. Private demand in Germany contracted only quite moderately in 2009: the growth contribution was –2.06 percentage points (–1.33 without inventories) and private consumption actually grew in 2009. In fact, this is not really surprising given that private demand grew so slowly even before the crisis. And the rather moderate increase in unemployment has also helped stabilize private consumption. Interestingly, the contraction of domestic demand in 2009 was smaller than in 2002, when it came to –2.25 percentage points (–1.68 without inventories), which was followed by three years of very sluggish growth (the average real growth contribution of private and government demand was respectively 0.12 and 0.00 percentage points of GDP in 2002–05). Nevertheless, the most recent German SP projects domestic demand to contribute 1.5 percentage points to GDP for three consecutive years in 2011–13 (implying a growth contribution of private demand of about 1.4 percentage points on average) – and the private financial balance to remain as high as 8.5 per cent of GDP in 2013. The projected pattern of growth in Germany for 2009–13 is illustrated in Figure 15.8.

We leave it to readers to decide whether they find the assumptions made in the SPs of other countries more realistic than those made by the German authorities. Yet it should be clear that if the largest economy within the euro area fails to achieve its plans, then this would almost automatically imply that most of the other member states will have failed to realize theirs.

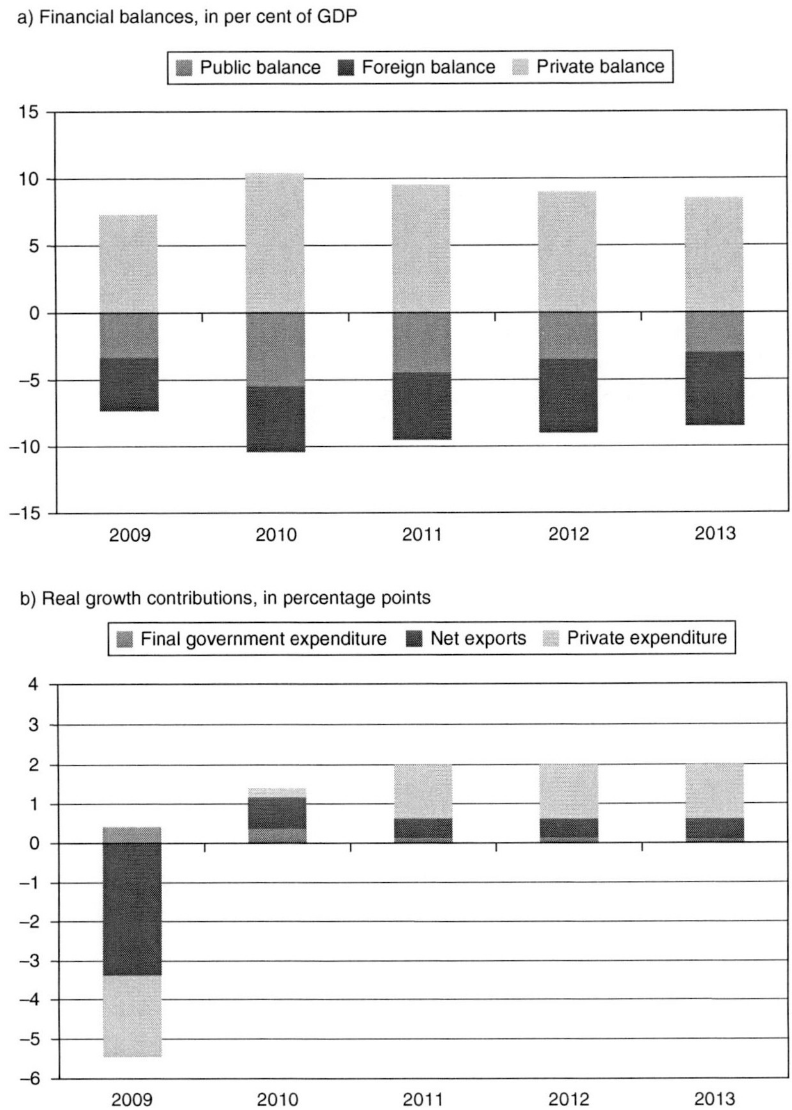

Figure 15.8 Pattern of GDP growth in Germany, 2009–13, according to the German Stability Programme
Source: German Stability Programme 2010 and authors' calculations.

15.7 Alternative scenarios for reducing government deficits, current account imbalances and unemployment rates in the euro area by 2013

Given the assumptions about GDP growth and public deficit reduction from the SPs, we can easily show the implications, in terms of the private financial balances, of a failure of the individual current account balances to evolve as projected. This is shown in Tables 15.5 and 15.6. In the underlying counterfactual exercises, we assume that the current account of the euro area as a whole remains constant as a percentage of the euro area GDP. This assumption would be justified if the recovery of global demand turned out to be weaker than apparently expected by the public authorities within EMU. However, we maintain the assumptions about government deficits from the national SPs.

In Table 15.5, we show what would have to happen to the financial balances in the countries with current account deficits if the current account surplus countries were to realize their SP projections given an unchanged current account position of the euro area as a whole. We also assume that the deficit countries will contribute to the implied deterioration of their deficits in proportion to the size of their respective deficits in 2009. Clearly, the implications for private and current account balances of the deficit countries seem highly unrealistic. In Greece and Portugal, private sector and current account deficits would once more rise to more than 10 per cent of GDP, in France the private sector balance would fall to around zero and in Spain the private sector would run a deficit of more than 4 per cent of GDP, corresponding to a current account deficit of more than 7 per cent.

In a second counterfactual exercise, we assume, albeit somewhat arbitrarily, that all countries with current account deficits in 2009 will reduce their deficits to 2 per cent of their respective national GDPs by 2013. Note that even such major rebalancing would still imply quite a substantial deterioration in the private financial balances of the deficit countries (for instance, they would be 1 per cent of GDP in France and Spain, compared to respectively 6.01 and 5.88 per cent in 2009). Here, we assume that the surplus countries will contribute to the implied reduction of their surpluses in proportion to the size of their respective surpluses in 2009. Based on these assumptions, we again solve our system of equations for the 16 private financial balances. The results are shown in Table 15.6.

In Figure 15.9, we illustrate what our assumptions would imply for the composition of growth in the largest surplus country, Germany,

Table 15.5 Financial balances, euro area countries, 2013, given surplus countries realize their plans but euro area as a whole fails to improve the current account

	In per cent of GDP			In billions of euros			In per cent of EMU GDP			GDP in billions of euros	
	Public	Foreign	Private	Public	Foreign	Private	Public	Foreign	Private		
Austria	−2.70	−2.90	5.60	−8.37	−8.99	17.37	−0.08	−0.09	0.17	310.10	Austria
Belgium	−3.00	−2.00	5.00	−11.69	−7.80	19.49	−0.11	−0.08	0.19	389.79	Belgium
Cyprus	−2.50	14.99	−12.49	−0.51	3.03	−2.53	0.00	0.03	−0.02	20.22	Cyprus
Finland	−1.90	−2.00	3.90	−3.94	−4.14	8.08	−0.04	−0.04	0.08	207.12	Finland
France	−3.00	2.95	0.05	−67.61	66.46	1.15	−0.66	0.65	0.01	2253.70	France
Germany	−3.00	−5.50	8.50	−79.98	−146.64	226.62	−0.78	−1.43	2.21	2666.13	Germany
Greece	−2.00	11.77	−9.77	−5.44	31.98	−26.55	−0.05	0.31	−0.26	271.84	Greece
Ireland	−4.90	4.04	0.86	−9.43	7.78	1.65	−0.09	0.08	0.02	192.53	Ireland
Italy	−2.70	3.18	−0.48	−47.61	56.16	−8.55	−0.46	0.55	−0.08	1763.37	Italy
Luxemburg	−1.10	−7.00	8.10	−0.49	−3.13	3.63	0.00	−0.03	0.04	44.75	Luxemburg
Malta	−2.80	4.07	−1.27	−0.19	0.28	−0.09	0.00	0.00	0.00	6.79	Malta
Netherlands	−3.00	−6.25	9.25	−19.13	−39.85	58.97	−0.19	−0.39	0.57	637.55	Netherlands
Portugal	−2.80	13.75	−10.95	−5.10	25.02	−19.93	−0.05	0.24	−0.19	181.98	Portugal
Slovakia	−3.00	6.49	−3.49	−2.69	5.82	−3.13	−0.03	0.06	−0.03	89.63	Slovakia
Slovenia	−1.60	0.97	0.63	−0.67	0.41	0.27	−0.01	0.00	0.00	42.16	Slovenia
Spain	−3.00	7.08	−4.08	−35.95	84.85	−48.91	−0.35	0.83	−0.48	1198.27	Spain
Average/Total	−2.69	2.73	−0.04	−298.80	71.25	227.55	−2.91	0.69	2.21	10275.94	Average/Total

Note: The three balances may not sum to zero due to rounding.

Table 15.6 Financial balances, euro area countries, 2013, given more significant rebalancing within the euro area

	In per cent of GDP			In billions of euros			In per cent of EMU GDP			GDP in billions of euros	
	Public	**Foreign**	**Private**	**Public**	**Foreign**	**Private**	**Public**	**Foreign**	**Private**		
Austria	–2.70	–0.36	3.06	–8.37	–1.10	9.47	–0.08	–0.01	0.09	310.10	Austria
Belgium	–3.00	–0.15	3.15	–11.69	–0.59	12.28	–0.11	–0.01	0.12	389.79	Belgium
Cyprus	–2.50	2.00	0.50	–0.51	0.40	0.10	0.00	0.00	0.00	20.22	Cyprus
Finland	–1.90	–0.25	2.15	–3.94	–0.53	4.46	–0.04	–0.01	0.04	207.12	Finland
France	–3.00	2.00	1.00	–67.61	45.07	22.54	–0.66	0.44	0.22	2253.70	France
Germany	–3.00	–1.00	4.00	–79.98	–26.70	106.69	–0.78	–0.26	1.04	2666.13	Germany
Greece	–2.00	2.00	0.00	–5.44	5.44	0.00	–0.05	0.05	0.00	271.84	Greece
Ireland	–4.90	1.60	3.30	–9.43	3.08	6.35	–0.09	0.03	0.06	192.53	Ireland
Italy	–2.70	1.30	1.40	–47.61	22.92	24.69	–0.46	0.22	0.24	1763.37	Italy
Luxemburg	–1.10	–2.22	3.32	–0.49	–0.99	1.48	0.00	–0.01	0.01	44.75	Luxemburg
Malta	–2.80	1.40	1.40	–0.19	0.10	0.10	0.00	0.00	0.00	6.79	Malta
Netherlands	–3.00	–0.79	3.79	–19.13	–5.04	24.17	–0.19	–0.05	0.24	637.55	Netherlands
Portugal	–2.80	2.00	0.80	–5.10	3.64	1.46	–0.05	0.04	0.01	181.98	Portugal
Slovakia	–3.00	1.90	1.10	–2.69	1.70	0.99	–0.03	0.02	0.01	89.63	Slovakia
Slovenia	–1.60	–0.30	1.90	–0.67	–0.13	0.80	–0.01	0.00	0.01	42.16	Slovenia
Spain	–3.00	2.00	1.00	–35.95	23.97	11.98	–0.35	0.23	0.12	1198.27	Spain
Average/Total	–2.69	0.70	1.99	–298.80	71.25	227.55	–2.91	0.69	2.21	10275.94	Average/Total

Note: The three balances may not sum to zero due to rounding.

over the period 2010–13. In these calculations (see Appendix for further details), we take into account the 2010 fiscal stimulus package and the strategy of fiscal consolidation to be implemented from 2011 onwards (as planned at the beginning of 2010). Clearly, the domestic demand boom required by these assumptions contrasts starkly with the German growth pattern projected in the SP (see Figure 15.8), which essentially replicates the pre-crisis export-led growth model.

It is clear that the scenario from Figure 15.9 is even more unrealistic than that in Figure 15.8. There do not seem to be any good reasons to expect the private sector to desire substantially higher spending relative to income over the next years. Given our assumptions, the implied growth contribution of private sector demand would have to be about 2.5 percentage points per year from 2011 onwards (even though we unrealistically assume that the current account surplus starts to decrease (and hence private demand to increase quite strongly) already in 2010, see Figure 15.9 and Appendix).[7] Of course, this seems even more illusionary than the projections in the official German SP.

Yet, as recalled in section 15.3 above, if the *ex ante* plans of both the public and foreign sectors are to improve their respective financial balances, GDP will be negatively affected, unless the private sector *desires* to worsen its balance by an equivalent amount.

Should the private sector not desire to reduce its financial balance to the required extent, the only way to achieve the projected growth rates given current account rebalancing, would be for the government to *willingly accept* higher public deficits over an extended period of time. It is clear from the analysis above that the German government may well have to accept deficits of significantly more than 5 per cent of GDP for several years, if the officially projected GDP growth rates and current account rebalancing are to be achieved within EMU. Although such a policy would currently be considered a breach of the 'debt break' rule, the deficit would still appear quite modest by international standards.[8]

15.8 Concluding discussion

In this chapter, our aim is to render explicit and to put into context the assumptions underlying the SPs of the euro area countries for 2010–13. We show that the rather optimistic assumptions about GDP growth and fiscal consolidation rely on a drastic deterioration of private financial balances in the deficit countries, strong global demand allowing the euro area to run a current account surplus vis-à-vis the rest of the

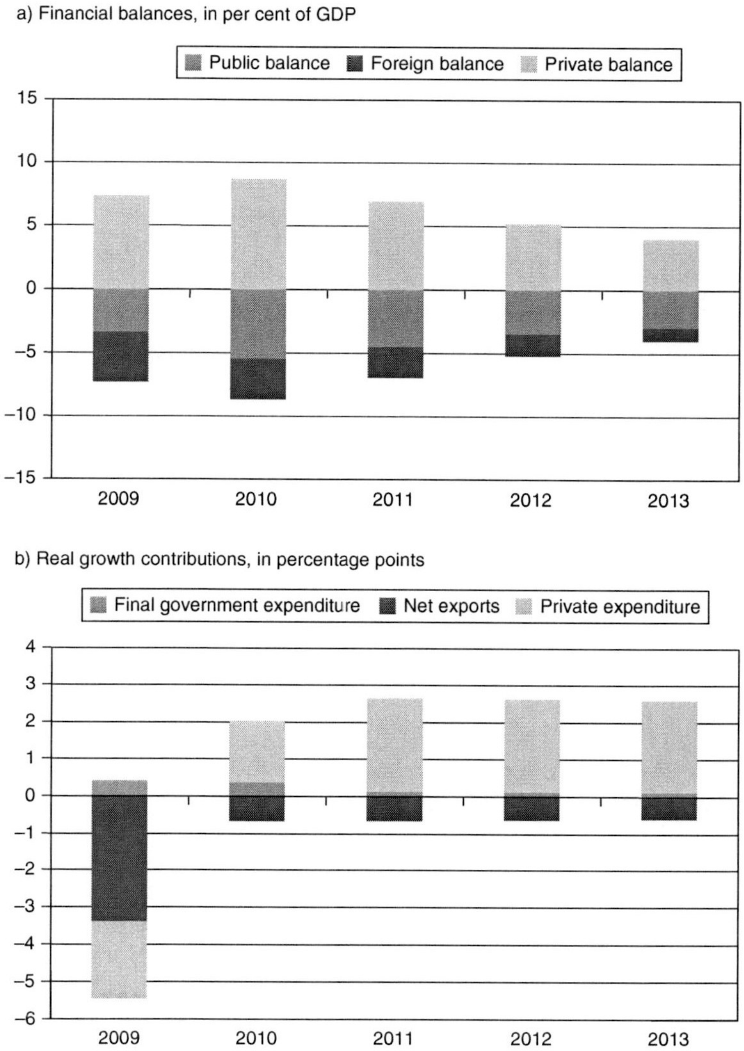

Figure 15.9 Pattern of GDP growth in Germany, 2009–13, given more significant rebalancing within the euro area (based on the SP's assumptions about public deficits and growth)
Source: Table 15.5 and Appendix; authors' calculations.

world, and the entrenchment of current account imbalances within EMU. Rebalancing current accounts at acceptable growth rates clearly requires stronger domestic demand in the surplus countries. Taking the case of the euro area's largest economy, Germany, as an illustration, we argue that it would, in historical perspective, be very risky to rely on the expectation of a private sector demand boom. Hence, the only way to achieve the GDP growth rates projected in the SPs (and, ideally, current account rebalancing) would be for the governments of surplus countries to run higher deficits over the next few years.

The approach chosen to argue the point is in a way almost embarrassingly simple. We say hardly anything about the behavioral mechanisms underlying desired changes in financial balances. To what extent do macroeconomic policies, unit labor cost differentials, demographic factors, productivity growth differentials, and so on, play a role in determining actual financial balances? And how do we know whether a particular financial balance is 'sustainable' in one country and not in the other? It would be beyond the scope of this contribution to address these questions. Instead, we simply take it for granted that: (1) the Stability and Growth Pact deems government deficits above 3 per cent 'unsustainable'; (2) current account imbalances within the euro area are still 'too large'; and (3) reduced unemployment and high economic growth is 'desirable' for the years to come. We then show that, under current circumstances, the simultaneous realisation of these three objectives is like squaring a circle.

It should be noted that our counterfactual exercises involve several more or less arbitrary assumptions, and that we are more concerned with qualitative conclusions than with putting precise numbers on them. For instance, we do not say anything about whether (or under which conditions) it is realistic to assume that euro area countries with current account deficits would benefit from a reduction in the current account surpluses of Germany and other surplus countries as implied by net exports and hence GDP. These questions would clearly deserve closer attention but would require one to make stronger assumptions than we deemed necessary in this chapter.

Despite these qualifications, our simple calculations seem to strongly suggest that euro area governments, particularly in countries with high current account surpluses and low foreign indebtedness, should be prepared in the years to come to accept substantially higher government deficits than projected in the SPs. If they do not – eyeing net exports to other euro area countries – it would seem rather hypocritical and irresponsible to criticise the high foreign debt and lack of 'fiscal responsibility' of those countries with current account deficits. In fact, sustained government deficits in the surplus countries may turn out to be the only way to effectively 'rescue' the European Monetary Union.

Appendix: Calculation of growth contributions (Figure 15.9)

As before, we define the three financial balances as

$$PFB = \text{Private financial balance} = S - I, \tag{A1}$$

$$GFB = \text{Government financial balance} = T - G - NTR, \tag{A2}$$

$$FFB = \text{Financial balance of the foreign sector} = M - X - NIA. \tag{A3}$$

where

S = Private saving,

I = Private investment,

T = Tax receipts including social security contributions,

G = Final government expenditures in final goods,

NTR = Net transfers from the government to the private and foreign sectors (interest payments on public debt, social security benefits and subsidies, foreign aid, etc.),

NIA = Net income received from abroad (including government and private transfers).

We want to calculate the growth contributions of (C + I), G, and (X – M) between t and t + i.

Because of GDP = C + I + G + (X – M), the growth contributions are given by

$$(\Delta GDP_{t+i})/GDP_t = (\Delta C_{t+i})/GDP_t + (\Delta I_{t+i})/GDP_t + \Delta G_{t+i}/GDP_t + [\Delta(X - M)_{t+i}]/GDP_t. \tag{A4}$$

We know PFB_t, GFB_t, FFB_t, GDP_t, C_t, I_t, G_t, $(X - M)_t$ (variables observed for t = 2009) and we make assumptions about PFB_{t+i}, GFB_{t+i}, FFB_{t+i}, GDP_{t+i} (for i = 1, 2, 3, 4), which are either based on the German *SP*, or implied by our assumptions in Table 15.5. Of course, we only have to calculate the growth contributions of G and (X – M) from (A2) and (A3), and we will then also know the joint nominal growth contribution of (C + I) via (A4).

From (A3) it follows that

$$\Delta FFB_{t+i}/GDP_t = \Delta(M - X)_{t+i}/GDP_t - \Delta NIA_{t+i}/GDP_t \tag{A5}$$

It seems reasonable to assume that[9]

$$[FFB - (M - X)]/(M - X) = \gamma = \text{const.} \tag{A6}$$

It would then follow that

$$\Delta(X - M)_{t+i}/GDP_t = -1/(1 + \gamma) * (\Delta FFB_{t+i}/GDP_t) \quad \text{(A7)}$$

In Figure 15.9 of the main text, we assume that the foreign financial balance is reduced in four equal steps from 2010 to 2013.

Analogously, from (A2) it follows that

$$\Delta GFB_{t+i}/GDP_t = \Delta T_{t+i}/GDP_t - \Delta G_{t+i}/GDP_t - \Delta NTR_{t+i}/GDP_t. \quad \text{(A8)}$$

Based on assumptions about changes in T and NTR, we can calculate $\Delta G_{t+i}/GDP_t$. In Figure 15.9 of the main text, our assumptions are calibrated to ensure that the growth contributions of G correspond to the projections of the German SP. We further assume that the price deflator increases at the same rate for all GDP components to calculate the real growth contributions for all sectors.

Notes

1. The government deficit is equal to the negative of the public financial balance.
2. The current account balance is equal to the negative of the financial balance of the foreign sector.
3. See Godley et al. (2007) and Hatzius (2003) for more detailed expositions of the financial balances approach.
4. Under the assumption of a long-run average nominal GDP growth rate of 5 per cent, the public debt-to-GDP ratio will not exceed 60 per cent in the long run, if the government deficit does not exceed 3 per cent.
5. Godley (1992, p. 3) emphasized early on that "the establishment of a single currency in the EC would indeed bring to an end the sovereignty of its component nations and their power to take independent action on major issues". Their financial position can, therefore, easily become unsustainable, as they "lose the power to finance deficits through money creation while other methods of raising finance are subject to central regulation" (p. 3).
6. As an example, in Ireland the public debt-to-GDP ratio was very low until recently, but it tripled between 2007 and 2009 as a result of the current crisis. Similarly, over the past two years, the Spanish government had to run very large deficits and substantially increase the public debt relative to GDP, after it had run surpluses for several years before (while the private sector had very high deficits during the real estate boom).
7. If we assumed that the deficit countries reduce their current account deficits to only 3 or 4 per cent, the implied annual private growth contribution in Germany would have to come to about 2.3 or 2.2 percentage points, respectively.
8. In fact, from the perspective of global imbalances, it seems rather irritating that Germany as one of the world's largest surplus countries wants to reduce the federal financial balance to approximately zero per cent of GDP by 2016,

whereas the US as the world's largest deficit country is projecting a deficit of more than 5 per cent for 2015, according to the Office of Management and Budget. This is all the more surprising as Germany is the only country (apart from Japan) for which the European Commission provides data, where real total government expenditure shrank(!) during 1998–2008 (the EU-15 average real growth rate of total public expenditure was 1.8 per cent per year).
9. In Germany, the current account balance and net exports have closely tracked each other over the past years.

References

Blanchard, O. and G.M. Milesi-Ferretti (2009) 'Global Imbalances: In Midstream?,' International Monetary Fund Staff Position Note, December 22.

European Commission (2010 *Stability and Convergence Programmes 2009–10,* http://ec.europa.eu/economy_finance/sgp/convergence/programmes/2009-10_en.htm.

Godley, W. (1992) 'Maastricht and All That', *London Review of Books,* Vol. 14, No. 19, 8 October, 3–4.

Godley, W., D. Papadimitriou, G. Hannsgen and G. Zezza (2007) 'The US Economy: Is There a Way Out of the Woods?,' Strategic Analysis (Annandale-on-Hudson, NY: Levy Economics Institute of Bard College).

Hatzius, J. (2003) 'The Private Sector Deficit Meets the GSFCI: A Financial Balances Model of the US Economy,' Global Economics Paper No. 98 (New York: Goldman Sachs).

Horn, G., H. Joebges and R. Zwiener (2009) 'From the Financial Crisis to the World Economic Crisis II Global Imbalances: Cause of the Crisis and Solution Strategies for Germany,' Report No. 40 (Düsseldorf, Germany: IMK at the Hans Boeckler Foundation, Macroeconomic Policy Institute).

International Monetary Fund (IMF) (2009) 'Sustaining the Recovery,' *World Economic Outlook* (Washington, DC: International Monetary Fund).

Wynne Godley – A Bibliography

Papers

1959

'Costs, Prices and Demand in the Short Run', reprinted in M.J.C. Surrey (ed.), *Macroeconomic Themes: Edited Readings in Macroeconomics with Commentaries* (London: Oxford University Press, 1976)

1964

(with C. Gillion) 'Measuring National Product', *National Institute Economic Review*, February

(with J.R. Shepherd) 'Long-term Growth and Short-term Policy', *National Institute Economic Review*, August

(with C. Gillion) 'Pricing Behaviour in the Engineering Industry', *National Institute Economic Review*, August

(with D.A. Rowe) 'Retail and Consumer Prices 1955–1963', *National Institute Economic Review*, November

1965

(with W.A.B. Hopkin) 'An Analysis of Tax Changes', *National Institute Economic Review*, May

(with J.R. Shepherd) 'Forecasting Imports', *National Institute Economic Review*, August

(with C. Gillion) 'Pricing Behaviour in Manufacturing Industry', *National Institute Economic Review*, August

1972

(with W.D. Nordhaus) 'Pricing in the Trade Cycle', *Economic Journal*, 82(327) (September): 853–82

(with J. Rhodes) 'The Rate Support Grant System', Proceedings of a Conference on Local Government Finance, Institute of Fiscal Studies, Publication no. 10

1973

(with T.F. Cripps) 'Balance of Payments and Demand Management', *London and Cambridge Economic Bulletin*, no. 82, January

1974

'Demand, Inflation and Economic Policy', *London and Cambridge Economic Bulletin*, no. 84, January

'The Concept of a Par Economy in Medium-term Analysis', in G.D.N. Worswick and F.T. Blackbaby (eds) *The Medium Term: Models of the British Economy* (London: Heinemann)

1975

(with A. Wood) 'Profits and Stock Appreciation', *Economic Policy Review*, no. 1, February

1976

(with T.F. Cripps) 'A Formal Analysis of the Cambridge Economic Policy Group Model', *Economica*, 43(172) (November): 335–48

(with T.F. Cripps and M.J. Fetherston) 'What is Left of New Cambridge?', Chapter 6, *Economic Policy Review*, no. 2, March

'The Measurement and Control of Public Expenditure', Chapter 8, *Economic Policy Review*, no. 2, March

1977

'Inflation in the United Kingdom', in L.B. Krause and W.S. Salant (eds), *Worldwide Inflation: Theory and Recent Experience* (Washington DC: Brookings Institution, 1977)

(with C. Taylor) 'Measuring the Effect of Public Expenditure', in M. Posner (ed.), *Public Expenditure* (Cambridge: Cambridge University Press, 1977)

(with A. McFarquhar and D. Silvey) 'The Cost of Food and Britain's Membership of the EEC', *Economic Policy Review*, no. 3, March, chapter 3

(with R. May) 'The Macroeconomic Implications of Devaluation and Import Restriction', *Economic Policy Review*, no. 3, March, chapter 2

1978

(with M.J. Fetherstone) '"New Cambridge" Macroeconomics and Global Monetarism: Some Issues in the Conduct of UK Economic Policy', in K. Brunner and A.H. Meltzer (eds), *Public Policies in Open Economies*, Carnegie-Rochester Conference Series on Public Policy, vol. 9(1): 33–65

(with T.F. Cripps) 'Control of Imports as a Means to Full Employment and the Expansion of World Trade: the UK's Case', *Cambridge Journal of Economics*, 2(3): 327–34

(with K.J. Coutts and W.D. Nordhaus) 'Industrial Pricing in the United Kingdom', University of Cambridge Department of Applied Economics, Monograph 26 (London: Cambridge University Press)

(with T.F. Cripps and M.J. Fetherstone) 'Simulations with the CEPG Model', in M. Posner (ed.), *Demand Management* (London: Heinemann)

(with R. Bacon and A. McFarquhar) 'The Direct Costs to Britain of Belonging to the EEC', *Economic Policy Review*, no. 4, chapter 5, March

1979

'Britain's Chronic Recession – Can Anything Be Done?', in W. Beckerman (ed.), *Slow Growth in Britain* (Oxford: Clarendon Press), pp. 226–35

1981

'Monetarism is Three Countries: United Kingdom', in D. Crane (ed.), *Beyond the Monetarists: Post-Keynesian Alternatives to Rampant Inflation, Low Growth and High Unemployment* (Toronto: James Lorimer), pp. 36–41

1983

'Keynes and the Management of Real National Income and Expenditure', in D. Worswick and J. Trevithick (eds) *Keynes and the Modern World* (Cambridge: Cambridge University Press), pp. 135–56

(with T.F. Cripps) *Macroeconomics* (London: Fontana)

(with M. Anyadike-Danes) 'Nominal Income Determination, Financial Assets and Liabilities and Fiscal Policy', *Brazilian Review of Econometrics*, 3(2): 105–30

1984

'Confusion in Economic Theory and Policy – Is There a Way Out?', in J. Cornwall (ed.), *After Stagflation: Alternatives to Economic Decline* (Oxford: Basil Blackwell), pp. 63–85

1985

(with K.J. Coutts and G.D. Gudgin) 'Inflation Accounting of Whole Economic System', *Studies in Banking and Finance*, 9(2)

'Unemployment in Europe: the Strategic Problem of the Mid Eighties', *Neuer Protektionismus in der Weltwirtschaft und EG-Handelspolitik: Jahreskolloquium*, pp. 99–108

1987

(with N.M. Christodoulakis) 'A Dynamic Model for the Analysis of Trade Policy Options', *Journal of Policy Modeling*, no. 9

(with M. Anyadike-Danes) 'A Stock Adjustment Model of Income Determination with Inside Money and Private Debt', in M. De Cecco and J.P. Fitoussi (eds), *Monetary Theory and Economic Institutions* (London: Macmillan)

(with N.M. Christodoulakis) 'Macroeconomic Consequences of Alternative Trade Policy Options', *Journal of Policy Modeling*, 9(3): 405–36

1988

'The Sensibility of Contemporary Institutions', *Theology*, March, 91(740): 89–94

1989

(with G. Zezza) 'Foreign Debt, Foreign Trade and Living Conditions, with Special Reference to Denmark', *Nationalokonomisk Tidsskrift*, 127(2): 229–35

(with M. Anyadike-Danes) 'Real Wages and Employment: A Sceptical View of Some Recent Empirical Work', *The Manchester School*, 57(2): 172–87

(with M. Anyadike-Danes) 'Real Wages and Employment: Response to Nickell's Comment', *The Manchester School*, 57(3): 285

'The British Economy during the Thatcher Era', *Economics*, 25(108) (Winter): 159–62

(with K.J. Coutts) 'The British Economy Under Mrs Thatcher', *The Political Quarterly*, 60(2) (April–June): 137–51

1990

(with K.J. Coutts, R. Rowthorn and G. Zezza) 'Britain's Economic Problems and Policies in the 1990s', *Economic Study* no. 6 (London: Institute for Public Policy Research (IPPR)) (with K.J. Coutts) 'Prosperity and Foreign Trade in the 1990s: Britain's Strategic Problem', *Oxford Review of Economic Policy*, 6(3) (Autumn): 82–92

'The British Economy Under Mrs. Thatcher: A Rejoinder', *The Political Quarterly*, 61(1): 101–2

1992

(with G. Zezza) 'A Simple Real Stock Flow Model Illustrated with the Danish Economy', in H. Brink (ed.), *Themes in Modern Macroeconomics* (London and Basingstoke: Macmillan), ch. 8, pp. 140–79

'Godley, Wynne (born 1926)', in P. Arestis and M. Sawyer (eds), *A Biographical Dictionary of Dissenting Economists* (Aldershot: Edward Elgar), pp. 193–201

'Britain and the Danger of the EMU', *Samfundsokonomen*, no. 7, November

(with K.J. Coutts) 'Does Britain's Balance of Payments Matter Anymore?', in J. Michie (ed.), *The Economic Legacy: 1979–1992* (London: Academic Press), pp. 60–7

(with K.J. Coutts and J.G. Palma) 'The British Economy under Mrs. Thatcher', *Economic Bulletin for Latin America*

'The Godley Papers: Economic Problems and Policies in the 1980s and 90s' (London: New Statesman and Society)

1993

'Time, Increasing Returns and Institutions in Macroeconomics', in S. Biasco, A. Roncaglia and M. Salvati (eds), *Market and Institutions in Economic Development: Essays in Honour of Paolo Sylos Labini* (New York: St. Martin's Press)

1994

(with W. Milberg) 'US Trade Deficits: The Recovery's Dark Side?', *Challenge* 37(6): 40–7

(with B. Rowthorn) 'Appendix; The Dynamics of Public Sector Deficit and Debt', in J. Michie and J. Grieve Smith (eds), *Unemployment in Europe* (London: Academic Press), pp. 199–206

1995

'The US Balance of Payments, International Indebtedness, and Economic Policy', Levy Institute Public Policy Brief, no. 23

1997

(with G. McCarthy) 'The Boskin Commission's Trillion-Dollar Fantasy', *Challenge*, 40(3): pp. 14–21

1998

(with G. McCarthy) 'Fiscal Policy Will Matter.', *Challenge*, 41(1) (January–February): 38–54

1999

(with B. Martin) 'America's New Era', *Economic Outlook*, 24(1) (October): 14–19

(with L.R. Wray) 'Can Goldilocks Survive?', Levy Institute Policy Note 1999/4

'How Negative Can US Saving Get?', Levy Institute Policy Note 1999/1

'Money and Credit in a Keynesian Model of Income Determination', *Cambridge Journal of Economics*, 23(4): 393–411
'Seven Unsustainable Processes: Medium Term Prospects and Policies for the US and World', Levy Institute Strategic Analysis, January

2000
'Drowning in Debt', Levy Institute Policy Note 2000/6
'Interim Report: Notes on the US Trade and Balance of Payments Deficits', Levy Institute Strategic Analysis, January
(with L.R. Wray) 'Is Goldilocks Doomed?', *Journal of Economic Issues*, 34(1) (March): 201–6

2001
(with A. Izurieta) 'As the Implosion Begins...? Prospects and Policies for the US Economy: A Strategic View', Levy Institute Strategic Analysis, July
(with A. Izurieta) '"As the Implosion Begins...?": A Rejoinder to Goldman Sachs' J. Hatzius 'The Un-Godley Private Sector Deficit' in US Economic Analyst (27 July)', Levy Institute Strategic Analysis, August
'Fiscal Policy to the Rescue', Levy Institute Policy Note 2001/1
'The Developing Recession in the United States', *Banca Nazionale del Lavoro Quarterly Review*, 54(219): pp. 417–25
(with A. Izurieta) 'The Developing US Recession and Guidelines for Policy', Levy Institute Strategic Analysis, October
(with M. Lavoie) 'Kaleckian Models of Growth in a Coherent Stock-flow Monetary Framework: A Kaldorian View', *Journal of Post Keynesian Economics*, 24(2) (Winter): 277–311

2002
(with A. Izurieta) 'The Case for a Severe Recession', *Challenge*, 45(2) (April): 27–51
(with A. Shaikh) 'An Important Inconsistency at the Heart of the Standard Macroeconomic Model', *Journal of Post Keynesian Economics*, 24(3) (Spring): 423–41
'Kick-start Strategy Fails to Fire Sputtering US Economic Motor', Levy Institute Policy Note

2002/1
(with A. Izurieta) 'Strategic Prospects and Policies for the US Economy', Levy Institute Strategic Analysis, April

2003
'Sauver Masud Kahn', *Revue française de psychoanalyse*, 67(3): 1015–28
(with A. Izurieta) 'Coasting on the Lending Bubble. Both in the UK and the US', Cambridge Endowment for Research in Finance Strategic Analysis
'The US Economy: A Changing Strategic Predicament', Levy Institute Strategic Analysis, March

2004
'Commentary to: Anne-Marie Sandler, "The Case of Masud Khan: Institutional Responses to Boundary Violations"', *International Journal of Psycho-Analysis*, 85(1): 27–44

(with D.B. Papadimitriou, A.M. Shaikh, C.H. Dos Santos and G. Zezza) 'Is Deficit Financed Growth Limited? Policies and Prospects in an Election Year', Levy Institute Strategic Analysis, April

(with A. Izurieta and G. Zezza) 'Prospects and Policies for the US Economy: Why Net Exports Must Now be the Motor for US Growth', Levy Institute Strategic Analysis, August

'Weaving Cloth from Graziani's Thread: Endogenous Money in a Simple (but Complete) Keynesian Model', in R. Arena and N. Salvadori (eds), *Money, Credit and the Role of the State: Essays in Honour of Augusto Graziani* (Aldershot: Ashgate), pp. 127–35

2005

'Commentary to: Anne-Marie Sandler, Réponses institutionnelles aux transgressions: le cas de Masud Khan', *L'Année Psychanalytique Internationale*, pp. 15–31

'Imbalances Looking for a Policy', Levy Institute Policy Note 2005/4

'Some Unpleasant American Arithmetic', Levy Institute Policy Note 2005/5

(with A. Izurieta) 'The US Economy: Weaknesses of the "Strong" Recovery', *Banca Nazionale del Lavoro Quarterly Review*, 57(229): 131–9

(with D.B. Papadimitriou, C.H. Dos Santos and G. Zezza) 'The United States and Her Creditors: Can the Symbiosis Last?', Levy Institute Strategic Analysis, September

(with M. Lavoie) 'Comprehensive Accounting in Simple Open Economy Macroeconomics with Endogenous Sterilization or Flexible Exchange Rates', *Journal of Post Keynesian Economics*, 28(2) (Winter): 241–76

2006

(with G. Zezza) 'Debt and Lending: A Cri de Coeur', Levy Institute Policy Note 2006/4

(with M. Lavoie) 'Features of a Realistic Banking System within a Post-Keynesian Stock-flow Consistent Model', in M. Setterfield (ed.), *Complexity, Endogenous Money and Macroeconomic Theory: Essays in Honour of Basil J. Moore* (Cheltenham: Edward Elgar), pp. 251–68

2007

(with M. Lavoie) *Monetary Economics: An Integrated Approach to Credit, Money, Income, Production and Wealth* (Basingstoke: Palgrave Macmillan)

(with M. Lavoie) 'A Simple Model of Three Economies with Two Currencies: The Eurozone and the USA', *Cambridge Journal of Economics*, 31(1), pp. 1–23

(with D.B. Papadimitriou, G. Hannsgen and G. Zezza) 'The US Economy is There a Way Out of the Woods?', Levy Institute Strategic Analysis, November

(with D.B. Papadimitriou and G. Zezza) 'The US Economy: What's Next?', Levy Institute Strategic Analysis, April

2008

(with D.B. Papadimitriou and G. Zezza) 'Prospects for the United States and the World: A Crisis That Conventional Remedies Cannot Resolve', Levy Institute Strategic Analysis, December

2009
'The Developing Recession in the United States', *PSL Quarterly Review*, 62 (248–51): 87–92
(with A. Izurieta) 'The US Economy: Weaknesses of the 'Strong' Recovery', *PSL Quarterly Review*, 62(248–51): 97–105

Working papers

(with C. Taylor) 'Public Spending and Private Demand', Economics Reprint No. 339, 1971
(with T.F. Cripps) 'Local Government Finance and its Reform: A Critique of the Layfield Committee's Report', Department of Applied Economics, 1976
(with T.F. Cripps) 'The Planning of Telecommunications in the United Kingdom', 1978
(with K.J. Coutts) 'Introduction to a Synthesis of Macroeconomic Theory Based on Tobin's Nobel Lecture', Department of Applied Economics, Working paper, 1984
(with K.J. Coutts) 'Outline for a Reconstructed Basis for Macroeconomic Theory', Department of Applied Economics, Working paper, 1984
(with N.M. Christodoulakis) 'A Dynamic Model for the Analysis of Trade Policy Options', Dept. of Applied Economics, University of Cambridge, 1986
(with K.J. Coutts, Robert Rowthorn and Terry S. Ward) 'The British Economy: Recent History and Medium Term Prospects', 1986
(with K.J. Coutts; Juan Carlos Moreno-Brid) 'Industrial Pricing in UK Manufacturing Industry Under Conditions of "Stagflation"', 1987
(with M. Anyadike-Danes and K.J. Coutts) 'IS-LM and Real Stock Flow Models: A Prelude to Applied Macroeconomic Modelling', 1987
(with G. Zezza) 'A Simple Real Stock Flow Model Illustrated with the Danish Economy', Department of Applied Economics, Working paper, 1989
'Time, Increasing Returns and Institutions in Macroeconomics', Cambridge Working Papers in Economics, 9023, 1990
'A Macro View of the Danish economy', Department of Applied Economics, Working paper, April 1991
'Britain and the Danger of EMU', Department of Applied Economics, Working paper, April 1991
'US Foreign Trade, the Budget Deficit and Strategic Policy Problems: A Background Brief', Levy Institute Working Paper, no. 138, 1995
'A Simple Model of the Whole World with Free Trade, Free Capital Movements, and Floating Exchange Rates', Unpublished manuscript, Levy Institute, 1996
'Money, Finance and National Income Determination: An Integrated Approach', Levy Institute Working Paper, no. 167, June 1996
'Macroeconomics Without Equilibrium or Disequilibrium', Levy Institute Working Paper, no. 205, August 1997
(with B. Martin) 'America and the World Economy', Research Group Occasional Paper no. 3, Phillips & Drew, December 1998
(with A. Shaikh) 'An Important Inconsistency at the Heart of the Standard Macroeconomic Model', Levy Institute Working Paper, no. 326, May 1998
'Open Economy Macroeconomics Using Models of Closed Systems', Levy Institute Working Paper, no. 281, August 1999

(with M. Lavoie) 'Kaleckian Models of Growth in a Stock-Flow Monetary Framework: A Neo-Kaldorian Model', Levy Institute Working Paper, no. 302, June 2000

(with A. Izurieta) 'Strategic Prospects for the US Economy: A New Dilemma', Centre for Financial Analysis and Policy, November 2002

(with A. Izurieta) 'Balances, Imbalances and Fiscal Targets: A New Cambridge View', Cambridge Endowment for Research in Finance, University of Cambridge, 2003

(with M. Lavoie) 'Two-country Stock-flow-consistent Macroeconomics Using a Closed Model Within a Dollar Exchange Regime', Centre for Financial Analysis and Policy, Working paper no. 10, November, 2003

(with M. Lavoie) 'Features of a Realistic Banking System Within a Post-Keynesian Stock-Flow Consistent Model', Centre for Financial Analysis and Policy, Working paper no. 12, 2004

(with M. Lavoie) 'Simple Open Economy Macro with Comprehensive Accounting a Radical Alternative to the Mundell–Fleming Model', Centre for Financial Analysis and Policy, Working paper no.15, April 2004

'Towards a Reconstruction of Macroeconomics Using a Stock Flow Consistent (SFC) Model', Centre for Financial Analysis and Policy, Working paper no. 16, May 2004

(with M. Lavoie) 'Simple Open Economy Macro with Comprehensive Accounting: A Two-country Model', Cambridge Endowment for Research in Finance Working paper no. 20, February 2005

(with M. Lavoie) 'Prolegomena to Realistic Monetary Macroeconomics: A Theory of Intelligible Sequences', Levy Institute Working Paper, no. 441, February 2006

Memoranda

'Measurement, Forecasting and Control of Public Expenditure', memorandum to Commons Expenditure Committee, 1970/71 (3rd Report), 1970

'Implied Price Relationships, Cmnd. 4234, Cmnd. 4578 and the National Income and Expenditure Account', memorandum to Commons Expenditure Committee, 1970/71, 1971

'Measurement, Forecasting and Control of Public Expenditure', memorandum to the Select Committee on Expenditure of the House of Commons (3rd Report), 1971

'Note on the Treasury Memorandum – Public Expenditure and Demand in Real Resources, 1971–1972' (7th Report), 1971

(with B. Stafford) 'Notes on Accounting Conventions with Particular Reference to the Treatment of Receipts', submitted to Commons Expenditure Committee, 1970/71 (3rd Report), 1971

'Notes on Public Expenditure to 1976–77 (Cmnd. 5178)', memorandum to Commons Expenditure Committee, 1972/73, 1972

'Public Expenditure and Demand on Real Resources', memorandum to the Select Committee on Expenditure of the House of Commons (7th Report), 1972

'Public Expenditure and Economic Management', memorandum to the Select Committee on Expenditure of the House of Commons (7th Report), 1972

'The Need for Further Information About Public Expenditure and What It Buys', memorandum to Expenditure Committee, 1971/1972 (8th Report), 1972

'The Supply and Disposition of Real Resources', note submitted to Commons Expenditure Committee, 1972/73 (11th Report), 1972

'The Measurement and Control of Public Expenditure', memorandum to Expenditure Committee, November 1973

'Public Expenditure and Inflation', memorandum to Expenditure Committee, (9th Report), Session 1974, HMSO, 1974

(with T.F. Cripps and M.J. Fetherston) 'Public Expenditure and the Management of the Economy', memorandum to Expenditure Committee, (9th Report), Session 1974, HMSO, 1974

'Reflections on the Control of Local Government Expenditure and Its Finance', Evidence submitted to the Layfield Committee, January, 1975

'Reflections on the Control of Local Government Expenditure and Its Financing: Evidence Given to the Committee of Inquiry Into Local Government Finance', Department of Applied Economics, University of Cambridge, 1975

(with M. FitzGerald Scott) 'The Arguments For and Against Protectionism', Papers presented to the Panel of Academic Consultants, no. 10, 1984

'Success in International Trade as the Key to Sustained Growth', London, TSB Group, 1993

'The Panel of Independent Forecasters February 1993 Report (Submission by W. Godley)', London, HM Treasury, 1993

'The Panel of Independent Forecasters July 1993 Report (Submission by W. Godley)', London, HM Treasury, 1993

'The Panel of Independent Forecasters October 1993 Report (Submission by W. Godley)', London, HM Treasury, 1993

'The Sensibility of Contemporary Institutions', Sermon before the University, Kings College Chapel, 31 May 1987, 1987

Articles in magazines and newspapers, letters to newspapers

'Economic Disaster in Slow Motion', *The Observer*, 27 August 1989

'Exposed: Lawson's Bogus Billions', *The Observer*, 9 April 1989

'Monetary Myths and Miracles', *The Observer*, 3 September 1989

'On Track for a Major Recession', *The Observer*, 15 October 1989

'The Mirage of Lawson's Supply-Side Miracle', *The Observer*, 2 April 1989

'Why The Figures Tell Another Story', *The Observer*, 5 July 1989

(with K.J. Coutts and G. Zezza) 'Is Britain in Credit with the Rest of the World?', *The Guardian*, 26 January 1990

'Recession Deep, Inflation High', *The Observer*, 19 August 1990

'Where Macroeconomics Went Wrong (A Review of 'A Market Theory of Money' by J.R. Hicks)', *Times Literary Supplement*, 18–24 May 1990

'A Long View', *New Statesman and Society*, 28 June 1991, pp. 18–19

'An Old Limousine', *New Statesman and Society*, 11 January 1991, pp. 18–21

'Bottoms Out?', *New Statesman and Society*, 17 May 1991, pp. 22–3

'Giving Up', *New Statesman and Society*, 29 March 1991, pp. 16–17

'New Consensus – Same Old Recession', *The Observer*, 12 May 1991

'Not a Dirty Word', *New Statesman and Society*, 8 February 1991, pp. 18–20
'Out of the Cul-de-Sac', *New Statesman and Society*, 18 January 1991, pp. 18–20
'Terminal Decay: There is Virtually Nothing That the Chancellor Can Do to Avert the Slump', *New Statesman and Society*, 15 March 1991, pp. 11–14
'A Severe Hangover', *New Statesman and Society*, 10 April 1992, pp. 26–7
'Escape from the Infinite Recession', *New Statesman and Society*, 20 March 1992, pp. 30–1
(with K.J. Coutts, J. Michie and R. Rowthorn) 'Hands-off Economics Equals Stagnation', *The Observer*, 19 April 1992
'Maastricht and All That', *London Review of Books*, 8 October, 1992
'No Cause for Optimism', *New Statesman and Society*, 17 July 1992, pp. 18–19
(with R. Rowthorn and K.J. Coutts) 'The Route Out of Recession', *The Observer*, 5 January 1992
'Derailed', *London Review of Books*, August 1993
'If in a Year's Time a Chancellor', *London Review of Books*, April 1993
'Letting Things Rip (review of T. Congdon, *Reflections on Monetarism*)', *London Review of Books*, January 1993
'Curried EMU: The Meal that Fails to Nourish', *The Observer*, 31 August 1997
'The US Economy: An Impossible Balancing Act', *Financial Times*, 19 February 1999
'Bush Should Triple His Tax Cuts', *Financial Times*, 22 January 2001, p. 15
'Recession, USA', *The Guardian*, 23 October 2001
'Saving Masud Khan', *London Review of Books*, 23(4), 22 February 2001, pp. 3–7
(with B. Martin) 'America's Years of Living Dangerously', *The Observer*, 1 September 2002
'Huge Fiscal Expansion Shortened U.S. Recession', *Financial Times*, Letters to the editor, 8 August 2002
'Kick-start Strategy Fails to Fire Spluttering US Economic Motor', *The Guardian*, 21 January 2002
'The New Interest-rate Orthodoxy is as Flawed as the Old One', *The Guardian*, 11 November 2002
'Forecasting is Defunct as a Means of Shaping Monetary Policy', *The Guardian*, 11 October 2004
(with L.R. Wray) 'Obscure Argument Not Easy to Follow', *Financial Times*, Letters to the editor, 17 February 2006
'Pensions £150bn Black Hole May Not be so Deep', *Financial Times*, Letters to the editor, 11 January 2006
(with L.R. Wray) 'The Balance of Trade, not Payments, is True Measure of a Deficit's Effects', *Financial Times*, Letters to the editor, 15 February 2006
'US Economy and the Deficit Predicament', *Financial Times*, Letters to the editor, 30 May 2006
'New Balance of Payments Figures May Transform Strategic Outlook', *Financial Times*, Letters to the editor, 28 December 2007
(with G. Gudgin, B. Martin and B. Moore) 'Bank Downplayed the Downside Risk', *Financial Times*, Letters to the editor, 20 November 2008
'Have Oxford Trio Built New Theory?', *Financial Times*, Letters to the editor, 1 May 2008
'Tackle Inflation with a Sensible Incomes Policy', *Financial Times*, Letters to the editor, 20 June 2008

'Immediate Cuts to Budget Deficit Will Worsen Recession', *Financial Times*, Letters to the editor, 9 October 2009

'An Expansionary Route to Cut Deficit', *Financial Times*, Letters to the editor, 20 April 2010

Index